Chink

Lavinia Greacen has been interested in Chink since 1974 when she first met his son Christopher. In 1984 she edited Chink's correspondence with Hemingway, which was published in the *Irish Times*. This is her first book, the result of five years' research and writing. A freelance journalist, she was born in England, met her Irish husband in London, and has lived in a whitewashed house overlooking Dublin for over twenty years. She has a son and two daughters. Her interests are reading, country pursuits and horse racing – not always in that order.

CHINK
A BIOGRAPHY

Lavinia Greacen

For Carol, who
meant much to Jim
Farrell, who — in the
Singapore Grip — was
interrogated by Percival,
Affectionately,
Lavinia

30th November 1991

M
PAPERMAC

First published 1989 by Macmillan London Limited

First published in paperback 1991 by
PAPERMAC
a division of Macmillan Publishers Limited
Cavaye Place London SW10 9PG
and Basingstoke

Associated companies in Auckland, Delhi, Dublin, Gaborone,
Hamburg, Harare, Hong Kong, Johannesburg, Kuala Lumpur,
Lagos, Manzini, Melbourne, Mexico City, Nairobi, New York,
Singapore and Tokyo

British Library Cataloguing in Publication Data
Greacen, Lavinia
Chink: a biography.
1. Great Britain. Army. Dorman-Smith, Eric
I. Title
355.3'31'0924

ISBN 0-333-55693-3

Typeset by Wyvern Typesetting Ltd, Bristol, England
Printed in Hong Kong

'To Chink Whose Trade Is Soldiering' and '[Some day when you are picked
up . . .]' from *88 Poems* by Ernest Hemingway, copyright © 1979 by the Ernest
Hemingway Foundation and Nicholas Georgiannis, reprinted by permission of
Harcourt Brace Jovanovich, Inc.

To my husband Walter, my son Robert and my daughters Amanda and Charlotte. My staunchest allies, always.

To Chink Whose Trade Is Soldiering

When you are picked up dead
Your face gone ugly tight
The situation clearly outlined
By the dead
We won't believe you're gone
Your boots have dropped too many times
We've drunk too much good beer
Watched the sun rise
And cursed the rain
That spoiled the piste
Or turned the river brown
So flies were useless

Ernest Hemingway, Paris 1924

Contents

Acknowledgements

This book could not have been written without help and encouragement from many people. I would especially like to thank the following for so generously giving me their time – in interviews or replying to letters – and in many cases extending their hospitality as well: Major-General G. E. Aizlewood, Rt Hon. Julian Amery, Lieutenant-Colonel Clive Auchinleck, Professor Carlos Baker, Mrs Maureen Baker-Munton, Mr and Mrs Correlli Barnett, Colonel D. T. L. Beath, Mr John Bowman, Mr Dan Bryan, Mr and Mrs Hubert Butler, Mrs Marie Carney, Field Marshal Lord Carver, Professor Giovanni Cecchin, General Sir Philip Christison, Sir Rex Cohen, Major George Connolly, Mrs Sally Corbett, Lieutenant-General M. J. Costello, Mr Maurice Craig, Lieutenant-Colonel Henry Cramsie, Mr Sean Cronin, General F. M. de Butts, Mr James Dillon, Mr Morgan Dockrell, Mr and Mrs Christopher Dorman-O'Gowan, Dr Victor Dorman-Smith, Lieutenant-Colonel John P. Duggan, General Sir Gerald Duke, Major-General Sir Charles Dunphie, Mr Michael Elliot-Bateman, Lieutenant-General Sir John Evetts, Mr William Finlay, Mrs Pauline Fitzsimons, Mr M. R. D. Foot, Lord Freyberg, Mr Douglas Gageby, Mr Robert Greacen, General Sir John Hackett, Mr Gerald Hanley, Field Marshal Lord Harding, Mr N. C. Harrison, Mr Denis Hart, Mr J. H. N. Hemingway, Sir Oliver Heywood, Mr Christopher Hibbert, Professor F. M. Hinsley, Lieutenant-Colonel Nicholas Holmes, Mr Joseph Hone, Sir David Hunt, Mr Bruce Hunter, Mr Brian Inglis, Mr Michael Jackson, Lieutenant-General Sir Ian Jacob, Mr James J. Kelly, Lord Kilbracken, Lord Killanin, Lieutenant-General Sir Henry Leask, Mr Adrian Liddell Hart, Lady Kathleen Liddell Hart, Major-General James Lillis, Miss Joan-Ann Lloyd, General Sir Charles Loewen, Mr Charles Lysaght, Mr Proinsias MacAonghusa, Mr Gerald McCarthy, Mrs Elise McCormick, Mr Brendan MacGiollachoille, Mrs Roisin

McHenry, Mr Eoin MacNeill, Mr Peter McNiven, Mr and Mrs John Madden, Brigadier Owen Martin, Mrs Elizabeth Mather, Mr Bryan Matthews, Ms Patricia Methven, Professor Jeffrey Meyers, Professor Norman Moore, Mr Charles Murphy, Mr Kevin Myers, Brigadier Andrew Myrtle, Mrs G. H. Nicholson, Mrs Stella Norton-Dawson, Mr Ruiri O'Bradaigh, Mr Conor Cruise O'Brien, Colonel Donal O'Carroll, Mr Ulick O'Connor, Mr Gearoid O'Cuinneagain, Mr Sean O'Faolain, The O'Grady, Mr Tom O'Neill, Major-General M. St. J. Oswald, Ms Katie Owen, Major-General Patrick Palmer, Captain Mungo Park, Mr and Mrs Barry Pitt, Captain W. F. Pringle, Mr John Profumo, Professor F. W. Ratcliffe, General Sir Charles Richardson, General Sir Ouvry and Lady Roberts, Mrs Ruth Connell Robertson, Colonel E. W. Robinson-Horley, Mr John Ross, Mr Peter Ross, Dr B. E. Schlesinger, Mr Michael Shaw, Lord Shawcross, Mr David Sheehy, Mrs Andree Sheehy-Skeffington, Mr Adam Sisman, Mr and Mrs Gerard Slevin, Mr and Mrs Daragh Smith, Mr Louis Smith, Mr and Mrs Michael Smith, Mr and Mrs Neil Smith, Mrs Elaine Strutt, Mr Paul Tansey, Mr Wynford Vaughan Thomas, Mrs Emily Thompson, Group Captain Charles Tighe, Mr Raleigh Trevelyan, Major K. M. White, Sir Edgar Williams, Mr Ernest Wood, Dr Margaret Wright, Commander Peter Young.

I am also grateful to the helpful staff of the Berkeley and Lecky libraries of Trinity College Dublin, the National Library of Ireland, the John Rylands University Library of Manchester, the Liddell Hart Centre for Military Archives at the University of London, King's College, and the Public Record Office in Kew.

I would like to thank the following for their kind permission to reproduce material from papers lodged in their possession or books published under their imprint: Christopher Dorman-O'Gowan, for extracts from his father's private papers; the John Rylands University Library of Manchester, for extracts from the Dorman-Smith/O'Gowan papers; the Trustees of the Liddell Hart Centre for Military Archives, at the University of London, King's College, for extracts from the Penney, Liddell Hart, Alanbrooke, Kirkman and O'Connor papers; the Royal Regiment of Fusiliers, for extracts from *The Fifth in the Great War*, *St George's Gazette*, and the *Regimental History of the Second World War*; The John Fitzgerald Kennedy Library, Columbia Point, Boston, Mass., USA, for extracts from early Dorman-Smith letters held in the Hemingway Collection; the University of Ulster Library at Coleraine, Northern Ireland, for extracts from the Denis

Johnston papers; Lieutenant-General Sir Ian Jacob, for extracts from his private diary; Jonathan Cape Ltd on behalf of the Executors of the Ernest Hemingway Estate, for extracts from *Fiesta*, *Death In The Afternoon*, *Green Hills of Africa*, *Across the River and into the Trees*, and *A Moveable Feast*; Collins Publishers, for use of quotations from *The Rommel Papers*, editor B. L. Liddell Hart, and *By-Line* and *Men At War* by Ernest Hemingway; Grafton Books for use of quotations from *Selected Letters of Ernest Hemingway*, edited by Carlos Baker; Harcourt Brace Jovanovich, Inc., for use of 'To Chink Whose Trade Is Soldiering' and '[Some day when you are picked up . . .]' from *88 Poems* by Ernest Hemingway; The Bodley Head, for an extract from *Jurgen* by James Branch Cabell; Pan Books, for extracts from *The Desert Generals* by Corelli Barnett; Curtis Brown on behalf of Lady Browning, for an extract from *The King's General*, copyright Daphne du Maurier 1946.

Finally, I wish to make clear that the account I have given in the following pages is my own, and should not be taken as representing the views of Chink's family or of any particular individual whose help I acknowledge above.

Lavinia Greacen
Co. Dublin, Ireland
March, 1989

Foreword

After Montgomery himself, the most controversial British figure of the 1940–3 Desert Campaign has remained Major-General Eric ('Chink') Dorman-Smith, acting Chief of Staff in the field to General Sir Claude Auchinleck during the First Battle of Alamein in July 1942. His critics have called him Auchinleck's 'evil genius', and made him the scapegoat for all that was amiss with the Eighth Army in the summer of 1942, such as its fragmentation into 'battle groups'; they have even largely blamed him for its rout at Rommel's hand in the Gazala battles in May and June. They have accused him of selling Auchinleck fantastic and impracticable offensive plans during First Alamein. Their opinions, privately conveyed to General Sir Alan Brooke, the Chief of the Imperial General Staff, helped to get Dorman-Smith sacked along with Auchinleck in August 1942. And his detractors have continued to denigrate him ever since, even as recently as Nigel Hamilton's biography of Montgomery, *Monty: The Making of a General* (1981).

Dorman-Smith's admirers, however, although acknowledging the quirks of character and flaws of personality so vividly portrayed by Lavinia Greacen in *Chink*, contend that he was one of the few original thinkers in a British Army largely led by orthodox and slow-minded officers whose attitudes had been formed by military life between the world wars when the army was hardly more than an imperial gendarmerie; polo-playing amateurs compared with their highly professional German opposite numbers. Dorman-Smith's admirers contend that it was his unorthodox plan of attack that enabled Major-General Richard (later General Sir Richard) O'Connor to win his sensational victory over the Italians at Sidi Barrani in 1940; that it was Dorman-Smith's brilliant use of Ultra decrypts of German Enigma cypher signals (giving details of Rommel's dispositions) that enabled Auchinleck to stop Rommel in full career during the First Battle of

Alamein and force him on to the defensive. And they argue that Dorman-Smith's and Auchinleck's proposed reorganisation of the Eighth Army into combined armour and infantry formations (later abandoned by Montgomery) foreshadowed the organisation of Nato armies today.

But behind this enduring controversy about Dorman-Smith the soldier lies the man himself. In *Chink* Lavinia Greacen reveals him for the first time as he really was. Basing her book on his unpublished letters and diaries and on interviews with his family, friends and military associates, she presents a fascinating, penetrating and in the end moving picture of an extraordinary man – the product of a strange Anglo-Irish upbringing who concealed sensitivity and self-doubt behind an outward intellectual arrogance and scornful wit; who as a young officer enjoyed a double life as a close friend of Ernest Hemingway and his literary circle at the end of the Great War and in the early 1920s; and who, after the collapse of his career, was to figure as the hero in Hemingway's novel *Across the River and Into the Trees*.

Lavinia Greacen shows how even at the period of Dorman-Smith's early military promise at the Staff College, he was making enemies of the second-raters who were later to take their revenge, and also earning the displeasure of soldiers senior to him such as Alan Brooke and Montgomery because of his outspoken comments and his failure to play the diplomatic game of the successful careerist. She demonstrates how Chink's long-standing love affair with another officer's wife during the Second World War (they later married) so shocked a stuffy military establishment that his private life too helped to abort his career. Especially interesting is Lavinia Greacen's account of Dorman-Smith's last posting, as a brigade commander in the Anzio beachhead in Italy in 1944, showing how his divisional general, a man of plodding mediocrity who had been the victim of Chink's wit at the Staff College, worked behind his back, and quite improperly in terms of military procedures, to get him sacked.

Lavinia Greacen's book ends with what in many respects was the most extraordinary episode in Dorman-Smith's life – his return to the family estate in Ireland and his assumption of an Irish name (O'Gowan) and an Irish persona, having rejected the Britain whose 'establishment' had, as he believed, destroyed him. Lavinia Greacen reveals through unpublished letters and interviews with IRA veterans (the old, relatively moderate IRA of the 1950s, not the Provo terrorists of the 1970s and 1980s) how Dorman-Smith became involved with the IRA as a military adviser and offered his estate as a training ground.

Chink is much more than another biography of a Second World War soldier – it is a picture of a complex, many-faceted character, highly strung, romantic, emotional, ambitious, self-questioning, flawed by pride; a man who saw that he was being left behind by less able contemporaries, and realised why, yet remained unwilling or unable to moderate his outspokenness or compromise on what he believed to be matters of professional principle, and instead play the world's game. Lavinia Greacen has written an intimate and very moving portrait of an outsider: what made him and what broke him.

Correlli Barnett

Preface

Chink Dorman-Smith, enigmatic and ignored, remains one of the last mysteries of the Desert War. The characters and skill of Auchinleck, Montgomery and Rommel have long been studied and dissected. Each battle has been fought and refought from numerous angles, switching the vantage point from general to that of private, from cavalry to infantry, intelligence and the Royal Air Force, from the British view to the German, and interpreted by a procession of military historians. Memoirs crowd upon each other, and the only major story still untold is that of the controversial soldier whose quick-thinking was behind the crucial battle of First Alamein, which is now generally acknowledged by historians to have turned the course of the war in the Middle East and the Mediterranean. Yet, along with his master Auchinleck, Chink was sacked by Churchill within the month and, unlike his contemporaries, sank back into anonymity.

Mention of his name continues to polarise commentators into two camps, and by far the greater number vehemently deride him. But final judgement on the events which took place only sixty miles from the vulnerable city of Cairo during that critical summer of 1942 requires his evidence as well. What has been left out so far? And why did he arouse such long-term hostility?

Chink was not a popular man, and he made no attempt to become one. In fact, he took such pride in being provocative that frequently one's sympathy goes out to his colleagues. This makes his story infuriating on two levels. The most popular conclusion is that he was his own worst enemy, and most certainly he was that. Had he cared to trim, to notch his career higher by subtle flattery, manoeuvring for position and above all keeping his thoughts to himself, he would have been heaped in due course with rewards, including the rank of general, a knighthood and an approved footnote in history. As it is, he retired as a colonel under obscure circumstances, which are revealed here for the first time, before the end of the war. The reality is that a conventional man working a conventional passage could never have possessed his military genius; conversely to be a military genius is to be politically naive.

It was who, rather than what, one knew that counted in the army, and average sound performance was instinctively preferred to scholarship-level brilliance. To be too brainy, in fact, was a handicap in the army of his generation, unless one had the common sense to hide the fact or the character to cushion it. Chink was scoffing openly at the gallant amateur code ten years before the Second World War began, and he proceeded to challenge it in both his military and his private life, disqualifying himself from being, to use Dr Johnson's rule of thumb, a clubbable man. The misuse of his ability was as much the result of the antiquated system as it was of the prejudice of the men who ran it.

A very different literary giant, Ernest Hemingway, made Chink his ideal. Hemingway put him, as the personification of integrity and honour, into much of his work, from poems and journalism to short stories and novels. That Chink should have inspired such feeling, and in turn been drawn to Hemingway and to other American expatriates in the Paris of the 1920s, including John Dos Passos, Scott Fitzgerald and Gertrude Stein, underscores his great individuality. It also sheds light on why so many of his relationships within the British Army ran into trouble. Erudite, anarchic and impudent, by the time he reached the Staff College his wit was barbed and his boredom threshold ominously high.

Acceptance in one world excluded him from the other. Hemingway, ironically, could never see that, and contemporary literature is as indebted as is military history to Chink's happening to be in the right place at the right time – in this case Milan in 1918. *Across the River and into the Trees* is now considered to be Hemingway's lament at the final outcome of Chink's career. And the fond portrayal of him in *A Moveable Feast*, completed shortly before the writer's suicide in 1961, shows that Hemingway never ceased his hero-worship.

Truth, they say, is stranger than fiction, and it is fitting that the life of the soldier who inspired some of the most important writing of this century should have a highly imaginative air to it, compared with predictable biographies of his military peers. To use his own description of Lawrence of Arabia, he was a poltergeist of history and, like all poltergeists, he seemed both mischievous and unreal. It was this that grated, even at the time. Post-war adventures could be said to justify censorious army opinion, but one must take into account his child-hood inheritance, the manner of his going and that personality which could never be pinned down and which always put principle before anything else – however much it cost him.

Would he have been more suited to the German Army, as is often claimed? The answer must be a qualified yes, since intellectuals could climb on the staff side alone, without having to qualify on the command side as well. But his outspokenness would have guaranteed his downfall with the advent of Hitler, and so cut short his career even earlier. Would he be edged out today, now that advances in technology dictate higher academic qualifications, now that many of his radical ideas are incorporated into conventional lore, and now that divorce is no longer unacceptable?

For the allied cause in the Second World War one can only conclude that it was fortunate that he was born when he was, and with the personality he had. If he had not been there – breaking the rules as defiantly as ever – at Auchinleck's elbow in July 1942, he would not have been able to influence the outcome of the war. Nor, of course, would he have incurred the distaste his name still arouses today. His story says as much about the army of his time as it does about the man himself.

Introduction

The tiny Protestant cemetery of Kilcrow, in County Cavan in the south of Ireland, was bleak and lonely. It was 14 May 1969, a rain-drenched day, with dripping trees, a low ceiling of cloud and gusts of driving wind. The cemetery nestled beside choppy lakes that separated the neighbouring estates of Bellamont Forest and Dartry, and the few mourners turned their coat collars up and gripped umbrellas firmly as they clustered around the open grave.

Surprisingly, to everyone who understood such matters, it was an ecumenical funeral service, being conducted jointly by the Catholic parish priest, Monsignor James J. O'Reilly, and the local Church of Ireland rector, Canon Robert Trenier of Kilmore. In the fixed tribal attitudes of 1969 this was unusual. Only the immediate family knew that the controversial service had been planned by the deceased well in advance, as a final tilt against sectarianism.

The widow, still beautiful in her fifties, stood beside a younger man, whom she would marry within eight months. The military bearing of her only son gave away his profession. A step-daughter, clearly distressed, stood with her husband's arm comfortingly at her elbow. A daughter, twelve years younger and as dark as the other was fair, showed no emotion. Among the handful of people, as the newly dug earth melted into mud and shoes absorbed the damp, were two Irish Army officers, incongruous, their heads bent. Hunched against the worst the weather could throw at them, Monsignor O'Reilly and Canon Trenier conducted the service with dignity, and without haste. Picking their way through the soaking grass afterwards towards cars parked in the lane leading to the solitary spot, the mourners were relieved it had gone off so well.

They could not know that the morning's events would be misinterpreted and that quite a different story would take shape. As soon as the

1

Canon began his prayers, it was soon whispered around Cootehill, the nearest town to isolated Kilcrow, the coffin had plunged of its own accord from the pile of dug-out clay, where it had been temporarily placed, into the grave below. This was because the Brigadier had wished to be buried as the Catholic that he was. The late Brigadier, known by his oldest friends as Chink, by his relatives as Eric and by the world at large as that odd fellow who changed his name after the Second World War from Dorman-Smith to Dorman O'Gowan, would have been wryly amused at this supreme irony. It made a good story, of course, but it was not true. And so it resembled so much else said about him in his lifetime.

Contrast that sparse attendance with the crowds that packed into Westminster Abbey in February 1985 for the memorial service for Lieutenant-General Sir Brian Horrocks. Her Majesty the Queen was represented, and the Prime Minister, Mrs Thatcher, sent her Secretary of State for Defence, Michael Heseltine. On velvet cushions the orders and decorations of the deceased were borne to the sacrarium past the ranked military attachés and representatives from a host of regiments. In the pews could be seen the uniforms of the Grenadier Guards, the Queen's Own Hussars, the Light Infantry, the Middlesex Regiment, the Royal Regiment of Fusiliers, the Black Watch, First Polish Armoured Division, the Royal Lancers, the Royal Tank Regiment, the Household Cavalry, the Devonshire and Dorset Regiment, the Royal Ulster Rifles, 8th Armoured Brigade, the King's Own Yorkshire Light Infantry, the Scots Guards, 13th/18th Royal Hussars, the Durham Light Infantry, the Royal Welch Fusiliers, the Fifth Royal Inniskilling Dragoon Guards, the Argyll and Sutherland Highlanders and the Royal Artillery. Here, too, were pinstriped or uniformed men on behalf of the Army Board, the First Sea Lord, the Admiralty and the Air Force Boards, the Commander-in-Chief, British Army of the Rhine, the Staff College and the Africa Star Association.

Two other representatives were also appropriate. Uppingham School and Uppingham Old Boys' Association were honoured to take part in this tribute to one of the school's famous old boys. Organ music swelled and the sense of occasion was tangible. Ageing contemporaries of 'Jorrocks', as the likeable General was referred to by most of them, greeted each other warmly in the crowd as they took turns to file out down the long central aisle, with the Uppingham men swept along with the rest. And it is they who provide the first clue to the connection between these two ceremonies.

Dorman-Smith and Horrocks, gauche fifteen-year-olds both, had entered Uppingham together in the September term of 1910, and left together for Sandhurst at the end of 1912. Who would have speculated then that the easy-going, sports-mad Horrocks, who scraped in second last of that Sandhurst intake, would reach such heights? Or that the flamboyant but diligently determined Dorman-Smith, who scored top out of the Uppingham candidates, would come to be so forgotten?

Even glimpsed together in 1958, the year when the two men last lunched with one another in London, it would still be hard to guess the outcome. An outsider would then have seen Horrocks leaning forward across the table to catch Chink's witty remarks, sympathetically emanating good humour. Chink, reeling off the expected anecdotes that were always lightly dipped in acid, would be putting on the best show he was capable of mustering. There would seem to be little to choose between them. Both men dressed conventionally and radiated an air of command, with Chink appearing the younger of the two despite an impression of nervous tension. Nostalgia for Uppingham days cut little ice with either of them, but a perceptive listener would quickly pick up the fact that there were subjects best avoided, and others to be approached delicately. The nuance was there for anyone not distanced by the clipped upper-class speech that eased into a drawl as they relaxed.

They always took it in turns to pay the bill at these lunches, so their income could be deduced to be on a par. Both were obviously army men, at home with army slang, and once this connection was made Horrocks would be instantly placed. In 1958 his face was becoming familiar as a result of his regular television programmes about battles in the Second World War. The observer would conclude that the General was out with a trusted old friend, and it would be a valid conclusion – except that Chink did not consider Horrocks to be an intimate any more. The gulf between them was immense.

Had the observer followed Horrocks back to work that afternoon he would have found himself at the Lord Great Chamberlain's office in the House of Lords, in time to see Horrocks greeted deferentially, as befitted the Gentleman Usher of the Black Rod. It would confirm the picture of a man at ease in the world of the Establishment, competently doing a historic job which he enjoyed and which was his as a mark of the country's respect.

But Chink, the retired brigadier who had briefly held general's rank himself, left the same restaurant for a very different world. He was returning in 1958 to a double life, being allegedly at that time a clandestine member of the IRA, which was then engaged in terrorist operations in Northern Ireland. Chink mentally kept his contact with Horrocks in a separate compartment and never once confused his diametrically opposed loyalties, but by now his disillusion with the system that Horrocks represented was total. It was a system he had once believed in himself and had spent his life serving, until events had taken place that set him apart. And for him there was no going back.

At home in Ireland, if tracked that far, Chink was viewed as a fortunate man, albeit with a chip on his shoulder, who had been blessed by worldly goods and a reasonable career; a conventional figure, almost a caricature of the classic British Army officer. He was taller than average and had the spare, straight-backed carriage of a soldier who had once ridden well. Quizzical blue eyes could still frown penetratingly and imply that an order was being given. They could also crinkle in contagious humour when he allowed himself to show his charm. A firm handshake, the brisk stride with hands clasped behind his back, and the energy of his movements showed that he enjoyed keeping fit and was competitive enough to want to dominate. Nothing unusual there.

Out of doors in winter he invariably pulled a tweed cap out of the pocket of his sports jacket, preferring the country camouflage so favoured by retired military men the world over. His hair was peppered with grey and beginning to recede a little at the temples, and outdoor life gave him a healthy glow. Usually the tie was a regimental one, his shoes were carefully buffed and certainly not new, and he drove an estate car that was indistinguishable from those driven by the rest of his generation. In the back could be seen a dog's rug and empty drinking bowl for long journeys, and maps were stuffed into the door flaps. It was a well-used car for getting adequately from A to B, and not for impressing the neighbours or making any sort of statement. Like many army men, he drove aggressively and well, losing his temper in traffic and whenever faced with idiotic behaviour by other road-users.

The impression was of a privileged, retired soldier, tweedy and energetic, concerned with nothing more momentous than paying school fees and keeping his estate in good order, even if that meant suing the local county council over a period of several years for pollution to one of his lakes. A man who enjoyed his shooting and never missed being near the wireless in time to hear the six o'clock news. A man who was always on the go and set a rather grating example to more indolent folk. The archetypal army man.

All these were characteristics as easily found in Cheltenham as in Camberley, but not frequently encountered in County Cavan, which is near the border with Northern Ireland. But then the reason why he lived there was entirely understandable. He had been born at Bellamont Forest and had inherited the estate from his father in 1948. The elegance of the house, with its Palladian portico and intact early Georgian interior, was a suitable background for him and, being considerably more impressive than the usual establishment retired officers can aspire to, lifted him into the bracket of landed gentry. He was fiercely proud, both of his home and of his Irish heritage.

It would be on this subject that Chink's true unorthodoxy tended to show in 1958. His were not the traditional Anglo-Irish views of a man born in Ireland and schooled in England who chooses to retire back home after an international career. Bitingly, indiscreetly and above all knowledgeably, he talked of the urgent need to get the British out of Northern Ireland once and for all, to the unease of most listeners. On this subject in the 1950s he was considered a bore; an eccentric who should have known better, but still a harmless crank. That he might have chosen to do more than talk would have been beyond comprehension, as were many of the subjects he liked to discuss if he took to someone. And the speed at which his mind worked could be equally disturbing. His need to dominate was more evident at close quarters. So, too, was the academic span of his thoughts.

He was familiar, it would transpire, with philosophy, the Classics, poetry, literature, current affairs, genealogy, obscure pre-Christian tribal movements and military history on the grand scale, down to minutiae of the Second World War. Contrasted with a general like Horrocks, whose simplified approach kept television audiences spellbound, the incisive comments of Chink's military analysis were on another plane. Gone then was the stereotyped brigadier, and fleetingly the layers that went to make up this man stood out. His searing bitterness about Sir Winston Churchill, already respected as a legend in his own time, also took people aback. Chink could laugh about most things, they soon found out, but not about the army and never ever about Churchill. Every time the ex-Prime Minister's name was mentioned it led to a lecture on Churchill's interference in the desert campaign of 1942 and the subsequent injustice done to General Sir

Claude Auchinleck by Auchinleck's successor as head of the Eighth Army, General Sir Bernard Montgomery. But if his Alamein views were attributed to personal loyalty and his IRA support to bitterness – the one stemming from the other – he could be comfortably pigeon-holed again.

It had to be faced, however, that the nearer anyone got to knowing Chink, the more often they had to revise their conclusion. He fitted into no category. He could be amusing one minute, woundingly sharp the next, intuitively wise but curiously insensitive, brilliantly up to date, as well as obsessed with the past, capable of being charming and also of being brutally rude, intolerant and yet generous, gentle but vindictive.

One characteristic knitted up all these strands, and this was an unwavering sense of principle. It was principle that had caused his emotional distancing from Horrocks and earlier still from the rest of his army world, and principle that kept Chink where he was now, on what he privately liked to call his patch of green and saffron. It was because of principle that there had been no lasting room for him on the neighbouring chequerboard square of red, white and blue.

1

Inheritance

At the turn of the twentieth century Eric Dorman-Smith, who was not yet known as Chink, was a thin, fidgety boy with a growing need for privacy. Alone in the beautifully proportioned library of Bellamont Forest, lying in front of the turf fire that tended to smoke whenever the wind was in the wrong direction, he was safe from his garrulous nurse and the other staff, and free to escape into the legends of King Arthur and his knights of the Round Table. There was ample time to commit the tales to memory and to absorb the chivalrous ideal, because he was left to his own devices so much.

He had been born towards dusk on the evening of 24 July 1895, in the largest bedroom of the house, on the hottest day of the year. His mother, twenty-one-year-old Amy, had been warned by her doctor to expect a long ordeal because her pelvis was narrow; in the event her labour had lasted over twenty-four hours. At news of the birth her husband Edward had ordered the estate bell to be rung, a bonfire to be lit on the Hoop Hill and free porter to be laid on for all employees. A name had already been chosen and four days later the baby was christened Eric Edward Dorman in the Catholic church that had been built by his grandfather in Cootehill. A nurse had immediately taken over the chore of looking after him and, being a healthy baby, he proceeded to thrive.

Amy had been married to Edward for fifteen months, and by the time of the birth she was already discontented with country life. She had been brought up in the style and bustle of Mayfair's Grosvenor Square, so the transition was abrupt; but to compound that she was urban by inclination and delighted in gossipy bridge games and the theatres of London's West End. The tranquil grounds of Bellamont Forest held little appeal for her, and the dullness of the small society in which she found herself made her increasingly outspoken. And it was not only parochialism that stifled her. Contrary to expectation, the newly married couple were snubbed by the land-owning families around them, and this threw them back on each other's company. She had already found that they had little in common, and their different religions did not help. Edward was Catholic and Amy Protestant; fortunately, neither was very devout.

Edward Smith was twenty-five when his oldest son was born, easy-going and unambitious. He was happiest out walking his dogs after woodcock, partridge and snipe, or shooting over his lakes for duck. Although fond of Amy, he was already awed by her impatient temper and the deftness of her scorn, traits which his first son was to inherit in full. Edward had the leisure to regret that it had been her wit almost as much as her auburn-haired beauty that had attracted him when they were introduced in Luxor, Egypt, where both had been despatched on grand tours with the unstated objective of finding a suitable partner.

Amy, in turn, had been impressed by Edward's good looks and the conventional pattern of his life. She had too little experience at the time to detect his lack of confidence, which resulted from incessant bullying at his public school, Ampleforth; so bad had this been that he had left two years early, refusing to go back. It never occured to Amy, either, that he might not be the scion of an established family, since he spent freely, wore all the right clothes and talked of his estate. They married without returning home, in the romantic setting of Monte Carlo, and the lack of curiosity shown by both families ought to have been a warning sign.

Edward's father, it transpired, had emigrated at fourteen, uneducated and penniless, but tenaciously ambitious. The Smith money stemmed from coal mines, and twenty-five years earlier the money had not been there at all. Amy minded about this greatly. Her own vivacious mother, Edith, had abandoned a husband who worked on the railways to set up home in Grosvenor Square with Charles Kettlewell, a member of the Prince of Wales's fast set, and even in the rapidly changing Victorian era this was impossible to live down. Much to Amy's shame, her father could still be seen at Marsh Lane station, near Bootle in Lancashire, where he had risen to become station master. Above all else, Amy had wanted a respectable match. Edward's uncouth local sporting friends were easily frozen off, but there was nobody to put in their place. Instead of marrying a squire, she had married a social liability.

From Edward's point of view, the bargain was not such a poor one.

Amy was lovely to look at and most congenial company when she was not in a bad mood. She had already given him a son and she made up for the loneliness of his earlier years. His father had died when Edward, the oldest of five brothers and sisters, was six, and in widowhood his mother had retreated into religion. The necessary financial decisions from which she had been insulated were too much for her, and her staunch Catholicism became fanatical. When Edward rejected the care of the Benedictine monks at Ampleforth and arrived home unexpectedly at the age of sixteen she gave in to his pleading and let him stay untutored at Bellamont Forest. On his twentieth birthday, when the estate legally became his, she slipped away with her younger children to live permanently in London, within walking distance of Brompton Oratory. Until Edward's marriage he had lived on at Bellamont alone, filling his time with shooting and rarely leaving his own grounds. The snobbish attitude of the local gentry merely confirmed the conclusions he had drawn from school.

For Eric, the consequences of such conflicting pressures would be lifelong, and the most influential would be that of religion. To appease Edward's mother he had been baptised in the Catholic church, but by the time Amy gave birth to a second son, Victor, within fourteen months, and a third, Reginald, in 1899, she had asserted her own authority. Both were christened in the local Protestant church. On Sundays Victor and Reggie walked beside Amy towards one teaching while Eric and his nurse separately approached another. In Cootehill, as elsewhere, the Protestant and Catholic churches expounded opposing myths and handed down individual strictures. It is no coincidence that Victor would grow up to be a conventional Anglophile while Reggie was to become the heartiest of Tories, or that both brothers should make their adult lives in England and rarely return, even for holidays. The more immediate development was that from an early age the younger boys had far more in common with Amy, and Eric felt excluded.

The most vivid of his early memories was the sound of the Protestant church bells tolling on Queen Victoria's death, associated with a bleak jealousy towards Reggie, the new favourite. Edward had left home before his youngest son's birth, having joined up as a volunteer with the 4th Leinster Regiment to fight in the Boer War. Alone at Bellamont, Amy cuddled her placid new baby, and Eric consoled himself in the library. Initially he was attracted there by the bloodthirsty Boer War drawings in the *Illustrated London News*, laid out on the table.

The smartly uniformed British corpses at Spion Kop compared admirably with the shabby Boers, and when no one was looking he liked to practise being shot in battle on the insulating fireside rug.

When Edward returned from South Africa, his enthusiasm for soldiering was infectious. Having set out apprehensively with the rank of captain to discover to his relief that his marksmanship was highly prized, Edward had flourished as he experienced the novelty of being popular. Regimental life suited him, and he wished it could have continued for longer. The Boer War books he brought back were given pride of place on the library shelves, beside pendantic tomes of more distant campaigns. As early as the age of seven, Eric's first choice was *Wars of the Eighteenth Century*, and his burgeoning interest in the army was whetted by learning that the first Victoria Cross had been created for a distant relation. Rapidly he graduated to Edward's military textbooks, using the time when he was supposed to be practising on the ornate grand piano; mechanically he would play reasonably proficient scales, while his book of the moment was propped up at eye-level on the music stand.

His reading was indiscriminate. By the time he was ten he was familiar with *The Decameron* and the works of Cervantes, Lewis Carroll, Dickens, Tennyson, Scott, Conan Doyle, Darwin, Jules Verne, Thackeray, Kipling and Rider Haggard, among others, as well as with all Amy's light romances. None, including *Don Quixote*, could in his opinion touch the Arthurian legends. He longed for someone to discuss them with, but Amy was unpredictable, preferring Reggie and the stolid Victor, and Edward would pleasantly rebuff him by saying that he had not managed to do much reading himself.

Eric was cut off from his own age group, with the occasional exception of John Charles McQuaid, a local boy whose birthday was four days after his own, and who also enjoyed collecting conkers, fishing with worms and exploring the estate. McQuaid was considered the most suitable available companion, since his father was the local doctor. He would call to play in the holidays, energetic and strong-willed but with a similar introspective streak; his mother had died shortly after his birth and sometimes Eric felt sorry for him. But the rest of the time he was alone: McQuaid attended school with a view to becoming a priest (impossible to predict then that McQuaid would become an archbishop, and that Eric would touch general's rank) while in term time Eric remained in the grounds of Bellamont Forest.

There had been a brief experiment of sending all three brothers to a small day school at the Methodist Manse, but as soon as news of that reached his grandmother in London Eric was switched to the care of a nearby order of nuns. The nuns won his respect but he was not allowed to stay for long, because Amy considered a governess to be more appropriate. The shy Miss Faith was installed, but proved no match for her strong-willed pupil. The solitary reading he preferred was sanctioned as education.

Eric developed into a secretive boy with a vivid imagination, and when not taking refuge in the library he was increasingly drawn to the servants' hall. Here he was made to feel gratifyingly important and was referred to as 'the Heir', which did a great deal to put his younger brothers in their place. One day all three were observed standing together on the stately Bellamont steps while Eric pointed out loudly that all the trees they could see belonged to him. 'Couldn't I have just one?' Reggie was heard to wheedle, used to charming his own way. 'No,' came the stern reply. 'I am the Heir.'

But usually the boys were too young to hold his interest, and they slept on while he was up and out of doors at dawn, his springer spaniel at his side, intent on keeping the private vigil. He had always displayed an insatiable curiosity, and from the staff he could be sure of stories in response, if not always direct answers. He learned that in the grounds there was a rath where it was unlucky to cut blackthorn, and he became fascinated by ghost stories. He spent eerie dusks trying to see the faint outline of a young woman who was said to have been hanged by her own brother from the stairs a century before, and even the library was supposed to have a presence – although a benign one that never frightened him. A series of uncanny presentiments convinced him that he possessed psychic powers, and this was a belief that he would never lose.

Out of loneliness, Eric began gravitating more frequently to the servants' hall, and here he picked up more than his parents could have imagined possible. During those years Ireland still belonged to the British Empire, but the hope of nationalism was spreading, and Eric was as intrigued by what he heard there as he was impressionable.

There was no reason why Amy should have forbidden him to be taken to watch the Orange military bands as they piped and swirled through Cootehill on parade. On the contrary, these were traditional treats for a child to marvel at in such a rural, quiet community. She could never have guessed that they might be seen from another angle. As Eric clutched his nurse's hand in the crowd, he could be sure of the electrifying whisper, 'These are not *your* people', at which the band took on an air of menace. He thought he glared back rather well.

By the age of seven he had pieced together enough of an exciting history to make his parents' world appear tame in comparison. His inheritance as the Heir was enhanced when he realised that the Smiths were descended from the Gaelic-named O'Gowans, once one of the ruling families of Ulster. They had come to Cootehill in the reign of James I, when Hugh O'Gowan was transplanted south for siding with the unsuccessful rebellion of Hugh O'Neill, and Eric's favourite version was the one in which Hugh O'Gowan first fled into the Mourne Mountains with his young son to avoid being killed.

Later in his life, when he had time for genealogical research, he fleshed out the details. The O'Gowans turned out to be a branch of the Cruthnean Dal nAraidi of counties Antrim and Down, with a surname first recorded in AD 955. In 1649, in exile, they had anglicised their name to Smith and taken up horse-dealing. The coat of arms, of three naked arms carrying burning brands and sword and the motto *Tenebras Expellit et Hostes*, commemorated a night raid by rivals, during which the Smiths seized back their horses and repulsed a second attack with brands from their fire. One member of the family subsequently fought on the losing Jacobite side of the Battle of the Boyne and was killed, with the result that the holding near Cootehill was forfeited and the family moved back to County Down. There the descendant who made the family fortune was born in 1807.

In childhood Eric heard many anecdotes about his grandfather, and also noticed how his parents changed the subject whenever he mentioned any of them. The story was not hard to put together. The child born in 1807 had also been christened Edward Smith, and showed further evidence of the family tendency towards a stubborn sense of principle. At fourteen he had left home on foot rather than take up the free education available if he agreed to become a Protestant, and worked his passage across to Liverpool. There he picked up lumps of coal on the docks to sell by the bucketful, until in middle age an overheard conversation about a flooded mine for sale at a bargain price brought him his opportunity. A prosperous town house, two more coal mines and a fleet of tugs were soon among Edward Smith's assets, and at the age of sixty he married a pious young wife and resolved to return to Ireland. Eric's father was born shortly before the move.

In 1874 Edward Smith senior aggressively bought the most illustrious property he could find near the site of his family's previous holding. Bellamont Forest was available because profligate descendants of the gentlemanly Cootes, who had originally built the house, had pledged the estate in a game of poker, which they lost. Edward Smith's successful bid did not, however, buy social acceptance. By the time he died, fifteen years before Eric was born, his sense of principle had hardened into bigotry and his bad temper was legendary.

The twists and turns of the tale impressed Eric. His people, he soon reasoned in agreement with his nurse, were not those whom the ceremonial Orange bands represented, the holders of British power and authority. They were really local chieftains who had long ago been dispossessed.

The contradiction was that his own father's new confidence after army service had resulted in the offer of appointment as Justice of the Peace for County Cavan, an honour Amy had urged Edward to accept. For the first time his parents were on good terms, and this was due to mutual allegiance to the Crown. Amy approved of anything that made the family more socially acceptable and she persuaded Edward to add Dorman to their surname. Acutely sensitive to the underlying tensions in the marriage, Eric kept his fascination with rebellion to himself. 'Children are sensitive to maladjustment between their parents,' he confided in a rare mood of candour many years later. 'I know that I was. When parents don't love each other the child, however it is reassured, feels that he, too, is insecure.'

All three boys were earmarked for a world outside Ireland. Chink was destined for the army, Victor for the Royal Navy and Reggie for a splendid career as yet unspecified; it was felt he would be able to tackle anything. They were dressed accordingly. Victor wears the sailor suit in family photographs, while Reggie is bland and confident. Eric looks out defensively, less robust but squaring his shoulders in the proper military manner and drawing himself up to his full height.

He had begun to observe soldiers at close quarters for himself, because contacts made by Edward during the Boer War were easing the Dorman-Smith's social isolation. The large British Army presence in Ireland formed a pool of congenial company for local families with a military connection, and through the 4th Leinster Regiment Edward had met officers in other infantry regiments, and took pleasure in organising shooting weekends in return. Eric studied the visitors in detail, approving of their neatness and aplomb. When invited back with Edward and Amy as regimental guests, he explored each barracks and was greatly taken with everything he saw. Much later he claimed that he had been forced into the army, but the truth is that he met his father's wishes more than halfway.

Although he spent so much time by himself, in retrospect it was a happy enough childhood. 'One of December's wet, warm days', he later recalled in the humidity of the Middle East.

> The bark of a fox, the call of a cock pheasant, the great threshing, splashing descent of a swan onto the water, the flutter of wild duck in the reeds, occasional woodcock. . . . We stoutly shod and not minding rain. Dogs and laughter, and the knowledge that on the hill behind stood a dignified, redbrick house which could be cosy in its strength, and log fires and lamplight and teas – such teas. Every believable kind of bread, far better bread than cake, barmbrack, soda cake, potato cakes, pancakes, honey, home-made jam. One would have to walk up a hill to the house to get that tea, and it would be worth it.

He was not unlike his father at the same age: both as boys were happiest alone, out of doors, and both poured affection on to animals, especially dogs. But otherwise they had little in common, and as Eric grew older this became more apparent. Edward was sufficiently mild to find his son's competitiveness irritating, and the first whipping was administered for boasting that the hassocks in his Catholic church were superior to those in his brothers' Protestant pews. As clashes became more frequent, a ritual evolved in which Eric was marched down to the lake shore and allowed to choose the stick with which he would be beaten. The relationship became progressively strained on Edward's side, faced with a boy who was silently self-absorbed one day and wearingly full of questions the next. Their happiest times together were when they were out shooting. At the age of nine Eric was given a twelve-bore, and it was a source of intense satisfaction to him that neither Victor or Reggie ever learned to shoot as well as he did.

With only a year and two months between himself and the extrovert, straightforward Victor, the gap between the two brothers slowly narrowed. Together they peeped through the keyhole as Miss Faith the governess took her hip-bath, and rowed on the lakes that were supposedly out of bounds, taking turns to swim. 'Floating out in the middle of Bellamont's biggest lake in the deliciously soft water, looking at light clouds against a sunlit sky,' he once recollected, 'that I've always regarded as the height of physical perfection.'

But the idyll could not last. Edward would have been content to stay at Bellamont forever, but Amy insisted that he had a duty to the boys. All three spoke with local accents, she pointed out, and Reggie was approaching preparatory-school age. Eventually Edward gave way. Arrangements were made to let the house and move to England.

'Childhood may be said to have ended', Eric wrote laconically in adulthood, by which time he had perfected a mask, 'when I went to prep school first. England marked a change in many ways. Anglicisation set in, and slowly asserted itself.' The painful reality was that at the age of twelve he was separated from the family and plunged into a class of hostile boys, most of whom had been together for the past four years, at St Anthony's Catholic school in Eastbourne, Sussex. He found he was thinner than most and his teeth stuck out more. Noisy derision at the strong Cavan accent he had until then been unaware that he possessed made him jettison it at top speed, but to his horror he developed a stutter that made him the butt of further sarcasm. The many books he had read meant nothing to most of the boys; the juvenile books he had not read were constantly pointed out to him. It was humiliating to have his untidy left-handed writing criticised, and games periods were a refinement of the ordeal since he knew none of the rules. The only consistency between his previous life and this one was the ritual of Mass.

The rest of the family were installed in a large rented house at Maidenhead; Queen Anne House, at Taplow, fronting on to the Thames. Amy flourished and Edward on official forms described himself as 'gentleman', contriving to fill his days. Victor had settled into Lambrook, a nearby Protestant preparatory school, and it was intended that Reggie should join him there. Eric wrote home and proudly kept his troubles to himself.

He was rescued after a year and sent to join Victor at Lambrook; his stutter vanished almost immediately. After the tribulations of St Anthony's he took the new regime in his stride, and his first report was satisfactory. '1908. *Classics:* Worked exceedingly well. *French:* Translation quite good. *Grammar:* Somewhat weak. *English:* Considerable promise. *Maths:* Good, inclined to work too quickly.

Drawing: Very good. Plays up hard in all games without marked success.'

But although the school suited him, he did not entirely suit the school. Victor was sound, the headmaster duly informed Edward towards the end of the first year, and Reggie had settled in excellently, despite his mother's fears. But the elder boy was a rebel, and in any organised society he would not go far. If one said 'Yes' occasionally, the headmaster explained, one went higher than if one always said 'No.' The interview worried Edward, and the summer holidays were used to good effect. Chink's next report shows that Edward still had a strong influence. '*1909. French:* Considerable improvement. *English:* Considerable general knowledge and has done creditably in Shakespeare. *Maths:* A great advance, both in knowledge and accuracy. Marked improvement – rather too easily discouraged. *Conduct:* Very good.'

His father's problems were harder to solve. England remained too large and too heavily populated for Edward's taste. Keeping up his army contacts, he had made a point of joining a London club, but he rarely went up unless he had to meet someone, and it was noticeable that he was in Amy's shadow. It was also apparent that he was the more careful of the two about money, and this was due to private alarm at the expense of their new life. His children took their financial security for granted, but from this time onwards lack of capital was a constant source of anxiety for Edward.

The problem resulted from his own father's will. In this, Bellamont Forest was entailed to the oldest son for several generations to come, and on the assumption that the estate and its income would remain valued at the sum paid in 1874, the inheritor was to pay interest to younger brothers and sisters who were unable to touch their share directly. That ground-rents might dwindle and rates and taxes multiply had never been envisaged, and as early as 1896, when Eric was still a baby, the result had been unworkable enough for the family to take an expensive court action in London, which resulted in the English Property Act of the same year. This stipulated that property could – henceforth – be transmitted only to 'life and lives in being', leaving Edward's position unchanged.

And Eric's imminent move to public school entailed greater outlay. Edward had selected Uppingham, because it was there that the individual 'house' system had originated, designed to provide a less institutional atmosphere for boys in the care of housemasters and their wives. The school dated from 1534 and was situated in the pretty

Rutland market town of the same name, which Amy was glad to discover had a sufficiently good hotel.

In September 1910 Eric was driven up to Rutland. As they approached, he was impressed by the way the school's pale limestone buildings dominated the town. He was less happy at the prospect of 432 other boys, ten times the number at Lambrook. Despite being better at mixing now, he remained self-conscious enough to admire the ease with which the other newcomers adapted, and as the names and faces took shape he attached himself to a cheerful boy who had been born at a hill station in the romantic setting of Kipling's India.

Brian Horrocks, soon known as 'Jorrocks', intended to join the army too, which was enough to draw them together in the first disorientating weeks. Although they were in different houses, they were able to meet regularly, both in the army class and in Horrocks's natural habitat, the Upper, the Middle, the Leicester and the Cambridge, as the Uppingham playing fields were called. Unlike Eric, Horrocks was more interested in games than anything else, but he never minded questions about his Royal Army Medical Corps father's life, and revealed that his mother came from Ireland. They had little else in common, except their similar height and angular build. Horrocks was impulsive and untidily fair-haired. Eric sleeked his own dark hair back and showed every sign of becoming a fussy perfectionist. Faced with his new friend's gregariousness, he kept up his guard. Horrocks's view that Uppingham was a reasonable prospect and bound to be fun was one he found reassuring.

Eric was in Lorne House, which had the reputation of being the unruliest of Uppingham's thirteen houses. Lorne House won most of the school sporting fixtures, and its senior praeposters, members of the top cricket, fives and rugger teams, lorded it over the thirty-six inmates without interference from the housemaster, 'Jocker' Weldon. 'It was openly stated,' a contemporary school memoir explained, 'that a house which made so much noise and was more or less at all hours in a state of uproar could not be up to any real mischief.'

Weldon was a figure of fun. He suffered from a speech impediment, which turned his strongest term of reproach, 'beastly', into 'beatly', and an ungainly walk due to a knee injury. The boys could mimic both to perfection, and bizarre Jocker Rags were a tradition. These varied from a Staccato Lunch, silent save when the hands of the clock reached each five-minute mark, at which conversation would break out for one minute precisely, to a mock fire, engineered by setting curtains alight in a downstairs study; during Eric's time this started a serious blaze. Preferring to observe, he sometimes envied Horrocks his quieter house.

Uniform was a black Marlborough jacket, striped trousers, stiff white collar, black tie and a speckled straw hat – forerunner of the many formal uniforms both boys would come to wear. As an advance on Lambrook, Eric had his own small study, and Lights Out was satisfyingly late. In the winter terms he went through two boxes of candles and one box of matches each month. Weldon did not visit the dormitories until 10 p.m., candlestick held at arm's length, and as soon as he moved on pandemonium broke out once more.

Quickly Chink assimilated Uppingham slang in his now very passable drawl: a sixpenny bit was a 'tizzy' and to make a major effort was 'to condescend'. Like all new boys, he resented the entrenched fagging system and yearned for more free time. He did not mind being caned by Weldon, who would allow five minutes for the reinforcement of trousers, but he loathed the praeposters' flaunting of their authority, which other boys appeared to accept without question. In one other way, too, he was already showing some individuality. The only school game he enjoyed playing was fives, and the rest he mocked. He took especial pleasure in teasing Horrocks, to whom all games were sacrosanct. 'Cricket, that mind rotter, bored me stiff,' he recalled afterwards. 'I have no talent for collective activities – everything done in rectangles with rigid rules.'

Very quickly he rated the school as uninspiring. By the end of the first year he had come to the conclusion that it was a necessary boredom to be endured before Sandhurst, the entrée to the army. The army class prepared boys who hoped for careers as officers, and the smug disdain of Classical scholars for himself and fellow members was too good to resist. A penchant for baiting those he despised began to make him enemies, and he enjoyed the reputation of being unpredict-able, which grew from capping patronising quotations and sneering back at the discomfited. He was proud of being in the army class; it taught science, a subject in which he scored good marks, and struck him as being the only class in tune with the twentieth century. It also attracted more than its fair share of obtuse bullies, however. But finding that ingenuity could get him out of most situations, unlike his father he reacted by provoking confrontations. It was a practice which Horrocks considered to be a total waste of time.

Eric's gangling appearance made him a natural target, and in the beginning he was picked on repeatedly, especially by a thick-set older boy named Groves, who had stayed down that year. Groves timed his attacks for when the master was looking elsewhere and, realising that he would come off worst in a fight, Eric decided upon humiliation as the best revenge. He took his time until he was equally sure of the routine. In due course Groves bent over a textbook in full view up on the dais for the maths master to correct his work, and Eric was next in line. He jabbed hard with the point of his compasses. 'Groves screamed,' he recorded 'and collapsed over the table with papers and ink everywhere, the class cheered and the master rose and felled me with a flat-handed blow.' He had to spend each half-holiday for the rest of term writing lines indoors, but Groves stayed away from him from then on.

On Officer Training Corps 'field days', Uppingham sent a contingent by train to take on other schools, and at the 1911 mock battle Eric's quick thinking gained him a more substantial triumph. Seizing the opportunity of being taken prisoner by the Rugby contingent, the apparent sincerity of his deliberate misinformation was enough to lead to the saving of Uppingham's military reputation. Back at school the commandant of the army class posted a citation on the school notice-board. Several masters in holy orders subsequently criticised the praising of a boy for telling lies. That winning should be confused with Christianity and playing the game struck Eric even then as ridiculous.

His own religious beliefs were by now thoroughly mixed up. Obediently he drifted along to school chapel with the rest, but he found it unimaginative compared to the flourish of Catholicism; the services did not touch him. Brooding during dull sermons led to the comparison of church teaching with the Arthurian code, and he came to the conclusion that chivalry was the only rule that mattered. 'I could never swallow Anglicanism,' he would write after many theological twists and turns, 'and found it difficult to return to early Catholicism but didn't want to be disloyal. The conflict resulted in neutrality.' He began poking fun at those who took the Bible seriously, but privately he sometimes wished that he too, like Horrocks and the majority, possessed an unquestioning type of faith.

He sat through hours of sermons and absorbed nothing. A glimpse of an unpleasant but not exceptional school incident, however, stayed with him for the rest of his life. Two Jewish brothers in the Lodge, a nearby house, were frogmarched one Good Friday to the top of their stairs and crucified upside down from the bannisters. Standing around beneath, the crowd jeered loudly enough to attract Eric's attention, and he was appalled to identify many of them as boys he had thought were friends of the victims. That vivid image came to haunt him.

'A delicate boy,' Weldon warned Edward in a letter the following term, and went on to recommend that more time should be spent in the gym, 'with a view to broadening out and becoming well set up'. The suggestion had Eric's full agreement because at sixteen, and on the verge of becoming clothes-conscious, he was anxiously aware of his narrow chest and buck teeth. Talk in Lorne House was salacious and increasingly about prostitutes, and, though his manners were polished and he was at ease with older women, he was mortifyingly gauche with girls of his own age. He had no experiences of his own to contribute. The cult of homosexuality disgusted him, but he evaded saying so directly by boasting that the cook at Bellamont Forest had once let him stand on a chair and look down at her breasts, after which all small boys were undesirable; being something of a flamboyant anomaly by now, he got away with the story. Out of the public gaze he spent hours in the school gym, but to little effect.

Too many hours, his father soon came to believe. Poor school reports showed that Eric was slacking in all other areas, and with the added expense of keeping Victor at Dartmouth, on course for the navy, and Reggie at Harrow, where Amy had insisted he should be sent, not to mention the drain of resources to the relations, the Uppingham fees appeared to be a waste of money. Enquiries among members of his London club revealed to Edward that the Sandhurst entrance examination could be taken at seventeen, and at the start of the autumn term of 1912 he proposed the matter to Eric's housemaster. 'Those responsible for his teaching do *not* recommend him entering for the next exam,' Weldon replied instantly. 'At present he is a weak candidate.... entirely a question of *when* he will be fit to go up.... Only fair that you should know this is *not* the date the Army Class masters would fix if the choice was left to them.' Bluntly Weldon pointed out that between 600 and 700 boys had sat the previous examination, some as old as nineteen. 'And while it is quite true we have passed boys into Sandhurst who were no better than him, this has been at times when the number of candidates has been normal.'

The army class masters, Weldon stressed, put December 1913 as the earliest he would stand a sporting chance. Edward did not agree. Suspecting the school of seeking to profit at his expense, he retorted that he would take his boy away if they were unable to provide the teaching he was paying for, and send him to a crammer. His letter had the desired effect.

Eric responded to the challenge. There were only two months to go and, although swotting was considered bad form, he worked as he had never done before. Nothing mattered but getting one of the 172 coveted places. Horrocks was entered for the same examination, but approached it in a characteristically relaxed way; Eric guessed that the new rugger season had his real attention.

The highly competitive Sandhurst examination was held at Burlington House in London's West End shortly before Christmas. Amy arranged for Eric to stay with her greatest friend, a young widow named Dora Gussett who had a house in Trevor Square, South Kensington, and laughter at her name was not enough to offset his dread of having to return to Uppingham branded as a dud.

'Dear Father,' he reported in muted fashion. 'Just a line to say how I got on in the exam. We had an essay in the morning which I did fairly well, then a précis. In the afternoon I had a geography paper in which I did fairly well, and then a general paper which I am afraid rather stumped me. Tomorrow I have history and French. I find the papers rather hard and am dreading the Maths.' But the chemistry paper, held out at Battersea Polytechnic, unexpectedly boosted his morale. Frowning over an important question that made no sense, he spotted a fault and went up to the examiner to point it out, only to be promised full marks if he would leave without another word. No other candidate presumed to double-check, and the implication was not lost upon him.

'His most serious deficiency,' complained that term's school report, 'is his deplorable handwriting and bad spelling. We regret he went up for an examination against the advice of those who had been entrusted with his preparation.' But the results vindicated Edward's judgement. When the successful names were publicly released, it was seen that Dorman-Smith had scored 6969 out of 12,600 – with 51 marks duly deducted for handwriting and 191 for spelling – and came sixty-ninth in order of merit, ensuring him a place. He had come top of all the Uppingham candidates, while to his relief Horrocks was also one of the successful ones; he had squeezed in last but one.

'Out of pique,' Eric wrote many years afterwards, 'my housemaster announced that since the exam had become too low in standard he would cease the practice of recording the names of boys who passed into Sandhurst on the school record boards.' As it happens he was never in a position to notice. Having left Uppingham, he never went back.

2
The
Military
Code

As soon as he ran his eye down the Sandhurst clothes list, Eric knew he had made the right decision. Six white evening shirts, six stand-up collars and one black satin tie promised much. But it was in the small print at the end that he found the real transformation from school. 'Revolvers of the Government calibre are allowed,' this sentence ran, 'but cadets must report possession. . . .'

His father's reaction to the long printed form was less euphoric. Edward had applied for a cut in the annual £150 fees on the basis of his earlier Boer War service, and had been refused. The expense could not be avoided, and there was not even an economical way around the lesser items.

Oblivious to these financial worries, Eric took the train to Camberley in Surrey in February 1913 and reported as instructed to B Company. The classic buildings of Sandhurst were very much as they are today, and at once he felt elevated into a most satisfying way of life. Defining it once, he said it had held all the freedom of a university, and that included a cross-section of fellow cadets. It was his first encounter with arrogant youths of vast private means, straight from Eton or Harrow and destined for the Household Brigade. But there were also many others like himself.

Initial relief at having Horrocks in the same intake did not last long. Eric's military dedication was so total that it was humourless, and he was offended by Horrocks's scruffy turn-out, general casualness and the same old sporting priorities. Soon Horrocks had taken to going to race meetings with a crowd Eric did not know – and did not want to know – and they saw much less of each other than before. The officer instructors and sergeant instructors, however, matched his expectations. All had seen active service, either in the Boer War or in lesser campaigns in India, and he respected them as he had never felt able to respect the masters at Uppingham. Weldon's advice about extra gym was one of the few legacies he thanked his old school for, but even so the punishing Sandhurst timetable wore him out until he had reached an adequate standard of fitness.

Every minute of the cadets' time was taken up in a regime designed over many generations to turn schoolboys into first-class officer material, and civility was high on the list. However rudely they were barked at by the instructors, whose policy it was to provoke, they had to keep their temper, but Eric's unforced admiration made this no problem. He could not even fault the teaching. '*Military History* – Peninsular War, well taught,' he noted. '*Tactics* – South African War, very modern. *Mapping* – very practical. *Field Engineering* – good. The outdoor stuff: *Riding* – tough. *PT and drill* – tough, and *TEWTS* (Tactical exercises without troops) – good.' Tough, from one perfectionist concerning another, was unstinting approval.

The riding school was gruelling, as he had never been taught to ride as a child. The classes were in four grades of ability, and he had to begin at the beginning. 'Dear Sir,' the Commandant wrote to Edward within the month, as he had to write to so many parents. 'Your son fell from his horse in the afternoon sustaining a contusion of the right elbow. It was not necessary to admit him to hospital but he is attending lectures and excused riding and gymnasium. The contusion was rather severe, but no bones broken.' Eric was not deterred; all higher rank officers, even in the infantry, were mounted, so it was an essential skill to master.

The Commandant was too remote a figure to register as a personality. To Eric, authority was represented by his company commander, Major Reidy, who soon came to personify all he most respected in a commanding officer. Reidy's hobby was military history, a passion Eric shared, and unlike the Uppingham praeposters he kept order laconically, without misusing his power. Their exercises were watched without comment, and after his second nonconformist tactical solution in a row Eric was summoned to report. In silence Reidy removed his monocle and began to polish it, glancing up only when he was satisfied with the shine. Quietly he enquired how it was that he arrived at his unusual ideas. The reply was one that would infuriate many soldiers over the years. When problems were handed out, this new cadet boasted, he preferred to wait to see which way everyone else was moving off, and then take the opposite direction. Reidy, unusually, was a kindred spirit. He let go of the monocle and smiled.

But compared in other ways to most of the cadets, Eric felt at a disadvantage. Horrocks never seemed to mind what he looked like on parade, but Eric was less secure. Being one of the youngest had its disadvantages, and he knew he looked even younger than seventeen. At six foot one inch he had stopped growing but had yet to fill out, and though razors featured on the Sandhurst list he had no need for one, and no amount of examination of his upper lip or chin made the prospect likely. In an effort to look older he had already begun to smoke, and he took great pains to be smart at all times.

To make the most of his one advantage, he concentrated hard on the work and by July had inched up to thirtieth in order of merit, gaining 3163 out of 4100 in the end-of-term examinations. It was the equivalent of 75 per cent, but not good enough to achieve his newest goal, which was to pass out of Sandhurst that December at the end of the second term. The odds against this were as long as they had been for the Sandhurst entry, since only the academic elite were allowed to leave early, but he was encouraged by his original success.

Lying in a punt on the Thames off Skindles Hotel that summer, he looked up often from his tactical books to listen to the river singers playing the new ragtime on mandolins or to watch the fun on Skindles Lawn, too self-conscious to join in. He was intent on proving to his parents that he at least had brains, principally to show up their favourite. 'The sun rises and sets on Reg,' he groaned resignedly to Victor, who was still at Dartmouth. But he did not tell Edward about his plan, in case it fell through.

Edward approved of his son's diligence and was relieved that he was not running up debts. In attributing this to thrift, however, he was wrong. Eric chose to drink beer rather than wine or spirits because he viewed drunken camaraderie as a boringly predictable way to court popularity. By now he had also reached the point of mentally dividing fellow cadets into Amateurs and Professionals, using the cricketing analogy. Amateurs were fellows who got drunk, paid too much attention to the form of horses, dined out extravagantly and hung around stage doors waiting for chorus girls. They were Amateurs because they were wasting a unique military opportunity. Professionals were people like himself.

During that second term another incident took place that was to have a permanent effect on him, underlining the impact of the

Uppingham mock crucifixion. Anti-semitism was rife at Sandhurst, and bullying a recurrent hazard. Both revolted him. Tipped off one evening that a rich Jewish cadet in his own company whom he liked was about to be given a humiliating ink bath, he determined to do something. His anger was the greater for having believed the intended victim to be safe because of his low polo handicap, confident, genial manner and generosity, yet the proposed ink bath traditionally ended with an after-dark hunt out of doors, chasing a naked prey. Only one other cadet, a powerful Scot named MacGregor Whitton, agreed to join the defence. Together they took up their stand outside the unsuspecting quarry's room armed with hockey sticks, the only weapons they could find.

'The ringleaders were upset at our lack of solidarity,' Eric noted later. 'But the passage was narrow and it was obvious that if they tried to take him out of the room, someone would get hurt. Whitton and I harangued them, telling them what we thought of them, and while this was going on I heard people moving in behind us, having come up another staircase. I thought we were in for it then, but in fact they were a few deserters shamed into joining us.' The brief victory reinforced his indelible distrust of mobs, and he had found another lifelong classification. The Mob could be composed of both Amateurs and Professionals, once the blood was up; he was reminded of Edward telling him as a child that the reason why his spaniel had to be kept in check out shooting was because it would kill sheep if it joined a roving pack. He worked harder still, to distance himself and to prove his superiority.

He continued to spend his free weekends at Maidenhead, where with Victor and Reggie away at school he enjoyed the novelty of being the centre of attention. He travelled there and back by train, and one autumn evening the return journey found him alone in the carriage, after several stops, with a Camberley girl, Ella Cox, whom the more worldly cadets boasted was readily accessible. Self-consciously he made conversation, only to be taken aback as she jumped up when the train came into the station, kissed him, and ran away laughing up the platform. It was a keen disappointment to find that she had behaved in the same way with a string of cadets, most of whom he considered dull and coarse, and he made no attempt to meet her again. The train journeys had a more formative consequence when towards the end of term he cut his return too fine and accepted a lift in a car that broke down on the way. Reidy glared through his monocle and confined him to college for two weeks, but added that he was doing him a favour. There would be no excuse now for not being among the first ten candidates, and he would be glad to give extra coaching in military history.

Eric took him at his word. In military history he gained 515 out of 600, and 2031 out of 2800 for general military subjects. In total, his marks were a creditable 7976 out of 10,500, putting him tenth overall. He was informed that he would be joining his regiment – still to be allotted – after the Christmas break. As he listened to Reidy's congratulations he jubilantly thought of Horrocks facing into a third repetitive Sandhurst term, and revelled in the triumph. For the last time as an officer cadet he went on parade, and was impressed enough by the staff sergeant's greeting never to forget it. It was an icy morning and their breath steamed as they were put through their paces. 'Gentlemen,' snarled Jock Worrall, famous for his ferocity, 'from tomorrow some of you'll be blooming officers and I will remain what I am, a blooming staff sergeant. But till then, you set of buggers, you'll move. Double march!'

Eric could not get out of Sandhurst quickly enough. But when it came, the letter from the Secretary of State for War – or God, as they had joked – brought him up with a jolt. It directed him to the 1st Battalion, Northumberland Fusiliers, instead of to his first choice, the Royal Fusiliers, whose officers had been the most frequent guests at Bellamont Forest. So sure had he been of getting his way that he had added the Northumberland Fusiliers only on Edward's insistence at the last minute, since one or two officers were also family friends. He still nursed a faint grievance when he reported to the officers' mess at the barracks in Portsmouth. It turned out to be empty, and the man who finally strode in, dignified and to Chink's mind old enough to be the Colonel, introduced himself as the Senior Lieutenant, adding to his sense of anti-climax. It was a sobering example of how slowly promotion was likely to come about, and the prospect of himself being a lieutenant still in twenty years' time was depressing in the extreme.

But nothing could dampen his spirits for long. He was introduced to the three most recently joined subalterns and quickly forgot his disappointment. David Coles had taken the full three terms to pass out of Sandhurst, but was pleasant and welcoming. Edward Boyd was a brilliant Cambridge athlete who had come straight to the regiment from university. And Richard Vachell, the strongest character of the three, was the son of the popular novelist Horace Annesley Vachell, whose books Eric had first read at Bellamont. He responded at once to Vachell's urbane wit, so unlike the schoolboy humour prevalent at Sandhurst, and had him to thank almost at once for his lifelong nickname.

On the first night in the mess Vachell made him stand by the door and studied him, then instructed him to walk forward and turn around slowly. Vachell nodded, remarking cryptically to Boyd that the regiment at last had its mascot back, and they explained that 1st Battalion had last been stationed in India, where their well-known mascot, a Chinkara antelope, had had to be left behind. Guiding him over to the mirror, Vachell showed him his narrow head and pointed ears, so like the Chinkara antelope in a picture nearby on the wall. He would be called 'Chink', Vachell announced, and this, more than anything else, made him feel accepted. Unlike most eighteen-year-olds, it was the first nickname he had ever had, a reflection on his self-sufficiency at Uppingham and Sandhurst. The name 'Eric', he decided, belonged to childhood, and he began referring to himself as Chink at once. The name stuck. So much a part of his identity did it become that he must be Chink in these pages from now on too.

The impression of an antelope was exact. It perfectly caught his wariness and quick movements, sprung with nervous energy. At eighteen he carried himself well and had none of the clumsiness of some tall youths. His thinness was evolving into elegance, accentuated by his long neck and the tapering fingers that were so well set off by the large gold signet ring given to him by his parents on his last birthday. His hands were one of the first things people noticed about him now. Whenever he forgot himself, as he tended to do when carried away in conversation, he used them to make points in a curiously European manner. And with his guard relaxed, the liveliness of his personality was unmistakable in his expressive, mobile face and sparkling blue eyes. With Vachell, Boyd and Coles he rarely stood still. He jinked about, shoulders shrugging, gesturing as he told a stinging anecdote, capping Vachell's quips, teasing Boyd about rugger, getting in digs at Coles for taking so long at Sandhurst, never missing an opportunity that slower minds would let pass. After the years of observing and standing back, he finally let himself go. He even allowed them to take him racing at Goodwood, and declared it was fun after all.

Everything in the subalterns' round was fun. In frock coat and sword he left the necessary visiting cards on admirals and generals stationed in Portsmouth. Cheerfully he submitted to drilling with the new recruits, amused that Sandhurst training was not considered up to scratch. Mastering regimental history for the necessary oral examination was sheer pleasure. He already knew the Northumberland Fusiliers were usually known as the Fifth Fusiliers, because they had been fifth in line when regiments were originally numbered, but he did not realise that they had been founded from Irish followers of the Prince of Orange in 1694 who moved into English service when he became William III. This put his own loyalty, he concluded wryly, in direct opposition to the ancestor who had fought at the Battle of the Boyne.

The Fifth Fusiliers, also known as the Old and Bold, had fought with renown under every great British commander and at every famous battle, and their resolute motto, *Quo Fata Vocant*, was translated as 'Where the Fates Call'. Two battalions had served in India for so long that Kipling had drawn many of his famous characters from the regiment, and the retiring colonel had been adjutant to the man who commanded the battalion in the Indian Mutiny. Tradition held that a Fifth Fusilier ought to speak his mind to his Prime Minister if he considered it his duty to do so. He had no more qualms about being stuck with his second choice.

In 1914 the ranks were mostly Irish, because it was easier to recruit in Dublin and Belfast; officers and NCOs were nearly all from England. At every rank family loyalties stretched back over the generations, and he could sense the pride in the regiment by the quality of the officers he met regularly in the mess. Low pay was accepted on the grounds that it ensured a better type – Edward had had to guarantee him £200 a year, twice the annual pay – and in another society, it occurred to Chink, many of the men would have been in monasteries, so total was their dedication. All could have made better livings in civil life, and all were individualists. One captain was an examiner in the higher standard of Pushtu, a Pathan dialect he had learned in India. Another had written a book about Hausa folklore. A third was an acknowledged expert on pugilism, and a fourth, Captain Gatehouse, had built his own boat and sailed around the British Isles. Chink's company commander, Captain Toppin, was a zoologist and explorer who had recently led an expedition to the High Andes in Peru. Once a fusilier, it was said, always a fusilier, and Chink was honoured to be one of them. At the General's inspection he carried the regimental colour with a swagger.

As the choice of regiment was a lifelong commitment – especially so, given the slow promotion – uniforms were correspondingly distinctive. A cap of raccoon skin gratifyingly replaced Chink's boater. The Adjutant had scrutinised everything as it was unpacked, since anything ill-fitting would reflect badly on the regiment. The Sandhurst list was sketchy in comparison to regimental needs, which included scarlet full-dress, an undress frock coat, blue serge jacket, scarlet mess kit with sword and sash, and impeccable Savile Row plain clothes, from evening tails to shooting suits. His tendency towards vanity gathered momentum, and it began to be noticed that he was unable to pass a mirror without glancing sideways and preening. Suits hung well on his spare frame and he knew it; however tired, he never tossed his clothes across a chair but always hung them up meticulously. He became fastidious. His hair was always trimmed short, his nails neat and his boots and shoes gleamed. It came as a shock to discover that his long-awaited beard was growing out auburn, taking after his mother, instead of being black like his own head of hair. He shaved with elaborate care, undecided about whether or not he would ever be able to risk a moustache.

At the annual Northumberland Fusiliers celebration of St George's Day on 23 April 1914, when he had been in the regiment two months, he entertained his parents with aplomb, resplendent in scarlet. One hundred and forty-four bottles of champagne were drunk that day in the mess and, careful as always about drink, since he hated the sensation of losing control, he arrived at the Sergeants' Ball that evening sober. Nursing his first hangover the following day, he held two NCOs responsible for deliberately plying him with whiskey.

In July he was dismissed from the barrack square, in company with Boyd and Coles, and to celebrate they bought a sailing boat between them. None knew how to sail and their worst moment, they agreed, was bobbing through the Home Fleet anchored in the Solent for the ceremonial Royal Review, to a storm of oaths.

He was happy. In the summer of 1914 he saw himself as a Professional among Professionals in the best of all regiments, and he had good friends. Reggie wrote admiring letters from Harrow, and he was well ahead of Horrocks, who was still stuck at Sandhurst. And on top of it all he had discovered the hero he had subconsciously been searching for. Lieutenant Lindsay Barrett, a subaltern four years his senior, was exactly the type of officer Chink intended to become himself, and unbelievably – since he still suffered from agonising bouts of self-dislike – Chink found that Barrett was very friendly in return.

They had been introduced in the mess, where Barrett was pointed out as having won the Sword of Honour at Sandhurst. The tall, fair-haired soldier who came across carried with him an absolute self-confidence, and so eclipsed did Chink feel that it was some time before he appreciated the mental agility which matched his own. Barrett never let a platitude pass, and was interested in anything that would make the army more efficient. He would argue on the side of idealism, but at the same time he was realistic and could laugh at himself. He detested snobbishness and was at ease with men of every rank, with an effortless assumption of authority that Chink longed to develop himself. Talking to him, as he made a point of doing whenever the chance arose, Chink came to look at their grand traditions with similar criticalness, and he was proud at being treated as an equal.

He modelled himself on Barrett completely. In any given situation he tried to envisage what Barrett would do, and he adopted all his mannerisms, down to copying his habit of studying *The Times* daily for military information. After a week spent with Barrett's hospitable family in Northumberland he got up the courage to invite him back to Maidenhead, and deliberately chose the weekend of Reggie's half term.

Two weeks before Chink's nineteenth birthday he noticed in *The Times* that a minor archduke he had never heard of had been assassinated in an obscure city called Sarajevo. It was so unimportant that he did not mention it to Barrett in the mess that night. His next orderly-officer duty was on 25 July, the day after his birthday, and as he soaked in the bath that evening, through the open door he admired the scarlet mess uniform laid out on his bed. Boyd called in to check the time and, seeing him in the bath, attacked with a towel. Chink scrambled out and made a grab for his sword. Flourishing it in the expected swashbuckling manner, he drove it finally not into the wooden floorboards, as he intended, but into his foot. The cut was a shallow one but it would not stop bleeding, and since it was strictly against regulations to fool about with swords Boyd helped him to bandage it and pull on his boot. Within the month Chink was using the same sword in earnest – this time at Mons.

3
A Hell
of a
Time

The British Expeditionary Force was quick off the mark. So quick, indeed, that there were no crowds to watch 1st Battalion, Northumberland Fusiliers as they marched to Portsmouth railway station on 13 August 1914, and no attention had been given to the matter of catering. It was assumed that meals would be provided en route between Southampton and Le Havre. Edward and Amy impulsively brought Reggie with them to say goodbye.

Disembarking in France at 3 a.m. that night, the battalion faced a longer march before they could catch a train to the front. The orderly column started off in style, Chink marshalling his platoon among the rest, but soon parade-ground smartness broke up as men began to faint from lack of food and the effects of last-minute enteric inoculations. The requisitioned horses, more unfit than the troops, jibbed and plunged, causing further delay. As the early Normandy sun came up they straggled on, only to find no food or shade when they finally made camp. It was late afternoon before supplies reached them.

None of this daunted Chink. It was adventure, and with the resilience of youth he bagged a window seat in the train taking them east, and waved back at the many old women who unbent from their work in the fields to twirl an imaginary moustache in imitation of the Kaiser and point towards the border, drawing the other hand sharply across their throats. It was immensely satisfying to know that Horrocks would not yet have got his final Sandhurst results.

The train stopped at Landrecies and the battalion marched on to Noyelles, where the BEF was assembling before setting off towards the enemy. By dawn on 22 August Chink was on parade with his platoon at Le Longeville, aware that they were about to take the offensive. He was the most minor of cogs in a massive wheel. B Company of 1st Battalion had become part of 9th Brigade, which was in 3rd Division of II Corps, under the command of General Sir Horace Smith-Dorrien; Smith-Dorrien in turn reported to the leader of the BEF, Field Marshal Sir John French. Chink was sufficiently detached as they approached the Belgian border to look out for the site of the Battle of Malplaquet.

The six-mile stretch of front allotted to his regiment ran along the Mons Canal from the village of Nimy to the steel bridge at Mariette, and it was Mariette that Chink's company was ordered to hold. South of the Mons Canal was a densely populated tangle of mining villages but north, where the Germans were said to be, the countryside was open. Marching towards the bridge they had to make their way between excited Belgian crowds pressing cigarettes, chocolate and cigars upon them. Chink was appalled to be singled out when women began to shout that he was too young, and some tried to pull him out of the column. He shook them off angrily, humiliated in front of Boyd whose platoon was also in B Company.

The sixty-foot bridge was a difficult proposition to defend. It was a double bridge, with a central towpath, and orders were vague. They had been instructed to maintain position for as long as possible, with the company commander, Captain Yatman, authorised to use his discretion about withdrawal. Nothing had been said about blowing the bridge, the only method of turning the canal into a serious obstacle.

Resemblance to the familiar training exercises was minimal. B Company shackled the level-crossing gates in the Germans' path towards the bridge, and wired these to the nearest buildings. Using his initiative, Chink broke off a length of ornamental iron railing from a nearby garden and jammed it across the bridge's northern end, explaining that they would be able to shoot through it and the enemy would not be able to climb across under fire. All nearby houses were evacuated and the cluster of barges sunk, but the defences were still unfinished by next morning when it was learned that the Germans were less than four miles away. Two of Chink's Dublin reservists chose their moment to ask if they could keep their rifles after the war. One thing at a time, he said tersely. The British attack was scheduled for 9 a.m.

The BEF had 70,000 men and 300 guns – against, as it would turn out, 160,000 Germans with 600 guns – and the roar of British musketry when it came was to Chink's right. He was exhilarated by a sense of

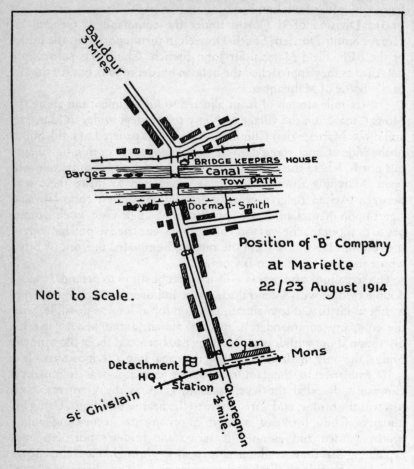

Baudour
3 miles

BRIDGE KEEPERS HOUSE

Barges   Canal
              TOW PATH

Dorman-Smith

Position of "B" Company
at Mariette
22/23 August 1914

Not to Scale.

Cogan

Mons

Detachment
HQ

Station

St Ghislain

Quaregnon
½ mile.

occasion, having pointed out to Boyd earlier that they were about to take part in the first British battle in Europe since Waterloo; the Crimea, he considered, had been further afield. But inside the hour German infantry poured into Mariette's main street and gained the safety of houses by the bridge. Using screaming local children as cover, they cut the level-crossing wire and swarmed forward. Chink memorised the *Pickelhaubes* and field grey uniform as he ordered his men to shoot, only to be told that the first shot had to be his. He took the proffered rifle and fired, counting three bodies before he handed it back. Rapidly the enemy gained control, and though the iron railings were still in place a field gun was being manhandled to the canal bank. By 3.30 p.m. German infantry and artillery were massing there, and the beleagured B Company had no way of knowing that their brigade had been ordered to withdraw an hour before. Their signaller had been killed in the first German rush.

For a further hour they fought on in the hope that orders would come through to demolish the bridge, but when casualties reached eight killed and eleven wounded the company commander ordered his men out. While they were falling back towards the town of Frameries the orders were rushed up by motorbike, too late to be effective. German columns could be seen moving in the same direction within half a mile, and Chink waited with Boyd and the rest until dusk to filter back. They slept as they were on the cobbled streets after a night of entrenching and building barricades, their rations one piece of bread each from the local baker's output, which had had to be shared among all the British troops. Chink raised a smile by reminding Boyd of the Biblical loaves and little fishes.

Frameries was attacked by the Germans at first light, and after two hours of hard fighting Chink realised that the Northumberland Fusiliers were in a tight spot. Regiment after regiment was pulling out around them in response to Field Marshal French's order to withdraw, but not until 9.30 a.m., with the town almost overrun, did their own orders come through. Drawing his sword, with Boyd similarly armed at his side, Chink made his escape. Behind the street barricades he could hear German soldiers hammering at houses in frantic attempts to knock out loopholes in the walls in time to fire at the British.

The long columns of infantry of 9th Brigade stretched out in retreat. Each man carried sixty pounds of kit and ammunition, and on the morning of 24 August they were worn out before they began. Chink was briefly cheered when the corps commander Smith-Dorrien rode past on horseback to rally them, but his enduring memory was of being among thousands of exhausted, hungry men who were too confused to do anything but keep up the pace. At Bermeries they slept out in the open and at 5 a.m. were off again, finishing the twenty miles to Inchy in punishing rain. At 10 p.m., still without food or shelter, they were allowed to rest till 2 a.m. and when he woke then Chink was glad to hear they could go back to sleep. He realised the implication of the reprieve later when they were told to stand to and fight at dawn. Clearly they were not retreating fast enough to avoid a confrontation.

Against the clock Chink helped to redig the shallow trenches, before going to take up position as a reserve platoon in a sunken road to the rear. But the German bombardment overshot the British front line, and exploded over the reserves. Chink was hit at once. As he regained consciousness he heard someone above him saying 'That poor bugger's got it;' to his surprise the blood he was soaked in came from a shrapnel wound in his left arm and from widespread surface cuts. In the chaos stretcher-bearers were everywhere, and finding that he could walk he was told to look for a field ambulance; disorientated, he then had to be pulled back from the direction of the German lines where he promptly headed. He was led to the hospital train which was waiting in a siding at St Quentin, and lost consciousness again. When he woke up he was in base hospital at Rouen.

His first reaction was to gloat that his name would be featured in casualty lists while some members of his old form were still hanging on at Uppingham in the hope of getting on one of the first sports teams. He knew Weldon took *The Times*, and that Lorne House would be following the war. He was sent back to England and as soon as he arrived at King Edward VII Hospital in London he sent a restrained telegram to Edward – 'Arrived 17 Belgrave Square this morning, slightly wounded' – and phoned home. But disconcertingly Amy accused him of being home from the war too early; as the telegram had not yet been delivered, and the casualty lists were not to be published till 5 September. The role of wounded hero appealed to Chink, however, and as he watched the matron approach him on the first ward round he composed himself for a compliment. She paused, enquired pointedly if he had brought his nanny with him, and then had him exhibited out on the balcony to prove to the crowds below how young their soldiers were.

The wound was in his upper left arm, its exit near his elbow, and his category was severe, but not permanent. He was given a month's sick leave, told he was too thin when he duly reported, and apart from applying for a new sword and revolver to replace those lost, all he could do was follow the war in the papers. A further month went by.

The battalion was in reserve near Kemmell when he got back to them in November, and he was in the front line next day. Horrified by the changes since he had last seen them, he contrived to hide his shock. Four officers were left out of the twenty-five who had sailed with him, and total strength had been whittled down to 200 men. Lindsay Barrett was Acting Adjutant, having taken over after heavy losses on 22 October, and Chink's company commander at Mariette Bridge, Yatman, was now the commanding officer. His first company commander had been killed at the Aisne on 15 September in a morning advance against Germans entrenched in a well-hidden position. In the following week of fierce fighting seven more officers had died, but none grieved Chink as much as the news that Boyd had been shot in the head by a sniper on 20 September, while pinned down in a trench.

The catalogue of loss was almost too much to take in. Coles was also dead, killed on 27 October at Neuve Chapelle after fourteen days of continuous fighting; he, too, had been picked off by a well-positioned sniper. Vachell had been badly wounded on 18 October at Herlies, in the fighting leading up to Neuve Chapelle, in pitiless shellfire that had wounded forty-one others that day and killed nine. The most recent nightmare was the disappearance of Captain Fletcher, the boxing specialist, who was known to have been killed with others on 1 November but whose body could not be found. That day's fighting at Wyttschaete was already recognised as a forlorn hope; only a miracle could have saved Fletcher and his men after vague instructions to advance in the dark over unreconnoitred ground towards an objective that could not be taken by such a small body of men.

Hunched in crowded, wet trenches as the weather got colder through the battles of Messines, Armentières and Ypres, Chink reflected on the reasons for so much loss of life, unable to stop thinking about Boyd and Coles; although there was little opportunity to talk to Barrett, the fact that he was alive nearby conveyed the only sanity. But he perfected a laconic, witty style to keep everybody at bay, including his family, and on 9 December when he was wounded again – in the calf this time – his letter to his father from the Duchess of Westminster Hospital, Boulogne, made no mention of the horrors.

'It's only a slight affair,' he wrote, passing off his wound. 'A graze just below the back of my right knee caused by a sniper who was enfilading our trench at long range. He got in some jolly pretty shooting, bagging two men and an officer – myself – in two shots, myself just as I had finished tying up the other two. I got down here yesterday and we are jolly comfortable. The Duchess, disguised as a hospital nurse, looks us up occasionally and usually manages to wound my feelings by saying I ought to be at school. . . . I'm told my wound was rather providential as my left foot might have got rather bad if I had stayed on up country. Its rather swollen and puffy with very little feeling in it, and the doctor is busy giving it iodine baths. . . . The trenches are very wet indeed. I am quite able to hobble about with the aid of a stick. It is jolly bad luck the way I am always stopping German bullets.'

On New Year's Eve he was allowed home and found himself the centre of Amy's matchmaking plans. Her wealthy friend Lady Watson had an eighteen-year-old daughter named Doreen who would inherit an income of £7000 per annum, and a tactful stay was arranged at the Watson's Scottish estate. He shot rabbits, escorted Doreen to a music hall and gallantly skated in the moonlight with her, but he fell through the ice, which did not improve his trenchfoot. On return to Maidenhead he insisted on rejoining the regiment's northern depot against his doctor's advice, where he fretted until the Medical Board passed him in March. On St Patrick's Day he lunched with Amy and Lady Watson at the Curzon Hotel and took Doreen to dinner at Pagani's. 'Eric back to those unthinkable trenches,' Amy recorded next day in her diary. Nothing definite had been said, but she was pleased with progress.

Chink was writing home simultaneously, excited at being free of inertia.

English Channel, 18 March 1915. The best crossing I have had. I went to sleep on my sofa just outside Southampton and didn't wake up until we were just off Havre. We are waiting till the tide rises enough to take us up river to Rouen where I pick up my draft. You had better start sending out a small weekly hamper with some cigarettes included. It helps the company Mess so much. I crossed with a fellow I had not met since prep school. We recognised each other immediately, isn't it a small world? I am awfully pleased with my new furlined coat and soft cap. It makes sleeping in one's own clothes so much easier. . . . I see our machine gun officer has been wounded again so I may get the guns if I am lucky. It would mean a lot to me to be MG officer – a horse to ride, living with HQ where I hear all the news and am usually with Lindsay. I ought to rake in at least a mention in despatches this time.

Lindsay Barrett was no longer Acting Adjutant. He had given Chink the news when visiting him earlier in Boulogne hospital that he was in the running for an independent company command, and his absence was a blow. The battalion, further depleted, was still in the Ypres salient when he reached them, within fifty yards of the Germans now and still without the initiative. Pinned down once more by snipers, he was alarmed at the proportion of untrained recruits around him, but was glad to meet John Lawson, a new subaltern the same age as himself. Lawson was already talked about as a character, and his phrase 'I want to go soldiering,' said to be his argument when requesting a regular army commission after his baptism of fire in the Special Reserve, had become a company catchphrase.

2.4.15. The post is pretty regular now and our servants bring up our letters when they take our grub in the evenings. . . . Things are pretty quiet – too quiet. There's a kind of lull before the storm feeling about it. . . . We live like dukes in the trenches these days. For breakfast we had bacon and eggs and rolls and ham and tea. For lunch we are going to have salted herring and bangers and bacon to follow. Tea and toast, if we can manage on a brazier, at 5 o'clock. . . . The German trenches run round our little redoubt on three sides of a circle. . . . I've not shaved for a week now nor washed my neck. Except for a slight throat caught through sleeping indoors, I am extraordinarily fit and cheery.

His promotion to lieutenant came through promptly, but someone else got the guns.

On 5 April they took over the defence of St Eloi, where the Germans had captured the vantage point of a mound which pinned down troops in the British trenches. It was frustrating that the enemy also possessed superior quantities of ammunition, and when German grenades burst above them one day without warning, leaving twenty killed and wounded around Chink, he could only help the new machine gun officer to bluff with a short double salvo in return.

24.4.15. I was pleased to see in last night's papers that we carried the mound and 500 yards of German trench – these journalists are the most marvellous folk I have ever heard of! I am still in the trenches and rapidly growing roots. I believe that when I come home again I'll build a dugout for myself in the back garden and only wash once in every three days. Irritating gases are the latest speciality. Beastly smell just like strong mustard and cress, and very irritating to the eyes. All the men were weeping with the beastly stuff. I was asleep so almost escaped. . . . I read one book of Vachell's since Monday and am halfway through *Lorna Doone* in my spare time. I hope you are not worrying or anything silly. Please don't, for I am most awfully careful nowadays and the rashness has gone out of me.

When a company officer went sick he was told to deputise for him in the front line, and jumped at the chance. '*30.4.15.* I came up last night and spent all today making a sketch of my trench and trying to dodge the German snipers. The whole trench has been so neglected that I don't know where to start. I have just sent in the deuce of a report to the brigade.' It is the first hint of the Professional at work. But the significance of their extra time in the forward trenches escaped him, and he did not realise that the trench they were simultaneously constructing in reserve was being dug in anticipation of the collapse of the salient.

The present was quite absorbing enough.

14.5.15. We turn in about 2 a.m. and I don't usually turn up again till 12 noon when I breakfast. Then we sit and read or play patience or write till teatime. At dusk the servants arrive with our mail, papers, grub etc., and we have dinner. After I usually go for a walk to stretch my limbs and as I'm now back in a support trench I walk around the front line and visit my various pals, taking a drink and a cigarette off each. This gin crawl usually lasts for an hour and is the cheeriest time of day. Everyone has a yarn and is jolly pleased to see a visitor. I nearly died of laughter last night. Lawson, my brother subaltern one month older, was coming with me over a particularly broken bit of ground. There were lots of spare bullets about and whenever a starlight went up we were exposed so I didn't want to hang about very much. John pretended he knew the ground and was just saying 'I know there's a six foot hole just here' when he vanished. I became so powerless from laughter that I only just missed falling in myself.

The only person who didn't see the joke was John. The hole was about seven feet deep, and full of tins.

Chink and Lawson shared a reserve dugout, and being equally fond of animals adopted a terrified local stray, which they called George. Whenever the artillery opened fire the dog cowered and whimpered in a corner or attempted to bolt away, impervious to soothing. To complete their domesticity they helped themselves to chairs and sofas from a smouldering château within walking distance at Potizhe. '29.5.15. We took over a new bit of the line last night. Poor trenches made by the French dug out like a pigsty. The second bombardment of Ypres has absolutely reduced it to ruins. It was still on fire when I went through last night and parts smelt terribly. The place, especially the low-lying dugouts, still smells of gas from the last attack. A sickly, cloying odour with a hint of chloride at the back of it. I don't think it's much to be afraid of if you get your respirator on quickly and get well out of the bottom of the trench. We wear the respirators for about half an hour every day, so as to breathe the solution on them well into our lungs and coat them with a protective layer.'

Although battalion casualties had topped 600 by now, the enemy remained invisible, which made everyone restless. 'I wish they'd give us a show,' Chink had let off steam to Edward a few weeks earlier. 'It's really very easy to go on once you've seen the enemy's trenches get shelled and got your blood up. The loss of whole platoons in an attack is not half so hard on the nerves as a few men shot through the head in trench work.' He was obsessed by Boyd's fate, the most athletic and daring of them all. When news at last came through that they were to attack on 15 June, it brought with it a charge of energy.

The complicated assault plan revealed at their briefing was intended to capture German positions further along the St Eloi sector of Ypres, attacking an area from Bellewaarde Lake to Railway Wood. It would have fitted easily into the Bellamont grounds beside the drive, he reflected, and was similar in terrain. Three regiments were to take part, leapfrogging over each other in separate waves of troops to carry the assault into backup enemy trenches. It was a complicated manoeuvre for such untrained men, and as their own artillery would be shelling the enemy to break morale and inflict maximum casualties, they were to be equipped with distinctive screens to show the British gunners when to pause. Bombardment was to start in the dark at 2.50 a.m. and lift at 4.15 a.m. to allow the first wave to go in. Chink and Lawson were detailed to wait with their platoons in reserve, and to go in with the second wave.

As the battlefield was eight marching hours away, the regiment paraded at 4.45 p.m. on the afternoon beforehand to be sure of reaching their positions on time. Each man carried two extra bandoliers of ammunition, one day's rations and iron rations, two empty sandbags and a waterproof sheet; the first reserves also had shovels slung across their backs. Four hundred hand grenades, carried on stretchers, would be shared between them on arrival. The long march took them through the battered town of Ypres and along the Menin Road, until they were held up by other troop movements at the aptly named Hell Fire Corner, where they had to wait, straining every nerve, for fifteen minutes. But they arrived on time – professional as always, Chink noted – and he and Lawson took up position in reserve from where they could see the first assault.

At 4.10 a.m. the British guns fell silent, and five minutes later the first wave of men rushed forward. Chink and Lawson watched helplessly as two of their company commanders, two younger officers they knew well, and many familiar NCOs and men were mown down by enemy machine-gun fire in no-man's land, before reaching the wire. It was clear as the assault built up that their marker screens were obscured by smoke and dust from shelling, because the British artillery was continuing the bombardment, following the timetable laid down by the High Command, and killing as many British as Germans. The front line, however, was carried.

Chink and Lawson set off with their platoons on cue, at once oblivious of each other. Scrambling into the captured German trench Chink set about counting platoon survivors in a mêlée of men from other regiments, pushed on by each new influx. With the regiments entangled, he was carried along over the top again, and raced towards the second objective, which was a further line of German trenches. Here only one frightened second lieutenant, young enough to look like a schoolboy, was alive. Chink took stock of the situation. The only protection for the men who were following him was in the centre of the trench where it was three feet deep. If they could not attack across the open towards the third objective it would be impossible to hold for long. But accurate German fire from the trenches beyond made advance impossible. There were three inexperienced junior officers with him now and leaderless men from a mixture of regiments. All dug furiously with entrenching tools in the hope of extra protection.

By midday the sun was directly overhead and a pall of smoke hung over nearby Ypres. From where Chink was trapped, almost blinded by his own sweat, he watched the British shells pitching towards them, hurling earth and metal into the trench, and longed to undo the cumbersome chinstrap of his helmet to wipe the sweat away. But it was against regulations to take it off. The trees of Railway Wood were blurred by shrapnel smoke and everywhere he looked he saw dead men, many of whom he knew. As he stared around, one blackened face moved in the pile of bodies beside his trench. 'The man did not call out,' he wrote years later, unable to forget.

He seemed like a curious bystander, propping himself up on his elbow to watch a sporting event. Suddenly I saw two of our fusiliers leave their digging and run back to him. I watched them stoop to lift him. They looked towards the trench, crowded and shallow. I wanted to say 'Bring him over' but my brain was working mechanically. The trench could hold no more and we had to have some freedom of movement to use our weapons. I heard myself shout 'Come back to the trench – put him down' and I could feel his eyes staring at me.

The picture returned in nightmares all his life.

He lost count of time. One of the young officers was wounded and evacuated, and by late afternoon the other two were so badly shot they could not be moved, though conscious and in severe pain. Reinforced German troops were massing for attack and Chink had few men left capable of handling a rifle. Without warning a concerted attack broke out on their left. Every foot of the parapet was raked by a continuous stream of bullets, and the enemy charged up the communications trench, bombing as they came. Grazed in the spine by a piece of shrapnel and dazed with concussion, Chink did not realise that he had four lesser injuries from rifle bullets as well. He could sense more German soldiers pushing up from the right and, pulling himself up, he found he was the sole survivor. Among the dead were the last fusilier bomber and both wounded officers.

'Then a young soldier of the Liverpool Scottish came,' reported the official regimental account subsequently, 'to tell Dorman-Smith that Germans were working up the trench to within 60 yards of where they were. Barely had this lad delivered his report than he, too, was shot dead.' Chink acted automatically. In the hope of finding more men alive he began to search in the direction of the enemy, and gathered up the few left. 'It was evident,' continues the gazette account, 'that if they were to escape capture or annihilation at the hands of the enemy . . . it could only be by risking immediate retirement across the open. It was thus . . . that Dorman-Smith and a mere handful of other ranks escaped from the position which their companies had captured and held for nine hours, and made their way back to the shelter of the old German front line.' For the coolness of his rescue he was awarded one of the first coveted batch of the Military Cross.

Recognising the scale of disaster, the British command had called off the attack some time earlier. Towards evening the 1st Battalion survivors began their eight-mile march back to the regiment's transport lines, and Chink's wounds prevented him from going with them. Against his will he was helped on to an ambulance lorry making its way to the nearest Red Cross post, but he was unable to rest. As the ambulance slowed in the military traffic that clogged the town of Poperinghe he climbed down and headed for the transport lines too, his head-start enabling him to reach them first. The sight of batmen running towards him, each man frantic for news of his officer or for any news at all, was another image of waste that would never fail to anger him.

The proud regiment was almost wiped out. Out of 645 other ranks, 486 were casualties, and of the officers only Yatman, the quartermaster, the transport officer and he were left on their feet. Lawson had been shot through the artery of his wrist jumping down into the first trench. 'All the other officers who were with me at East Boldon have been killed or badly wounded,' he wrote tersely in his next letter home. 'We move at 3 a.m. today. I am OC 2 troop.' But Lindsay Barrett, who was commanding his own company elsewhere, remained unharmed.

By the time his letter reached them, his parents' third buff-enveloped War Office telegram had already arrived. 'Regret to inform you . . . head and back, but not seriously.' Amy had become fatalistic. When, within the week, another was delivered during dinner to announce that he had reached London on sick leave, she felt no urgency. 'Packed Ted off at once to see him,' she noted in her diary. 'I went last time.' Chink was not home for long. The difficulty of replacing experienced officers was acute and the monotony of trench life began again within a fortnight, with new recruits making their numbers up to full strength.

'*28.6.15*. We are shifting to more stormy and gaseous quarters at 3 a.m.,' he informed Edward. 'The poor second battalion has had another cutting up. The second within three weeks, but has behaved very gallantly.' His father, frustrated in an army desk job in Scotland, wanted to pull strings to have him moved out of the front line, but he underestimated Chink's sense of duty. '*18.7.15*. It would be awfully nice to have a good job that showed more of the show than a company commander sees . . . but I'm much more use where I am . . . and though in quieter days my colonel might have recommended me, I'm sure he will not let me go with things as they are. I wish I could do it as it would save you all a lot of anxiety but regular officers, especially subalterns, are getting very scarce.' The rise from a platoon to a company within one year implied more rapid promotion than he could have hoped for before the war, but already the days spent sailing and speculating about the odds of promotion seemed to have happened to somebody else. '*24.7.15*. It's been a funny 20th birthday. The queerest I'll ever spend, I suppose. Still rather moist hereabouts and very hard to keep one's feet dry. The trench is built on clay and consequently holds the wet and makes drainage difficult. I'd quite a birthday party in my dugout this afternoon. Five people to tea – not so bad . . . Our tenth day [in the front line] and we're going to do a fortnight at least. However, I'm not complaining and all the men seem very cheery, too.'

It reads convincingly, but the optimism was to reassure himself as much as his parents. Each time that Chink had to force himself back under heavy fire now, it took a greater self-control, and the clarity of his imagination was becoming destructive. His habit of military analysis stoked a deepening anger. He was unable to stop thinking about the British mistakes, so evident in the crass stupidity of Bellewaarde Wood where a fine regiment had been thrown away without intelligent appreciation of the difficulties. He had always been highly strung, and now he was honed to a brittle edge, seeing his fellow soldiers in the trenches in two dimensions only – the dead and the not yet dead. He hated being pointed out as a celebrity to newcomers – the surviving hero – because he felt distanced further by every admiring glance. Nightmares lurched him awake so that he was able to sleep for only snatches at a time, unlike the spring when he had boasted about blotting out gunfire for twelve hours at a stretch.

On 2 August the battalion went back into a new section of front-line trenches, north-east of Ypres, for twelve days of constant shelling. It was very near the château of Potizje where he had shared his dugout with John Lawson, but there was little resemblance otherwise. Lawson was still in hospital in England and not expected to return, and George the dog had long run off. The friends they had visited each evening were all dead, and though the fusilier uniform and slang surrounding him was familiar, the men were too young and too vulnerably trusting. His strong compassion for victims everywhere was magnified by his sensitivity to atmosphere, and where another man would have been able to switch off and busy himself in trivia or daydreams, Chink had no escape route. His mind was the busy centre of the world, never in low gear, and he masked strain by a wit that was too sardonic to be humorous any more. At last his commanding officer saw behind the façade, and pulled him out. Diagnosis in the Fourth London General Hospital at Denmark Hill was nervous exhaustion caused by stress of active service and previous wounds, and he was not discharged. A crucial episode in his life was about to take place.

On the daily ward round six days later his bed was found to be neatly made – and empty. Search in the hospital grounds revealed no sign of him and his uniform was missing. When his family were contacted it was revealed that he had not been in touch with them at all. Amy's diary for 12 August 1915 reads, 'So very anxious. No news of Eric for days so Ted went to London by Midnight train.' They were living in Scotland to be near Edward's war work, and she felt as isolated as always when removed from the vicinity of London. '15 August. Wire from Ted. Eric left hospital. He has not arrived home. Am most anxious.' On impulse she wired Edward that she thought Chink might have gone to the house in Maidenhead, but Edward had already come to the same conclusion. He took a cab to the shuttered house and walked around the garden in the dusk, looking for some sign of occupation and furious that he had not brought the keys with him.

In an iron garden chair, facing towards the Thames, Chink was sitting motionless and did not turn around. Edward sat on the chair beside him and waited, too inhibited to take his hand. Eventually, in the darkness, he persuaded him to come with him. It would transpire that Chink had been there alone all the time, without food or warmth, and during the following fortnight's sick leave his sleep pattern remained disturbed. Edward treated him as he had when Chink was a boy. He took him shooting – pheasant, as they were in Scotland – and talked about country matters and his own childhood at Bellamont. For his part, Chink would make light of the experience subsequently, and never disclosed anything more than that he had been 'pretty well played out and sent home for a rest'. Nowadays it would popularly be called a nervous breakdown, and two weeks considered a ludicrously short time to obtain results; one can speculate about its part in the impatience and self-preoccupation that would come to antagonise so many of his contemporaries in due course.

Within a fortnight Chink seemed almost his old self again, although he refused all attempts by Amy to make him get in touch with Doreen. He insisted on going back to the regiment at their Newcastle training depot, and at the end of September was appointed instructor in bombs and grenades at the Army School of Trench Warfare at Wrotham. His only stipulation was that he must be allowed to go back to France at short notice as soon as the opportunity arose. On 14 January 1916 his MC was announced in the *London Gazette*, and he pestered the regiment with requests. In February, with substantive captain's rank, he was allowed back to the front line.

The war had scarcely moved in his absence. The battalion was still at Ypres, and reserve was in Poperinghe, where he had got down off the ambulance. Once more everything felt unreal. 'I am the only com-batant officer who sailed with the Battalion in 1914,' he wrote to Edward, more man to man now. 'Very cold. Heavy fall of snow today, some inches. Thank goodness we aren't in trenches. . . . The Bosche are having a hell of a time at Verdun, tremendous casualties – worst in the war.'

It was while in reserve, after a long trench duty near the Ypres Canal, that he again met Lindsay Barrett, who happened to be serving in the same war-torn area. To be a temporary lieutenant-colonel at the age of twenty-five and hold his own command was a distinction, and Barrett had become a by-word in the regiment. He was as friendly and interested in Chink as before, however, and insisted that they dine together at once. Barrett's grasp of his job, with his unassumed dominance over the men Chink met in the strange mess, impressed him as much as before the war. But it was his pungent criticism of the way the war was being run that was most reassuring. 'It's very nice seeing him again,' he wrote home before going to bed, and they spent the following morning together as well. Lunching at Barrett's mess, Chink listened without interruption when told that he must take Edward's advice and try for a staff job in Divisional Intelligence. He had more than done his duty in the trenches, Barrett argued, and noticing Chink's hesitation pressed the point. He himself would do so, he said, if he were in Chink's shoes. Before he left, Chink agreed to apply.

Within twenty-four hours he was in the same stretch of the St Eloi trenches that he had spent so long in the previous year, but casualties were low and the staff-job decision brought a rare sense of relief. On 19 March the battalion marched back in the bright sun to reserve once more, and a day later their mail caught up with them. Chink had difficulty comprehending what he read. Lindsay Barrett had been shot through the head by a German sniper three days after their lunch and had died at once. Dick Vachell, who had volunteered for the Royal Flying Corps on recovery from his bad 1914 wound, had been killed the same week. Numbly he wrote to Edward. '*21.3.16*. That divisional job has been hastened by the fact that the CO wanted to send me home again because my nerves are as bad now as they were last August. Lin's death has been a most awful shock, on top of the whole business. At any rate, I protested at being sent home after getting out here with such difficulty, and explained to the Brigade Major that if I went home again I'd be stuck on the sick list for more months. . . . One thing's certain. Trench work has finished as far as I'm concerned.'

He had never been given to taking the easy path, and he did not seek sympathy now. Barrett's death became a closed subject, even to his parents. 'His death was a supreme shock, my particular loss,' he was finally able to write eleven years before his own death, 'from which I took long to recover.' A recurrence of his breakdown, which Edward dreaded, did not yet come about, presumably kept at bay by shock. There was little time to brood, in any case. As Amy recorded in her diary on 15 April 1916, 'King presented Eric with the Military Cross this morning at Buckingham Palace. Lunched at Romanos and dined there with Edward who came down to see Eric. Went to "Tina". A *little* disappointed.' '*16 April*: Eric remained in town for a few days.' Chink himself draws a discreet veil over his reasons for not going home with them, but the war, as he did tell friends later, brought unexpected opportunity for affairs. He did not seek out Doreen, dashing Amy's lingering hopes, and reported back to the trenches without seeing Reggie, who was still at Harrow. His application for the staff had gone forward.

His commanding officer was more perceptive than Amy had been, and sent him straight back again. On 28 April, in London, the Medical Board confirmed nervous disability resulting from shellshock at St

Eloi the previous March, for which the treatment was rest. Taut with the need to conserve the manpower he had seen so wantonly thrown away, he argued that training recruits would speed his recovery, and was relieved to be sent to teach trench warfare to youngsters who had not yet seen the Western Front.

As details of the Battle of the Somme were disclosed his bitterness increased. On 1 July 1916 19,000 British troops alone were killed, and by 19 November casualties on each side mounted to well over half a million men. He cut out every statistic from the newspapers and attempted to read between the lines of battle reports, obsessed not by morbidity but by the implications of deaths on such a scale. Posted during this time to Northern Command in York – 'clever', they reported back to the War Office, 'and of good type' – he was impatient enough to volunteer for the Royal Flying Corps as Vachell had earlier, only to be told that his unique army experience barred him. He agitated to get back to France again but the same experience was making him more valuable for training in England. In January 1917 he was posted to the Northern School of Instruction – 'above the average', it was recorded – and he continued to buttonhole anyone who might get him across the channel.

'19.7.17. Rather sudden, wasn't it? The War Office shot me over here in about 24 hours. . . . I hope my kit arrives OK, it was packed in rather a hurry. . . . By Jove, it's a relief having left.' He found himself stationed at Brigade Headquarters, in the area where he had served in December 1914, but this time the countryside was transformed by acres of canvas, both training and convalescent camps. Deliberately he turned his back on the past. 'The brigade run a jolly good Mess,' he was informing Edward within days of arrival. 'If you can buzz out any game that's going they say they will keep well enough, and I'd like to make the general a present for his hospitality.' By the time the grouse arrived, however, they were too high – 'several ardent fishermen nearly went off their heads when they saw the maggots,' he teased Edward – but a good impression had been made.

He was next temporarily attached to 12th Battalion, the Durham Light Infantry in a sector where he had spent several months in 1915 and, much as he tried to live in the present, he found the contrast with his memories painful. '3.8.17: The trouble is the junior officers,' he confided to Edward. 'I'm fairly broadminded but they are rather terrible. They aren't even the beginnings of soldiers as we know the meaning of the word. . . . Never open their mouths on the march and seem afraid of the men. From all telling they are very gallant fellows, though. The saving of the place is the excellent officers' club. I spend most of my time off parade here.'

His break came almost immediately, and at the age of twenty-two he exulted at being appointed Acting Major in the 10th Battalion of his regiment for a relief period of three weeks. 'Twice the work in commanding a company than doing second in command,' he wrote home proudly. 'I'm now Major Dorman-Smith, terrific, isn't it? I'm tickled to death when sentries present arms and aged subalterns salute.' By now he would have been furious if they had not. The immature face was dignified by an auburn moustache, in startling contrast to his black hair, and the enthusiastic boy who had once headed his Flanders letters 'Sandbag Hall, Bombed Street, Telegraphic address: Whizzbang' had become a martinet. There was no sign of his breakdown, and the year of teaching awed recruits had left him arrogantly confident.

In the autumn of 1917, to his intense regret, he was posted to a backwater of the war, the Italian Piave Front. Here he was attached to 68th Infantry Brigade School, and the transition from boy to man was more marked than before. 'At last mine enemies are scattered,' he told Edward almost immediately. 'The Commandant has gone and various other lazy devils whom I fought against have been relegated to the limbo of failures. Such a clearance was badly needed, too. . . . Busy training the whole time we're out of the line and really the battalion is damn smart. Lecturing morning and afternoon is not easy, but I think it's useful work and that's the great thing.'

Useful work . . . After the slaughter he had seen he was voluble about the need for sound training before men went into action, but it was difficult to get this across to men who had not seen the chaos of battle for themselves. He could think about little else. 'Of course the modern infantryman should be a much more highly trained individual than the prewar private,' he lectured Edward, his captive audience, in a typical letter. 'He has to possess the prewar excellence in musketry and in addition have a working knowledge of the rifle grenade bomb and the Lewis gun, one of which he has to know thoroughly. A company has a very complete system of signallers, eight under an NCO, and also a few really well-trained scouts. It has as transport a limber for the four Lewis guns and a cooker which can carry one day's rations. It should be able to operate apart from a battalion for at least two days without much replenishment of ammunition etc. unless heavily engaged. All this requires development and working out, and this is what I am trying to do.'

He had found his métier, and one suspects that the men who were the centre of his attention would much rather have been left alone. Life in Italy was relaxed, and the sight of Chink buried in his translations of foreign textbooks – 'He's a sound fellow, this Boche,' he even lectured one day – was bound to give rise to nudges. The hard shell of his concentration, however, remained unbroken. He was beginning to see the army in a new light, as an inefficient machine that could be stripped down and reassembled more effectively. At Sandhurst the teaching of strategy, tactics and logistics had intrigued him theoretically, but viewed through accumulated images of war their potential was tantalising. To think about tactics and war had become his obsession, and this was evident by the first months of 1918.

'*21.5.18*: I'm a little tired now,' he admitted in one letter home. 'It's a long time without a break of any sort. I'm beginning to forget what you all look like, it's so long since we met. One gets into a sort of coma when one has been away from people for so long. England's got very visionary in consequence.' A presentiment of the constant ruffled feathers ahead in his career came when he was attached as adjutant to 12th Durham Light Infantry once more, now on the Asiago Front, and tipped to rise to second in command, which would supersede officers with similar service. But hostility from men he discounted had never bothered him, and it did not do so now. '*7.7.18*: I stayed as the Brigadier's guest for two days and he offered me the choice of two vacancies as major,' he kept Edward posted. 'Chose to stay with my present CO as Adjutant and in my absence the second in command has been sacked. Excellent, as my name has now gone in as temporary major.' He believed he deserved the job and would in due course get it, but he took every factor into account except one. Gastroenteritis was endemic among British soldiers in Italy and he went down with an attack at the crucial moment. It was severe enough to need lengthy hospital treatment in Genoa.

And so he finished his war, with a star added to his MC and having been mentioned three times in despatches, in a convalescent's job. On discharge from hospital he was given the misleadingly important title of Commandant of the British Troops and sent to Milan, known to be a soft billet. Here, he did his best to take stock. 'I saw how pitilessly horses were destroyed in modern barrages,' he summed up his conclusions. 'I saw how senseless it was to use men against metal in frontal attacks. If there was such a thing as military science, the war had shown little evidence of it.' And while so absorbed he was about to make the most important friendship of his life.

4

Ernest Hemingway, a.d.c.

Autumn tightened into a bleak winter. In Milan the streets were icy and the game hanging outside butchers' shops – deer, pheasant and rabbits – was lightly powdered with snow, fur and feathers ruffled by a wind that blew straight down from the mountains. Inside the tiny Anglo-American club it was warm and comfortable, and they served a fine German export ale taken from a captured ship. Chink's duties commanding the British troops in Milan were light, and he had plenty of time to kill.

Around noon on 3 November 1918 he was alone, nursing his pint and savouring the tranquillity that enabled him to read, when a uniformed young Red Cross officer limped in on crutches and made his way laboriously to a deep leather-cushioned armchair by the window. Discreetly Chink identified the Croce de Guerra, Italy's second-highest decoration, but he did not speak. He dealt with far too many strangers as it was, since all British officers coming to Milan had to report to him. But from the corner of his eye he watched, reminded irresistibly of Reggie by the build and the broad shoulders. The fellow had placed one crutch beside the chair, he noted, and taken up a magazine, clearly the object of the exercise. Silence settled over the small room again.

It took the interruption of news of the Armistice, signed that morning with Austria, to bring Chink and Ernest Hemingway together. He looked a decent sort, the youthful Major Dorman-Smith concluded, and he condescended to address him. 'So that is that,' Chink said. "Have a drink!" ' Another version he occasionally gave was that they exclaimed simultaneously, 'So we are to go on living!' That thought more probably occurred with hindsight.

If Chink saw Reggie in Hemingway, Hemingway's first impression of Chink was of a pair of smart leather boots that were immaculately polished, because in covert glances he had been memorising the shine so that he would be able to describe it in exact words later. A drink seemed an excellent idea, and that led to lunch and a leisurely afternoon. Hemingway turned out to be Reggie's age, nineteen, and possessed the same confident, infectious smile. The more Chink looked across at him, the more uncanny the resemblance seemed. He was charmed by the pithy accent and the exuberant response to everything he said, and curious to know how an American had got an Italian medal in a European war.

Hemingway had not been over long, he soon learned. He had been a reporter on the *Kansas City Star* as recently as April, only six months earlier, when a Red Cross campaign for ambulance drivers had at last provided the opportunity to get involved. Within a month of his arrival he had been wounded. Awed by Chink's three prominent wound stripes, Hemingway hesitated at this point. He had been hit leading Arditi storm troops on Monte Grappa, he said, and Chink took him at his word. And the fact that he did, so matter-of-factly, convinced Hemingway of the immensity of his battle experience. If he had dared to tell the truth, which was that he had been blown up while distributing chocolate and had won his medal for rescuing a more serious casualty despite his own wounds, Chink would have thought no less of him; the experience would have been very like his own at Mons.

Chink was pleasantly aware of the awe, but not of its cause. He did not realise that this casualness about his own medal ribbons and his assumption of military confidence made him the sort of soldier Hemingway longed to be himself. And with a receptive listener and a couple of bottles of wine Chink proceeded to monopolise the conversation. Delighted to find that Hemingway knew little about the war in France and wanted to know more, he held forth about the bad British generalship he had witnessed with flashes of angry pessimism – 'all cooked' – that fascinated Hemingway by their contrast with his debonair good humour. The young American was flattered to be talked to as a military equal and riveted by the Mons and Ypres anecdotes Chink used as illustrations.

As Lindsay Barrett had seemed to hold all the answers for him, so Chink, although he did not know it, was taking shape as Hemingway's hero. Even the age gap between them was identical. By the end of the afternoon, when they arranged to meet the next morning as soon as Hemingway was allowed out of hospital again, Chink had teasingly appointed him his a.d.c. It was a role Hemingway was proud to accept. He, like Chink five years earlier at the same age, had been searching for someone to model himself upon, someone who would live up to the standards that intensive reading of Kipling had led him to expect. Chink impressed Hemingway as the quintessential Kipling hero, and he could scarcely believe his luck.

They had enough in common to achieve an immediate rapport. They were intellectually well matched, and both were widely read and idealistic. They were mutually determined to succeed on their own terms, without compromise, at whatever personal cost. They enjoyed field sports and country life, and were both left-handed, with birthdays within three days of each other. Chink liked Hemingway at once, and that freed the personal charm he had kept damped down since the loss of comradeship with Boyd, Vachell, Coles and Lawson. He was stimulated by Hemingway's American irreverence, almost shocking after years of English conformity, and it threw a sudden light on answers he was seeking himself. 'Hem was sufficiently remote,' he explained once, 'from my own stereotyped world for me to be able to see that world through his eyes.' It was deference to tradition, he began to recognise now, that stultified military evolution – and would continue to do so, given English society. A disciple sparked his own creativity, and to cement the friendship it was Chink who possessed the whip hand of authority, as had subconsciously become essential to him. He dubbed Hemingway 'Popplethwaite'; just right, they both thought, for an ambitious a.d.c., and in due course this became shortened to Pop.

Chink was exceedingly bored with his job and ready to be distracted. Milan was little touched by war and the British troops he was supposedly commanding consisted of a sprinkling of Ordnance, Repair and Clerical recruits who lived together in a billet, rendering him superfluous. His subsidiary role of Assistant Provost Marshal was equally insubstantial, despite the trappings of an office on the same floor of his hotel and a Milanese assistant named Soldato Valli, who in civil life was a director of one of the major perfumery businesses and was old enough to be his father. Being Assistant Provost Marshal was a tedious job. Milan was at the centre of inter-Allied communications and the city where British officers were most frequently given leave; looking after stray drunks and smoothing over ugly incidents called for patience. Chink had been intolerant to begin with. His experience in Milan was accelerating the tendency.

It was heady to have such a willing pupil in Hemingway after the loneliness of the last months, and he could not have asked for a more attentive one. 'All I did mostly was hear guys talk,' Hemingway revealed once. 'Their experiences get to be more vivid than your own. You invent from your own and from all of theirs. . . .' Chink's sense of drama, his ability to tell a good story, his Irish use of language and his flair for the imaginative touch were compelling. Although only twenty-three he appeared much older. His elegance had become instinctive and he was as assured to the young Hemingway as Barrett had once appeared to him. Chameleon-like, he responded to admiration, and the disgruntled officers he had superseded before his illness would not have recognised the man Hemingway saw. Carried away as ever by ideas, he used his hands more expressively and his voice with deliberate effect. He was conscious of showing off but could not help it. Talking to Hemingway, who hung on every word, he found himself saying things out loud that he had not been aware of thinking until then. And, much to his surprise, he enjoyed teaching someone who so clearly wanted to learn. Hemingway was as avid to know more about the Classics as he was to soak up army matters, and endearingly open about admitting the gaps in his education. Even his clipped accent, Chink realised after a while, was being copied, and he had no need to remind himself that imitation was the sincerest form of flattery.

On 11 November, the day the Armistice was signed on the Western Front, he found he had a rival for his pupil's attention when Hemingway announced that a nurse who had looked after him in his early days in hospital – and had seduced him before he could stand up – was due back from temporary duty in Florence. Reggie, too, was good with girls, and Chink prepared to be put to one side, but Hemingway would have none of it. He wanted both the people he liked most to like each other, he insisted, and they did. 'Very nice,' Chink rated Agnes von Kurowsky subsequently. 'Not pretty, but vivacious.'

He felt prim when the other two were together, and could not get over the fact that Agnes was older than himself. But her novel lack of reserve fascinated him, as Hemingway's spontaneity continued to do. He was untravelled enough to miss her American accent and too polite to test his theory that she was from South Africa; personal questions were not on. They took him along with them to informal parties, where he made an incongruous guest with his unbending military stance and elaborate good manners. The affairs, if any, in London on war leave had done little to add to his sexual confidence. He was envious of Hemingway's ease with Agnes and gullible enough to believe they were lovers. He longed for a similar relationship, and promptly fell in love with someone unattainable.

Cora Chase was American too, a fresh-faced eighteen-year-old soprano who was taking her first small roles at La Scala, and he met her at an official function in his capacity as Commandant of the British Troops. From the first, his attempts to prise her away from her mother, who was chaperoning her around Europe, were hopeless. 'Sweet and lovely,' he described her euphorically to Amy in his letter home that evening, and he was in his seat in the third tier, army field glasses in one hand, the following night. The mirrored entrance hall of La Scala, entered directly through central double doors at the top of a flight of steps, had reminded him at once of Bellamont Forest, though created on a smaller scale. But the first person he identified inside was Mrs Chase, who frowned and looked away.

The opera house was situated within a few hundred yards of the Anglo-American club and just across the square from the bustling, mosaic-floored Galleria where he had taken to drinking at Biffi's and Il Gran Italia, or the Cova nearby, with Hemingway, convenient for a sprint across at the last minute. Occasionally Hemingway accompanied him, when he would allow more time to reach their seats, and attempt to ignore Hemingway's nudges each time Cora Chase appeared on stage.

On 20 November, however, for the emotionally-billed 'Evening in Honour of the Allies', he attended in style, and Hemingway was relegated to observer. In full-dress uniform as the invited representative of Great Britain's army, Chink was ushered into the Royal Box, which was decorated for the occasion with British, Italian and French flags. Taking his seat beside General Angelotti of Italy, General Fischer of France and the Belgian Minister, M. Dossogne, among other dignitaries, he was astounded by the ovation that greeted his entry. La Scala was filled to capacity, with the audience overflowing into gangways and the orchestra pit, and when the curtain went up over 1000 singers were revealed on stage. To delirious applause, 'Long Live England' struck up.

As a prelude to the musical programme, a silence was called for speeches. A stocky, confident man whom Chink did not recognise stood up, stilled the tumult, and proceeded to heighten the mood. By the time his oration was over the audience was roaring approval, and Chink had managed to find out his name. He watched, fascinated, as Benito Mussolini acknowledged the wild applause and looked directly towards the Royal Box. Then the passionate chorus of Va Pensiero from Nabucco swept Chink up with the rest, and his own moment was imminent. A tenor in the costume of St George came down to the front of the stage, the signal for the familiar strains of 'God Save the King', and it was time to do his duty. Self-consciously he stepped forward and stood to attention at the salute for the duration of the solo, as flowers rained down and handkerchiefs fluttered at him from every tier of the vast auditorium.

The occasion did nothing to diminish Hemingway's admiration. He was attending the Ospedele Maggiore as an outpatient by now, and as his mobility improved they spent increasing hours exploring Milan together on foot. Until Chink read *A Farewell to Arms* ten years afterwards he had no idea of the amount of topographical detail his friend was absorbing along the way, despite being the one who acted as translator. Hemingway introduced him to the race track at San Siro, and as the weather sharpened they took to drinking hot rum punches – 'Every sort of luck!' was Chink's habitual toast – while roasted chestnuts bought at street braziers did double duty as handwarmers in the pockets of their coats. One day they paused beside an old pavement artist to have their silhouettes snipped out of black paper and pasted on to card, and after Chink's death his picture was found uncreased among his papers. Hemingway chose to preserve his in words.

They talked nonstop, master to pupil, and one Shakespearean line that Chink recited whenever they discussed courage – as they frequently did – meant so much to the untried Hemingway that he asked for it to be written out. 'By my troth, I care not,' this ran. 'A man can die but once; we owe God a death, and let it go which way it will, he that dies this year is quit for the next.' Hemingway was unsure of his own courage in the face of death, and the quotation became his lucky charm, one that he would often quote in his books. It is a shame the English master at Uppingham never realised that his insistence on learning by heart when the army class did *Henry IV, Part 2*, would field the line into twentieth-century literature.

They also spent a great deal of time sitting down, to give Hemingway's wounded leg more chance to heal. Inside the Cova it was noisy and smoky, and Chink doodled the café's Art Nouveau trademark as they chatted, the large capital C sweeping around to enclose the other letters, and soon applied the same design to his own signature. It was the final touch to handwriting that after painstaking practice had become rounded and neat, and that at twenty-three he was still perfecting.

His job took up so little of his time that when Agnes was posted away to a field hospital in Treviso he and Hemingway became inseparable. On 9 December he took some overdue leave to accompany Hemingway on a 200-mile journey east to visit her, and organised a visit on the way to a unit of the Royal Garrison Artillery, some of whose officers he had looked after in Milan. Here they were put up on a couple of army horses for a day out with the local Montello Hunt, and his Sandhurst expertise showed him up to further advantage. Revealingly he chose to stay on with the hospitable colonel while Hemingway sought out Agnes. It was not his form to butt in, but the main reason for his tact was the lure of being with soldiers again. The break showed up his Milan life for the exceptional interval that it was, and all the more precious for being about to end. His own posting was a temporary one, and Hemingway was due to be repatriated.

Although the obliging Soldato Valli was always glad to deputise, Chink's work became more time-consuming as Christmas approached, bringing with it a predictable upsurge in the numbers of British officers applying for leave, as well as extra functions to be attended in his capacity as Commandant. Demonstrating how relaxed he had become in the short time since he had met Hemingway, he coaxed Valli into standing in for him whenever possible, and continued to have fun. He found no further opportunity to talk to Cora Chase, but he kept up his vigil in La Scala for the bittersweet hopelessness of it as much as for the bristling effect he had on her mother. There was another reason, as well. Music, which he had not until now appreciated, could lift or depress his mood as no book had been able to do for some time. He did not tell Hemingway about the tears he shed in the anonymity of his cheap seat during especially poignant arias. It was the music of Verdi and Rossini, almost as much as Cora herself, that drew him back – but only if there was nothing more exciting on. While to Hemingway he was the complete Kipling hero, the ideal of honour and tradition, all he really wanted was to let himself go.

Approaching the Cova one afternoon where he had arranged to meet Hemingway among the riot of demobilised Italians who were celebrating inside, he passed a temporary shop selling mistletoe for charity, run by the usually inaccessible daughters of Milan's top families. He covered the distance to the Cova in record time. 'The entry of Chink with the great news,' Hemingway wrote nostalgically many years later. 'We sort out a battle patrol as rapidly as possible, eliminating Italian inebriates and all ranks above that of major.' In three raids they bought up all the stock, and left one sprig in place for their objective, which was to kiss the blushing girls. Before he met Hemingway, Chink would have been too inhibited to think up the idea, let alone take part. On Christmas Day he skated through his duties and joined Hemingway at a dance in the Cova straight from the official British church service, still in uniform. And when that was over there was another party.

Hemingway was scheduled to sail from Genoa on 4 January, and Chink's busiest period in his office, reaching a crescendo on New Year's Day with the number of drunken incidents to be smoothed over, coincided with Hemingway's absence in Sicily for a few days. They made the most of their remaining time together, and Chink helped him to pack and say goodbye at Biffi's, the Cova and Il Gran Italia. And Hemingway left him as he had begun, with a tall story. This time it was about his sexual adventures in Sicily, and the reason for the lie was the same as before. Disciples always strive to impress.

On his own, Chink found the smallness of the city centre oppressive, and welcomed his posting to the Military Landing Staff at Taranto. Here his closest companion became a spaniel pup he bought locally, calling the dog George after the Mons stray. 'I am in deadly danger of growing respectable,' he teased Hemingway by post. 'Come over into Macedonia and help me.'

But over three years were to go by before they met again, and by the time they did, Hemingway had married. 'I'm prepared to take Mrs. Popplethwaite to my heart, metaphorically speaking,' Chink wrote on receipt of the news in January 1922. 'But it is to be remembered, a de c, that the friends of bachelordom are seldom the friends of married life! Although I hardly ever drink and have abandoned the tobacco of my youth . . . the lady may decide that I have a bad influence on you. It's a risk I'm prepared to take for the sake of meeting you again but, Popplethwaite, it's a real risk.'

Soldiering and the Atlantic, however, kept them apart. He was spending his 1922 leave quietly in Paris with his parents – 'I only got away for one amusing evening' – when Hemingway breezed into his hotel bedroom without warning, to proclaim that he was taking him to Switzerland there and then. Amy, equally charmed by the resemblance to Reggie, allowed Chink to go with a good grace, and he was out of the hotel 'like a bat out of Hades'.

He was off the parental leash, it was spring, he was happy to be with the Hemingways, and he approved of everything. His a.d.c. had managed to return to Europe as a freelance journalist and before starting work in Paris the couple were holidaying in a 'Swiss pub – just the spot Hem would choose', in Chamby, a village between Montreux and Les Avants. Chink's apprehensions about Hemingway's bride Hadley turned out to be groundless. Quickly he recovered from the surprise that she was four years older than he was himself, and therefore eight years older than Hemingway. She reminded him of Agnes von Kurowsky in that regard, and she was unaffected and friendly enough to make the age-gap insignificant. 'Hadley was nice,' he recalled in more worldly middle age. 'Plain looking but bedworthy . . . but my behaviour was ultra non-sex.'

Still guarded with women at twenty-seven, he was touched by her evident need for him to approve of her – so contrary to his expectation – and he let down his own defences in response. There was none of the atmosphere Amy could generate if her husband or sons paid more attention to anyone else, and as neither was possessive about Hemingway they did not see each other as a threat. He could tell she was as reassured to be addressed as Mrs Popplethwaite as he had been by his own belated nickname in 1914, and as he got used to the strangeness of talking openly to a woman after his all-male world she became his first female friend. In some ways she was easier to talk to than Hemingway, for whom he instinctively put on a slight act. Soon he thought of Hadley as the sister he had never had.

The small wooden Chalet Chamby was not really a pub; it was an inexpensive, well-run pension which Chink would later recommend to army friends going on leave. In the distance the Dent du Midi towered beyond the veranda and the air exhilarated him with its scent of narcissi in flower. His bedroom had a featherbed and duvet and was heated by a square porcelain stove. The couple who ran it, Herr Gangwisch and his maternal wife, were glad of the extra income and unobtrusively gave them the run of the place. His sole discomfort came from Hemingway's incessant sexual boasting (for Hadley's sake as much as his own) although she did not seem to mind. 'They were very much in love and used to disturb my breakfast coffee by reciting, blow by blow, the events of their nights,' he wrote. 'Hem's delight was for me to come into them at breakfast and over croissants hear about their amorous nocturnals. I was a little shocked as he debated whether it was five times or only four.' There was no question, however, of being made to feel left out for long.

'It's great down here,' Hemingway informed his father in America. 'My old pal Major Dorman-Smith has been spending his leave with us and we've been trout fishing and mountain climbing. . . . Today we climbed Cap au Moine, a very steep and dangerous climb of over 7000 feet and had a great time coasting down the snow fields, coming down by simply sitting down and letting go. Just below the snow line when we climbed the Dent du Jaman the other day we saw two big martens. We have climbed all the high peaks near here and are about ready to start on the best ones again.' 'Climbed a couple of mountains with Chink,' he soon told his new Paris literary mentor, the formidable Gertrude Stein. 'And then he climbed one himself and nearly got killed on Ascension Day coming across a torrent that was too deep and fast for him, and met us at the Bains des Allies and we drank 11 bottles of beer apiece with Mrs. H. sleeping on the grass, and walked home in the cool of the evening with our feet feeling very far off and unrelated and yet moving at terrific speed.'

Chink's abstemiousness in the mess had an element of defensiveness about it. Now he could be himself, and Hadley did not sulk if they went down without her to the beer halls in Montreux. It was the start of a Jekyll and Hyde way of life that no one in his regiment was ever told about. One evening when they stood up from their stein-studded table the regular patrons rose from their chairs and bowed; it was the sort of compliment he had never had before. 'God, what literary discussions we had,' Hemingway would write in *Green Hills of Africa*. 'Beer was mostly those years just after the war with Chink and in the mountains. Flags for the Fusilier, crags for the Mountaineer, for English poets beer, Strong beer for me. That was Chink, then, quoting Robert Graves, then.' The nearby Bains des Allies ran a beer-drinking contest and they weaved their way back, disappointed at not having won the prize of a calf, along the curving mountain road with moonlight glinting on the narcissi. Decently Hadley said nothing even then.

On the days when Hemingway fished for trout, Chink would lazily read and talk with her before they strolled on to meet up at Hemingway's usual spot on the Stockalper River, where the Rhône runs into Lake Geneva outside the village of Aigle. All three walked on together when Hemingway was ready to put his rods away. The master–pupil relationship reverted, and Chink's zest for military history seized on every coincidence. Along this road, he would instruct, Napoleon's army had marched towards the high St Bernard mountain pass into Italy, and the Romans had built it in the first place to propel their armies into battle. At Aigle they usually headed for the café opposite the station, with its circular veranda overhung by a massive purple wisteria. Collapsing at the green tables, they called for the potent 17 per cent dark beer. Meanwhile Hemingway was making use of everything. 'The beer comes foaming out in great glass mugs that hold a quart and cost forty centimes,' he filed to the *Toronto Star*. 'And the barmaid smiles and asks about your luck. The trains are always at least two hours apart at Aigle, and those waiting . . . wish they would never come.'

It was at the little Aigle café that Chink declared that a poem Hemingway had just written about fishing in the valley was too stark, and Hemingway attacked back by criticising his florid Victorian favourites. (Chink's rucksack book in the trenches, he had been forced to admit, had been *The Oxford Book of English Verse*.) Now Chink took hold of the poem, fleshed it out in the style of Tennyson – 'and very well it looked, too' – and at the table copied out both versions, one beneath the other. He presented the page to Hemingway. Later that afternoon, making their way back to the chalet with some difficulty, they argued about a definitive description of the chestnut blossoms overhead, and agreed finally on 'waxen candelabra'. 'Hadley packed up,' Chink noted, 'and had to lie down for a bit. The assiduous Hem accompanied her even then.'

They always brought the day's catch back for supper, wrapped in backnumbers of *La Gazette de Lausanne*, and Frau Gangwisch cooked the trout *en bleu*, poached in wine vinegar, bay leaves and a dash of red pepper. With this they drank a white Sion wine. Far below the steep drop from the veranda miniature trees marked out the twist of river where their meal had been caught. 'I think that for Hem, as well as Hadley and myself,' Chink would write in old age, 'those days were supremely happy.'

With only a week left of Chink's leave they decided to show Hadley Milan, which could easily be reached by train; Hemingway also wanted to assess Mussolini's much publicised Riparto d'Assalto troops for his paper. Chink raised the stakes. He dared them to climb the St Bernard Pass with him, in Napoleon's footsteps, and none of them paid any attention to warnings about heavy snow. It meant travelling light and an early start – something both men were used to – and going up to the bedroom at the last minute to hurry Hadley up, Chink found her in tears. She had had a row with Hemingway about her make-up bottles, which would not fit into her pack. Diplomatically he put them in his own.

Leaving the train at Bourg St Pierre, they began the climb. 'Soon after reaching the snowline the going became very heavy and deep,' Chink recalled later. 'Then Hem got mountainsick. He could just about keep moving without his pack if Hadley helped him along. So I portered the three packs up that damn pass. I had to carry them in relays, one at a time; on a hundred yards, dump, back to the next; on a hundred yards, dump, and back again, with Hem being sick, Hadley scared and fatigue gaining on me. The route was marked by the heads of stakes protruding from the snow. Nothing has ever seemed so endless.' Hemingway never forgot the sensation that he and Hadley had that day of being protected. 'I hope Chink will come,' he put into *A Moveable Feast*, which was published posthumously. 'He takes care of us.'

In the late afternoon they met monks on skis who indicated a monastery in the distance. Chink saw it theatrically as a stone fortress in a lunar landscape. 'I went ahead to the entrance hall, accompanied by an enormous St. Bernard dog,' he recorded, 'and the bell labelled Almonier was behind the dog who obviously disliked strangers. . . . I edged to the bell, my back to the wall, with him growling at me whenever I moved. . . . But I made it, got the Almonier, very surprised to see me, and together we went back to Hem and Hadley.' The Hospice of St Bernard was 6000 feet above sea level and the monks turned out to be 'damn nice', providing dry clothes, bedroom slippers and a huge meal laced by a litre of wine. Chink's Catholicism remained dormant. 'All that cold night,' he added, 'I had bitter indigestion and sat up reading Chekhov and looking out at the frozen lake between belches.'

In the morning they inched their way down into Italy, supporting the blistered Hadley between them. She had gone against their advice and worn light tan Oxford shoes – chiefly to impress Chink, she later admitted – which had split soon after the start. Chink always referred to the climb afterwards as 'Across the St Bernard in Street Shoes' in honour of her ordeal. The train journey to Milan was an anti-climax. 'Made 57 kilometres in two days with Chink the Captain doing the Simon Legree on us,' Hemingway briefed Gertrude Stein. 'It took the combined efforts of the Captain and Mrs. Hemingway and a shot of cognac every 200 yards to get me up the last couple of kilometres of snow.' It was their own brandy; the famous St Bernard dogs had proved a severe disappointment.

And so was Milan. At Biffi's they treated themselves to the fresh fruit-cups they had told Hadley about, and they dined her at the Cova. They pointed out the Anglo-American club, the hospital and La Scala and went to a race meeting at San Siro. Here there was a new track and grandstand, making it impossible to deny that they were raising ghosts. Everywhere felt different. Uniformed Fascisti were all over the city and Hemingway grew truculent. Chink was not sad when his leave was up, and left with his pupil's admiration intact. In Paris that summer, emulating him, Hemingway began to grow a moustache, and in the autumn of 1922 they made plans to spend Christmas together at the Chalet Chamby. 'Chink is coming the sixteenth,' Hemingway enthused to an old friend expected to join them later. 'You'll like him any amount. . . . We'll have a lot of stuff to read and if you've any of the new American stuff, bring it along. Chink does a book a day when he's in his stride.'

But the holiday got off to a disastrous start. When Chink reached Chamby he found Hemingway tight-lipped and Hadley more upset than he had thought possible. She wept as she told him that the suitcase containing everything Hemingway had written, with the exception of two stories in the post, had been stolen from her side at the Gare du Lyon. Chink was always good in a crisis, and he did not fail now. He teased Hemingway about the loss of his own Aigle poem, packed with the rest, but the lack of response showed that his friend was in danger of losing his writing nerve. He resorted to his officer habit of leadership. Turning round a disaster could only be done by not becoming obsessed by the casualties; in battle, he reminded Hemingway sharply, that was how generals and staff planners coped. It was how he was going to have to cope as well. In military terms, introspection and regret were liabilities, and that was why officers were trained to snap out of them. His straight talking did the trick. Describing how he showed one of the two salvaged stories to a friend later, Hemingway wrote: 'Chink had taught me never to discuss casualties . . . and I told him all that stuff you feed the troops. I was going to start working and writing stories again, and as I said it . . . I knew that it was true.'

Chink's arrival was fortuitous. He was at his most amusing

whenever trying to divert someone under strain whom he admired – having had plenty of practice on the Western Front – and he set out to change the atmosphere. Each day a cogwheel train lifted the three of them to the top of the Col du Sonloup, from where they luged down the icy road until Hemingway and he were able to graduate to the steeper road between Chamby and Montreux, which the more experienced favoured. Chink deliberately called it bobbing, knowing Hemingway's competitiveness about language. He reeled off all the distractions he could. The casualties beside each run reminded him of a French battlefield, he mentioned one day, and Hemingway took up the idea in his next article, likening the resort hotels to field hospitals. In the evenings Chink taught them both bridge, having learned the card game from Amy, the severest of coaches. He even went to the length of prescribing a cheerful song – 'Hi ho, says Roly' – to be sung while skiing.

In winter, snow transformed the chalet, packing smooth and hard over the pine logs that were stacked as high as the roof at one side, and softening the contours of the valley so that it merged into one with the peaks. A thin ice formed overnight on the water in the jug on Chink's bedside table, and out of doors the air knifed into his lungs. He kept his footing on the icy roads with the aid of nail-studded boots, and despite Hemingway's despair exulted in being there. He walked him along to Montreux for the latest newspapers and the beer hall – both good for morale – and in the opposite direction was the Bains des Allies, where they drank steaming *glühwein*. His high spirits were contagious. By the time of the impromptu Christmas concert at the Grand Hotel in Les Avants, Hemingway was back to his usual aggressive form. Usually Chink preferred to avoid the Grand because it had too many English guests for his liking, and he accompanied Hemingway that evening with bravado. 'Hem took the stage with a blackened face and sang a really bawdy German song about somebody's shwester who sits in Zukhaus and alles is gebraucht,' he recalled with mixed emotions. 'Well, as he sang he got no applause. Then back came his head around the fallen curtain to remark "I seem to have offended the better elements in this audience" in an upstage Bostonian accent.' No Northumberland Fusiliers were on Christmas leave there with their families – but they might have been. Chink was flirting with danger, and he did not care.

That Christmas of 1922, he always maintained, was the happiest of his life. It was the same for Hemingway, who wrote about it twenty years later in the middle of the Second World War. 'I reached up with a boot and banged on the ceiling,' he began his nostalgic description then.

'Hey Chink – it's Christmas.' 'Hooray' came Chink's voice from the little room under the roof. . . . Chink knocked at the door. 'Merry Christmas, mes enfants' he grinned. He wore the early morning garb of big woolly dressing-robe and thick socks that made us all look like some monastic order. In the breakfast room we could hear the stove roaring and crackling. . . . Against the tall white porcelain stove hung the three long skiing stockings, bulging and swollen with strange lumps and bulges. Around the foot of the stove were piled boxes. Two new shiny pairs of ash skis lay alongside the stove, too tall to stand in the low ceilinged chalet room. . . . We ate breakfast in the old, untasting, gulping early morning Christmas way, unpacked the stockings, down to the candy mouse in the toe, and each made a pile of our things for future gloating.

After breakfast they took the train up to the Col du Sonloup to try the new skis.

Soon the three of us were high above the shoulder of the mountains that had seemed the top of the world. We kept going up in single file. . . . At the brow the skis seemed to drop out from under and in a hissing rush we all three swooped down the slope like birds. On the other side it was thrusting, uphill steady climbing again. The sun was hot and the sweat poured off us. . . . There is no place you get so tanned as in the mountains in winter. Nor so thirsty. Finally we hit the lunching place, a snowed-under old log cattle barn. . . . Everything seemed to drop off sheer below us. The air at that height, about 6200, is like wine. We put on our sweaters . . . unpacked the lunch and the bottle of white wine, and lay back on our rucksacks and soaked in the sun. Coming up we had been wearing sunglasses against the glare of the snowfields, and now we took [them] off and looked out on a bright new world.

Hadley was sunburned but scoffed at Chink's army advice to use lampblack on her face; he was glad to see she responded to teasing again. They practised until she awoke, and then, taking off the sealskins and waxing their skis, plunged down in powder snow to the crowded road which wound past the station. 'It was too steep and slippery to stop,' continues Hemingway's account. 'We could see [Hadley's] blue beret occasionally before it got too dark. Down, down, down the road we went in the dusk, past chalets that were a burst of lights and Christmas merriment in the dark.... As we dropped past ... we heard a shout from [one] lighted doorway. "Captain! Captain! Stop here!"' Gangwisch was on the alert at the Chalet Chamby and in peacetime Chink had reverted to substantive rank. 'Inside was a big Christmas tree and a real Christmas turkey dinner, the table shiny with silver, the glasses tall and thin-stemmed, the bottles narrow-necked, the turkey large and brown and beautiful, the side dishes all present, and Ida serving in a crisp new apron.'

Chink spent less time alone with Hadley but one January afternoon, shortly before his leave was up, he walked with her to Montreux. Sitting in the beer hall afterwards, as they gathered strength for the climb home, he surprised himself by prophesying that she was going to have a son within the year. 'At their high copulation average it was a fair bet, and the son only a 50/50 chance,' he shrugged nonchalantly in due course, but at the time his remark had the force of a psychical experience. Hadley was equally taken aback.

When he next saw them it was summer, and her pregnancy was confirmed. He arrived at their Paris flat expectantly, and was delighted to find the poet's garret of his imagination. Their cramped fourth-floor flat at 74 Rue Cardinal Lemoine had open pissoirs on each landing and a workmen's rowdy Bal Musette throbbed at night beside the front door. The drunks, the prostitutes, the sewers and the poverty were exactly as he had hoped, but on home ground Hemingway was less of a pupil than before. His need to assert himself had become more marked, and it was on this visit that the respectful 'Popplethwaite' evolved into the more equal 'Pop'. 'The summer training by Hemmingstein,' Chink ribbed on return to his regiment, 'has used up any facility of expression my poor pen may ever have possessed. . . . I hardly dare write . . . for fear of falling into Hackneyed Expressions.' He was a little more hurt than he revealed.

But it was still fun, and he was determined to enjoy himself. He was taken to meet Sylvia Beach at her bookshop Shakespeare and Company in the pretty Rue l'Odéon, primed with a copy of James Joyce's *Ulysses* which she had just published – and which later scandalised the mess. And it is tantalising to speculate about converging circles: another of the book's first subscribers was Winston Churchill. Browsing often in the small bookshop, Chink came to like Sylvia Beach very much. The kindly Ezra Pound was next introduced, and presented a volume of his poems which Chink thought 'damned fine'.

Hemingway was too harassed to be a full-time guide, however. He was under pressure to expand the few writings he had left into book size because the Three Mountains Press had already announced the imminent publication of *Blank* by Ernest Hemingway, and after Chink and Hadley retired to bed he wrote on, fortified with a bottle of bourbon whisky. 'By morning,' Chink noted, 'the bottle was empty.... He wrote and rewrote, until all the fat had been boiled out and the essential meat alone survived.... I could not see the need for such stark writing, anymore than I could understand ... Joyce.' He was proud to learn that two of his Mons anecdotes were to be included, and Hemingway handed over three longer stories for him to read when he could and give an opinion. That undid much of the sensation of being outgrown.

He was not pleased, however, with Hemingway's cavalier treatment of Hadley and the barrage of his complaints about having to return to Canada for the birth. By the end of the visit she had his entire sympathy. 'I want to know all sorts of things, Pop, but first and foremost about Hadley,' he reproved when they failed to write from Canada, where Hemingway had joined the staff of the *Toronto Star*. 'I'll be anxious as the devil till I know.' 'For the love of Mike,' he persisted when there was still no reply. 'Tell me what's going on. I'd hate to tell you both how often in a day you're in my thoughts.'

The Hemingway's baby, a boy, was born prematurely on 10 October 1923 and they did not tell him for three months, when they asked him to be godfather in the next sentence. 'I got your letter just as I was going out shooting,' he wrote straight back. 'Nearly let off my fusil in the hall of the mess with delight. Couldn't shoot a thing all day but I fired several salvos to the health, luck, happiness and success of John Hadley Nicanor. I feel rather like the old lady in the New Testament – with the suitable masculine variations – in that I foretold this event pretty completely.... If he was a triple deformity I'd stand godfather to him.... I think it's as well, though, to have him christened.... Just as soon as you settle down in Paris again, Pop, I'll be with you.'

Hemingway's first book, *In Our Time*, in which the Mons cameos appear, was dedicated to Chink when it came out that winter, as promised. But Amy did not boast about it among her friends, because the author was unknown, and keeping his worlds apart Chink did not tell anyone in the regiment about it. Until meeting Hemingway he had not been as aware of being bored by his army colleagues as he was now, and the sense of isolation spilled over into his letters from barracks.

10.15 p.m. I've just been reading your three stories again, old friend. It's warm, steam heated and fuggy in the anteroom, and the wind's howling like the devil outside. . . . 'My Old Man', of course, I read at Chamby. When I read 'Up in Michigan' and 'Out of Season' before I couldn't get at what you were driving at. I see it now. . . . Just reading your stuff made me want to talk to you. I wish you two were at Gang's little room with a decent fire going and the room thick with yarns and cigarette smoke. What a lot I'd give to get that back! . . . I shan't be happy till the three of us are anchored in one room again with all of a long evening and nothing to do. Fools go to the theatre. . . . I've so much to say that it's no good writing.

It was not until the beginning of March 1924 that he was able to join them again in Paris. The Hemingways had taken a larger flat this time in a better district at 113 Notre Dame des Champs, near the Luxembourg Gardens. It was on the second floor, over a noisy sawmill that cut timber for picture frames, and it was as bohemian to him as their previous flat. 'The sawmill apartment always had a few fleas around,' he would remember fastidiously. 'At least, that was the best explanation as to why I frequently picked up fleabites while staying with them. The bites,' he added quickly, 'were worth it.' The buzz of the saw under the spare-bedroom window woke him early each morning and the baby, known as Bumby, cried in the night. Humdrum daily life to the Hemingways, but definitely slumming it to Captain Dorman-Smith MC.

His advice about the christening having been ignored, he suggested it again. Hadley prevaricated, explaining that Hemingway was an agnostic and she was afraid to bring the subject up. 'However, as I his godfather I stuck to my guns,' he noted with satisfaction. 'There was then a debate as to which church he should be committed to. Gertrude Stein was nominally the other godparent, a canonical impossibility since she was not a Christian, but let that pass. In fairness to some abstruse principle thought up by Hem, Nicanor could not be a Catholic because I am one, and equally to be Jewish was debarred by Gertrude's position. Besides, it was a bit late to circumcise the poor scrap.'

A compromise was thrashed out in Gertrude Stein's studio flat at 27 Rue de Fleurus nearby, and they settled for American Episcopalian, which was the religion of Hemingway's dominant mother, but more to the point it had the least dogmatic strings attached. Chink came to dread his visits to Gertrude Stein's flat. Her autocratic flaunting of the role of lesbian patron of the arts had too much of the bully about it, and everything about her offended him. She sat aggressively in at discussions, knees apart and feet solidly planted on the ground, determined to get her own way. His inclusion in the christening group evidently puzzled her, and he found it novel to be considered a philistine soldier for a change. In due course Gertrude would dismiss him in her memoirs as an English war comrade of Hemingway's, impervious to his personal charm but genuinely fascinated – if he had but realised it – by war. As the christening was debated he studied the galaxy of Picasso nudes that covered the walls and, gratified at his lack of shock, Stein lectured him on Picasso's importance. The name was as unknown as Hemingway's still and he was unconvinced. However, he took care to address her as 'Miss Stein', more at ease with her than with her subdued but somehow menacing lover 'Miss Toklas'.

The most convenient christening choice was St Luke's Episcopal Chapel, tucked among local artists' ateliers in the gaudy little Rue de la Grande Chaumière, which branched off their road opposite Pound's flat. The minister's address was easily found by trailing him home after morning service. 'Hem would not approach him because he had not shaved and his pants did not match his jacket,' Chink described the scene subsequently. 'So I sent in my visiting card. . . . He was a little puzzled as to what Captain Dorman-Smith of Bellamont Forest, County Cavan could be doing in the Quarter, but he was delighted to arrange a baptism. Clearly he thought Nicanor was my child. I had an awful job making him understand. Was I married? No. Well, that frequently happens but the baby should be christened all the same. But I'm not it's father. Who is, then?' Chink pointed down to Hemingway who, stubble-chinned, was leaning against a lamp-post opposite, reading a torn scrap of newspaper which he had picked up from the gutter.

The christening took place on 10 March, before Vespers, and James Joyce's shy nineteen-year-old son Giorgio played the organ, despite being unbaptised himself; the threat to have this done was the surest way to stop Joyce drinking, Giorgio's mother Nora Barnacle had found. It was not a ceremony that fellow officers of the 1st Battalion would have found impressive. Hemingway and Hadley stood beside the two godparents: Chink, spruce and upright, and Gertrude in her carapace of self-preoccupation. Few attended, and at one point she interrupted the minister to rasp out loudly, 'Chink, what *is* the Apostle's Creed?' During the party in her studio afterwards, over champagne and sugared almonds, he did his best to explain, but saw she had already lost interest. 'We christened the baby with Chink's aid Sunday,' Hemingway informed the absent Ezra Pound with a dart of irony. 'I've got nothing further to worry about him.'

And his fellow officers would have backed away from the talented people Chink now met. James Joyce, increasingly handicapped by bad eyesight, was well mannered and reserved. Chink found Joyce 'kind', remembering nothing more tangible than goodwill, and his own Irish nationality went unremarked. Ford Maddox Ford, testy editor of the *Transatlantic Review*, on which Hemingway was currently working, smoothed walrus-moustaches and pigeonholed him accurately down to the fusilier roots, amused to find the source of Hemingway's mannerisms. Ford needed to classify people. Faced with heiress Nancy Cunard, whose large eyes appraised him briefly from behind a long, slim cigarette holder and then dismissed him, Chink bridled at the magnetism between her and Hemingway and suspected it to be the beginnings of an affair. Her apartment on the Ile St Louis was also crammed with modern paintings, but the wilder surrealism of Picabia was not interpreted for him, and he was glad to get away. 'Hem was pleased to be in contact with even a déclassé member of the great British Upper Class,' Chink sniffed afterwards. 'I think he was flattered to meet them.' It is ironic that the two models for famous literary characters – Nancy appears in the writings of Aldous Huxley and Michael Arlen and he himself would inspire Hemingway – did not take to each other at all.

The snobbishness he detected in Hemingway was a reassuring foible in a disciple who was fast developing leadership qualities which Chink sometimes wondered if he possessed himself. And he continued to like him unreservedly. 'The great charm of Hemingway in those days,' he wrote in his sixties, 'was his youth, intelligent gusto and single-minded ambition to write in the way he wanted to write.' That would not have been a charm widely appreciated by members of the British Army at the time.

It was on this Paris trip, too, that Chink bought the book that would have the greatest single effect of distancing him from his contemporaries. In Shakespeare and Company he flipped through the banned *Jurgen* by James Branch Cabell, already infamous, and liked it enough to ask for a copy to be wrapped for him. He identified eagerly with Jurgen, the anti-hero of the allegory, 'a monstrous clever fellow', dark-haired and set apart. Jurgen took pride in trying every new drink once; so did Chink. 'Jurgen was no more able to give up questioning the meaning of life than could a trout relinquish swimming; indeed he lived submerged in a flood of curiosity and doubt as his native element.' Chink recognised himself. Jurgen relished being a rebel but was rent by his inability to be the same as other men; it was the same acute loneliness. From now onwards he always kept the book to hand, and each time he read it he was struck by the fresh aptness of a line. Cabell's book had been banned for its sexual symbolism, but it was its celebration of the outsider that was to influence Chink.

Rather than have Hadley cook, they ate out at the inexpensive Negre de Toulouse and kept to the Left Bank, except when they threaded their way over to Zelli's in Montmartre to dance the Black Bottom; Chink observed instead, greatly taken by the black musicians. There was always a party if they wanted one, where sex was talked about easily and explicitly, but he stayed celibate. He met no one who appealed sufficiently – 'some deeper attraction is always necessary,' he admitted significantly – and the spiderweb of gossip horrified him. But he was not a prude, as his reaction to Gertrude Stein's Picassos had demonstrated, and he was interested in everything. 'My first view' he noted of the student Bal Bullier ball in Montparnasse, 'was of a really magnificent mulatto woman in a loge, completely naked. . . . By the end, when the prettiest models were carried round in procession by students, all naked, half the assemblage had no clothes on.' He was in the other half, needless to say. He rolled up his shirtsleeves.

Whenever he was alone with Hemingway, they talked as they had always done. But the exchange was less one-sided now that Hemingway was older than he himself had been when they first met. At the Closerie des Lilas, a few hundred yards from the flat, the statue of Marshal Ney flourishing his sword defiantly beyond the laurel hedge tended to prompt conversations about honour and principle, conversations which made Hemingway angry these days. Chink was heading for disillusion, he went so far as to taunt one morning, because soldiers were only dupes to keep the status quo ticking smoothly. Ruling classes everywhere were crooked, he sneered, because that was how they came to rule in the first place; they were on the same side as war profiteers and politicians – their own side. Chink was hurt to realise that Hemingway's perception of him was changing so rapidly. He had no idea, smartly blue-suited and vibrant as they drank out of doors, with the sun flashing from his signet ring as he argued back, that Hemingway's imagination was projecting the same protective horror which he himself had felt for fellow soldiers in the trenches after Bellewaarde Wood. Hemingway did not explain. He did not show him the poems he was writing, either, in which Chink is described as flyblown and stiff, his trust in higher authority betrayed.

The reason for the Spanish Nicanor in his godson's name had been Hemingway's newfound enthusiasm for bullfighting, and the San Firmin festival at Pamplona in 1924 was their next rendezvous. It was fortunate for Chink that he was not possessive by nature, because he was by no means the centre of Hemingway's attention here. Instead, he found himself one of a group, and the only non-American present.

John Dos Passos was a compulsive traveller whose novel *Three Soldiers* had already made his name. Don Passos wore glasses, rarely drew breath and disconcertingly from Chink's point of view shared a room with his student girlfriend. Donald Ogden Stewart was equally likeable – 'full of wild fun' – and had a dry wit that reminded him of the dead Vachell. Stewart could not have been more different otherwise, however, being a Yale graduate who specialised in humorous fiction. Bill Bird, who ran the Three Mountains Press which had published *In Our Time*, was academic and easy-going, and devoted to his wife Sally, whom he had brought along to keep Hadley company. On being introduced to Robert McAlmon, however, Chink was reserved. McAlmon, suspected of living off his heiress English wife and called McAlimony behind his back, was a dilettante, malicious publisher who at once struck Chink as being as self-absorbed as Gertrude Stein. His Contract Editions had scooped Bird's company by bringing out Hemingway's *Three Stories and Ten Poems* in shorter time; the three stories of the title were the ones Chink had read the previous year. And lastly there was an uncomplicated eighteen-year-old, George O'Neill, son of an older friend of Hemingway.

It was a strange milieu in which to find a British regimental officer, but with his Jekyll and Hyde facility Chink fitted straight in. 'There were two trips to Pamplona,' Don Stewart recalled. 'The second was the one usually thought of as the model for *The Sun*. The first is the one

I remember with the most pleasure. It was a masculine time. Things were great. Pamplona was ours. No one else had discovered it. I have nothing but the most satisfying memories.' Dos Passos labelled it a Cook's conducted tour with Hemingway as master of ceremonies, and members thought of themselves as blood brothers. Their base was the Hotel de la Perla, across the square from the Hotel Quintana, which Chink came to regret when he got to know Juanita Quintana, whose knowledge of bullfighting was encyclopaedic. It was swelteringly hot. For camouflage as well as protection they bought black Basque berets, and proceeded to lose each other regularly at first in the crowded streets. Nobody, it appeared, ever refused a drink or went to bed before dawn, at which hour – to Chink's delight – a Spanish military band played reveille in the plaza. McAlmon was the only odd man out. 'McAlmon gave me a queasy feeling,' admitted Dos Passos. 'There was something disarming about the guy, too, that made me feel guilty for thinking he was such a heel.'

Hemingway was in his element, leading and instructing, and Chink stood back, too stimulated by novelty to mind the lack of deference in his one-time a.d.c. But Hemingway's macabre insistence on bullfighting being a beautiful dance of death against which all men needed to test themselves soon irritated the others. McAlmon grinned when Stewart whispered that it was better to save one's courage for a crisis, but Chink took it more seriously. He was appalled at such a public obsession, and took Hemingway aside to say that death was an unpleasant subject best avoided. It was bad form to be morbid, he pointed out, in an attempt to play on Hemingway's snobbishness. 'Never discuss casualties' had this other implication as well. But the rebuke administered, he turned to distracting him in the old way. 'We used to take and/or defend Pamplona,' Hemingway would recall, 'till it was worse than Fort Knox. I would tell him that I could come through the pass of Roncevaux and he would say "You can not."'

Pamplona was quiet till noon. Then the café terraces filled up in the space of five minutes and noise erupted until it fell quiet again in the siesta. Chink was reminded of the Staccato Lunches at Lorne House. At 6 p.m. he met the others in the shade of the arcade around the square, where announcements of bull-unloading times were flyposted to each pillar. Here they braced themselves for the throng of Spaniards about to pour in from the countryside, garlanded with garlic, smelly goatskin winebags adroitly plied among the crush, in a cacophony of deafening riau-riau music.

On the third day he was in position at 6 a.m. in the boarded-up street leading to the bullring to watch as the bulls ran past. Above him the balconies were crowded, and his hangover amplified the noise and smells. At the roar signalling their arrival in the bullring he followed Hemingway, with Stewart, McAlmon and O'Neill on his heels. The ascetic Bill Bird watched, as did Dos Passos in charge of the camera. In the ring Chink was pleased with his army fitness. Despite padded horns the steers were aggressive and as Stewart put it afterwards, 'balls or no balls, they were mean as hell'. Stewart had two ribs broken and Hemingway was tossed, but plying his jacket as Quintana had advised Chink stayed on his feet, unscathed.

His first reaction to the disembowelling of picadors' horses in the formal bullfights was one of horror; it reminded him of similar carnage in the war when horses were no match for the guns to which they were exposed. But he listened as Hemingway explained ritual and technique – always ready to try a new drink once, like Jurgen – and absently munched shrimps and shared the beers. By the time Manuel Garcia Maera, Belmonte's banderillero, vowed to place four pairs of banderillas at a dangerous angle, Chink was rising with the rest of the crowd and shouting at him to stop, caught up in the spectacle. He knew Maera had not been to bed the night before, because he had shadowed him, fascinated by the thin-lipped arrogance.

The courage of John Annlo, Nacional II, touched him even more, and when a Spaniard near them yelled abuse at Annlo's cruder style it was Chink with whom he had to contend. Meanwhile Hemingway was studying each one of them in turn, building up his casebook for *Death in the Afternoon* where 'Capt. DS' duly appears. 'Suffered sincerely and deeply at what happened to horses at first bullfight – said it was the most hateful thing he had ever seen. Continued to attend, he said, in order to understand the mentality of people who would tolerate such a thing. At the end of his sixth fight, understood them so well that he became embroiled in a dispute. . . .' McAlmon needed his hipflask to get through each session, and accused everyone else of posing.

It was a relief at the end of the San Firmin festival to get up into the cool mountains of their war games at Roncesvalles – the setting, as Chink reminded Hemingway, for the Carlist wars – and unwind. He was content for a while to idle at Burguete with the group and discuss 'whimsies' such as *The Song of Roland*, while Hemingway fished the Irati River undisturbed. Chink knew he wanted to concentrate on an unfinished story which, he had confided, he had with him and in which his aim was to 'do the country' like the impressionist painter Cézanne. While at Burguete Hemingway sought Chink out to show him *Big Two-Hearted River* and ask his opinion, which he readily gave.

'I liked the first part where the man just catches trout,' he recalled later, 'but in the second part Hem set his hero down to smoke and think. . . . His hero's reverie was strictly psychological, some of it relating to myself. I thought that part was phony . . . and said so. My view was that the chap had better catch some more trout and leave Freud to the intellectuals. . . . I was surprised that he took the piece, tore it up and began again. . . . I was also surprised that I could influence Hem so easily.' That was protesting a little too much. He had been criticising Hemingway's style since they met – 'Anyway, even if you can Hiawath' he had written in a characteristic 1919 jibe, 'it's not as good as my effort. I find your effusion Browningesque in its cryptic obscurity' – but by 1924 the number of people prepared to criticise Hemingway's writing was becoming small, and Chink's influence was correspondingly greater. And that cutting of the reference to himself is one of the earliest indications of his self-effacement when confronted by a cause. 'I have decided that all that mental conversation in the long fishing story is the shit and have cut it all out,' Hemingway informed McAlmon that September. 'I got a hell of a shock when I realised how bad it was and that shocked me back to the river again and I've finished it off the way it ought to have been all along. Just the straight fishing.'

With a fortnight of leave left Chink suggested a long walk, and Dos Passos, McAlmon and O'Neill volunteered, Dos Passos's girlfriend having gone back to university. Hemingway, with reluctance, had to stay behind with Hadley. They planned to hike along the chain of mountains as far as Andorra, undeterred by the lack of a compass and relying on an old army map of Chink's that was blank on the Spanish side. Dos Passos, whose scholarly looks belied a driving stamina, had every faith in him, considering him 'just the kind of reliable man you would want to climb a mountain with' (the reverse of later army criticism), and O'Neill was young and energetic. McAlmon, they agreed, was going to be the problem; and McAlmon began literally on the wrong foot by wanting to wear canvas alpargetas.

'Chink Smith, the Army man, had the maps,' McAlmon's version began, 'and while swearing that he wouldn't try to show up the rest of us, he noted that Dos Passos and George both set a pace hard to follow.' They did thirty-five kilometres the first day, forty the second and sixty on the third, losing their way twice, and that night they slept in haystacks. 'My recollection,' wrote the educated Dos Passos, 'is of a succession of high passes and the scenery unrolling on either side like the painted panorama they used to unroll during the Rhine music in *Siegfried*. The mountains were green towards France . . . toward Spain dry and lion-coloured.' Curious as always, Dos Passos tried to prise out Chink's real opinion of Hemingway, but met with a brick wall. Hemingway was a likely lad, Chink always countered, deploying regimental slang but enigmatically using the past tense. Dos Passos gave up.

They bought their food as they went along, and with money running short reached a village -- hardly more than a shack and a pigpen, to McAlmon's jaundiced eye – where O'Neill found a letter propped on a fencepost addressed to him; by coincidence he had seen the name of the village on a map before starting out for Pamplona, and his father had sent on his allowance. At Luchon Super Bagnières they ran out of money again, and sat on the pavement 'like tramps' according to Chink while shoppers skirted around them. 'And we said rude things to them,' he added, 'because we were hungry and they had obviously had good breakfasts. The only free thing in Luchon was the public baths; we had them and felt better. The money came in the evening, by which time we were plotting to burgle something.' The contrast with his very correct Northumberland Fusilier life could not have been more extreme.

Picturesque as the mountain villages were, the food was monotonous and the steady diet of goat's cheese, black bread, tortillas and coffee with goat's milk sickened McAlmon, making him as awkward as they had anticipated. On the fifth day they knocked on an isolated door, pesetas in hand, and were invited inside. 'We seated ourselves in the peasant woman's kitchen,' recorded McAlmon indignantly, 'and in the corner was an old hag certainly past a hundred years. At short intervals she coughed and gurgled as though it were her death cry. Chink Smith and I didn't feel like eating then . . . but Dos Passos . . . loved it all.' Next day McAlmon baled out for the French border, complaining that long trips were fun only if taken leisurely.

The remaining three hacked on. By the time they had covered 460 kilometres and were nearing Andorra they needed nips of brandy to keep going, but being taken for smugglers by a conspiratorial elderly Spaniard spurred them on. Even the enthusiastic Dos Passos, however, had his limits. Stumbling down the long track into Andorra in a thunderstorm after dark, unable to see, he clung to Chink's pack and shouted that they had lost the road and were on a river bed. Around midnight they limped into Andorra and found everywhere shut, with the exception of one rough-looking inn. 'They led us upstairs to an evil-smelling room with three beds,' Dos Passos recounted. 'We were absolutely worn out. Our legs ached. Our feet were sore and bruised. We were desperately sleepy. The minute we stretched out in dry clothes the bugs came like shock-troops, wave after wave. George and I lay there inert, but Chink amused me by jumping out of bed, dressing carefully and sitting up solemnly in a chair for the rest of the night. His attitude was that it didn't behove an officer in His Majesty's Army to suffer indignities at the hands of the natives. I esteemed him for it.' Chink did not labour the point that he had learned about bugs in the trenches.

Fiesta/The Sun Also Rises was begun in July 1925 after Hemingway's third trip to Pamplona, and founded his literary reputation. As soon as it was published an absorbing guessing game began for those in the know, identifying the real-life characters in the novel. Don Stewart and Bill Bird were recognisable, as were many who had not been in the Pamplona class of '24. (Chink got Brett Ashley wrong, always remaining convinced that she was Nancy Cunard.) Most were sly verbal caricatures, and though some victims were amused, the majority were not. Only one character is treated with affection, and that is the 'exemplary Englishman named Harris', as Hemingway described him to his editor Maxwell Perkins. 'You know, my name isn't really Harris,' the exemplary Englishman introduces himself in the book. 'It's Wilson-Harris; all one name. With a hyphen, you know.'

Hemingway had constantly been skimming accents and phrases into the small notebook he carried with him, and many of Chink's words reappear. 'I've not had so much fun since the war,' says Wilson-Harris/ Dorman-Smith. 'Be a good chap.' 'Is that a pub across the way? Or do my eyes deceive me?' 'Jolly good show.' Even lazing beside the Irati he had been observed. 'Wonderful', Wilson-Harris/Dorman-Smith rejoices, 'how one loses track of the days up here in the mountains.' But Chink made no connection between the character in the bestseller and himself, and a more self-important man would have read the book from that angle alone, expecting to find himself there. More significantly, the fact that Hemingway used his dialogue and mannerisms alone for an untwisted portrait proves that he remained the hero at a time when Hemingway's pattern of exploiting friends was established.

They did not meet again – 'I'd give a great deal to be with you,' he replied to the next Christmas invitation, 'and I would be, if this cursed work hadn't got me by the thorax' – until the spring of 1926. The chance then came to accompany an army rugby team to Paris. 'It's like this, Maestro,' he contacted Hemingway at once. 'I'll arrive in Paris on the 14th April. . . . The night of the 15th the French officers here are preparing an orgy which will probably beggar description – I hope so. . . . Get us some rooms at the Université, if you can, like a good a de c, decent rooms with a bath adjacent. . . . Hadley and I will show you round Montmartre. All except one flat – magnificent. I think Bumby better come too in the pram. Wheeled by Gertrude!! I may have to appear at this function in uniform. Will the Quarter mind? You may, if you wish, avoid me at that juncture. Stories! I've got heaps of stories. We'll get busy on them when you please. . . .'

And at first no change was evident. Hemingway appeared no different, being as impressed as always by inclusion in army events. 'Went with Chink and many generals etc. to see Sandhurst play St. Cyr,' he promptly boasted to his rival Scott Fitzgerald. 'He and I are going to walk from Saragossa across the Pyrenees by way of Andorra end of July.' Sitting in the Closerie des Lilas as of old, Chink enjoyed hearing about Scott Fitzgerald, who was infuriating Hemingway by aimlessly touring Europe with his capricious wife Zelda, borrowing money and feeling sorry for himself. As usual Fitzgerald was hard up again, despite recent publication of *The Great Gatsby* and an advance of film rights, and they examined his problem without sympathy, as Hemingway's letter shows. He was going to make Fitzgerald his heir, he continued. 'Chink says he'll leave you Bellamont Forest too, if you like. Pauline Pfeiffer says you can have her job on *Vogue*. I've written Scribners to send all my royalty checks to you. . . .'

But behind the banter lay tension, and the clue was in that letter. Hemingway was not being straight with Chink. He was involved in a serious affair with Pauline Pfeiffer, who was much richer than Hadley, and felt guilty enough about it not to introduce her to Chink, although she was in Paris at the same time. But the situation was soon clear enough and, when he found out, Chink's allegiance – as Hemingway had known it would be – lay with Hadley. He was saddened to see her throwing away her advantages by the disastrous tactic of following Hemingway about in tears. 'I warned her that nothing could be more fatal,' he revealed once. 'She was an unattractive weeper.' He hated emotional situations, and he shied away from this one. Hadley was distraught, Bumby fretful, the weather was bad and Hemingway so defensively on edge that it became a strain to be with him. It was hopeless for anyone who wanted to work to stay in Paris indefinitely, Hemingway blustered finally, so he and Hadley would probably be going back to America. Impossible to pretend that things had not changed, and would not change even more.

'Pop, I had a feeling you were pretty tied up one way or another,' he wrote when thanking him. 'I'm so sorry your plans have gone to pieces so completely. . . . It's the very devil how all these things go wrong, but anyway Bumby is better which is something. . . . Hell, but I wish I was in the Quintana now. It's six 30 o'clock. We'd be in the white chairs with an absinthe to be destroyed.' Hemingway pressed him to come down to Cap d'Antibes for August, explaining that it was all fixed with the hospitable Gerald and Sara Murphy, who owned the Villa America; he did not mention that he was staying there in a destructive limbo with Bumby – and both Hadley and Pauline. But instinctively Chink recoiled. 'It's very nice of the Murphy's to ask me, but I feel in need of tackling a piece of country on my hind legs somewhere. Andorra, Austria, Switzerland. . . .' He sent a Christmas card that year, scrawling 'Good Luck' across the conventional greetings, but by then the Hemingways had separated.

Hadley divorced Hemingway in March 1927, and in May that year the marriage to Pauline Pfeiffer took place. Disgusted by the break-up and absorbed in his demanding army career, Chink allowed the friendship to lapse for the time being, and refused a pressing invitation to stay with Hemingway and Pauline in Key West in 1930. He visited Hadley and Bumby whenever he was in Paris but that was not often, and he was a careless godfather, forgetting birthday and Christmas presents.

But by being the one to cut the friendship for reasons Hemingway could only respect, unintentionally he retained the advantage. Hemingway was the one who dropped people. He had quarrelled with every one of the Pamplona band of brothers by this time, except Chink, and with most of his old friends and contemporaries. The irresistible, dynamic youth had become a touchy celebrity, cornered by his own success.

Chink had not changed so fundamentally. The influence of Jurgen the outsider was an alienating factor, but otherwise he remained intrigued by novelty and increasingly engrossed in military potential. He did not suspect that the very quality which had slotted him into Paris circles so easily could be a handicap in a conforming world. But as he had influenced Hemingway, so had Hemingway influenced him. The stimulation of new experiences, the pursuit of intellectual honesty, the fascination with language and ideas, the company of creative people like Hemingway, Dos Passos, Gertrude Stein, James Joyce, Nancy Cunard, Sylvia Beach, Don Stewart, Ford Maddox Ford, Ezra Pound and the many other writers, painters and eccentrics he had mixed with, had raised his expectations. He suffered fools less gladly now, and he knew his own worth. And the timing, as far as personal army relationships was concerned, was to have disastrous consequences.

5

Leaping Ahead

Alone among the drab khaki, shining out like a master of a hunt, Colonel Yatman insisted on wearing his red mess kit. One evening a mess waiter passed in front of him, balancing a single glass of stout on a tray. For Yatman, sitting glowering, it was the last straw. He kicked up savagely, sending tray and stout flying. 'We don't drink stout in this mess,' he bellowed. 'We drink sherry *wine*.' Chink was sympathetic, but he was seen to smile. In the post-war army in England the mood was one of anti-climax. It was appropriate, Chink often thought, that his new hunter, a fast bay called Quits, had been wounded on the same day as himself at Le Cateau. They were both survivors, conditioned to pre-war standards, and so was the man who had guided him through the chaos of Mons and Ypres, promoted now to command his regiment. Readjustment was painful.

A year to the day after his meeting with Hemingway in Milan, Chink was drawn up outside the gym at Aldershot in the guard of honour for the visiting Shah of Persia. A light drizzle seeped out of a grey sky, and it matched his spirits. Dining out had been ruined for him on his first evening in London when his companion had glanced around the restaurant and remarked that there was nobody pre-war to be seen. The shrunken ranks of the regiment on St George's Day 1919, compared to the massed scarlet only five years earlier, had been infinitely depressing.

He was Adjutant, right-hand man to the Colonel, and their job was to rebuild and reorganise; for him this meant putting across frequently unpopular orders and bringing efficiency up to scratch. Even Sandhurst, it was known, had dropped its entrance standards in a bid to combat the fall in recruitment. He hurled himself into his work, and his newest enemy was sport. In peacetime the army's greatest attraction was the opportunity it gave officers to hunt, shoot, play polo and take up whichever game they preferred; transforming amiable sportsmen into military professionals was a guarantee of frustration.

Sport infuriated him – but sport also saved him. He remained approachable because he joined in. He entered point-to-points, riding Quits to qualify for the top Hampshire event, watched by the Prince of Wales, whose brother was in the same race. And out of the saddle he was competitive as well. He finished near the front in the three-mile relay race at the Aldershot Tournament and represented the regiment regularly in miniature rifle marksmanship contests. 'Most targets almost invisible,' he needled after one victory. 'A fine example of the practical joke department in the War Office.' It was a new voice, witty and sarcastic, and quite unlike the general tone of the time. As 1st Battalion editor of *St George's Gazette*, the regimental magazine, he took every opportunity to say what he thought, and rarely was it approving.

His belief in looking forward extended to shepherding his officers by bus to Aldershot to hear the most up-to-date lecturers, who included the new Commander-in-Chief, Lord Cavan. From the back of the hall he studied the face of General Sir Henry Wilson, another speaker, simultaneously fascinated and repelled. In every way he tried to keep up the momentum. Hearing that the Machine Gun Corps was being disbanded and its guns allotted to suitable infantry battalions, he put himself down for a course and came back with a distinguished certificate, ready to train a platoon. The extra pay from being adjutant made him financially independent, which he relished, and he gave up cigarettes to pay for the keep of his horse. He was not acquisitive, and because of his wit he could count on dinner-party invitations to give his vanity a fling in top hat and tails.

The extremes in his life stimulated him. In the mess he was the adjutant, perfectionist but prepared to be reasonable. At dinner parties he shocked, irreverent but always knowing where to draw the line. With Hemingway he was the reassuring veteran who read and talked about everything and anything. At home he was an enigma, compared to Victor who did as he was told and Reggie who did everything right – even to squiring Amy's choice, Doreen Watson, about the nightspots, despite being so much younger himself. On his own he was Jurgen the sceptic, amused by people's foibles and cut off from them.

In June 1921 a more complicated role presented itself, putting his ambivalent Irish loyalties to the test. Extra British Army reinforcements were needed to contain the Sinn Fein rebellion, and when news came that his battalion was being included he refused to use his Irish origin as a ploy to stay behind. On the contrary, he insisted that professional soldiers were insulated from political events, even in their own country.

The posting got off to a good start, because on the boat crossing to Dublin he was reunited with Brian Horrocks, against whom he at once privately measured himself with considerable satisfaction. Horrocks had joined the Middlesex Regiment on leaving Sandhurst and reached the war quickly enough to have been in the retreat from Mons. But there their paths had divided. Horrocks had been captured on 21 October 1914, during Chink's first sick leave, and had spent the rest of the war in German prison camps, making a series of fruitless escape attempts. Chink felt older and wiser when it came to war, to the point of being protective about Horrocks's undiminished sporting approach to life. But he envied him his post-war adventures with the army in Russia, which had culminated in capture by the Red Russians, because in 1919, after leaving Milan, Chink himself had put in a request to be sent there. All in all, however, he congratulated himself on moving much faster ahead. Horrocks had the rank of captain, too, but had not been appointed adjutant. Battle experience was a distinct advantage.

Before disembarking, he bet Horrocks provocatively that he was bound to be stationed in Cavan because the War Office would never have checked up on his address. Horrocks took him up on it and won, a bet he claimed as soon as realised he was being sent to Cavan himself. Horrocks would spend the next six months not just in Cootehill, but camped with his regiment along the drive of Bellamont Forest. Chink's destination turned out to be the martial-law county of Kilkenny.

1st Battalion, Northumberland Fusiliers disembarked with full military precautions. Magazines were charged, covering parties out, the hotel across the road held by Auxiliaries, while an armoured car waited to escort them to the station. It bore no resemblance to coming home on pre-war holidays, and he recalled an incident on his brief visit in 1919 which he had thought comically exaggerated at the time. Dining with his father at the Shelbourne Hotel in St Stephen's Green, Edward had called for champagne to celebrate his sons' safe return from war, only to be taken aback as fellow diners threw their hands in the air or dived to the floor when the waiter pulled the cork.

But both had missed the build-up of tension. The rising had broken out nine days after the presentation of Chink's MC in 1916, during the period when his commanding officer had been making up his mind to send him back from the trenches for treatment. His knowledge of it was correspondingly blurred, and the Somme had had far more impact. But he had kept up with events from a distance, noting while serving on the Piave front that his old Commander-in-Chief at Le Cateau, Field Marshal Sir John French, had been appointed Lord Lieutenant. The job was such an unpopular one, he had guessed with army loyalty, that no professional politician would handle it.

Confronted now with the reality, he still saw it from a British, rather than an Irish, viewpoint; from the soldier's angle, not that of the private citizen. And to a soldier it was the worst possible work – being a military policeman in a deadlocked situation. Law and order were in the hands of the Black and Tans, demobilised war recruits whom the Northumberland Fusiliers would not have signed on in the first place, and whose violence was disowned by regular British Army officers in the privacy of the mess. They were equally scathing about the Auxiliaries, a mercenary force whose commanding officer's confidential admission that they were insubordinate, dishonest, sadistic and drunken had quickly circulated. On both sides the legacy of casualties was mounting up. In the first three months of the year 462 had been killed and wounded for the Crown, and 602 against. Seventy-three suspected spies had been executed, and reprisals sanctioned by Sinn Fein and the Irish Republic Army.

Throughout the country tribal loyalties had been accentuated. At Bellamont – although Horrocks was unaware of such a complication – the housekeeper was an IRA sympathiser: the local IRA brigadier was now brother-in-law to Chink's ex-nurse. Meanwhile Edward had been appointed High Sheriff for County Cavan and divided his time between England and Ireland, where he received regular threats in the post. He took these more seriously after an inflammatory sermon was preached in Cootehill Catholic church in 1920 – the one with the superior hassocks – and six shots rang out shortly afterwards as he was strolling down the long drive with twenty-one-year-old Reggie. Reggie pushed him behind a tree and the aim was a poor one, but in his anger Edward stormed to the butcher's shop kept by the local IRA brigadier, slammed the most recent anonymous letter on the counter, and swore that if anything more happened to him he had three sons in the services who would get their own back. It had only been to assert a position, he was assured. Apologies were accepted.

Chink's own emotions were divided. Black and Tans had raided

Cootehill with such venom that, when tipped off about a further raid on a visit the previous winter, he had warned the housekeeper and helped to bury the small cache of hand grenades in the grounds. But that was the full extent of his involvement. He did not know – nor, of course, did Horrocks – that the local IRA brigadier was intercepting most orders for the Middlesex Regiment. And the interacting relations between the family and the IRA may explain why Bellamont escaped burning, despite its open associations with both the British Army and the Crown.

Chink considered himself impartial. He plunged into work and kept introspection at bay by ensuring that his own battalion behaved itself. They were in the Curragh 5th Division, and patrolled the martial-law county of Kilkenny from their headquarters in Carlow town. The barracks were in a rambling quadrangle which had previously held a cavalry regiment, and a series of companies were stationed in outposts throughout the counties of Carlow and Kilkenny.

'Difficult to say at times,' he wrote on arrival, 'whether we are performers in a harlequinade or a tragedy.' On their first day an army lorry waiting at the station was burned out by armed men, and three local girls had their hair shorn for talking to soldiers. A youth was tied to the chapel gates, with 'convicted for aiding the enemy' scrawled on a placard round his neck. It was hard to know who was in the IRA and who was not, as the trenchcoat was standard dress. 1st Battalion, with morale still low from the war, had to oversee the curfew and send out patrols in Crossley trucks to clear roadblocks, protect bridges and pick up wanted men for internment in the Curragh Camp. Extreme boredom alternated with extreme tension.

Unlike Northern Ireland after 1969, however, the IRA were concentrating not on the British Army, but on the Black and Tans, the Auxiliaries and the Royal Irish Constabulary. There were off-duty invitations for officers to tennis parties and private homes, and later that year the local hunt relied on their membership subscriptions to keep going. In contrast to those serving in more violent areas, like Cork, it was impossible for those with Irish backgrounds to take Sinn Fein's threats seriously.

When the Truce was announced on 16 July the level of tension dropped, but the battalion found themselves in a more invidious position. The catchy air of 'Kevin Barry' haunted them in the street, and in barracks they whistled it among themselves. They went about off duty unarmed, and were taunted by Sinn Fein members waving revolvers. 'We have been busily engaged in eating mud,' Chink let off steam in the *Gazette*. 'Most of the patriots that our comrades and ourselves have been at such pains to catch and intern are out and about again. Those patriots who ... dared not show their noses ... now swagger up and down their villages. We have to deal with Liaison Officers, such mirrors of murderous patriotism ... and as a reward for our forbearance platoons of flat-footed rebels dare to drill within sight of barracks.' His printed comments found their way to the *Morning Post* in London, where they appeared on the front page under the headline 'What the Soldier Thinks', and he was given an official reprimand which bounced off him. 'As if,' he snorted to Hemingway, 'soldiers *ever* think.' But the press had not seemed accessible until then, and the realisation that news might be manipulated was thought-provoking. A more conventional man would have resented being put in such a position. He was flattered, and saw only opportunity.

Local IRA headquarters were in Duckett's Grove, a house six miles from Carlow. Here on 13 August the incoming officer listed strength as one battalion staff commander, six company commanding officers, nine half company commanders, thirty-nine other ranks and five fianna boys for cookhouse work. 'The men are willing but untrained,' he noted. 'Arms in a very bad condition. I have ordered a week's training starting immediately – there is no ink to hand, so I have had to write in pencil.' Within six days the IRA had mustered twenty-three commanding officers, fourteen battalion staff and fifty-one officers of all ranks, plus fifteen other ranks and seven cookhouse staff. British Intelligence consistently underestimated the organisation, and Chink was no exception. 'Promising rebels being sent to study most modern methods of murder,' he ridiculed. 'Kidnapping in full swing, training camps in existence. There is a Republican variety in their headgear, a Republican ease in their slouch and a very Republican dislike on their faces as they pass the representatives of Hated England.' But he was still able to reconcile being one of those representatives himself with his act of burying the grenades at Bellamont.

Although the British Army felt superior, they could not wait to be gone. There was no overnight leave from barracks and troops chafed at being pinned down. The return of patrols was awaited anxiously because the IRA were believed to string wire ropes across roads to behead drivers; Chink had little patience with such rumours. Newspapers frequently mentioned the shooting of soldiers in other counties and law and order in their own district was increasingly hard to maintain. There was little to do and yet they could not relax, because security was always under threat. Even their orders had to be brought by motorbike from the Curragh as it was assumed their post was being intercepted.

They were correct. In Carlow post office the IRA member kept a kettle boiling on the range in the back room, ready to steam open all letters to and from the barracks. And through his hands, as a matter of course, passed the correspondence between Chink and Hemingway. Not only was it tantalisingly out of the ordinary, but it presented a curious picture of British morale. 'Remember, I prythee, my Hemmingstein, that I am absolutely poverty-stricken as befits an Irishman,' one typical effusion runs. 'I have no means but debt and live on the credit I obtain by producing my card with my high sounding home address on it at appropriate intervals.' Did Chink's letters repay a second reading, or were they tossed aside? The fact that he was thinking of himself as an Irishman, however, is significant.

Although the local Sinn Fein members were too amateur to identify with, his imagination had been caught by Michael Collins, chairman of the Irish provisional government. All he read and heard convinced him that Collins was a man of vision and integrity, not to mention a Professional in his organisational ability. By the time it was reported that Collins had signed the treaty in London on 6 December, agreeing to an Irish Free State and allowing the North one month to opt out and so antagonising everyone who wanted a thirty-two-county republic, Chink's emotions were involved. The inevitability of Collins's assassination preoccupied him, and he began wondering about his own contribution. Once it was over, he rarely mentioned his service in Ireland, and on Collins's death the following August he swung around to outspoken criticism of partition for its inevitable long-term challenge. The border now ran within eleven miles of Bellamont Forest, making it an ever-present reminder.

But ratification of the treaty allowed the British Army to leave, and his regiment withdrew with dignity, unlike the Black and Tans and the Auxiliaries. The Northumberland Fusiliers held a ball, gave a variety show and two band concerts and were about to auction off superfluous equipment when the Irish Free State announced that barracks were being taken over as they stood. Shortly before the handover an IRA representative came across from Duckett's Grove in lounge suit and Sam Browne belt on behalf of the new regime. Hands were not shaken and lunch was taken at separate tables in the local hotel, but the

Quartermaster Sergeant was meticulous about the inventory. Beds, cooking equipment, furniture and lorries were left behind. Only the horses remained the property of the regiment.

Ritually the flag was hauled down. As Adjutant, Chink folded it, placed it under his arm and saluted, before the flagstaff was snapped off to prevent the Tricolour being hoisted where the Union Jack had flown. When the trenchcoated IRA marched in, arms were presented, and presented in return as the 23 officers and 338 men of 1st Battalion, Northumberland Fusiliers marched out. 'The scene was heartening,' reported the *Carlow Nationalist*. 'Carlow Military Barracks, one of the oldest in Ireland, was taken over by the forces of the Irish nation.... Perhaps one of the best comments on the incident was passed by one old lady who tearfully exclaimed "Thanks be to God." '

On 8 February 1922 Chink boarded the SS *Strathmore* as the wind got up and flames from Cahills, a large printing company on fire at Ormonde Quay, were symbolically reflected in the water. He was relieved to be free of the Irish problem and unaware that up in Lurgan, on the far side of the new border, a meeting of Orangemen was being addressed by the Unionist MP, Colonel Sir William Allen. 'They say we can have peace if we come into an all-Ireland conference,' Allen declaimed as the *Strathmore* edged out of Dublin Bay into rough sea. 'Thank you for nothing. We are not coming in. . . . They must realise it means bloodshed worse than Ireland has ever known.'

Six months later Chink was snapped to attention on the Dom Platz in Cologne as Lord Cavan, in full regalia as Chief of the Imperial General Staff, inspected the Rhine Army. What would his own feelings be, he mused in a letter to Edward afterwards, if the position were reversed and it were England that was occupied by German regiments? Parades and marching competitions were a way of displaying garrison strength and proclaiming the British military presence, and they made a pleasant change. 'At Carlow it was "Occupy by all means but don't hurt the inhabitants and keep off the flower beds",' he had quipped when they joined 11th Rhine Army Brigade. 'Well, now, we did lick the Hun, didn't we? So we are all trying to look very fierce and martial and domineering . . . but it is hardly possible after being booed out on home ground to come here and try to exult in the success of the fixture list before that.'

As adjutant in Germany he had a higher standard to enforce, and the British were more popular than the French, who provoked violence in their zones. Their sector included Godesberg and the

Remagen Bridge and they provided guards for the British High Commissioner's residence in Koblenz. The spit and polish suited him. He was in barracks every morning before 7 a.m., despite rarely getting to bed before 3 a.m. 'Oh dear,' one groan appeared in the *Gazette* from the ranks. 'You know what Adjutants are, so for further security we have men posted to prevent entry until such time as we shall have put on our boots and coats, brushed our hair and are quite ready.'

In the mess at Marienburg Barracks, Cologne, their pre-war scarlet was restored, set off again by a backdrop of silver, mahogany and pictures. Conversation, however, was limited. No mention was allowed of politics, women, religion or professional 'shop' and anything intellectual was suspect. It reminded him of school. Few officers kept abreast of military development in other countries, or troubled to plough through the foreign journals he read. In his Jekyll and Hyde way he kept most of his interests to himself, including his growing curiosity about the interplay between politics and war and the likelihood of subjectiveness in the reporting of news. When it came to reading newspapers, the usual form was to turn to the sports pages.

Sport was the universal panacea, and he fought boredom with his Irish ability to wear different hats in different company. His *Gazette* barb 'When all is said and done, life in any garrison is as monotonous as a neutral Harris tweed' referred surely to the dull military routine, not to parochial tedium. Or did it? Nobody could be entirely sure.

But even the most obtuse member of the mess was voluble about the fall of the mark. As recently as August 1921, when they had been in Ireland, it had seemed stable at 250 to the pound. But when it became clear that Germany was not going to honour her war reparations the value fell so swiftly that the exchange rate was 5000 to the pound by the time they had been there a month. Company cash was drawn from the bank in oat sacks, and soldiers paraded for pay with kitbags or suitcases, while officers came off better still as their pay went straight into London bank accounts in sterling. On Chink's arrival a couple could stay at a *de luxe* hotel full-board for 600 marks a day. By May the following year a sandwich cost 900 marks in a station buffet. By 1924, when he was still there, the price of a newspaper was 300 million.

And the non-payment of reparations had a delayed effect on his work. When the French decided to help themselves to the sum owed by sending troops into the Ruhr basin in January 1923, the strikes that ensued threw transport and communications into chaos. 11th Rhine Army Brigade were in the thick of it. So anarchic did the general situation become that when Hemingway visited him on behalf of the *Toronto Star*, Chink felt it necessary to issue him with a safe conduct pass. 'R.T.O. Cologne, Main', he wrote with a touch of the Heir about the wording. 'The bearer, Mr. R.E.K. Hemingway, has been staying with me. He is going back to Paris. I would be obliged if you would do anything in your power to assist him on his journey. E.E. Dorman-Smith, Cologne. Captain 5th Fusiliers.'

The unrest also confronted him with the most chilling example of mob hysteria yet, when the regiment had to clean up after a German policeman's murder by a mob of previously stolid Cologne citizens. The experience remained in his mind, reinforcing the lessons of the Uppingham and Sandhurst incidents. So unpleasant did conditions become that he waited for a nationalist backlash, but when details that November of an attempted *coup d'état* by the National Socialist German Worker's Party in Munich reached the newspapers, it was the uniformed presence of Field Marshal Ludendorff that caught his eye, and he paid no attention to Ludendorff's thirty-four-year-old companion, Adolf Hitler. He was distrustful of Germany's aims, and the continued backwardness of British training was pointed up by the tension around them. He dared to say things now that he would not have said earlier.

'The British nation is always engaged in a detailed study of the lessons of the last war,' he pointed out in the *Gazette* in his customary light style. 'As opposed to the more theoretical task of forecasting the methods of waging future wars. . . . Up to 1914 we had our hands full with Brother Boer. He was always attacking convoys or occupying kopjes . . . while we plodded about in tenacious and surprisingly successful pursuit. . . . By the time we had defeated Bruder Boche, we were far too fond of him lightly to leave him. We still give him credit for his past glories and struggle with him in trench attack. [Our] enemy never has tanks or low-flying aeroplanes [and] the query as to what does an attacking company do if it is itself attacked by a tank remains unanswered. The tactical scene of today puts the art of Jules Verne and Rider Haggard in the shade.'

As early as 1923 he was promoting his ideal of an integrated all-service college in the *Sandhurst Journal*, and by 1924 he was finding it difficult to contain his seriousness. Perennial regimental jokes at the expense of the Staff College got a testy response. He found the mess claustrophobic and opinions there puerile. 'Not got anything to talk about or anyone to talk to if I had,' he confided to Hemingway. 'My brain is steadily becoming atrophied and its place being taken by a mixture of Rhineland fogs and short drinks.' The highest ambition of the majority of his fellow officers was to command their regiment, and he too had once thought in those terms. But change could only be achieved from a higher rank, which meant going to the Staff College and stepping away from the regiment. He no longer saw it, however, in the simplistic terms he had ten years before. Regimental pride, he was now convinced, was more of a weakness than a strength. It gave men a cause to fight for that was greater than themselves. But, by elevating unchanged tradition too high, it perpetuated technical backwardness.

Leaving the Northumberland Fusiliers was a more poignant break than leaving school, made worse by its being entirely his own choice. Eventually his rustiness at a course at the Hythe Small Arms School made up his mind for him, but even then he decided to compromise. He applied for a Sandhurst instructorship because it would reflect well on the regiment if he were chosen, leave the door open to return and place him advantageously for the competitive Staff College entry. He did not expect to be turned down and nor was he. Comparing himself as always to Horrocks when the good news came, he patted himself on the back for having raced even further ahead.

Ten years after leaving Sandhurst as a cadet he reported back in plain clothes as an instructor in the autumn of 1924. And apparently he had changed little. The staff sergeant on duty barred his way, growling, 'None of your public school jokes from now on, Sir, if you don't mind me telling you for your own good.' He grimaced at being taken for a cadet all over again.

He was honoured to be among soldiers of such high calibre. He was immediately impressed by the Sandhurst adjutant, 'Boy' Browning of the Grenadier Guards, and for the first time since Barrett's death put aside his reserve and made an army friend. Behind the briskly handsome exterior, Browning was humorous and widely read, the reverse of the stereotype of a guardsman. Browning took fitness equally seriously, and they jogged around the grounds together every morning discussing books. But Browning's predecessor, Arthur Smith of the Coldstream Guards, called forth all his infantry disdain. Discovering that Smith was a Christian Scientist, Chink responded whenever they met afterwards with an irreverence that made the antagonism mutual. He would not have done so before the Hemingway years.

Alec Gatehouse, an ex-fusilier related to the captain killed on the Aisne, was also an instructor. Gatehouse had transferred to the new

Tank Corps and could talk of little else, but it was a subject Chink was already interested in, and only too glad to discuss. The man he most admired, however, was Richard O'Connor of the Cameronians, whose war experience was a byword among cadets and staff. As light as a jockey and with a courteous, matter-of-fact manner, the more senior O'Connor had none of the assertiveness of some small men. His mildness cloaked the qualities Chink liked most – original thinking and decisiveness. It was a mutual love of long-distance walking that narrowed the gap in rank between them, and at the end of the first term they planned a walking holiday together. At Chink's suggestion they decided to follow the trail of the Alpini infantry through the Austro-Italian Alps, and in Innsbruck before starting O'Connor took him to Maximilian's tomb in the Silver Chapel, where he modestly indicated King Arthur as his favourite knight on the frieze. Chink looked from the carved figure to O'Connor and back again, and thought how alike they were. The chivalrous ideal was possible; it did exist.

Together they walked from Innsbruck to Maloga, and from Val d'Isère to Zermatt, less exalted in mood but talking all the way, oblivious of their difference in height. Unlike the walks with Hemingway and later Dos Passos, Chink was the subordinate, but O'Connor made little of it and so did he. It was his first opportunity to discuss soldiering constructively with someone of the same mind, and moving along at a crisp pace as usual fired his imagination. O'Connor found him entertaining and full of ideas. 'Very argumentative and cocksure,' he would recall. 'But I learned a lot from my association with him, all the same, and we were on speaking terms at the end of the fortnight.'

On Boxing Day 1925 Chink went back to Switzerland by himself, despite his excuse that year to Hemingway about hard work. Wanting to be alone, he booked into a small hotel in Maloga where he was introduced against his will to another dedicated mountaineer on the first evening. Leo Amery, Colonial Secretary and Secretary of State for Dominion Affairs in the Conservative government, was staying there with his family, and while most regimental soldiers would have backed away from a politician, Chink was soon so charmed that they climbed together every day. Army isolationism seemed increasingly irrelevant as Amery allowed himself to be indiscreet. Eyes twinkling behind prim glasses, his stories about clashes with Winston Churchill, whom he had been senior to at Harrow and considered disastrous at the Treasury, made Chink conclude the two worlds were not so very dissimilar. Each had cliques and personalities and inefficient men in key positions, but whereas politics was capricious, army evolvement was static. On the last afternoon they brought Amery's six-year-old son Julian up with them, governess in tow, and as it was the child's first ascent Chink christened the peak Pitz Julian in a theatrical small ceremony on the summit.

He returned to Sandhurst stimulated by the political insight, and it threw a harsher light than ever on military limitations. He enjoyed teaching but thought the low entrance standards were attracting too many Amateurs. He respected his fellow instructors but they were the exception to the rule. Anything innovative was frowned upon, including his harmless proposal for an officers' ski club. Needing a patron, he approached a member of the Staff College directing staff who was said to be a keen skier, but as soon as he broached the subject Colonel Bernard Law Montgomery quenched the idea. 'He would not play,' Chink noted, 'excusing himself for being too junior and unimportant.' It seemed one more small example of the inertia that surrounded him. 'It's hell,' he wrote at this time. 'I'm getting very bored with it all. Nothing of great interest is happening to me. Whatever my professional progress is, mentally I stagnate and I suppose in the end what one does mentally is all that is of interest.' (The club eventually came about, under Montgomery, in 1947.)

He could not bear to be underutilised, and at Sandhurst there was more free time than he had been used to as Adjutant. He fretted in the leisure other men enjoyed, and envied Gatehouse his involvement in the creation of a new military venture. While Gatehouse frowned over designs for a distinctive Tank Corps uniform that would also be practical, Chink reeled off suggestions. When consulted about a hat, he did not hesitate. The specifications were that it had to protect men's hair from the oil in a tank but not take up space in the cramped interior, and he led Gatehouse straight to his room. Hanging on the wall was his Basque beret from Pamplona. He tossed it across, and Gatehouse gingerly tried it on. The beret design was adopted, and one of his sardonic consolations after Alamein was to speculate about Montgomery's reaction if told that his famous beret had links with the unorthodox Hemingway set.

There was only one escape from tedium, and that was the Staff College; he had realised for some time that he could not bear to go back to the regiment. Characteristically he went about getting a place obliquely. Instead of applying for the nomination which his instructorship entitled him to, he gambled on sitting the stiff examination, knowing that he did well under pressure. It was in the spirit of taking the more difficult line in the hunting field, he assured Browning. Horrocks was not among the other candidates, he was pleased to learn. The questions turned out to be well within his scope, and he approached the Strategy paper confidently. Candidates were asked to comment on one of three quotations, two of which were well known. Resorting to his original tactic of going in the opposite direction to the majority, he chose the third, an enigmatic remark by Marshal de Saxe.

'In the hope of disguising my ignorance, I began "Marshal de Saxe was given, in his day, to disguising his profound knowledge of war behind a flippant pessimism," ' he recounted jubilantly afterwards. 'And after referring to him as if I knew his works well, I went on to deal with the substance of his argument.' It was Chink's good fortune to have an examiner who was as unorthodox as he was himself, and he was awarded 1000 out of 1000. Colonel J. F. C. 'Boney' Fuller's aim, even in 1927, was to admit students who were capable of teaching themselves, because he believed it was only through free criticism that truth could be thrashed out. It would transpire that there was a row about the marking of Chink's paper, and that Fuller was unapologetic. He ought to have given 2000 marks, he was heard to shout, since Dorman-Smith's answers were 100 per cent better than any which he could have given to his own question. It is a record that still stands.

Chink was elated, and he did not trouble to hide it. It had been ten marks for accuracy, he challenged openly, and 990 marks for unorthodoxy. He had no doubts any more about his mental superiority, and likened himself even more to Jurgen, who saw things differently to other men. 'I defeated the examiners handsomely,' he exulted to Hemingway by post at once, 'and passed in fairly high up.' It would have been wiser to arrive with less of a fanfare. It was a two-year course, with an annual intake of sixty students, and one of its most useful benefits was the network of 180 contacts for subsequent careers. And of course this can work both ways. The word was out that he was conceited and intellectually arrogant, and he did not help matters by boasting that 95 per cent of men bored him to tears. It was not the recipe for a good clubman, the Staff College criterion of soundness. In the official photographs Chink looks no different from anyone else. He sports the uniform, the standard posture and the regulation moustache. Yet not only did he feel set apart, but he distanced himself further deliberately. The cult of Amateurism operated there more flagrantly than in a regiment, and he announced that it made the 'profession of arms' a joke. If they had to divide themselves into gentlemen and players, he was soon mocking, then he preferred to be a player.

It appeared to many that he was asking for trouble. His sense of humour was ironic and could hurt. There was a staginess about him, and it was clear he was aware of the effect he had. Spruceness was approved of in the army on the grounds that a tidy body reflected a tidy mind, but he was a dandy and that was bad. It would have been sensible to be honest about his determination to live on his pay, but in refusing to take an allowance from Edward he took such exaggerated care of his clothes that the pose was remembered, and the thrift discounted. He would smooth out a handkerchief over one knee before crossing his legs – to save wear on the cloth as much as to imply the fop. It was easy to tease like Oscar Wilde, and not at all easy to correct that impression. One thousand out of 1000, inevitably, remained a black mark.

In the stark, square building that looks down on Sandhurst in the same Camberley grounds there was an atmosphere of elitism and constant mutual assessment. Students kept their seats in syndicates of four, with a passage separating each group, for the entire course. Chink's syndicate put him in close daily contact with Ronald Penney of the Royal Signals, and Philip Christison and Angus Collier, both of the Queen's Own Cameron Highlanders. These three, along with Robert Bridgeman of the Rifle Brigade and Oliver Leese of the Coldstream Guards, became his constant companions, and soon he resented the popularity of Leese, who everyone expected to achieve most. An Old Etonian, as was Bridgeman, Leese was a classic Amateur in Chink's book. He was a big, broad extrovert, had a natural presence and took pride in being casually dressed. His careless assurance threw Chink into sharp relief, and nowhere more so than in the mind of Penney, the son of an Edinburgh doctor and Leese's greatest admirer.

The only opinion Chink and Penney had in common was dedication to the British Army. Penney venerated games, having represented the army as a three-quarter back in rugby, and was a keen fly fisherman. But it was his lack of any sense of humour, combined with religious complacency, that irritated and then infuriated Chink. Penney's reaction to the ribald jibes that had been second nature among the Paris set was one of affront, and he never masked his distaste. So easy was it to get this response that Chink deliberately set up situations, and found them more piquant by imagining Penney as a trout rising to each expertly cast fly. It was dangerous self-indulgence, and took no account of the possibility that Penney might end up senior to himself. But in 1927 the prospect was an unlikely one. Penney's corps, the Royal Signals, not being one of the 'teeth' arms, rarely produced generals in charge of fighting divisions – the working relationship most likely to bring them into proximity in future. Bridgeman was worldly, and sided with Chink whenever Penney overreacted. Christison had the wider perspective of having already been to university, and Collier enjoyed a joke and liked everybody. But, as luck would have it, it was Penney who sat next to Chink day after day for two years.

There was a build-up of tension between them. 'One day', as Christison recalled much later, 'Penney, who was ambitious and looked a leader with a handsome face and the high cheekbones of a Scot, said to Chink "As a Signals Officer I can never hope for high command of troops, but you need not, either. You are doomed for the Staff!" ' And Penney had put his finger on something that engrossed them all. To reach the top meant succeeding on both the staff and the command side of the army, and summing each other up was instinctive. Chink's *cri de coeur* earlier about what he did mentally mattering most showed his bent towards theory. The streak of dumb insolence he occasionally let slip did not go unnoticed either. It indicated that he might be a difficult colleague in high office when the time came for teams to be assembled.

Busy with study and work, Chink did not give a damn about what they were saying about him behind his back. Learning stimulated him, and he was ready for new ideas. Dick O'Connor had become one of the directing staff and he enjoyed being taught by him, but was careful not to trade on their friendship. Although Fuller, nicknamed 'Boney' because he looked like Napoleon, did not teach directly, he had influenced Chink already through his writings. Another member of the staff had equal impact. 'Fuller taught me to see in the first place,' he once summed up his time there, 'but it was Paget who taught me to arrange my thoughts into meaning.' Bernard Paget was not at first sight an obvious hero, being a gentle, religious man, the son of a bishop, but he had the gift of constructive correction, and it was Paget who instilled Chink's lifelong preference for looking at military problems through the analysis of an Appreciation. The standard method taught was to examine situations under headings: the objective, factors for and against, and possible courses open, leading to a recommendation. Chink seized on the method, and tended to approach each category with the depth of an examination. Today the example taught at the

Staff College as the best of its kind is that drawn up by him on 27 July 1942, concerning the position at Alamein.

But his hopes were too high and he was bound to be disillusioned. Before the end of the first year he had come round to seeing the Staff College as the 'high temple of orthodoxy', its teaching a 'pedantic réchauffé' of the techniques of past wars. He criticised the inflexibility of battlefield thinking. Students were given the classic groupings of troops to work with, and his suggestion that a division could be advantageously reorganised was ignored. He complained that directing staff taught that the right ground was all-important, when what mattered more was the way the enemy's mind was working. One theory he preached was that history and foresight had to be correctly combined – principles from history and practice from foresight – and that the greatest enemy of foresight was rigidity of organisation. 'Chink did not need much teaching,' Paget privately commented. 'His trouble was that he was a bit intolerant and would not suffer fools gladly . . . and there are an awful lot of fools.'

He was no respecter of persons. After one exercise about an Indian North West Frontier expedition, in which administration was given more emphasis than the method of fighting, he pinned some verse to the main notice board:

I can't subscribe to the belief,
That wars are fought with bully beef;
I cannot quite believe it true
That whole campaigns are won by Q. . . .

The instructor for administration – 'an honest, stupid fellow', was not amused.

But it was the senior lecturer, Bernard Law Montgomery, who drew most of his fire. Montgomery and he could have had a great deal in common from their shared formative experiences, but they had drawn opposite conclusions. They had been born within fifty miles of each other and had both served in the army in Ireland in the Sinn Fein rebellion. Montgomery hated Ireland and the Irish, whereas Chink by this time liked his friends to call him O Gowan, an Irish translation of Smith. More importantly, both men had been caught up in the random slaughter of the Western Front, and had sworn that such mistakes must not happen again. Chink was convinced that prevention lay in imaginative tactics, open-mindedness about deployment of troops and speed of reaction. Montgomery believed in taking every precaution before committing men, however time-consuming, and above all in numerical superiority.

The two had first met over Chink's proposal for the ski club, when they had parted without making an impression on each other. But their Staff College relationship was at once abrasive. Chink interrupted an early lesson on the faults of pre-1914 doctrine to ask the senior lecturer what he thought future generations would regard as errors in their current teaching. 'There are no errors,' Montgomery snapped. The next clash was more direct. In a Junior Division exercise the enemy opened fire from two farmhouses on the far side of the Blackwater, and Chink's proposal was to send over strong fighting patrols on a wide front, because the untested enemy force might be a small one. Montgomery poured scorn on it. His solution entailed halting for twenty-four hours to bring up artillery for a divisional attack, at which Chink muttered carryingly that Montgomery's only notion of tactics was to take a sledgehammer to crack a walnut. The exercise was over by lunchtime, and he was perched on the bumwarmer in the crowded students' anteroom enjoying a sherry when Montgomery unexpectedly came in. Conversation froze. 'He strode in his little-man walk up to me,' Chink noted, unabashed. ' "What's this I hear, Dorman-Smith? You think my idea of tactics is to take a sledgehammer to crack a nut. Is that true?" "Perfectly true, Colonel." "Preposterous, preposterous." ' There was silence as Montgomery stamped out.

Dorman-Smith, Montgomery announced in class, allowed cleverness to precede thoroughness. But this was a military approach he had thought through. Even when playing war games with Hemingway in Pamplona three years earlier he had rebuked clumsy moves by pointing out that the best way to break a nut was to use another nut and one's finger and thumb. Sledgehammers were crude. 'Professionally, I'd rather beat the enemy at a game of which he didn't even know the rules than have to win a slogging match,' he had already written. 'I regard unnecessary bloodshed as the hallmark of the Amateur. The job is to know what is necessary. The emphasis is on skilled prediction of the technique most likely to save lives.' However, he was not totally immune to Montgomery's technique. He had all but been persuaded, he admitted once, that the secret of successful battle lay in the obviousness of the approach. 'Almost,' he added with a glint. 'But not quite.'

It was Ireland that brought their most open confrontation, when the

Staff College was informed of an imminent visit from two Irish Army officers. The Irish Minister of Defence had been reproved, off the record, for the practice of using Fort Leavenworth in America instead of the Staff College, and had been invited to see British Army facilities. Montgomery promptly ordered a boycott against, as his notice put it, 'shaking the bloodstained hands of Sinn Feiners'. When the two twenty-three-year-old major-generals arrived, their ranks trimmed to colonel for the occasion, they found the building deserted except for the Commandant and one student. Chink was determined not to let Montgomery dictate to him and equally curious about the training of the Irish officers, foreseeing more dangers in isolationism than in working together. It would have been wiser to apply the same overview to his own career.

With their antagonism out in public, he treated Montgomery with disdain. He cut his class on the Registering of Personality, dismissing that as 'fundamentally hokum', and saying that successful tactics and planning owed nothing to promotional tricks. And when Montgomery announced before he left at the end of their junior year that anyone who wished to know what he thought about their future could come for an interview in his office, everyone turned up – except Chink. 'Most disliked what he told them,' he observed. 'My view was that if he had anything adverse to tell me, he could send for me. If nothing adverse, I was not concerned with his opinion one way or the other.'

Instead of queueing up to see Montgomery, he used the time to tidy up his affairs as Assistant Secretary of the Staff College Drag before handing over to Gerald Templer, an incoming student. Hunting remained a passion, though he had vowed never to point-to-point again after Quits had been killed under him in a fall, and through organising the Drag he had got to know the whippers-in, approving most of 'Ginger' Hawkesworth and 'Jock' Whiteley. Two 1928 whippers-in would make strong impressions. He became full of praise for John Harding, independent of mind and small of stature, and scathing about cavalryman Richard McCreery, whom he dismissed as a dolt.

In that second year he was usually to be seen buried in a book. He joined the Library Committee and swept through the works of Clausewitz, Liddell Hart, Fuchs and many more. He lingered over Bird's *Directions of War* and Van Overstraaten's *Principes de la Guerre à Travers les Ages* – 'a goldmine properly used' – and Wellington's cold efficiency stood out as a benchmark. Stonewall Jackson's motto

'Mystify, mislead and surprise' struck a chord, as did Sherman's maxim of putting the enemy on the horns of a dilemma. As his own views were clarified through studying the great commanders, he concluded that direct confrontations rarely succeeded. It was the psychological impact on the enemy that mattered – out-guessing and anticipation – if casualties were to be kept to a minimum. But his reading looked like a pose, compounded by his ostentatiousness. He began boasting that he had to jettison obsolete 'rubbish' continually to maintain a mind of relevant information, and so his personal motto was 'Empty that Ye May be Full'.

His reputation spread, and he was asked to write the 1928 Staff College pantomime. 'It may be a fair assumption that Dorman-Smith the author, kept reasonably in restraint by the producer, has at least given us something we can laugh at', a critic predicted in *Owl Pie*, the college magazine. But he was not kept in check. His creation was the struggle of a Utopian island, Pacifica, under attack from the owl of Bellaria – the Staff College emblem is an owl – and in his barbed plot Bellaria was defeated because it relied on directing staff solutions.

One act lampooned Montgomery, another the Army Council – he cheekily named his generals Bombastes, Glorioso and Armadillo. The politician Pomposo was modelled on Churchill, after Amery's tales, and everyone's religious susceptibilities were bruised by the high priest, Globular. And so it went on. He cast Oliver Leese as Charon the Vulgar Boatman and Penney as Diligens the sanctimonious head neophyte; and when the curtain went up laughter greeted the typecasting. Leese took the joke against himself well. Penney did not.

When the Commandant sent for him to point out that the Army Council had been sitting in the front row, Chink was unrepentant. He had his seat on the Embankment among the tramps already picked out, he said, for when he was heaved out of the army for dangerous thoughts. At the final combined exercise of a corps of two divisions he commanded one of the four mixed syndicates and Leese commanded another. No hard feelings were noticeable on either side. 'He was extremely clever and did well at the Staff College,' O'Connor summed up, but added, 'with some reservations. He was rather supercilious and arrogant, and talked down to people and certainly made no pretence of hiding his feelings if he disliked or despised anyone.'

On 28 December 1928 Chink passed out Grade A in the top four. Publicly he burned his lecture notes, with the announcement that he was setting out to teach himself as the curriculum had left off where it ought to have begun. His period of intensive study and disagreement had steeled him, and he intended to change things for the better. But he was not in a society that liked flamboyant gestures, and he had failed to understand the most important lesson of all. The part goodwill plays in a career.

6

New Food
for
Thought

Estelle, Lady Berney, saw life as one long houseparty to be enjoyed. She was in her early twenties, tiny at five foot one, and so used to ordering people about that her father's pet name for her had been the Little Queen. Men commented on her huge eyes and vitality, but she was shy about her appearance and beneath the light steely touch not as confident as she appeared. And from Chink's point of view she was safely out of marriageable bounds. She already had a husband and a daughter.

She met him when he was still a Sandhurst instructor, and her first impression was a disapproving one. Persuaded by a plump, plain friend to lend moral support for a trip to see a Sandhurst admirer, she realised within minutes of arriving that the officer was more attracted to her. She decided to put him in his place. A threadbare pin-cushion on his desk gave her the opportunity she was looking for and, picking it up, she remarked in her most domestic voice that he was setting a bad example for the boys so she would have it mended for him. He said he would come and collect it in person as soon as she invited him. 'Very bawdy but very nice,' she concluded, unable not to like him. He was at her home in Norfolk the following weekend.

Emphasising her marriage had been a mistake, since it only accelerated his interest. Chink loved women, was highly sexed and had no intention of losing his independence, and affairs had for some time answered all three needs. He was thirty when they met, with his youthful appearance as much of an asset in his private life as it could be a handicap in his professional one. Sexually he had been a late developer, but he had more than made up for it since. The days of standing back at Paris parties had given way to a succession of affairs with women who were safely married, though never to army colleagues. He adored racy elegance and wit and the intrigue of an affair, and appreciated his freedom even more each time he got bored.

Amy had done her best to introduce him to suitable débutantes, without success. He had taken the dancing lessons she insisted upon in 1920 to equip him for the Season, and had been seduced by his instructress, who made a better living away from the dance floor. He lost her soon to a richer man who set her up in a Hampstead house, but not before she had sent a pencil sketch of herself naked, which created ripples in the mess. There had been a young widow, again to Amy's displeasure, and in Germany he had been embroiled in a long affair with the wife of a senior civil servant. 'The lady in question has a husband whom I like which makes my situation more hopeless because it precludes me doping his tea,' he gloated to Hemingway. 'She is nearer 40 than I care to contemplate, has a grown-up family and a daughter she wants me to marry, doesn't like her husband, is a confirmed flirt but the Almighty has fastened her Grecian head to a perfect neck and shoulders by a process which has not been repeated, and all the artist in me which will never get out goes mad about it.' The fact that he was one of several lovers made her initially more desirable, but by the time he left Germany, shortly before he met Estelle, he was glad to escape.

Jurgen's maxim – Always try every new drink once – suited him well. His opinions on marriage, he claimed, were so well known that to congratulate friends on their engagement was hypocritical. He had been stunned when Reggie at the age of twenty-one had married Doreen Watson and rapidly become the father of two daughters. Victor, to his relief, was determined to stay single. The collapse of Hemingway's ostensibly happy marriage had shaken him more deeply than he was prepared to admit. He did not intend to put himself in the same position, and he was content.

He dined out sufficiently often to pick and choose his affairs, and his sense of fun and ease with older women was so disarming that his self-preservation offended no one; indeed with many women it was a distinct advantage. Emotionally he was self-sufficient, sexually there were as many opportunities as he cared to take up, and he envied none of his married friends. It had been the unambitious regimental officers who married early, and he equated late marriage with high achievement. When told by a London fortune-teller in 1925 that he was going to marry within two years, he was disbelieving enough to try to get his money back.

He spent most weekends in Norfolk, content to play a waiting game, and studied Estelle. She was so hospitable that there were always people staying, and the efficient way she ran her large house and staff made light of it. He liked her fondness for animals and the way she was so very much better with people than he was. Like Amy, she played cards to win and joined in all games competitively, but unlike Amy she could laugh at herself. As he got to know her he realised how often she disparaged herself, and found that endearing. Her daughter charmed him, making him wonder why he had never noticed children before.

None of this might have touched him sufficiently had he not also watched as Estelle's marriage broke up, reminding him of Hadley's misery. She began to confide in him, and he learned that her husband's latest girlfriend was pregnant and that she herself could never have another child after septicaemia following her daughter's birth. She blamed herself for breaking the continuity that had passed the estate from father to son since the fourteenth century, and felt she had to allow remarriage for the sake of the unborn child. But she dreaded a public divorce, with every detail in the gossip columns, and it was the chivalry of her motive as much as her courage that touched him. If she went through with it, he promised, she could count on him at the far end. Later he would claim that he married her out of pity rather than love. She always said he pulled her up from the ruins when she was left alone. Her daughter came to believe that they fell in love before, but that as a divorce would ruin his career the break-up was providential. Certainly the fact that she was the innocent party and that Chink did not figure in the case eased matters.

Amy saw Estelle as a threat, and made her disapproval plain by refusing his request for an engagement ring to be made up from stones taken from his grandmother's jewellery. She told him bluntly not to marry Estelle, adding that she knew that the fact she had said so was going to create a permanent gap between them. Without hesitation he took Estelle's side. He had a guarded relationship with his mother at the best of times, and she had greeted him earlier that year with the jibe 'My son, I doubt your morals and I hate your politics but I am very glad to see you. Come in.' He knew she discussed him in detail with Doreen, and he avoided both of them unless absolutely necessary. Edward said nothing, but Estelle reminded him of the women who had cut his own mother. Completely in Amy's shadow by now, he lived all year round in England and enjoyed playing with Reggie's little girls.

The marriage took place as soon as Chink could fit it in, on 29 December 1927, the day after term ended at the Staff College. His appearance at Holy Trinity, Brompton on crutches prompted one of Estelle's aunts to say fondly that it was so like her to marry a wounded soldier. Estelle smiled. He had broken his ankle leaping in the air to demonstrate a trick to her daughter Elaine, who called him Buzz because he was always buzzing about. The crutches did not deter him from a climbing honeymoon in Snowdonia.

He was surprised at how happy he was. Difficult though he could be, she brought out his latent tenderness and cosseted him in return. 'Estelle's whole field of aesthetic expression is in household management,' he wrote after several years. 'At her hands it becomes a high art and ritual.' And he was not being patronising, although by then there was regret. She spoiled him with treats like walnuts in the best light port and was fiercely loyal, supplying the common sense he lacked. He introduced her to Rupert Brooke and Graves and read the *Rubaiyat of Omar Khayam* aloud to her beside the fire. Both mad on dogs, they were happy to sit on the floor if the chairs were occupied, and whenever he brought a new puppy home she took it in without question. 'At one time you were a mother, at another a sister, at another something else – we were very close,' she said of him. 'He had very correct ideas about men and women. We have one job and men another, but we need each other.'

But emotionally they were opposites. She had a sharp temper and could as quickly forgive. He hated quarrels and forgot nothing. He was not demonstrative, and could not learn. She was not sensual, and he could not teach her. The 'something else' was a barrier, and they talked about everything in bed but sex. He sublimated his disappointment in hard work and thought it probably happened in all marriages. To his dismay she never became a reader, and she had to accept that the army came first. 'We followed him,' she said wryly. 'He liked his comfort but home was a place to live in, no more. I learned to become the most wonderful mover. The last thing ever to go into the van was his study, and he'd find it all as usual in a new setting. I said one day "We're only baggage, aren't we?" "Yes," he said. "I'll call you that from now on." And he did!' She was the perfect army wife.

All his ideas about marriage somersaulted. So much did he recommend it that when 'Boy' Browning confided that he had fallen in love with the contemporary writer Daphne du Maurier, who was refusing to marry him on the ground that she did not believe in marriage as an institution, he was appalled. He made a point of meeting Daphne and, taking to her at once, exerted all his charm. Browning adored her, he argued, and his career was bound to be ruined if he lived with her openly, as she proposed. But there was an immediate attraction between them also, and he flirted with her outrageously, to which Browning turned a tolerant eye. Daphne's quick mind and introversion fascinated Chink, although publicly he agreed with Estelle that she was hard. The sparring matches had an undercurrent beneath the teasing, and eventually he had to be as firm with her as he had been with Hadley over the christening. But when asked to be best man by a grateful Browning, he backed away, and subsequent friendship between the two couples was laced by his keen interest in Daphne, which she did not appear to return. Her short story 'A Borderline Case', however, which was published after his death, reveals that she was equally intrigued by him. But if Estelle sensed this at the time she gave no sign of possessiveness. Her lack of jealousy was a continual source of relief to him.

She took him at face value, and did not learn about Bellamont Forest till they had been married for several months and he surprised her one day by suggesting a visit to his Irish property. She had no idea he was Irish until then. They would camp at Holyhead overnight, he informed her, because he refused to pay the exorbitant hotel prices. She pointed out that he was spending even more on camping equipment, and he said it was a matter of principle. It was on a later trip that he watched impassively as customs men tipped out her home-made jam instead of paying the duty demanded, which he considered wrong.

The gates of Bellamont Forest were broken, the drive overgrown and the house neglected by the caretakers. 'I will never forget his face,' she said later. 'He was heartbroken. He had expected it to be the same as when he was a child.' Despatching him to the woods where they could hear the sound of trees being felled, she had one bedroom and sitting room scrubbed out as a base, and took charge. That night they vowed to put it back together again. The trees, it transpired, were being cut down on Edward's instructions, breaking the entail. He had that stopped. Strangers came up to her in Cootehill to say how much they admired the Bellamont cutlery and linen, and she was touched that nothing had been taken in their absence, despite so many people going through the house. He made no allowances. 'Squalid, shabby and totally neglected,' he noted in his diary, and resolved to live there permanently when he retired from the army. Ireland reabsorbed him.

He lectured Estelle on the need to get rid of the border, taught her Irish history and picked out books for her to read. She came to see that Bellamont meant as much to him as the army.

Lovely fires and lovely beds, she declared characteristically, instead of feeling relegated to third place. The delicate matter of their marriage receded; in Ireland, unlike England, divorce was not recognised and so their ceremony was considered invalid. But though most people referred to her as Lady Berney, instead of Mrs Dorman-Smith, she attributed it to fondness for a title, and was not hurt. The nuns who had briefly taught Chink came to tea – 'they were fond of him and he of them' – and on his advice she talked to everyone. They threw a huge dinner party – the first of many – and out of curiosity everyone accepted. Each day, whatever the weather, they swam in the lakes, and they marked out the empty ballroom for badminton. 'I must say, Padre,' she heard him tease the local rector one evening. 'Thy service is perfect freedom.'

At every leave after that they came back, and they kept a low profile in the post-civil-war regime. But one afternoon in the 1930s she was sunbathing on the steps when a car braked with a scrunch on the gravel below and five men got out, hats pulled low. She ran down instinctively to protect him. 'I don't know what I could have done,' she explained later, 'but I expected guns.' She did not recognise Eamonn de Valera, leader of the party in power, Fianna Fail. But Chink did, and he invited him in. For once he made no mention of what they discussed, but de Valera's policy was to heal rifts – to the extent of allowing pro-Treaty officers, his old enemies, to remain at the head of the Irish Army – and professionalism was the quality he respected most. International military developments fascinated him, and he remained anxious about the standing of the Irish Army. Chink's military experience was common knowledge and his presence would have been reported by local party members.

Slowly the house took shape, though they had little money to spend on it and never enough time. It was like an enormous holiday cottage, and as his work increased it became doubly precious as the only place where they could be themselves. Elaine got to know him there, and never thought of him as a stepfather. He teased her till she could not speak for laughing, and he always drove at breakneck speed up the long drive, singing loudly. He never, as far as she could see, stopped fooling. When it rained he read her stories, and his favourite was Wilde's 'The Jackdaw of Rheims'. She was encouraged to sit up late at dinner and to learn from adult conversation. She thought him brilliant, and the only beating he ever inflicted on her she considered fair when he explained it was a matter of principle: she had broken her word. She gravitated to the basement kitchen – much less busy now – and watched the horse plod in a circle by Dromore Lake pumping up their water. There was no electricity, and to go to bed she had to climb two flights of stairs past a vast mirror which lit up as her candle neared it. He was thoughtful enough not to tell her the ghost stories.

While Estelle bustled about, he read widely, and took care to add each new Hemingway title to the library. But although he was delighted to hear about the Pulitzer Prize win in 1933, he did not write to congratulate him. Their friendship was a thing of the past, he told Estelle. In 1936, however, he bought an English first edition of *Green Hills of Africa* and discovered a mention of himself. 'I hung my booted legs over the side to let my feet cool and drank the beer and wished old Chink was along,' Hemingway had written when describing the white hunter known as Pop. 'Captain Eric Edward Dorman-Smith MC of his Majesty's Fifth Fusiliers. Now if he were here we could discuss how to describe this deer-part country, and whether deer-part was enough to call it. Pop and Chink were very much alike. Pop was older and more tolerant for his years and the same sort of company. I was learning under Pop, while Chink and I had discovered a big part of the world together and then our ways had gone a long way apart.' A long way apart. . . . From his new height in the army those days seemed to have happened to somebody else. But still he did not write, and nor did he trade on his association with a by now world-famous writer. And in the wider circles he now mixed in there was plenty of opportunity.

His climb was rapid. In 1929 he had become the first infantryman to hold the coveted post of instructor of tactics at Chatham, the sapper's equivalent of the Staff College. 'Don't say sappers like flappers,' he corrected Estelle as they drove up. 'Say Royal Engineers.' He was proud at having been picked out not only by the Chief Engineer, but by the Military-Secretary's department in the War Office as well. He took the trouble to find out that Horrocks had not yet gone to the Staff College.

Perhaps Chink should have been a sapper all along, commented one infantry general many years later. He had a point. Students at the sapper colleges of Woolwich and Chatham considered themselves superior to those at Sandhurst and the Staff College because entrance standards were higher. Conversely, the cavalry and infantry, who prided themselves on closing with the enemy in battle, dismissed sappers as brainy mechanics, no more than a service to the Service. Usually the separate colleges did not mix, and so Chink was the first infantryman his students had met. They expected an oaf, and were confronted with a razor-sharp intelligence that encouraged unorthodox questions.

Chink's approach made the dull subject of tactics interesting. He preached the value of surprise, the last quality infantryman were believed to specialise in, and the solutions he propounded were often unconventional. After TEWTS he held uproarious post-mortems over lunch in the local pub where he was admired for his style. But the martinet could blank out the sense of humour unexpectedly, and if hangovers showed on the morning exercise after a guest night for Young Officers, who joined every six months, he never saw the funny side. That was amateur.

No criticism attached to Chatham. He was a good mixer, a cheerful master of the Royal Engineers Drag, and he entertained with Estelle. His career soared. That year he was asked to write a textbook on military tactics, which led to an official army handbook, *Infantry Section, Leaders' Training* within two years. To his amusement a sporadic correspondence with his *bête noire* Montgomery began; he was sent the ex-senior lecturer's own book, *Infantry Training*, in draft form and was asked for his comments. And the army's brevet system, which recognised merit without extra pay, leapfrogged him ahead. In July 1931 he was appointed Brigade Major to 6th Experimental Brigade at Blackdown, near Aldershot. Here his brigadier was Archie Wavell, author of *The Palestine Campaigns*, which was one of the books he most admired.

Wavell deployed two monocles; one to read through and the other to camouflage the eye lost, as they discovered to mutual surprise, at Bellevaarde Wood on the day Chink won his MC. It was rumoured that Wavell raised a monocle to the false eye whenever shown a proposal he disliked. A stocky, short man, he could appear terrifying and rarely spoke. At forty-eight, he was twelve years older than Chink and he seemed more. He had been at Blackdown for a year, and the malicious were whispering that he was past his peak.

In the snakes and ladders of army fortune, however, Chink had made the right move. Wavell was an original. He was comfortably at home in an academic's maze of poetry and history, and was innovative about battle technique. He believed in flexible military thinking, considered no rule to be unbreakable, and welcomed an imaginative second-in-command. To Chink's delight, Wavell passed even his childhood test of chivalry in the way he dealt with men of all ranks, and their relationship was harmonious from the start. Junior officers came upon them chatting together on subjects as diverse as Lawrence of Arabia – 'he understood his intellect and heroism,' wrote Chink, 'but could not fathom his search for degradation which atrophied these' – to the need for mechanisation of troop movements. They were of the same mind about tank potential and the obsolete values of the cavalry. 'Trot on, Algy!' was Wavell's favourite command overhead during a previous spell with a guards regiment. It perfectly caught the horse preoccupation and elitist familiarity.

But it was a different matter when Wavell's wife was present, the influential Queenie; and Chink was soon in disgrace, demonstrating yet again his naivety about the need for sponsors. As he had run drag hunts before she asked him to do the same at Blackdown, and he replied that he intended to succeed on a professional basis, not as a 'social stooge'. It was a relief when she refused to accompany Wavell to the Bellamont shoots, where away from Blackdown they were determined to relax. Despite the loss of his eye Wavell was the better snipe shot, and when he fell in a boghole he took it with equanamity. Estelle was in her element. She brought out duck sandwiches at lunch, and they would pick a ruined cottage, make a fire from sticks, and cook potatoes in an iron pot. After dark they read by oil-lamps beside the library fire in silence, whiskey and soda to hand. 'They are just two men who like each other,' she noted with satisfaction. '*Very* close.'

Aldershot was the hub of the military world. It contained a corps of two divisions under the command of General Sir Henry Jackson, and 6th Experimental Brigade was given its head. But in 1931 the army was in the doldrums. The barracks of corrugated iron were icy cold in winter and so many men were serving overseas that no more than 500 were present at any one time; in practice four men and two ropes equalled one platoon. Equipment was minimal and the atmosphere was one of farce. Their few Austin Sevens were driven by majors in spurs, and so unable to accelerate uphill. The solitary one-tracked vehicle slipped its track and charged when passing a general at salute. They were armed with the out-of-date Lewis gun, and their anti-tank rifle bounced off armour but broke a man's shoulder. Usually flags stood in for weapons.

Wavell's aim was to speed up mobility, and exercises were devised to simulate the chaos of war, so that men had to make decisions while exhausted, baffled and unbriefed. Chink's imagination was given full rein, and his plots often involved fancy dress. He was fully stretched and content to be with Wavell, because the more he saw of him the more he was learning from his approach. Battlecraft, preached Wavell, was no more than the cunning of a successful criminal, and the British were too gullible, as his time in Palestine had shown. Lecturing about the constant likelihood of spies one day, he mentioned two who had successfully slipped through his own lines in a baker's cart. There was a show of hands – 'I say, that's cheating,' exclaimed one young officer – and Chink was seen to nod vigorously when Wavell lost his temper. To test men to the limit they were made to go seventy-two hours without sleep. 'Very valuable, but we didn't think so at the time,' recalled one guinea-pig. 'It was original, diverting, and terribly hard work.' Wavell's nonchalant method of command impressed Chink too. He approved of the way he would watch without interference, rarely saying anything more than his celebrated 'Very well', but was always about when needed.

But Wavell was bored by technical minutiae, and it was Chink's responsibility to tighten response throughout. He fizzed out ideas. Hating the cumbersome Vickers machine gun and complaining that the army was 'nailing itself down by the foot', because it had to be fired from the ground by a crew of six, he worked out a drill for it to be fired from a vehicle, with a crew of two, for use as an assault weapon. And why not make firepower more effective by motoring advance troops forward beyond marching infantry? Word came back from the orthodox Netheravon Machine Gun School nearby that they were splitting up the regulation unit. He organised a demonstration of their new techniques, only to be told that anything not in the machine gun manual was out, and the Netheravon Commandant was said to refer to them as 'unsound iconoclasts'. They took the rebuke as a compliment.

Breaking traditional rules, Wavell did not keep a general reserve of men back during manoeuvres, and repeatedly beat fellow brigadiers before all their forces had been committed; his and Chink's sweetest triumph was at Divisional Exercises, the climax of the season. It was the first working relationship for many years that Chink had found satisfactory. When beneath one of his tactical proposals he saw an inked-in comment by Wavell warning 'Remember that a little unorthodoxy is a dangerous thing,' his disappointment was short-lived. Turning the page, he discovered 'But without it you cannot win battles.' 'Wavell taught me how to turn the practices of warfare inside out while retaining the principles intact,' he wrote once. 'How to empty the bathwater, without spilling the baby.' The longer Chink worked under him, the more convinced he grew that it was time the classic infantry brigade was reorganised.

His interest in tanks had swung around to the opinion that they were very useful but had less flexibility and striking force than mechanised infantry, and Percy Hobart, who commanded 2nd Battalion Tank Corps a short distance away at Farnborough, was sufficiently annoyed to challenge him to put it to the test. Hobart brought over his battalion and afterwards Chink pointed out that even against 6th Experimental Brigade's flimsy anti-tank defence, the attack would at best have succeeded with considerable losses. 'Blasphemy!' shouted Hobart, climbing back angrily into his machine. Chink stuck to his opinion and continued to plan new combinations of transport weapons and men.

The objections of Netheravon Machine Gun School grew louder. Finally a summons arrived to a Salisbury Plain conference at which the Commandant, the CIGS and a majority of the Army Council would review their results. Chink briefed Wavell on their conclusions and waited anxiously, but Wavell returned shaking his head. Word filtered back that when asked to present his case, Wavell had replied that he had nothing to say. 'Archie was the one person who could have devised a genuinely new school of tactics in the 32/38 period,' Chink wrote after the Second World War. 'But there was this curious oscillation between originality and orthodoxy in his make-up.' It occurred to him that a mind steeped in the Classics might be more ready than most to accept fate, which says much about his respect for Wavell. Normally he had no use for excuses.

His posting had been for a year, and when he left Wavell presented him with a copy of *The Palestine Campaign*, inscribed 'In grateful memory of 1932 and with best wishes for 1933. A last ounce of optimism is sometimes a better general reserve than many men.' The last ounce of optimism became his precept, as anger at Wavell's silence at Netheravon gave way to gratitude for the 'magnificent solvent' he had provided for dissolving Staff College orthodoxy. But the partnership benefited Wavell equally, as he acknowledged in due course. 'I believe it was this season that probably determined my future career,' he revealed in his memoirs, 'in that I was always afterwards chosen for command, and never again for the Staff.' The signs were there that Chink was a catalyst – but only for a man he respected.

His ingenious mind had not gone unnoticed, and his corps commander predicted that he would go far on the staff. Next he was asked to
update the textbook *Elementary Tactics*, which he subtitled *The Art of
War*, like a chess manual. He was tipped for a second brevet and it was
said he would be going to the War Office the following January on
Dick O'Connor's recommendation. When the half-yearly lists came
out he was at Bellamont, and so was kept in suspense for an extra
twenty-four hours until *The Times* reached Cootehill. Estelle threw a
party at once. 'To be brevet Lieutenant Colonel at the age of 39 is a
great achievement,' remarked his regimental gazette. 'But those of us
who have had experience of his enthusiasm, knowledge and industry
will know that it is no more than he deserves.' At the party his speech
contained only one serious sentence, which was that every nerve must
be stretched to prepare for the come-back of Germany. It was
considered unnecessarily dramatic.

Estelle found a top-floor flat at 65 Overstrand Mansions in Battersea
on his instructions that they must live within walking distance of the
War Office, and he reported to his desk in January 1934 with alacrity.
He had not been exaggerating at the party. He was convinced that
Germany was taking advantage of starting with a clean slate to create a
modern mobile army, and that a 'return match', as he put it, was only a
matter of time. But while in 1914 it had been possible to produce an army
of men and horses at short notice, a mechanised army needed thorough
advance planning. His attitude at Whitehall can be gauged from his taunt
that he was prepared to divide army officers into two types – those
who were bone from the neck up, and those who were solid bone. He
saw horse sentimentality as the main problem to be overcome.

Winding up the Army Estimates debate in the House of Commons
in March, the spokesman for the War Office, Duff Cooper, said it was
too early to assume that the horse was finished. A letter appeared in the
Daily Telegraph the following day: 'It would be interesting to hear
from Mr. Duff Cooper what new conditions would change for the
better the natural vulnerability of the horse. For it seems only possible
if the War Office could produce a scheme for breeding bulletproof
horses. . . .' It was signed not by Chink, but by a name increasingly
irritating to the military establishment, the crusading military journalist Basil Liddell Hart. And Liddell Hart went on to point out that the
British Army contained twenty horsed cavalry regiments, as well as
sixteen yeomanry and twenty-one Indian Army, compared to four
battalions of tanks. In 1935, promoted to Secretary of State for War,

Duff Cooper's opinions had, if anything, hardened. Military experts, he declared in his annual Commons speech on the Army Estimates, would recommend exchanging the last horse for a bicycle and pushing the last infantryman into a tank. 'But I have had occasion during the past year to study military affairs both in my public and my private life, and the more I study them, the more impressed I become by the importance of cavalry in modern warfare.' Chink followed the exchange with more than usual interest, exasperated by the knowledge that Duff Cooper was writing the biography of Haig in his spare time. But by then little surprised him.

Every day when he left the War Office for one of his clubs – he was a member of the Athenaeum and the Naval and Military – he ritually doffed his hat at the same lamp-post. Soon, as he intended, somebody asked why. He explained that he hoped to see a Secretary of State for War hanged from it one day for having neglected to prepare the army for the coming war. Black humour was bad form, and his second theory was equally macabre. Annually at the Cenotaph ceremony, he proposed, a Cabinet minister should commit hari-kiri as an act of contrition for the Cabinet's collective responsibility for the next holocaust. If they wanted peace, he would add, they must be prepared for war. As he mastered his desk job in SD2, the department responsible for development and yearly estimates – the first hostage to the second – he became more precise. He now broke down British casualties over the first year of any major war into three categories: 25 per cent caused by enemy action, 25 per cent by indifferent generalship and accidents of war, and 50 per cent by the penny-pinching Treasury. It was no accident, he took to remarking, that the Cenotaph was situated in Whitehall.

The freedom of his work with Wavell was over. In SD2 he felt cramped by the six layers of authority above him. Beyond his colonel was the Director of Staff Duties, beyond the Director of Staff Duties was the CIGS, beyond the CIGS there was the Army Council with its imbalance of cavalry generals, and beyond that was Finance. But the Director of Staff Duties, 'Guffin' Heywood, was forward-looking, and John Dill, Director of Military Operations and Intelligence, was sympathetic. Chink respected Heywood and warmed especially to the gentle Dill, whose open-mindedness was in direct contrast with the attitude of the new Inspector of Regimental Artillery, Alan Brooke, who joined the War Office within a few months. In Chink's eyes, Brooke epitomised everything he most disliked about the complacency of the upper classes, and he attributed the hostility he sensed in return to Brooke being in the Horse Artillery, one of his targets for mechanisation. 'Dill was as spiritually sensitive,' he said once 'as Brooke was insensitive.' He did not mind how many enemies he made.

From his desk Chink could look across the courtyard into the office of the Permanent Under-Secretary, Sir Herbert Creedy, which gave him new food for thought about the contribution of civil servants to the slowness of military evolution. 'Creedy knew everything about the British Army,' he concluded, 'and nothing at all about war.' The only civil servant to pass muster was Archie Rowlands – 'sharp little chap, full of brain' – who had won a scholarship to Oxford from a poor Welsh background and was about to be appointed Assistant Under-Secretary. Antipathy between the soldiers and the frocks, in Henry Wilson's phrase, was endemic in the War Office, and it is one more indication of Chink's unconventionality that he should choose to make a close friend of Rowlands.

But the first familiar face he met brought him up with a jolt. Brian Horrocks had already spent a year in another War Office department, instead of being safely outdistanced as Chink had thought. He was in MS2, the Military Secretary's branch that dealt with promotions up to the rank of Lieutenant-Colonel, and he had access to confidential reports. Horrocks quickly righted the balance by saying that he considered himself to be on a much lower level, because Chink's file – as he would admit many years later – showed that he was heading for the top. And, with the edge he needed, Chink relaxed. Hearing that it had taken Horrocks five attempts to get into the Staff College, he was at his most charming.

They got on better than they had done at school, and as both felt cooped up in the massive stone building they regularly strolled out to Battersea Park and back after lunch, usually discussing army reforms and personalities. Horrocks had gone directly to the War Office from the Staff College, where Chink's boss John Dill had been a respected commandant, and now that they had more in common they were glad to meet again. At last Chink was prepared to allow that Horrocks had got his priorities right by relegating sport to second place, and he had also served not only in Ireland – an interlude that seemed distant to them both – but on the Rhine and at Aldershot. They found it easy to pick up the threads, helped by the fact that neither had changed much physically, although they were nearly forty. They were naturally spare, showed no sign of losing their hair and were equally fit. Chink dominated the conversations, striding along as briskly as Horrocks, hands flourishing, stopping to make one of his points about brigade reorganisation or mechanisation. Horrocks tended to listen and butt in when necessary, never slow to correct but seeing himself as the sounding board. Chink, of course, took that for granted. He was astounded to realise they had known each other for so long. Apart from John Charles McQuaid, who had become a priest and had not been heard from for years, Horrocks was his oldest friend.

He was pleased that Estelle thought Horrocks charming too, but meeting him again also confronted him with a regret that was becoming more insistent. Horrocks had married shortly after his own wedding, and talked proudly of his daughter. Estelle's inability to have children was something Chink could not bring himself to disclose, to Horrocks least of all. But he saw a great deal of him and he missed him when Horrocks was in due course posted to Aldershot in Chink's old role of brigade major, with Archie Wavell as his divisional commander. The smallness of their world appealed to Chink – as long as he was ahead.

He often thought back to Aldershot and Wavell, because the potential of his development brief was so wide that he blessed his time with 6th Experimental Brigade. He believed that, to bring the army up to date, it could be rejuvenated by cutting out horsed transport, improving infantry armament, mechanising and re-equipping artillery with long-range weapons, and modernising the cavalry by substituting tanks for horses. But tactically it would be unimproved. His preference was for the more radical – and expensive – approach. He longed to introduce heavy tanks for frontal assault, mobile tanks for rapid penetration, armour-protected infantry for fast follow-through, reorganisation of brigades and supply, and fire support from the air. It was frustrating to be limited by funding and to realise that the RAF came higher in the rearmament pecking order. At an early meeting Heywood stated that they were going to have to compromise with infantry modernisation, and Chink put his ideal mechanised battalion across. Too complicated, he was told.

He re-examined the weapons in use. The Bren, a Czech import, was superior to the Vickers, but he was told that the army had to buy British weapons: he soon circulated a Kipling verse about intelligent men tied to obsolete machines. Eventually that point was won. But his seeing each decision in more black-and-white terms than anyone else added to his feeling of tension. He found it hard to switch off and have patience with more easy-going men. When one senior general inspecting an experimental armoured car with him observed, 'It looks ugly, and I have found that ugly-looking things are seldom efficient,' he gave him short shrift.

The power of vested interests added to his cynicism. His ideal ratio of one mechanised vehicle per platoon for infantry called for a cheap, easily produced lorry with a good road speed, able to carry fifteen hundredweight. The Vickers model in production had a fuel radius of less than forty miles and a top speed of 10 m.p.h., so through a contact in Morris Motors he pushed through a better and cheaper alternative, only to be shown a letter from Vickers to the CIGS pointing out that retiring Army Councillors could not expect to join the Vickers board with that sort of treatment in favour of competitors. Drafting parliamentary answers showed him how frequently public officials prevaricated, ostensibly for the nation's good. Now his barbs were directed at new targets. When the Royal Ordnance Factory wanted to know why the new Morris lorry was called the Infantry Truck, since it was their prerogative to name new vehicles, he retorted that soldiers were fond of a short four-letter word that rhymed.

He went into the empty office every Saturday morning, a practice which paid one spectacular dividend. Towards the end of 1934 he found a note requesting a horse-drawn brigade as the League of Nations force for the Saar plebiscite in January; deleting the horses, he mechanised it from RASC sources. It was, he remained convinced, the first all-mechanised force to leave Britain. (The result of the plebiscite was less auspicious; over 90 per cent voted to join Hitler's Reich.) By now his ability to churn out novel ideas was more marked. He proposed a single common pool of postings for all infantry officers, irrespective of regiment, and designed more practical field uniforms based on the freedom of his skiing clothes at Chamby. Next he turned his attention to the necessary equipment.

But this was tinkering with accessories, compared to the army's reliance on horses. He had no sympathy any more with the widespread emotional tug towards hunting and country life that supported it, and when Heywood despatched him in 1935 to lecture to cavalry regiments about mechanisation, he did so with relish. He would goad his audiences by announcing that it was high time they got off their 'blooming' horses and on to trucks, and his speech usually began with the taunt that muscles were about to yield to machines. Back once more in the War Office, he measured progress by the depth of animosity with which Brooke snubbed him.

The CIGS, Field Marshal Sir Archibald Montgomery Massingberd, had given a newspaper interview in which he said there was a danger of going too fast in mechanisation. 'We should,' he cautioned, 'go slowly.' In his regular *Daily Telegraph* column the journalist Basil Liddell Hart pounced, pointing out that emergencies did not always wait while changes were being slowly made. Chink cut out the article and took it into Heywood to discuss his thoughts on the manipulation of news. Liddell Hart was summoned to the War Office for an off-the-record briefing, and afterwards wrote that Heywood's attitude was refreshingly progressive, 'and even more so that of his assistant, Lt. Col Eric Dorman-Smith, who gave the detailed explanations of the new programme. So I came away with higher hopes . . . although I had criticised the infantry bias of the new programme.' They were never to be in agreement about the proportions of infantry to tanks, but that meeting was the beginning of a lifelong friendship.

Liddell Hart had joined the army in 1914 after only one year at Cambridge and had been wounded on the Somme, where he was so horrified at the ineptitude and losses that he devoted himself from then onwards to bringing the army up to date. He had tried to educate from within, writing a pamphlet on platoon tactics while convalescing and updating the official manual *Infantry Training* after the war. He was ostensibly invalided out in 1924 and continued to chivvy from outside. As military correspondent for *The Times* and the *Morning Post* as well as the *Daily Telegraph*, he was afraid of no one. With the fervour of an evangelist he promoted the use of tanks, excoriated reliance on horses and criticised low funding. It was both to get information and to exert influence that he liked to woo the brighter minds in the army.

Chink was delighted to be invited to lunch at the Athenaeum within the week; instead of turning it down, as most soldiers would have done, he could not wait. And on the day he found they had a great deal in common. They were of the same age and had witnessed similar trench casualties close up. Both were romantic idealists and shared with barristers the ability to abstract whatever was needed for a convincing case. They were tall and slim and could be superciliously smug, though Liddell Hart's spectacles gave him a donnish air. Militarily they spoke almost the same language.

Liddell Hart had studied twenty-five centuries of warfare, closely examining the methods used by – among others – Lysander, Hannibal, Scipio, Cromwell, Marlborough, Napoleon and Sherman. In the majority of decisive battles, according to his analysis, the victor had always put his opponent at a psychological disadvantage first. The Macedonian, Roman and British empires had been founded on the same principle, which led him to formulate definite conclusions. No general was justified in sending his troops against an enemy in position and on guard, and attack should never be renewed on the same line if it had once failed. A defensive battle was a stronger form of strategy, and more economical in lives and weapons. In a campaign against more than one army it was more effective to wipe out the weaker partner first. Alternative objectives distracted the enemy's mind and split up his forces. By luring or startling the opponent into making a false move, his own effort – as in judo – turned into the lever of his overthrow.

Basil had formulated his theory of the indirect approach, in which to outwit the enemy it was necessary to use a strategy of either 'elastic defence, calculated withdrawal, capped by a tactical offensive', or of 'offence, aimed at placing oneself in the position most upsetting to the opponent, capped with a tactical defensive'. Both employed the psychological pressure of a trap or lure, and he pointed out that the enemy's rear was the most demoralising line of approach. 'An army, like a man, cannot defend its back from a blow,' he argued, 'without turning round to use his arms,' and losing balance. In contrast, confrontation only consolidated balance and increased resistance.

Liddell Hart advocated always seizing the psychological advantage by choosing the line of least expectation, putting oneself in the enemy's mind to guess where this would be, and planning operations that indicated alternative objectives. Both plan and dispositions had to be adaptable to changing circumstances, and provision had always to be made for the next step – whether failure, success or, more probably, partial success resulted. He was convinced that the new mechanised mobility and increased danger from air attack made concentration of force less effective than ever. 'Under the new conditions of war,' he had already written, 'the cumulative effect of partial success at a number of points may be greater than the effect of complete success at one point,' and 'Fluidity of force may succeed where concentration of force merely entails a perilous rigidity.' Overall, it was the value of cool calculation and co-ordination that counted. His maxim envisaged three steps: first, dislocate the enemy; next, deliver the main blow; lastly, immediately exploit the advantage.

Above all, he warned against the frontal approach that Chink, too, despised.

> Experience of history shows that, save against a much inferior opponent, no effective stroke is possible until his power of resistance is paralysed. . . . The training of armies is primarily devoted to developing efficiency in the detailed execution of the attack. The concentration on tactical technique tends to obscure the psychological element. It fosters a cult of soundness, rather than of surprise. It breeds commanders who are so intent not to do anything wrong, 'according to the book', that they forget the necessity of making the enemy do something wrong. . . . In war it is by compelling mistakes that the scales are most often turned.

The urgent need for the development of mobile warfare was the theme he most constantly returned to.

Ironically, although he did not know it, his keenest readers were in Germany. The writings of Liddell Hart and Fuller were being translated by Blomberg, the Minister for War, and von Reichenau, Chief of the Defence Staff, for the benefit of non-English-speaking officers. 'Liddell Hart,' it was officially pointed out, 'is not . . . following obsolete theories but setting new rules.' Devotees included the younger officers Erwin Rommel and Heinz Guderian; writing about tank warfare after 1945, Guderian stated that it had been 'principally the [work] of the Englishmen Fuller, Liddell Hart and Martel that excited my interest. Deeply impressed by these ideas, I tried to develop them in a sense practicable for our own army.'

In the oblivious security of the Athenaeum, Chink and Liddell Hart enjoyed each other's company and the complicity of being angry young men. 'The professional mind in all professions is an amusing study,' Chink wrote to him afterwards, following up one of their points of agreement. 'It is really the second rate mind defending itself – the soft shelled crab going into any borrowed shell. The main characteristics seem to be the reliance on traditionalism and precedent as a defence against having to face facts. It usually means the professional has dropped behind in his trade.' 'I am glad,' Basil wrote back, 'that you appreciated the humour as well as the gravity, but then I knew you would, which is what I have found so refreshing in our comparatively short acquaintance. And also,' he added carefully, 'your discernment.' Both were vain and susceptible to flattery. In his diary, however, he was no less complimentary. '[Chink] is the liveliest in mind', he noted privately, 'of all the soldiers I have ever known.'

Chink was frustrated enough to find Liddell Hart's interest – with its potential for reaching readers and manipulating policy – irresistible. But he was taking a grave career risk, as there was a War Office ban on regular contact with him which he was insolently breaking. In April Liddell Hart sent him a copy of *When Britain Goes to War: Adaptability and Mobility*, inscribed 'to E.E. Dorman-Smith, for whom my subtitle is exceptionally appropriate'. They continued to see a great deal of each other and their self-interest grew into comradeship. But Chink did not invite him home to meet Estelle.

Both men were appalled at the direction of events. Four months after their first meeting, Hitler announced the reintroduction of conscription to create an army of thirty-six divisions, which would be three times the size of the British Army and five times the number permitted under the Versailles Treaty. But in the same week when the annual Army Estimates were announced in London there were two very indicative sums. Expenditure for hay was increased by £44,000, while petrol was allotted £12,000. 'A milk and water reaction,' Chink wrote disgustedly to Liddell Hart.

Other countries were more adventurous. He talked to officials who had visited the Russian Army, which appeared to have taken the lead in mechanisation and air support. He saw the situation in France for himself. At short notice he stepped in as military assistant to the Master-General of the Ordnance, Hugh Elles, on a plain-clothes visit with the CIGS and his assistant. They were shown the Maginot Line and were impressed – till it ended abruptly on the Belgian frontier. 'On top of one of the vast forts,' he noted, 'Hugh Elles pointed to one of the armoured observation post cupolas and said "The real problem is how to put a sack over that thing."' Their smirking was brought to a halt next morning when General Gamelin showed them the French secret weapon, a group of powerful tanks with four inches of armour which under the 1925 Locarno Agreement was illegal. They raised their eyebrows at Gamelin, who exclaimed, 'Je m'en fiche de Locarno.' When they asked about the moral significance of the pact they were told that the Germans had something very similar.

Back in London he sent in his blueprint for a British mobile division, with the specification of a sixteen-ton tank with heavy armour which he called the I – for infantry – tank. 'I had all the ideas before but here was the ideal argument,' he recalled later. 'If the French had made as much progress as this, we were foolish to lag behind.' And some of SD2's planning was bearing fruit. It had been decided to convert transport of infantry divisions to a motorised basis, except for divisional artillery, and to reorganise brigades. In addition, a battalion of I tanks was agreed for each. By December 1935 the department had the details worked out, but Finance approved it only for the army at home. Seeing the policy so near fruition made Chink's frustration the more intense. When he was appointed a member of the Chemical Warfare Committee shortly afterwards the parallel with 1915 stoked his notorious impatience.

His anger grew to the point where he almost believed a rumour that the field army was in danger of being abolished to finance an RAF bomber programme. And when news came that he was about to be appointed an instructor at the Staff College he decided to act while he still could. It was time for the political stroke. Reggie had more than achieved Amy's high hopes, having become a Justice of the Peace in Surrey and President of the National Farmers' Union before his recent election as Conservative MP for Petersfield in Hampshire. At the beginning of his election campaign Chink had taken pleasure in slipping into the back of meetings and heckling him, though Reggie always saw through the assumed voice. Lately Chink had recognised the usefulness of having him in the House of Commons, and he decided to use Reggie now to go behind the Army Council's back. It was taking a chance, for he would be in serious trouble if his seniors heard of it, but he persuaded him to set up a private meeting with the Secretary of State for War, Duff Cooper, so that he could put across his view of the army picture. Reggie, a keen territorial, agreed.

Dinner was arranged at Reggie's comfortable Lansdowne House flat and, discarding small talk, Chink plunged straight in. Whatever Cooper was being told by his advisers, he stressed, as soon as Britain was involved in war France, Belgium and Holland would be the weak spots. He produced, like a rabbit out of a hat, seven overlaid maps he had made featuring a German advance through the Low Countries which focused on the same territory in sequence, and showed how a mobile army could concentrate overwhelming force at selected tactical points; it was a forecast of the *Blitzkrieg*. 'The point was, this was possible with the army we ourselves had in mind, and for which approval had already been given in principle,' he wrote afterwards. 'I had checked and rechecked the damn things and convinced myself of the feasibility. . . . Far from losing defensive power, modern armies regain offensive potential.' So it was madness, he persisted, to cut back expenditure on the army. Cooper thanked him through the cigar smoke and enquired why, if it was so, the CIGS had not mentioned it? Because, Chink predictably replied, only three people in SD2 knew, and he was the only one who knew it all. He had to leave it at that and nothing apparently came of his gamble, although Cooper did not give him away. But for a man in a hierarchy it was the first sign that he might no longer be able to fit in. As yet he had not faced up to this, telling himself only that a Northumberland Fusilier considered it his duty to speak to the Prime Minister, if necessary.

At Camberley in 1936 he was taking the place of another rising star, Archie Nye. Fellow directing staff included Bill Slim, whom he respected, and his erstwhile fellow students Philip Christison and 'Ginger' Hawkesworth; soon 'Sandy' Galloway, a like-minded radical from 6th Experimental Brigade, joined them. But the Commandant, to Chink's dismay, was Lord Gort VC who, though a legend of bravery to the public, to him personified military backwardness. 'Hippophil conservatism,' he snorted to Liddell Hart on arrival. 'Utterly bow and arrow.' Gort was still tanned from his time in India, where he had been Director of Military Training – training for past wars, as Chink was fond of saying.

His subject was staff duties, and he found he was expected to put across lectures that had been out of date when he first heard them as a student; after modernisation, stemming from SD2, they had little relevance. The established theories of logistics, tactical handling and staff duties had to be tailored to faster mechanisation techniques, and Christison and he worked them out in their spare time. Within three weeks Gort sent for him to say he was taking them 'too far, too fast'. 'Is this what you really mean?' a frowning Gort asked him another day, 'or are you taking us on a red herring?'

Tactics remained his obsession, and he fitted them into his subject whenever he got a chance. Study the enemy's mind, he instructed; and he liked to work out counter-strokes as each lesson's action developed, so students could oversee both sides. His favourite quotation was by Napoleon, and though it had appealed to him when he found it as a student, mechanisation made it more relevant than ever. 'I will tell you the mistakes you are always making,' Napoleon had criticised a lesser general. 'You draw up your plans the day before the battle, when you do not know your adversary's movements. I never issue orders long in advance. I survey the field myself and keep my troops concentrated as long as I am still in doubt. Then I hurl myself on the enemy, attacking him wherever the ground makes the attack more favourable.' The lack of a Channel tunnel to get men and weapons across to the Continent fast was a drawback he often referred to.

Very quickly he began to wonder if he was achieving enough where he was, when international events were moving so swiftly. 'I don't think that I do like my new job very much at present,' he reported to Liddell Hart. 'Having been ground to small powder in Guffin's crucible to produce this reorganisation, I am being ground even finer to revise all the schemes which it has rendered obsolete. . . . We are beginning to discover a number of amusing and interesting reactions on the fighting habits of that Dodo, the Infantry Division, as the result of our gland grafting.' Impediment to progress also came from the textbooks they were using. Wavell's update of the *Field Service Regulations*, the army's bible, had been completed before the mechanisation reforms, as had Montgomery's *Infantry Training*. The sensation of pressure tightened.

In March 1936 Hitler invaded the Rhineland unopposed, and that May Mussolini completed the conquest of Abyssinia. In Spain civil war broke out in July, and Italian and German troops backed the revolutionary General Franco. The British, meanwhile were hypnotised by the scandal of King Edward VIII and Mrs Simpson. Inside the Staff College speculation was as rife as elsewhere, and Chink was not immune. The directing staff were sure that publicity would force the King to give her up, and they waited with interest for the official royal visit in December. When he arrived, Edward VII was dressed in a kilt as Colonel-in-Chief of the Seaforth Highlanders and sported a black eye. His younger brother, the Duke of Gloucester, was a student in the Junior Year, and they sought him out to enquire. 'From me,' came the tight-lipped answer.

It was a welcome moment of light relief. Gort's backward thinking had been confirmed for Chink and Christison by his plan for the annual Winchester Exercise – so named because students spent the night in hotels in Winchester, and the culmination of the Junior Year. Christison taught tactics, the subject he knew Chink would rather have had, and when summoned for the briefing reported back to him that Gort intended to use an old exercise from his Indian days, which had no bearing on the work they were currently doing. Chink advised him to go back and tell him the scheme was out of date. To Christison's dismay, Gort remained silent, but then instead of a reprimand he was ordered to redraft it with Chink's help. When told that that was not possible, Gort authorised them to replan it on modern lines and Christison assured him that that was undoubtedly why they had been sent there. The anecdote shows up Gort's humility but it also pinpoints the difference between Christison and Chink. Christison, like most officers, saw himself as part of an evolving system, while Chink saw himself as a solitary prophet.

His impatience was a byword now. At an artillery demonstration that year at Larkhill, the School of Artillery on Salisbury Plain, each observer found a kit on his seat in the bus giving full details of the day ahead. On arrival, the officer in charge recited the contents of the pack, word for word. Gatehouse, also there for the day, asked Chink in a whisper why they bothered to repeat it. 'Don't you know?' Chink's reply rang out. 'None of these old buffers can read.' None had any trouble with their hearing. And so when Gort was promoted to Military Secretary in the spring of 1937, Chink's reaction came as no surprise. Gort, he stormed, was going to put the clock right back to where he could tell the time.

He did not have long to fret. A posting to the Staff College was normally for three years, but later that same spring, after only sixteen months, he was presented with the dream of every regimental soldier and appointed Colonel of 1st Battalion, Royal Northumberland Fusiliers, out in Egypt. (Two years earlier the 'Royal' had been bestowed.) He could not help comparing himself with Horrocks, who was still a brigade major. He was fed up with teaching, only too glad to ensure that his regiment, at least, was prepared for war, and confident of going higher. Traditionally all directing staff are presented with a silver owl at their farewell dinner, and when he stood up to make his speech of thanks they braced themselves. Instead of chatting genially about personalities, he lectured them on Mussolini's recent Abyssinian campaign, commended the Italian high command for 'logistical elasticity', and went on to say that in similar circumstances their own best military minds would be 'mule-bound'. He misinterpreted the immediate clearing of throats.

There was a final holiday in Ireland with Estelle and Elaine before leaving for Egypt, and three family snaps remain. Chink and a friend in solar topee and shorts, rifles slung over their shoulders, set off on mock safari in the first. In the second, they aim and fire, and in the third they stand triumphantly on the steps of Bellamont, with Chink's foot planted on a rounded skin rug. Inside the rug, hides Estelle, laughing. It is a bubble of carefree optimism. Everything lies ahead.

7

Stepping
up the
Pace

'The month of May was a memorable one for this Battalion,' announced *St George's Gazette* in 1937. 'Not only did we celebrate the Coronation of our new King and Queen, but we also welcomed our new Commanding Officer and his wife. Lt. Col and Mrs. Dorman-Smith . . . are known to many of us though they have been away from the Regiment for some years. Our new Commanding Officer comes straight from teaching at the Staff College, so we should all gain through his experience.' It is what is *not* written in the gazette, however, that has lingered in regimental minds the longest.

The battalion had been in Egypt for over three years as part of the Cairo Brigade, and were stationed at Abbas Hilmi Barracks in Abassia, three miles from the city centre. The city's impact on Chink was amplified by his fastidiousness and imagination. It was raucous and overpoweringly smelly, and after flinching he exulted in it as the most vivid place he had yet been in.

The Anglo-Egyptian Treaty recognising Egypt's independence was one result of Mussolini's attack on Abyssinia, when official eyes had been opened to weak defence spots. British and Egyptian armies were now allies, but although liaison was the policy, private regimental opinion had not moved on. 'Gippies?' the most tolerant version went. 'They're the idlest people you've ever met in your whole life.' As King Farouk attained his majority, the British presence remained as pronounced as ever, and the coronation of King George VI was celebrated by a parade at the Gezira Sporting Club on its exclusive island in the Nile. A display of planes flew overhead and the new mechanical transport and marching infantry swanked past the ambassador, Miles Lampson, to the beat of massed bands. Everybody was satisfied –

everybody but the new arrival Dorman-Smith. He summed up his new charge as a flatfooted, lackadaisical, polo-playing unit. Very, very smart, they thought of him in turn. A beautifully dressed officer, beautiful boots and breeches but. . . . Both views would harden.

He saw himself as a consultant with a little black bag, entrusted with the task of turning the regiment round, and as the War Office had passed over three officers for him to do the job he was going to cure the ailments and transform them into a mobile machine gun battalion, whether they liked it or not. If necessary, he wrote privately, he intended to knock hell out of them by day and night. He announced that they would have the best health record in Egypt because there was going to be no time to be sick, but they seemed to have absorbed the Egyptian philosophy of *Bukra fil mishmash* – 'Later, when the apricots bloom' – all too well. Swiftly he diagnosed sport as having a stranglehold.

The Royal Northumberland Fusiliers had won the coveted Regimental Handicap Polo Tournament outright in 1935, and as the 1937 final approached they were the only team left representing an infantry regiment, having beaten three crack Canal teams to get there. Polo was the pride of their Egyptian identity. Chink began by curtailing the regular weekly practice, but not out of 'bloodymindedness', as they concluded. He saw it as an inadequate focus for ambition, a distraction that put a break on other progress and took up valuable time. They had to content themselves with practice on Saturdays only, a Moslem holiday, and simmering resentment lies behind the bland remark, 'We have been on the whole remarkably lucky being able to get so much polo during the training season,' which slips through in that year's gazette. Gossip soon percolated through the colony. He was not the expected paternal colonel, and when he identified the inadequate he said so.

Egypt was a soft billet and motivation was low. He was a disciplinarian who knew what he wanted. As the battalion became fitter and able to do without food or sleep on exercises, his disapproval increased against those whose approach differed from his own. He was considered arrogant and ruthless, and the men did not take to him because he harangued them. 'He thought everyone was a bloody fool,' said one. 'Except him.' 'Thought he knew it all,' said an officer, 'and jolly well didn't.' Possibly he was as brilliant as everyone said, they agreed – *too* brilliant. Estelle noticed women holding on to their husbands at cocktail parties to stop them coming up to her to complain. It is worth remembering that Montgomery nearly provoked a mutiny for the same reason when commanding his own 1st Battalion in India.

Chink was more of a perfectionist than ever. 'I'm always dissatisfied with the way I do a job and I always know it can be improved,' he wrote when on his own. 'I cannot bear the thought of anything in which I serve not being topnotch, or that it should fail to be excellent through any fault of mine. I will never compromise with inefficiency, high or low.' It came across as inflexibility. Instead of his customary high spirits he seemed withdrawn, presumably regarding the outwardly splendid infantry battalion with contempt. 'I have this cursed urge,' as he confessed once, 'for truth inside me.' He confided in no one now but Estelle, and kept to himself. 'Nobody really trusts left-handed Irishmen with looking-glass minds,' he said dismissively of this period later. 'Like the lady who disapproved of Oxford bags because she liked to know what chaps were thinking about – nobody really knew me.' To his subalterns he appeared a loner and most certainly not a womaniser. He hated two things above all in the British Army: a certain sexual smugness, and the scorn reserved for foreigners, so evident out in Egypt.

Two Egyptian companies were attached to his battalion for machine gun training, and he refused to treat the senior officers in the conventional paternalistic way. When 1st Battalion threw a party and the Egyptian officers turned up without their wives, he accepted the return invitation but arrived without Estelle. 'But you haven't brought your ladies,' he recounted the exchange to her afterwards. 'Well, you didn't bring your own to us, so you can't expect to share ours.' 'But they don't know what yours do.' 'Then it's time you taught them.' Teasing on the same level was bad form. The traditional view was that Egyptian women never went anywhere and it was nonsense to suppose they might. Typical Chink.

The first cadre of officers and senior NCOs finished their machine gun training on time, and 200 soldiers commenced. An issue of Morris trucks arrived, and a driving course rushed out two classes. As horses gave way to trucks and even the new machine gun textbooks were found to be out of date, new weapons drill and tactics had to be worked out by him as they went along. As the work became more technical the calibre of men enlisting grew in importance. 'We simply cannot afford the recruit of low mentality,' he pointed out, 'however willing and healthy.' Training was stepped up. A fully mechanised rifle company motored 180 miles over desert track from Cairo to the Gulf of Suez and back to teach control of a column of twenty-five vehicles. 'We feel,' he quipped on return, 'there must be more in the biblical legend of the failure in pursuit of Pharaoh's armies at the Red Sea than meets the eye.' All officers and NCOs had to learn to ride motorbikes, and he gave the lead wearing brown dungarees, disappearing in a cloud of dust down the Suez road. By 10 October, on target, reorganisation was complete.

Compulsory exercises for officers on the barrack square at 5.45 a.m. were introduced. His reasoning that they were liable to get unfit with so much driving was derided, out of earshot. It was the hour when two rival cavalry regiments went to stables, and hoots of laughter made the edict resented even more. When wives were roped in and a squad of female volunteers began PT before breakfast, stories multiplied. His energy is evident in contemporary accounts, rallying over PT, loudspeaker and microphone, at last no longer shackled by tradition. 'It has been a particularly momentous year for the 1st Battalion,' he concluded, summing up 1937 with satisfaction. 'Its opening saw it still organised as a mixed battalion, on its feet literally speaking. The close finds it organised and trained as a mechanised machine gun battalion. . . . No longer shall we see the mounted officer draw in to the side of the road to view his command marching into barracks. . . . Looking back, the transformation is remarkable.' If discontent was reaching him, he did not acknowledge it.

By January 1938 over 300 men were trained to drive and maintain vehicles, and another 300 were under instruction. Twelve thousand miles had been covered during training. Road driving was simple compared to desert driving, with its hazards of wadis, rocks, sand, gravel and unpredictable weather. During a February course a sandstorm was followed by hail and thunder, and breakdowns in the rush to reach the road in daylight had to be towed in after dark, by which time rain had turned the sand into axle-deep clay. He was reminded of only one image: a wet night at Ypres.

The more he learned about the desert, the more its military implications fascinated him. 'It forced me to re-appreciate the art of war in the light of space, freedom of movement and freedom to move through mechanisation,' he wrote later. 'To lose my Western ideas about infantry.' He began to develop a theory about 'Extensive' fighting, more suitable for wide-ranging Middle Eastern fighting than the

European 'Intensive' fighting for which the army chiefly trained. Day-to-day experiments proved the scope of desert mobility. He got out Wavell's *Palestine Campaigns* again to study from this angle, and it was as he expected. 'Written in 1931,' he annotated the margin. 'Many of the deductions . . . are now out of date. e.g. Modern mechanised troops can move down from Arsuf to Damascus on one fill of fuel. They can be maintained there from Arsuf with three echelons of transport. Incidentally, mechanised troops moving via the Msus pass would have reached El Aule by midday if unopposed.'

His concern with accuracy boiled over publicly after one Canal Brigade exercise in which the established thirty-six-hour timetable was expanded so that everyone could be properly fed and rested and have adequate time for manoeuvre. The Royal Northumberland Fusiliers's role was to provide cover for Fayid station, on line from Cairo to Suez, and the opposing side was allocated two ancient transport aircraft because the brigade major happened to have them on hand. After dark the planes landed and two fusiliers, asleep, were captured. A roar of laughter went up throughout the brigade at their expense and Chink was furious. He complained that it had been absurd, as no attacking regiment would have had planes. It had been a Boy Scout game, not a useful exercise with Wavell's necessary ingredients of exhaustion, panic and confusion. He came across as a spoilsport.

Official British policy was not to offend Italy, which put the places he most wanted to inspect, like the tactically important port of Sollum, out of bounds. But in the autumn of 1937 1st Battalion were told to reactivate the defences of Mersa Matruh, also on the coast, and he went up in plain clothes to design the fortifications, which he based on the original perimeter. 'Inevitably I had to produce something like the linear defences made by the Italians coping with similar problems at Bardia and Tobruk,' he wrote later. 'Only I think our combination of machine gun posts, anti-tank guns and anti-tank ditches and wire was more formidable because it was closer-knit in defensive fire plan.'

But Mersa Matruh shared something else with Tobruk: tactically it was less significant than it appeared, since it was out on a point and could be bypassed by forces in the high desert inland. When he remarked, in his cocksure way, on the futility of refortifying it because Alamein, further to the east, was bound to be the decisive battleground for Egypt, he was told not to be stupid and made to apologise. It was one of the many occasions when he warned Estelle to get ready to pack. At social events conversation irritated him by being as insular as ever, despite Hitler's ominous dismissal in March 1938 of his army chiefs, followed by the swift annexation of Austria, the stop before Czechoslovakia. The reasonableness Chink had displayed as adjutant in his twenties was no longer in evidence. Privately labelling himself a single-minded military spiv, he pressed on without minding how many he offended, and gave no quarter.

Returning late from a long desert manoeuvre at Repeiqui Camp at the end of March – 'sufficiently workmanlike,' he allowed, 'though a very great deal to be done' – he was stunned to find a letter from the War Office offering him the post of Director of Military Training for India, Gort's old job. There were thirty minutes left in which to make up his mind, but one would have been sufficient. He jumped at it, surprised that Gort, who was now CIGS, should have approved and nursing a suspicion that Liddell Hart, who had been taken up by the Minister for War, Leslie Hore-Belisha, had something to do with it. In this he was partially right. 'In 1937,' as Liddell Hart pedantically confirmed many years later, 'I compiled at Hore-Belisha's request a nine page list of Some Noteworthy Officers from general down to lt. cols, classifying them into Outstanding and Close Up. . . . For Lt Cols I did not give any comment beyond putting an A+ against a few names. Eleven were classed as outstanding, and of these five as A+. You were one.' The means to the end were unimportant. It was a plum post given only to men expected to go right to the top, and the army in India badly needed to be brought up to date. At last the hard work was paying off. His elation was sharpened by knowing that Horrocks was now two rungs behind him, currently teaching at the Staff College.

At the St George's Day parade that April he took his last salute as the colours were carried past – the King's Colour, presented at the Delhi Durbar by King George V in 1912, the Regimental Colours, and the Drummer's Colour which commemorated a brave moment in the Peninsular War. Briefly, he was content. 'I saw the St. George's day parade in Cologne in 1923,' the new brigadier at HQ Cairo Infantry Brigade, Ian Grant, wrote to him afterwards. 'You were Adjutant and myself a company commander in the Camerons. It must be a source of particular pride to yourself to see, as Commanding Officer, that in spite of the very great strain placed on the Battalion by reorganisation and mechanisation, the same very high standard of close order drill can still be attained.' That was the only assessment that mattered.

A final act of regimental splendour enclosed him at the annual St George's Ball that evening, held in the magnificent 500-bedroomed Heliopolis Palace Hotel. Two scarlet-coated fusilier sentries guarded the entrance to the terrace as he approached with Estelle. Buttonholes of red and white roses were banked on their drums for guests, and beyond glimmered the familiar silver mess trophies on maroon silk-covered tiers behind the Regimental Colours, beflanked by two more sentries with fixed bayonets. Every regimental chord in him responded, bringing on a temporary depression. 'I am sorry to be leaving Egypt so soon,' he confided to Liddell Hart. 'I would have liked another year in command. . . . For ten years now I have been connected in one way or another with modernisation and advanced soldiering, and I will find a return to the Middle Ages extremely difficult. It will be a sort of military Berkeley Square without any romance.'

The local newspaper covered his departure in May 1938 for Port Said, where the SS *Cormorin* waited to sail for India. 'All the officers of the battalion, many of other regiments and several of the Egyptian Army who had been associated in training with the Royal Northumberland Fusiliers,' the report attested, 'were at the station to bid farewell to Colonel Dorman-Smith.' The sigh of relief was not mentioned, nor the attitude of members of the polo team who had been pipped so closely by the 8th Hussars in the final that special silver tankards had been sent for at half-time to be presented, uniquely, to the runners-up. They were heartily glad to be rid of him.

Against that has to be weighed a statement in the subsequent regimental history of the Second World War. 'In 1937,' it runs,

the Battalion was organised and equipped as 3 MG Coys and 1 A/T company, all mobile. . . . It was clear that the old Battalion control would not operate and that companies, platoons and even sections must learn to be independent in both command and administration. The foundation for this revolutionary change in outlook was well and truly laid by Dorman-Smith. . . . How sound was this foundation can be gauged from the fact that about 40% of the original Morris 15 cwt trucks issued found their way back to Cairo at Christmas 1941 after the siege of Tobruk, returning to the desert in 1942. In summary, the Battalion entered the war . . . well trained in its weapons, with company and platoon commanders ready to act on their own and full of confidence. . . . The greatest change since

1914 was in the mobility [which] made possible their use in every campaign.

The specialist with his black bag had effected a cure, as he had always known he would, even if the patient would continue to query the bill for some time.

The heat of India was stupefying. From his train window, as Estelle and Elaine dozed and their small terrier Mac leaned his head against the iceblock, Chink summoned up stanzas from Kipling to lace the discomfort as he gazed out at a vista of open grassland, twisted hills and jungles of unrecognisable trees. There were monkeys everywhere, people everywhere, and gradually in the distance an indistinct range of mountains took shape in the blue haze. The iceblock had formed a shrinking puddle, lapped desultorily by Mac, long before they changed trains at Kalka in the foothills for the four-hour climb to Simla.

Escaping the shimmering heat along the toytown narrow-gauge track, his mountaineering eye delighted in the peaks about them until the accumulation of smug overheard conversations contrived to infuriate him. His black mood was aggravated by a sight that charmed most visitors. At the minuscule station rickshaws were the sole transport, because only three cars were allowed in Simla – one for the Viceroy, one for the Commander-in-Chief and one for the Governor of the Punjab – and he was tugged further uphill by a crew of four jhampanies; his heavy luggage, he was told, was following on the backs of coolies. He was shocked that men should be downgraded to a pony's job. As they were pulled through the steep narrow streets with English names at every turn – their hotel was in the Mall – he groaned aloud to Estelle.

So he began his time in India with reservations, and he would end with even more. Within days he was writing about the 'pomposity' of the country and complaining about provincialism, and by the time he was able to distinguish between the tall Punjabis with their dark faces and rapid gestures and the more mongoloid hill people, he had also identified the sahib 'brontosaurs', and was taking active precautions to avoid them. His and Estelle's social life started as it threatened to go on when an elderly officer boasted to her that he had spent forty years in India without crossing a native's threshold once, and nudged her to emphasise the falling standards of Indians no longer stepping off the pavement and furling their umbrellas when a white man approached. (It is an ironic fact that as he was speaking a local Sikh carpenter, Zail

Singh, was a prisoner of the Maharajah of Faridkot, whose invitation to the incoming Director of Military Training prompted the outburst. By 1984 Zail Singh occupied the Viceroy's House, renamed Bashtrapat Byhavan, in his capacity as President of India and was proud to entertain Queen Elizabeth II. He spoke so little English, however, that an interpreter was necessary.)

Army Headquarters, when Chink reported like a businessman to his office in the old War Office way, was a huge wooden building – Simla was entirely built of wood – on the side of a hill. Stairs linked the many levels, and he took them two at a time. He was ninth in the hierarchy, but close to British policy-making since power was in the hands of a small nucleus of men. The bureaucrats and top army brass worked side by side, spending the hottest months in the mountains at Simla and moving to Delhi each October. But the men Chink had to work with were Indian Army and proud of it. It was made clear to him that no English service officer – especially a newcomer – knew anything.

As DMT he was responsible for training half a million men, some 55,000 in the British Army stationed there and the rest in British-officered Indian regiments. It was the largest repository of British soldiery in the world. Sometimes he compared the scope of his job to Horrocks's, and thought back to their schooldays. His charges included the Quetta Staff College, the Dehra Dun Military Academy, the many Indian battalions and all the forty-seven British battalions dotted around the vast country; the story went that as there were only forty-six barracks, one battalion was always shuttling between by train. Internal security, the duty of the majority, was considered dull, but the North-West Frontier occasionally provided action and the training he had to oversee inevitably favoured the skills of mountain fighting. The Indian Army's state of preparedness for war, as he realised from the start, was in his keeping. His view of its role, however, ran counter to general opinion at AHQ. Indian military philosophy thought in terms of defence of India alone, not what might have to be contributed globally. It was believed she would never be asked to send forces outside her own borders, and the men he had to work with had no intention of changing their minds.

When he inspected the four army headquarters at Bombay, Madras, Calcutta and the North-West Frontier he found the situation worse than he expected. No SD2 changes had reached India. At his most generous he dated development at 1916, in the trench warfare period. As far as modern tactical thought went, the Indian Army was 'in the dark ages', and at Quetta instruction was 'obsolete'. 'I have begun to see this Army from close up,' he was soon writing to Liddell Hart.

Very useful tour of the NW Frontier. How Lewis Carroll would have revelled in that land of Paradox where all the political officials are standing on their heads, and many of the soldiers too. The only sensible people are the tribesmen who have discovered how to make money out of our obtuseness. . . . I have now motored and flown over a good part of northern India. . . . This Army is ripe for modernisation. . . . What makes it all the more difficult is that the next war is going on all the time. Ethiopia, China, Spain, the occupation of Austria and the Sudetenland. The Russo–Japanese encounters in Siberia and Palestine . . . are all part of this next war business.

Both divisions on the North-West Frontier had an inadequate arsenal. There were sixteen horsed regiments, no tanks, and everyone worked on a London directive which stipulated that their role was a defensive one. He resolved to cancel this – 'in such a vast space an Army geared solely to defence will soon have its flanks turned and be out-manoeuvred' – as soon as he had drawn up a substitute. He crisscrossed his massive training ground in a concentration too single-minded to take in anything but the matter in hand. Burning funeral ghats, poverty, mutilated beggars, stench, overcrowding and flies all pass unnoticed in his writings, which are solely concerned with military shortcomings and the means to correct them. Gort had recommended his own bearer who knew whom to see and where to stay, but Chink did not take him on. He was determined to approach his job from the outside to evaluate the true state of affairs, and the bearer told Estelle he was most put out. But much as Chink longed to dispense with red tape it is significant that the only Hindustani words he would remember were *Hookum hai* – 'That's an order.'

As usual he saw no point in keeping his thoughts to himself. Sneers about an army fit only for tribal warfare were too strong to swing support around to his own view, and he rushed in where generals fear to tread. And at his level it was a very small club. At the pinnacle was the Viceroy, Lord Linlithgow, who was far-seeing but not concerned with army priorities. They got on well, however, and through Linlithgow Chink met a man whom he respected even more, the Governor of Bengal, Lord Brabourne. Later that year the constructive Brabourne sat in as Viceroy while Linlithgow visited England, and undeterred by Chink's deepening intellectualism became a close friend. Brabourne made every effort to persuade him to move to Bengal, but Chink refused. The army was the only thing he wanted to change.

The Commander-in-Chief was General Sir Robert Cassells, a gaunt cavalryman twenty years Chink's senior. He had the conventional passion for polo, and was brusquely hardbitten. Cassells's temper was legendary. He hurled books at staff and a current junior a.d.c. kept his job through the ploy of picking up each tome and handing it back for a second throw. Undeterred, Chink liked Cassells personally, but thought him professionaly uninspired. It was an opinion he did not bother to disguise in front of Cassells's loyal senior a.d.c. 'Bunny' Careless, who hated his arrogance from the start, whenever they encountered each other at social functions. In Cassells's absence the two were soon having 'sharpish' sessions, and these increased as the months went by.

His working hours were spent closeted with 'out of touch' chiefs of staff, Indian Army 'know alls', and finance experts with whom he was at once at loggerheads. These included Roger Wilson, the complacent elderly Adjutant-General whose habit of sweeping past without a reply when greeted by junior staff endeared him to few, and the civil servant Finance Member, P.J. Grigg. The crunchpoint of most meetings was the sum allocated for training, and study of the figures for Defence Funding showed Chink that India was the poor relation of an impoverished empire. Wilson he soon despised, and Grigg he judged to be clever and likeable but blind to army needs.

Grigg was a small man with an alert, intelligent face, who unlike everyone else had not gone to public school. He had been in India since 1935 and freely admitted that he had arrived a liberal but was now imperialist. England, he argued, had done everything for India and would continue to do so, and he saw no reason why the army should take money which the country needed as a whole. In meetings he made Chink furious, but out of the building they got on so well that Grigg and his wife became Estelle's favourite guests. Friendship between the two couples grew. The Griggs could have no children either, and similarly poured their affection into dogs. P.J. had once been Private Secretary to Churchill and over dinner added to Leo Amery's anecdotes, unintentionally rounding out Chink's mental picture of the politician he most despised. As they got to know each other better, Grigg revealed himself to be sensitive about snobbishness and endearingly dogged, as Chink saw it, about his own more bourgeois values. There were two faults that he would never condone, whatever the circumstances, and these were deceit and immorality; it was a touching idiosyncrasy to someone much of the same mind himself.

It was a less isolated life than Cairo. In India Chink built up a circle of friends, aided by Estelle's hospitality, but they were not conventional ones. Unlike his colleagues he invited very few army men home, dismissing most as bears of little brain. One frequent guest was his old War Office companion Archie Rowlands, who was seconded to the government as Defence Finance Adviser, with virtually full powers over defence funds. The intellectual Sir Theodore Gregory and the novelist Edward Thompson were often to be found there. Different, again, and it did not go unnoticed.

Everyone at that level in India watched everyone else. To men who had known him at the Staff College or at Chatham he appeared much more driven now. His thinking was concentrated and definitive, and his opinions more original. But he himself had no time for nostalgia, and he paid little attention to Oliver Leese and other contemporaries who were serving there as well. Fellow radicals were in a minority but they did exist, though he never thought to mention them subsequently. He was very much the prima donna by now.

But one senior ally was about to appear. A veranda linked Chink's hillside Simla office to all those on the same floor, and he noticed that the next-door room's occasional occupant, a tall man with a long freckled face carved out of granite, sometimes went out for a breath of air to lean on the rail and contemplate the ring of peaks. 'Deputy Chief, General Staff' read the sign on that man's door, and using the mountains as an excuse Chink introduced himself. Claude Auchinleck was approachable but reserved. They were soon close companions, however, their fellowship brought about by mutual indignation at the vulnerability of the army. At Auchinleck's suggestion they began a regular routine of brisk hill-walking before breakfast, during which they analysed shortcomings and tried to work out how things could be improved. Chink was often reminded of his Alpine trek with Dick O'Connor. 'We discussed war and training – training mostly, and I found him very intelligent and very valuable to talk to . . . very valuable indeed,' Auchinleck said many years later. 'Very imaginative. Not popular, because he was a little bit inclined to state his opinions very openly, and the less intelligent didn't like him much. But I had a very great opinion of him.'

An unaffected, almost naive man beneath his shyness, Auchinleck was very powerful in his chosen world and ill at east outside it. The social territory of his flirtatious, self-absorbed wife Jessie, whom Chink and Estelle instantly distrusted, was anathema to him. He had an inner humility Chink was unable to understand and a dedication to India he did not share, but the same horror of military backwardness. Auchinleck insisted on the need for modernisation, and his responsibilities included Indianisation, the phasing out of British officers for suitable Indian replacements, and the updating of equipment and training. The latter overlapped with Chink's job, and he lost no time in explaining his SD2 theories on mechanisation and mobility, estimating that he got these across within a week. Already he was being classified as one of Auchinleck's men by the personality watchers at AHQ and it was not a bad tag to have, as Auchinleck was immensely popular. On his advice Chink roped into his office Francis Tuker from the Frontier forces, a brilliant soldier whom he found impressive but disconcerting and praised as a 'practical visionary in his own right'. As a guide around the enormous military structure, however, Tuker was invaluable. In 1940 Chink made him his deputy.

Auchinleck took up Chink's proposal that an overall modernisation plan could be worked out by a small think tank, and Cassells sanctioned the idea. Under Auchinleck's chairmanship, the internal committee was composed of the Director of Staff Duties, the Director of Military Operations and Intelligence, and the new Director of Military Training. Superimposing planning as it evolved on a large-scale map of India, they looked at modernisation under the headings of Frontier Defence, Internal Security, Coastal Defence, External Defence and the General Reserve of 4th and 5th Indian Divisions, which would automatically be involved in any international war. The mechanisation and modernisation of these two was given priority and put under Chink's care, and it was agreed that the military schools should be brought up to date. But there his influence stopped and that of the Indian Army took over, as Auchinleck was not usually present to back him up. Trying to get the others to see during one session that Singapore was more crucial to India's defence than the North-West Frontier, Chink challenged the DMI to say which had the greater strategic importance: Razmak, up in the local trouble spot of Wazaristan, or Singapore? 'Razmak, of course.'

But Auchinleck kept them together as a team, and by September 1938 the committee's report was ready. Changes were to be financed on the necessary 'no cost' basis by disbanding seven regiments, and Cassells initialled it. A copy was sent to each of the five army commanders, and the author of the squib enclosed – 'I have read the report on the modernisation of the Indian Army. I have/am resigned' – was easily identifiable. Events overtook them, however. After the Munich agreement between Chamberlain and Hitler that month a Whitehall lens swung in India's direction, and the high-profile Chatfield Committee was appointed by London to examine the same subject. Auchinleck was co-opted on to it, and Chink privately took the credit for his career leap, more aware of cause and effect than he had been at Blackdown. Their report eventually formed a large part of the Chatfield conclusions, and the Imperial Exchequer came to the rescue of the threatened regiments. But by then he was almost too cross to care.

Predictably he was outraged by Munich and went around saying it was 'a disgrace and a disaster'. He was tactless at Linlithgow's functions, likening Indian policy to a 'distant echo of Downing Street', and each time he read about conciliation or the Cliveden Set his anger mounted. 'The day before yesterday I visited the residency in Lucknow,' he raged to Liddell Hart when turning down due to pressure of work his invitation to write a book on tactics. 'Something seems to have happened to our race, or perhaps we are suffering from leadership by Cawnpore wheelers and have yet to find our Lucknow Lawrence. So much to say which can't be said in official circles – and there are no other circles in Delhi.' The 1939 appointment of General Sir Eric de Burgh, whom he had no time for, as Chief of the General Staff, indicated that the old guard were going to go on filling the top Indian posts.

The more keyed up he became the harder it was to hide his disdain for men he considered amateur. Visiting Southern Command to see an exercise by 5th Indian Division, he judged the solution of the cavalry-man in charge, Frank Messervy, to be 'so fantastically obvious and clumsy that I had to observe on it'. And so he began with the sarcastic remark that Messervy was accident-prone with divisions, and finished by observing that it might be brave, but it was other men's lives he was throwing away. 'Poor Messervy was a product of the Staff College school which always looked it up in the book,' he said dismissively afterwards. 'But the books are always obsolete.' Pointing out the correct answer publicly, he sped on, leaving Messervy with his thoughts.

But behind the cocky façade he was as self-critical as ever, and his own work dissatisfied him too. 'How contented should one be?' he asked himself late at night on paper. 'Not at all, I think, until you achieve perfection. To relapse otherwise is to betray one's guest.' Linlithgow's secretary, who was half-Russian, astounded him one morning by asking why he would never let himself be happy, and for once he was stumped for a reply. Brabourne's suggestion about Bengal came to seem attractive as his frustrations mounted, but then word came that Brabourne had died suddenly, in his early forties, so that escape route was blocked.

If everything and everyone has a *dharma*, a natural role, as Hindus hold, he was following his to the letter during 1939. Everywhere he went army preoccupation with horses mocked him. Polo cost little in India, there was even hunting after jackal in winter, and horse 'infatuation' rankled more than ever. Told once too often that a tank would never be able to do everything a horse could, he circulated a tank design with a special attachment lever. Out would come horse manure, instructions stated, when this was pulled. His impatience at social occasions was more marked than before, and he attended mainly to cut through red tape. Although the best string band in India, featuring thirty musicians culled from British regiments, played seductively at dinners and parties in Linlithgow's superb Lutyens palace in Delhi, Chink preferred to talk. On one occasion he leaned across to demand why one of his men had been stopped at the frontier; at another he prised out the Viceroy's real opinion of Churchill, Anthony Eden and Duff Cooper, and filed away the information that it was the same as his own. Following Grigg's departure in April 1939 he took the chance to cultivate his successor, Jeremy Raisman, but thought him unpromisingly concerned with small print.

He had another reason for avoiding army functions. The scale of bigotry alienated him, and he found he had this in common with Auchinleck too. In Delhi he preferred to go out of his way to meet members of Congress, the eventual Indian national government, and although most did not impress him, he was much taken by the magnetic Jinnah, who led the Moslem League. And it was Jinnah, a barrister who had learned his excellent English at Lincoln's Inn in London, who initiated him into the swirl of conflicting Indian views. Through him Chink met Bhulabhai Desai, a scorching nationalist lawyer who shared Jinnah's disillusion with Gandhi's mainly Hindu Congress, and both came to dinner frequently, where they talked long after Estelle had gone to bed. Jinnah's attitudes were hardening to the point of planning a separate Moslem state, and Pakistan would eventually come about under his leadership in 1947, shortly before his death. Another Indian who became a good friend was Mohammed Ali, Deputy Finance Adviser in the Indian Civil Service; in 1953 Ali would become Prime Minister of Pakistan. But in 1939 these were unpopular guests to have. Chink was unconcernedly saddling himself with the reputation of being pro-Indian, which added to the disfavour in which he already stood.

But fascinating as the Indian question was, the undeniable graph plotted by newspapers and radio bulletins made it a provincial one. In July 1939 Chink presented a Simla paper on 'Command in the Indian Ocean' in which he proposed Ceylon as a sounder base for GHQ, and his audience was convulsed. 'It is quite impossible,' he fumed afterwards, 'to get over the obvious fact that any war will inevitably expand to include India, and therefore India is directly interested in not only a Russian threat to NW India, but Iraq, Egypt, Malaya and Burma.' Undiscouraged, he went about forecasting that command would be moved to Ceylon eventually, and in the spring of 1940 returned publicly to the charge. 'Nobody,' he began trenchantly on this occasion, 'can conduct a real war from the stagnant pool of Delhi/ Simla,' and he went on to advise a joint India/UK planning and communications staff in Ceylon while it could still be set up, before Japan intervened. He was told it was not for the DMT to make such suggestions. In 1944 Mountbatten made the move, the Chiefs of Staff in London having recommended it from June 1943 onwards.

On 1 September 1939 Germany invaded Poland. 'Hitler has pushed our old gentlemen beyond even their dirt-swallowing capabilities,' he commented, and two days later was in position beside Estelle to hear Linlithgow's formal broadcast of the declaration of war. Shortly afterwards he overheard Cassells instructing Raisman by phone that he could not commit him to any extra expenditure, and using his trick from War Office days sent around the Kipling poem 'Mesopotamia 1915'. 'But the men who left them thriftily to die in their own dung, / Shall they come with years and honour to the grave?' Elaine's coming-out dance was due to be held within the week and invitations had been accepted, but he cancelled it when news came in that the first ship had been torpedoed offshore. He would never have it said that they had danced while others mourned, he told Estelle. Most unfair and unnecessary, remarked Lady Cassells sympathetically.

In Delhi that autumn everyone flocked as usual to the parties given by the Japanese Consul, including the Linlithgow girls. He would not allow Elaine to go. Sickened by the 'obscenity' of formal junketing, he turned down all invitations except those of close friends, and Estelle contrived to defuse awkwardness by entertaining anyone on the verge of taking offence. She was well aware that he sparkled more tolerantly in his own home, against a hospitable backdrop. In public he was unpredictable. His sense of irony was liable to offend anyone who took religion, the army code or family virtues over-solemnly.

Auchinleck had been out of the country when war broke out, and when he returned he recoiled in the same way at the prevailing nonchalance, taking Cassells's a.d.c. aside to say – nicely – that it was high time they got out of their bright uniforms. But he was not destined to be a comfort to Chink for long, because in January 1940 Auchinleck was given a corps command in England. They walked, the morning after word came, around the lovely Delhi ruin of Pmana Killa, and Auchinleck knew him well enough by this time to admit his apprehension. With all the charm he had used on Hemingway in 1922 after the loss of the suitcase, Chink eased him back into good humour. Privately he was jealous, and disgusted at being left behind to watch the war from the sidelines.

The campaign in France was a 'pathetic spectacle'. Simla that spring felt like the Kipling poem about the town where the obvious and the commonplace and the trite reign supreme. 'It must have been pretty bloody,' he scrawled, 'even fifty years ago.' Claustrophobia and uselessness were aggravated by having become caught up in a row between the Adjutant-General and the Commander-in-Chief. Cassells had sent for Chink the previous December to ask if he would chair meetings on the expansion of the officer corps in the new war situation because Wilson – 'woolly-minded', Cassells had shouted angrily – refused. Setting about the job with characteristic energy, Chink had promptly quarrelled with Wilson himself, explaining only that he had caught Wilson lying and so would not speak to him again. When Wilson complained to Cassells, pressing negative financial counter-arguments to expansion, Cassells did not support Chink. Chink burned with annoyance at being manipulated into an invidious position, and Archie Rowlands, the only man whose advice might have helped, had long been summoned back to England.

Frustration at the waste of India's twelve-month breathing space made him more provocative than ever. Of every three soldiers killed in action during the first year of war, he took to repeating, one at least had been earmarked for death by the Treasury. India was timidly dipping in her foot when she should be going in up to her neck. He had criticised Grigg's approach, but now he longed to have him back. 'Raisman keeps referring to HMG's war,' he noted, 'in which India is financially neutral. Always HMG's war!' Exasperated, he worked harder, concentrating on 4th Indian Division, which was likely to be called upon first. Modernisation had been carried through in both General Reserve divisions after much harassment of Raisman for equipment, and teaching in the schools was reorganised. But he was dissatisfied with general progress, and pessimistic about improvement.

His walks were solitary now, but he continued the routine because he needed to be alone. One evening early in June 1940 he climbed the 8000-foot Mount Jakko, prominent above Simla, as he had often done before, and sat on the spur looking out over Kasauli. The Netherlands were occupied, the Belgian Army had just surrendered, and the French were once again facing the Germans along the Somme. 'Suddenly,' he recorded afterwards, 'I had an experience of complete illumination, and with it the certainty that the Germans would not win the war. It was entire certainty, factual and emphatic. I could justify it with a reasoned appreciation that they had made a great training mistake in not taking time to prepare, but its source was quite otherwise.' He believed in his own second sight, and the optimism that was to be so criticised subsequently grew out of that moment.

A week later he was asleep when the phone rang as Elaine was tiptoeing in from a party. She answered it in a whisper. A clipped voice said that Italy had come into the war, and she wrote this across the mirror in lipstick, where he found it in the morning. In July tentacles of the Italian Army spread out from Abyssinia, first north into British Somaliland and then west into the Sudan. The 'flaccid' Indian reaction disgusted Chink so much that he resolved to stir things up in a lecture he was due to give to the United Service Institute of India in the first week of August, always a full-dress Simla affair. As a theatrical touch he barred women in advance, on the ground that it was too depressing a recital of male stupidity.

The Middle East was the base from which to wage war against Italy, he commenced, because with two armoured and two mechanised divisions the British Army could possess North Africa and invade Sicily. Advocating Liddell Hart's theory of the indirect approach, aware that his listeners would flush collectively at that name, he stressed that an army equal to its enemy in fighting power but 50 per cent more mobile 'can do what it pleases with its enemy. . . . There is nothing in the world to stop us winning . . . except the relics of ignorance, timidity and financial turpitude. . . . Our first action must be to review the lessons of the war. . . . We must free our minds from all preconceived tactical ideas and strive to remodel our land forces objectively. . . .' Reaction was not long in coming back. Clearly impractical, he heard above the polite applause. Undismayed, he boiled down his talk for a national broadcast, and added for good measure that the Italians were about to be 'licked' in Libya.

Nothing changed. All around him, he complained to Estelle, were inertia, complacency and flagrant careerism, and he said as much openly. At Simla in August 1940 they were still wearing plain clothes on duty as if it was peacetime, glad of the reprieve, and no one paid any attention when he said there was symbolism to consider. 'Coma in Simla', he headed one letter, odd man out as always.

One morning a file was handed to him as DMT, and opening it he found a request from Archie Wavell, now Commander-in-Chief, Middle East, for a successor of brigadier's rank to take over from 'Sandy' Galloway as Commandant of the new Staff College at Haifa in Palestine. He had not seen Galloway since Camberley or Wavell since Blackdown. It meant an abrupt £1000 per annum loss in pay, but on impulse he sent his own name in. He wondered if Cassells would refuse to let him go, and it was a test, of a sort.

Cassells did not attempt to hold on to him. Chink was furious initially, and then quiet whenever he was alone with Estelle. He was annoyed that he had himself handed the Old Guard the dagger, since they had not hestitated to use it. With the appointment due to start at once he tried urgently to get permission for Estelle to join him after Elaine's imminent wedding to Kenneth Bols, one of Cassells's a.d.c.s. Permission was refused. He applied directly to Wavell, who phoned him back but, he suspected, took refuge behind the War Office when he said it was impossible. The prospect of being without the prop of Estelle's rock solid good sense was alarming. They spent four days alone at Cariguano, the Commander-in-Chief's summer house, and in his superstitious way he was unable to shake off the sudden conviction that it was the end of their time together. He slept badly and woke with nightmares. It was a relief when the four days were up.

Leaving his substantial library of books in Simla and everything else that would not fit into one trunk and one suitcase, he said goodbye to

Estelle and took Mac the terrier with him in the rickshaw as far as the station. 'Not a good journey,' he noted. 'Pad, pad, pad, pad, Hut! Khabadar. But Mac loves a rickshaw and didn't realise.' It was cool and fresh, and Elaine and her fiancé were at the station to take the dog from him, and wave.

He took the narrow-gauge railway down for the final time, and stared out at the pines, wracked with emotion. He was conscious of feeling no longer young, poor and not at all successful. Mentally he was worn out, having had no leave since Egypt and little for ten years. 'Stupid of me, perhaps,' he noted, 'but I feel still that the real work of a trained military brain should be done *between* wars. Once they begin, there is very little scope.' Reggie was in the government as Minister of Agriculture, and that did not help.

It would have consoled him to know that Cassells thought better of him than he believed. 'Dear Wavell,' his chief took the trouble to cable next day,

> Dorman-Smith is just off by air to take over your staff school and I am sorry to lose him. He was very keen to go, although it meant a heavy loss of pay and no increase in rank. You already know him well, but I would like you to know that he has been a great success out here as DMT, and I have a very high opinion of his energy and outstanding ability. He was due to complete his tenure as DMT in May, but he is unfortunately junior as a colonel so there is no immediate prospect of fitting him into a major general's appointment as he would have had to pass over many colonels senior to himself. I am sure he will do you well.

And he was not as friendless as he supposed. Although he had lost his political pull, in London Liddell Hart was drawing up another list – this time headed 'Commanders of Outstanding Promise with the Quality of Audacity' – with only fourteen names upon it. These ranged from general down to brigadier, and Chink was one of them. Unaware, bleakly hugging the novel sense of failure, he headed south into the heat. Estelle would never see him again.

8
Crossroads

The state of the war in the Middle East in the autumn of 1940 looked decidedly bad for the British. Stripped of their fallen allies, the French, the British barred the way to a critical prize and were facing an Italian enemy ten times their number. If the Italians broke through and reached the oil stocks in the Mosul, Iraq and the Persian Gulf, British tanks and trucks would be unable to roll, British aircraft would be unable to fly and British ships would be unable to keep the seas. Hitler and Mussolini would dictate their terms.

As Commander-in-Chief at such a critical moment, Wavell's command covered an immense territory compared to the speck on the map where 6th Experimental Brigade had operated. He was responsible for three and a half million square miles and nine countries, straddling two continents, and his resources were proportionately even more minimal. Where four men and two ropes had once done for a platoon, now he had to make do with the tiny Western Desert Force for an army.

Wavell's most vulnerable point was Libya, the setting for Chink's broadcast prediction of victory. And it was from Libya on 13 September that the Italian Tenth Army moved out into Egypt towards the Nile Delta and the oil-rich Persian Gulf. Under the cautious command of Marshal Rodolpho Graziani the four divisions – which included a motorised brothel – maintained a ponderous top speed and paused four days later at the seaside town of Sidi Barrani. Here they were seen to consolidate in a semicircle of defensive camps, in territory Chink knew well.

Eighty miles away, ready to take them on, waited a man whom Chink knew even better. Dick O'Connor was commander of the Western Desert Force, which by now included Chink's protégés, 4th Indian Division, and fifty-seven of the I tanks he had pushed through at the War Office. And O'Connor was making his stand, David to Goliath, at Mersa Matruh, where Chink had designed the defences only three years earlier. Tactically it had to be held, because from Mersa Matruh onwards the British fleet base at Alexandria came within range of air attack.

As he headed towards the Sea of Galilee in the flying boat *Caster* to take up his teaching post, Chink's stinging regret was that he could not be at O'Connor's side. Everyone else seemed to be fully stretched: from Horrocks, who had already been commanding 2nd Battalion of the Middlesex Regiment in France, to the gentle John Dill, his senior at the War Office, who was now CIGS. But at least he would be nearer the war here than he had been in India. By the time he climbed into the car sent for him at the pier at Tiberius he was in a more equable mood. He had brought a Bible with him, read a more up-to-date history of Palestine and worked out his curriculum priorities. He was ready for anything.

The fact that the Haifa oil refinery was under regular air attack from Italian planes based on the Dodecanese Islands made up for the initial disappointments. In Haifa, the room booked for him in the annexe of the Windsor Hotel was small, and Teltsch House, the staff college on Mount Carmel, still looked like the holiday-resort hotel it had been before the war. And the standard of teaching was no better than he expected, either, with pre-modernisation exercises making little allowance for the real desert fighting his students would face. Excited by the distant bombing, he began drawing up a new syllabus at once. 'Several beds which needed considerable weeding,' he noted in the laconic style he always used when caught up in something new. 'Not to mention trees of knowledge with no fruit, authorised or forbidden.' Haifa was a whitewashed, lemon-scented port on the Mediterranean, and beyond was the Egyptian coastline which so absorbed him. Like Jurgen he was prepared to try any new drink once.

None of his recent dissatisfaction showed. He was decisive, sure about what he wanted taught, and on the surface as arrogant as ever. He knew the team he wanted, and it did not include men who reminded him of Gort, like his Deputy Commandant Brigadier 'Sharks' Tiarks. Tiarks was an elderly cavalryman old enough to be his father, and though he grew fond of him personally, he was contemptuous of his lack of interest in mechanisation. Tiarks's range of vision stretched no further than 1st Cavalry Division, stationed around the corner with a full complement of horses. 'Tomorrow I go out for the morning with the Cavalry Brigade,' he fumed in his cramped basement room while settling in. 'The bit I'm seeing is not horses – I cannot waste time on horse soldiers. . . .' In discussions about the type of instructors he wanted – men who could teach but also analyse current operations and anticipate developments – he could tell that Tiarks was humouring him.

But he was pleased with the senior lecturer he inherited, who had been a favourite pupil at Camberley four years earlier. Freddie de Guingand's amiable good manners masked a managing director's grasp of essentials, and his wit and urbanity were a relief after the last months in India. Like all able men, however, de Guingand ached to move on and they worked together for only six weeks before he lost him to a new school nearby, followed by a posting to the Joint Planning Staff in Cairo. He had submitted a list of names before leaving India, and one successful application was for a young sapper he had noticed ten years before at Chatham, Charles Richardson. He wanted Richardson not only for the aptitude he had shown then, but for his topical battle experience in France. It was imperative to make the teaching relevant.

As reverses to the British Expeditionary Force in France threatened to lower morale, he worked instructors and students to the limit, with no qualms about pushing them too hard. Better they cracked there, he always countered, than in the field. 'We have had a year of war, full of useful lessons, most of which I predicted,' he noted. 'Don't see why people who blunder should get off scot free. Just been debunking the staff's carefully prepared and over-elaborate work. . . . I am not sure we have the *best* syllabus yet.' With the zeal of an evangelist he assumed that everyone else shared his own beliefs, and to point the way he pinned up a quotation from A.A. Milne in his office. 'The third-rate mind is only happy when it is thinking with the majority. A second-rate mind is only happy when it is thinking with the minority. A first-rate mind is only happy when it is thinking.' But by then de Guingand had moved on, and the directing staff left did not take kindly to the implication that he was the only one with a first-rate mind.

He came across as personally ambitious, and they resented the way he would correct them in front of students, or in his subtle cat-and-mouse way lure them into making mistakes in public which he would immediately point out. He made no allowances, met nobody halfway, and deployed sarcasm more frequently than charm. His narcissism was more evident than ever and his fastidiousness about his clothes and appearance alienated many, including the previously impressed

Richardson. As Commandant, Chink's vanity was as pronounced as when he had been a student at Camberley, and the recent sharp drop in his income threw him back to a thrift he did not care to explain. He had little to spend on uniforms, and to eke out his pay he wore battledress whenever he could. In due course he moved out of the hotel to a room in the school to save £10 a month.

But the students saw a more pleasant man, and his lectures were popular. 'We were better staff officers after three months at Haifa than a year at Camberley,' summed up one graduate who would become a full general, John Hackett. 'The latter we felt were boy scouts in comparison. I learned so much there that I felt quite able to face huge demands.' Chink did not endear himself to all students, however. Some, like the future field marshal Lord Carver, recoiled from him and considered him dangerously exhibitionist. But away from his polished manner on the platform, behind the confident tone and compelling gestures, Chink was uneasy about holding court, and suffering from a new and painful self-doubt.

'Today,' he agonised before putting on the mask, 'I am saying goodbye to the students. Here is one of the many matters in which I fail. I cannot bear pep talks, either to give or to receive.' 'Wish I was a real one-piece human being and not a two-piece person with each piece watching the other to see what a mess it is making,' he confessed after a long afternoon lecture. 'Today was the kind of day in which one definitely listens with detachment to oneself speaking and thinks "What a damn silly thing to say."' He missed Estelle's no-nonsense approach, which had kept introspection at bay before, and the unaccustomed solitude brought on bouts of self-loathing that no one irritated – or charmed – by his confident exterior detected. Complex, prone to melancholia, he worked himself harder still and expected the same dedication from everyone else.

On behalf of the students as much as for his own interest, he longed to study the fighting in Egypt at first hand: lessons from the battlefield, as this was called in the curriculum. And he did not have too long to wait. In spite of Wavell's high command, their taciturn accord picked up where it had left off as soon as he reported to him in Cairo and adjusted to the difference nine years had made. Wavell's hair was thinner, the lines in his face etched deeper, but he was as pugnaciously thickset as before and brushed the matter of rank aside. Chink felt he himself had changed the most; he was no longer the buoyant second in charge but an outsider – 'a caretaker and a pedagogue' – and the uncomfortable sensation took some getting used to. But Wavell knew him far too well not to pick up his frustration, and promptly put him at his ease by saying he would be calling on his good judgement often. On 9 October he stopped Chink as he was about to leave and asked him to look into the feasibility of a Western Desert offensive against the Italians. It was the instruction he most wanted to hear.

Between 9 and 24 October he visited each unit of the Western Desert Force and talked at length with O'Connor, their rapport as effortless as it had been on the Swiss holiday. His pleasure at meeting him again, after years of working with less compatible men, intensified the exhilaration of planning tactically at last, and as O'Connor had recommended him for SD2 he knew they thought alike. Happily he drove about Mersa Matruh, pored over maps and aerial photographs, conjectured and analysed, and came to the conclusion that taking on the massive Italian Tenth Army was not as mad as it seemed. Reporting back to Cairo, he told Wavell that it would be practicable, but only if it was carried out before the Italians reached Mersa Matruh. Without a word Wavell nodded and reached into a drawer for an order already written out, authorising a five-day raid with the same proviso. Chink's dart of envy at O'Connor's chance vanished at Wavell's parting command. He was to drop everything on receipt of a personal message and go to assist O'Connor with the planning.

He bounded back to Haifa, where the directing staff resented his obvious attention elsewhere. His absence was attributed to opportunism, the desert excursion no more than an excuse to be on the spot to take over if someone happened to be killed in battle. He could make no mention of Wavell's confidence, but nor could he give any indication of the chief reason for his air of suppressed excitement, which had nothing to do with the army at all. He was falling wrenchingly, elementally, in love.

'At least there is someone in the dining room worth looking at,' he had written to Estelle on his first lonely night in the Windsor Hotel, but after that he had taken care not to mention the matter again. Alone at a table near him each evening sat a lovely blonde in her twenties, and as meal followed meal he assessed her over a book propped in front of his plate. Her innate dress sense delighted him and so did the mystery, since she was far too attractive to be on her own. Each evening his eyes sought her out from the doorway, but as Commandant he could make no move without gossip, and the crowded room was full of observers. But at a party held a week before his first trip to the Western Desert he spotted her among a crowd of younger officers and when the lights were suddenly extinguished by an Italian bombing raid, used the chaos for a quick introduction.

Her name was Eve Nott and that appealed to his sense of destiny: Estelle, Elaine, and now Eve with, he learned with a twinge of fatalism, her own small daughter Elizabeth, who was the same age Elaine had been when he met Estelle. Continuing to play the commandant in front of his students he kept his distance, and let her be swept off to a dance. Alone, he sipped the pink gin he now favoured and lit up a cheroot, feeling every one of his forty-five years.

He had not been faithful to Estelle, but none of his three affairs had threatened his marriage and he had ended each one as soon as he was bored. For the past three years there had been no one else, because in the small circles abroad he had not wanted Estelle to be subjected to malicious innuendo. And as long as he remained confident of eventual army fulfilment he had been content enough. Wryly aware of lost illusions, he thought a great deal about Eve Nott, and finding her absent from the dining room on his return from Mersa Matruh, he made discreet enquiries. Her room, he discovered, had been next to his own all the time. The small basement area shared a single door for access, and he began to monitor her night life possessively, unable to sleep till he heard her come in. On 1 November he gathered up his courage and invited her to bring her daughter with her for a picnic on the beach.

If Eve had been exciting when dressed, in her swimsuit the dusting of blonde hair on her brown skin tantalised him, and he was delighted that she chose not to shave beneath her arms, so setting herself apart from other European women, and from Estelle. Five-year-old Elizabeth splashed in the sea, and the hands of the clock raced backwards as he basked in the novelty of being teased once more. That evening it was Eve who came to his room, saying she felt unwell. He poured her a brandy and sat her on his sofa, ready to prompt adroitly. Her husband, he found out, was a junior officer serving in North Africa who knew nothing of the complicated affair – her second, she confided, in six months – that was making her so unhappy. He was an attentive listener and in no mood to force the pace; to travel hopefully, as he had always agreed with Victor, was usually the better part. She showed him the small scar beneath her chin that was the only mark from a recent case of smallpox and told him at length about the doctor packing her in mud to protect her.

In the morning Wavell's promised summons was delivered, and he knocked on her door at once. 'The moment when I told you I might have to go away to Dick and you came across the room into my arms really clinched matters,' he wrote eagerly from the desert. 'For we were not then lovers, we had never kissed even, and that was the first physical acknowledgement of each other.... We've thoroughly awakened each other in a way I never expected to happen to me, and that sort of awakenedness doesn't go to sleep again. This is the first time in my life that I have been the greater lover of the two and I find the experience desperately strange and extremely disconcerting.' It was a sexual revelation, and he was still stunned that she should respond to him in a city packed with younger men. His maturity, however, was his strongest card.

At twenty-eight Eve was tired of being married to a man of her own age, and more than ready for adventure with someone older. She was used to getting her own way because she was the youngest, prettiest child of a rich family, pampered and indulged. Her parents had divorced when she was fourteen, and she had sided with her father, who found her irresistible and treated her as an adult. His influence remained the stronger, and she had inherited his iron will and capacity for self-deception. He preached stringent socialism and lived in luxury in Park Lane. Eve professed a dedication to world good and lived for herself. She was a flirt and men adored her. Most women distrusted her, and the few female friends she had were expected to give uncritical devotion. Housework and cooking were something to be done by others, confidences made amusing small talk, and every man was fair game. She could not have been more unlike Estelle. She was quick, intelligent and completely self-absorbed. She also had a vivid imagination.

He believed her when she said in her breathy, debby voice that she had been forced to leave her husband because he drank, and had walked alone with Elizabeth across the desert. In Cairo she had had to shoot an Arab gardener because he was climbing in through her ground-floor army accommodation window to rape her, and to avoid a scandal she had been hastily moved to Haifa where no one knew what to do with her. She always slept with a jewelled pistol under her pillow, she explained; at least, she had till it was confiscated. The tale was better than he had hoped for and he was captivated, telling her something of his own life in return. They reflected a delicious image back to each other. He saw the perfect sensual and mental companion. She saw a brilliant brigadier who needed her as his inspiration. He never questioned her portrayal of herself as a victim, and loved the protectiveness she brought out in him, as well as the intoxication of so much becoming possible. 'Our little son,' he heard her whisper after they made love for the first time. It was indelible, as much later he suspected she had known it would be.

'I found in you something I thought I had said goodbye to forever – my boyhood again,' he wrote from O'Connor's camp.

I should theoretically be able to dispose of such distressing and inconvenient obsessions with a laugh and a shrug, but enormously powerful forces have hold of me. I have always before played for safety and avoided giving myself completely for fear of hurt, kept some armour on and sentries out, however secure the position appeared. . . . The first reaction was to release a very tied up sense of fun – just to talk to you meant laughter. Estelle cares for me a great deal but I doubt whether all her love and caring would help her to sustain the bubble-over of conversation which I fizz with when with you.

The new perspective showed him and Estelle up as a childless couple tagging through a daily round in friendliness and security, with little in common. 'Both becoming middle-aged and lacklustre. I'm sure this is exactly what Estelle hopes to happen, just quiet and comfort in Bellamont, the occasional trip to Dublin, visiting friends, shooting. Well, perhaps I could have done it if I hadn't met you. But how is it possible now, with every sort of adventure calling us?' After the zest of the second visit to O'Connor there were only a few days together before Eve and Elizabeth were despatched with the rest of the British women and children in Haifa to safer accommodation in South Africa, giving them less than three weeks in all. 'Only responsibilities which I cannot evade without cruelty will keep me from you,' he promised, distraught. 'I am ready to walk on bare feet across the world to you forgetful of any obligation or duty, decency or honour. . . . What in Heaven's name are either of us going to do?'

He began a stream of letters, alive only in his room with her photograph within touching distance. She had been the teacher sexually but here the power was reversed, and he projected all his charm, terrified of losing her. 'I want so much to write to you all the time. I ought to see more people, of course. I suppose a decent brigadier would call on the commissioner and entertain, but everyone but you bores me. I daresay my reputation is that of a conceited, casual, offhand, standoffish blighter who thinks himsef too good for local society, which isn't true.' He left parties early and turned down the customary New Year Fancy Dress Ball at the Haifa Club, writing compulsively to her instead. Re-reading *Jurgen*, he found her there too, beside his distancing from Estelle.

'I only seem to be reaching maturity,' he marvelled, 'having lived in suspended animation for 15 years.' He told her of his longing to walk the Silk Road and climb the Andes, to lose himself in modern poetry and opera again. He found a local bookshop and read widely once more, and works by Virginia Woolf and André Maurois jostled with studies of philosophy and sociology on his desk one January evening in 1941. 'I sip from each like a bee from a bowl of flowers. How unformed my brain is, and how incapable of close and delicate reasoning years of soldiering have made it. I sit puzzling away like a Simla rickshaw coolie trying to learn to read.' At a dinner party he met Freya Stark and reported before sleeping that she was plain but fun. Everything led back to Eve. He sent her reading lists and she was more responsive than Estelle had been. Love revitalised him. He looked at contemporaries and was horrified at how old they had become.

Her letters back were like an electric shock. In between descriptions of new admirers in South Africa and complaints of ostracism by the other women, she sowed seeds – on fertile ground – about conspiracy against him. His duty, she urged, was to post-war society, not to an army which did not appreciate or deserve to have him. 'I am clearing my mind fast,' he replied obediently, 'and becoming left and more left.' It occurred to him that service to society would justify the hurt his love for her was bound to cause, in the manner of a prisoner paying his debt; quite what form this would take neither of them defined. His childhood dream of knighthood made the notion doubly persuasive. Despising wealth, fighting wrong and defending the oppressed would be completed by worshipping the beauty Eve provided. But her lack of a sense of humour had been camouflaged by flirtatiousness. Already she was liable to take offence if not deferred to all the time, and when a stiff letter accused him of implying that she was limited, he had to reach for his pen at once. 'Did I really say that? Well, so is the ocean and so according to the physicists is space, so you are in good company. In fact, all the best companies are limited. . . .' He failed to see the danger sign.

Alone at Haifa he wrestled with his conscience, loath to hurt Estelle.

It is so enticingly easy to become slippered. I have only to think to see the lamplit library of Bellamont lit by an enormous fire. Myself slippered after shooting, a cold wet night out of doors. 6 p.m. and the wireless on. Alcohol lurking an obedient demon in the background. Great curtains drawn across high windows and all the shabby comfort of a well-used evening room. No! Lovely as it all would be, it isn't for me. . . . Estelle has been so kind and is so dear, but should we fade childlessly into a Darby and Joan inertia? My role would be to grow old in an atmosphere of kindness and care, a pottering purposeless background to E's fulfilment. Bless her. There is nothing 99% of men would like better, but to me the prospect appals. It is awfully unfair of me to say all this, more than unfair – unjust, to someone who has spent 14 years of her energy on my dull self. Bless her again. I am very, very fond of her and I hate the idea of making her unhappy – *hate it.* I feel most desperately selfish, but I simply can't die in my socks while still walking about at my age. I understand why men die when they retire. The world would be flat.

But as the relationship with Eve grew more insistent, so did the urge to be honest with Estelle. He felt divorced from her and knew she continued trustingly as his wife in India, smoothing his career path through everyone she met. If he really hated duplicity, he asked himself, why was he doing what he most despised? But then wasn't it selfish to tell her now with the risk that he might be subsequently killed in action? He decided to put off confession until after the war.

But it was naive to suppose that no one would find out. Twice that year he lectured Smuts's officers in South Africa as an excuse to stay with Eve, and he was too much in love to be discreet. On his return to Haifa after the second trip he was hailed by a man among a noisy group whose wife was also down there, and realised from the innuendo that his secret was out. Kenneth Bols, Elaine's new husband, was posted to the Middle East and called to see him unexpectedly. Chink found him in his hotel room appreciatively studying Eve's studio portrait, and took it from him without explanation; he despised Bols, and had done everything he could to prevent the marriage. De Guingand probed with his hunch for intrigue, and Chink told him everything in confidence. De Guingand was very understanding, but soon far more people knew than Chink assumed.

It was Wavell who broke the news to Estelle, when he called to see her on return to India. She took it in her stride, and mentioned it in her next letter. 'He wrote back about how annoyed he was with his job,' she explained once, 'and said "You see, Baggage, Eve has nothing to do with the case. She wiles away the dreary hours of the night." I'm quite serious that I didn't mind. They *all* had girlfriends, and I was happy for him because it was the thing; no one knew how long the war would go on. When Archie told me, I wrote out a list for her, with all his favourite things on it so she would make him comfortable – the way he liked his shoes cleaned, his shirts ironed, his favourite recipes.' But Chink's clumsy attempt at reassurance was dishonest. He was pledged to a future that did not include her.

And, as so often, he took pride in being different. 'Emancipated as our love affair is,' he instructed Eve, 'our responsibility developed from the first time we admitted its existence. Otherwise we will come to look on ourselves as just another pair of physically minded people dressing up their philandering in high-flown sentiments. Hateful.' But conventional army philosophy accepted a pair of physically minded lovers – if they were discreet. What it could not accept was the breaking up of a marriage. To abandon one's wife was considered appalling, and Estelle's loyalty was so well known that it was widely believed he owed much of his career to her. A blatant affair with a junior officer's wife when her husband was at the front broke another unspoken rule. It is ironic that Chink was about to become infamous as a 'ladies man', because he could not approve of philandering. 'Orthodoxy with orthodox monogamy as its overt expression,' he hooted to Eve. 'We rarely become adult in the way that Latins and Levantines are. I thank God that I am not as other men are – a little, thanks to contact with Hem and his left bank clique.' Conveniently he forgot his own strong reaction when Hemingway left Hadley for Pauline.

Wandering out of a Cairo bookshop one morning, a copy of Julian Huxley's *Philosophy and Living* tucked under his arm, he was accosted by a palmist, and he hesitated. His unusually long index finger indicated purpose and idealism, the patter began, but also lack of interest in money and personal gain. The man had his full attention at once. Confused patterns on his upper palm, the reading continued, pointed to a troubled life. 'He was insistent on this,' he wrote, describing the encounter to Eve that evening. ' "Family troubles.

Crises in your family life. It is all there in your hand." ' The loss of a great friend was mentioned – Lindsay Barrett – and the small lines branching off the line of life indicated wide-ranging opportunities.

He wrote out as much of the conversation as he could, before he forgot it. ' "You received sudden promotions between 40 and 44." "But that is all over for me now." "Oh no, there is more to come. You are never content till you have thought a subject out to the end. You are kind to the wrong people, but if a person harms you, you never forget it. The area X is higher than the area Y. General Wavell attacks, and I am sure his area Y is big. You are a defender. I would give you a city to defend, not to attack. You have two children." "No." "But of course you have." "My wife is childless." "How long have you been married?" "Fourteen years." "Well, you will have two children. Not one in a thousand has lines like you. Take two regiments and look at all their hands. . . . Take my card and you will remember what I say and write to me someday to say that I told you the truth." ' Here was the permission he had been looking for.

He began to think practically. Amy had never stopped criticising Estelle, so she would be sympathetic. And why not? Everyone else had what they wanted. Reggie had been knighted and was now Governor of Burma, where he appeared content. 'Would Doreen's £7000 per annum have made me a civilised, respectable member of society in place of the restless tilter at windmills I have remained?' he speculated on hearing the news, after writing to remind him that he had once given him his cast-off clothes. 'Amusing to think that two people I have known so well will shortly be immersed in all the pomp of oriental rulers – entry through double doors, the national anthem and every wish anticipated. How I'd chuckle.' Victor, rising high in the navy, had married a seventeen-year-old when quite old enough to know better and now had a small son. Horrocks had been given his own brigade in England, under Montgomery. Even Basil Liddell Hart had recently remarried, after an earlier divorce. 'I hate this childlessness,' he resolved. 'Somehow I must make it possible to have and maintain those two unborn children which my hand shows so clearly.'

The bond with Estelle, however, was not lightly broken. One night he dreamed so realistically of India that he woke at 3 a.m., shaken. He had been at a railway station and a bearer brought Mac the terrier to him. 'I felt his cold black nose against my cheek and his rough strong coat and taut little muscles,' he recorded next morning. 'And he was so pleased to see me, the little chap, and then they took him away.' He was convinced that the dog must be dying because as soon as he went back to sleep he dreamed of him once more. A few nights later he jerked awake, and lay in the dark, mourning. Estelle's next letter was to inform him that Mac had died that night, and that the vet had suddenly been sent for on the previous occasion. 'Such grief over what I knew,' he wrote to Eve, 'and I am so sad for Estelle. We met on common ground in the happiness we shared in our dogs who were a substitute for our children and a very powerful link between us. I can't bear to think of her loneliness.' But it was not enough to make him do more than glance back, and the timing was to be decisive. He had antagonised nearly everyone who knew them as a couple, and not only was he dispensing with a winning advocate, but from now on he would be relying on inappropriate advice. Lovely and exciting as Eve was, she could not supply the balance he had taken for granted.

But in the Western Desert everything was fresh. Rushing apologetically into O'Connor's underground operations room, now at Maarten Baggush, on 25 November, after being held up on the way by a broken fan belt which Egyptian mechanics had taken twenty-four hours to fix, he put the emotional complications out of his mind. Dick O'Connor knew nothing of his love life and all that mattered was the planning of Wavell's raid. Here personalities were unimportant and appearances did not matter. The diminutive O'Connor was dressed for action in comfortable corduroy trousers, well-worn leather jerkin, faded cap and tartan scarf. In the circumstances his conspicuous Italian Silver Medal for valour, awarded in 1918, boded well. O'Connor's authority was low key but absolute, bringing out the best as usual in everyone. For once Chink was aware of being among like-minded friends.

He was glad to see the acerbic 'Sandy' Galloway again, his predecessor at Haifa, because they had worked well together at Camberley in 1937. Galloway was also on loan, being Brigadier General Staff to the Commander of British Troops in Egypt, General Maitland 'Jumbo' Wilson. And Chink also approved of John Harding, O'Connor's BGS, whom he had got to like in the Student Drag at the Staff College ten years earlier still. Gatehouse, black beret at an angle, was there in charge of his tanks, and he recognised Beresford Peirse – 'no Napoleon, but a very genuine personality' – of 4th Indian Division, also once at Blackdown. Everything seemed to be coming together.

In 1946 Freddie de Guingand was to enjoy a post-war correspondence with Basil Liddell Hart in which the subject of Chink inevitably came up. 'Chink certainly produced a number of excellent ideas,' replied de Guingand patronisingly. 'But he also provided a very large number of others which were anything but sound. He was so prolific of ideas that it was inevitable that few would be a real winner.' Liddell Hart put his finger on the factor de Guingand had missed. 'He jumps to ideas so quickly,' he wrote, 'that he is often inclined to propound before he has weighed them up properly. But there is great potential value in such stimulation.' In preparations for the attack on the Italian Tenth Army O'Connor made proper use of Chink's creativity by sifting out the impractical, as Wavell had intended. And the winner very quickly emerged.

They had agreed on his first visit that the chain of Italian camps at Sidi Barrani was vulnerable because they were spaced too far apart, and they had discarded O'Connor's initial plan to fight around Matruh in favour of striking unexpectedly at them at Sidi Barrani. Now he was briefed that something more daring than a five-day operation was under way. A week earlier the entrance gap between the two most accessible camps had been seized – 'the foot in the door' – and the follow-up attack was about to be finalised. His instructions were to observe the dress rehearsal, referred to by them all as Training Exercise Number One, next morning. He was not at all pleased to learn that Messervy, Beresford Peirse's second in command, was responsible for its design; Messervy's tactical thinking was unlikely to have improved since his time in India.

Watching the exercise, he recognised the textbook method from the official pamphlet *The Division in Attack*. It was quite unsuitable for the lightning move necessary if they were to achieve surprise. In Messervy's plan two hours were spent waiting in daylight at the assembly area while artillery registered the enemy defences, followed by a frontal attack by tanks and infantry on foot in classic Western Front style. Protesting to Gatehouse that there was nothing to stop the 'unfortunate Indians' from being bombed to pieces in the assembly area, he sought out O'Connor and took it apart. O'Connor tossed the ball back by asking how he would go about it.

Chink studied the replica of the 'damn camp' from every angle, before joining the others down in the operations room. There would be less danger of air attack if instead of approaching from a distance they pounced directly alongside, using the Italians themselves as cover. But a new problem was revealed by the air photographs he called for, which showed a minefield in the direct path of the infantry. The answer was to be found in the same aerial shots. All Italian wheeltracks led to the well-protected north-west corner of the camp, showing the path through the mines. 'Why the hell not?' he was heard to muse. If Gatehouse could get his tanks within striking distance, he suggested at last, they should go in there before daylight with lorried infantry at their heel, and simultaneously let go with an unregistered barrage to hide the noise of the tanks, achieving panic rather than destruction.

It was too unorthodox to pass at the Staff College, but Gatehouse said his tanks could do it and after working the details out Chink informed O'Connor that it was really only a matter of getting troops into position on time. 'It was a sound plan,' O'Connor said in 1960. 'A bit complicated perhaps, but I had every reason to rely on my commanders, their staff and the troops.' Chink's finished paper 'Assault on a Desert Camp' was accepted by Wilson at a conference the following evening, on condition that the first wave of infantry reached the perimeter within five minutes of the leading tank. He flew down to Wavell with the draft, and Wavell approved. Gleefully over dinner he toasted the 'round the back of the arse' attack with de Guingand, but to his chagrin was ordered straight back to Teltsch House. 'I reached Dick's HQ on Sunday and since then I have been busy with this and that,' he wrote guardedly to Eve from his Cairo hotel before leaving. 'I am gradually getting a lot of my ideas into circulation in these parts which pleases me, if only because of my powerlessness at Haifa.'

But his reputation was spreading, to the extent that he was already being described by some as a nanny with the candle, visiting children in the dark. Those superseded were less appreciative. There was also an increasing number who resented his sudden appearances and the way he was treated as Apollo the divine messenger by HQ in the field. Messervy had been made to lose face again, and he chalked up one more grievance.

On 7 December 1940, using Chink's unorthodox plan, the Western Desert Force attacked Nibeiwa camp before breakfast and the operation went like clockwork. They swept on to take the next two Italian camps, Tummar West and Tummar East, using the same method, and then all the others, one by one. Operation Compass had begun. Within three days O'Connor's men had captured Sidi Barrani and taken 38,300 prisoners, 237 guns, 73 tanks and over 100 vehicles, at the cost of 634 casualties, killed, wounded and missing. It was the first British military victory of the war.

Chink was ecstatic. 'One cannot help feeling the excitement,' he wrote on 12 December, 'as news comes in of more and more prisoners and enormous captures of weapons and gear. It is so wildly beyond our hopes. I curse my stars that I was not permitted to take an actual part in it, but that is the personal side which doesn't really count. What matters is the immense effect the victory is bound to have. All the little quislings who have been fence-sitting between Cairo and Calcutta will be busy climbing down onto our side. . . . The chaps here are frightfully pleased and almost too excited to work.'

An appreciation of the value of post-mortems was one of the most useful legacies of his time with Wavell, and he wrote at once to O'Connor – 'My dear Dick' – to point this out.

> I only hope that you and your leaders and staff are not too exhausted and I also hope that the Force has not suffered too many casualties. If things have gone as I hoped they would, that should not be so. It will be a matter for regret to my dying day that I had no part in, in my opinion, the first truly modern battle. . . . As such, a full analytical study of all its aspects. . . . should be made at once and passed around the outer Army. . . . As soon as your headquarters are less busy I would very much like to visit you again – walk the course of the battle, vet the orders and get on with the first rough historical analysis. . . . I am grossly underworked and in any case I want the material for the school here.

A cryptic note from Wavell promised that he would not be kept at Haifa if the chance came for closer connection with operations, and with that he had to be content. Remnants of the Italian Tenth Army recrossed their own frontier and took cover in the Libyan coastal fortress of Bardia, which was promptly encircled by O'Connor's tanks. 'We seem to have the better part of two divisions penned up,' Chink reported gloatingly to Eve. 'The only reason why we might draw off would be shortage of water and difficulties of supply. Germany is still strong and capable of much damage but she has lost this war inevitably. Isn't that a bold prophecy for 1941?'

Dining indifferently in the Windsor one evening, a void without her, he tried to concentrate on philosophy while two couples talked golf loudly at each other across the room. Closing his book in annoyance, he wondered what the golfers would say it they knew about Eve or, as he reflected in his room, 'that the contents under my hat gave Dick the key to the doors of a place initialled SB'. It had been a justification of all his conclusions about imaginative thinking and speed, and if he had been delayed one day longer by the listless mechanics repairing his car, he told himself, the battle would have had a very different result. He had to force himself to concentrate on college affairs, and resented his job even more after O'Connor wrote to break it to him that he had been overruled about having Chink as his BGS when last choosing one. 'What the devil are they playing at? I couldn't ask for a better job.'

Precise information was hard to come by at his distance, and he could not understand why the pursuit was now slowing. But the unexpected triumph of Compass had brought in a political factor beyond the range of his comprehension. Conflicting claims on Wavell's small army had led to 4th Indian Division being switched down to the Sudan as soon as success was judged sufficient, and the Western Desert Force was now halved. But Bardia cracked at last on 6 January, yielding 45,000 prisoners, 462 guns and 129 tanks, and British armour lumbered on west to pin down further Italian resistance in the fallback fortress of Tobruk. Here they were compelled to wait until 6th Australian Division, replacements for the Indians, caught up with them. Tobruk fell on 22 January, the most exciting prize yet.

Envisaging it all from Haifa, Chink swept mentally on as far as Benghazi and beyond. His prophecy about pushing the Italians out of Libya appeared to be on the verge of fulfilment. Reading that his *bête noire* Winston Churchill, now Prime Minister and Minister of Defence, was praising the 'daring and scope of the original conception' in the House of Commons, he forgave him everything. And at last Wavell's message came, taking him at his word. He was to observe and report the campaign from Sidi Barrani onwards, which he interpreted as picking up progress where it stood and studying previous lessons when time allowed. Flying down to Cairo on 26 January, he drove on through dust storms for forty-eight hours to reach O'Connor's makeshift headquarters in an aircraft hut at Bomba, well beyond Tobruk. 'Directly one pokes one's nose into one corner of war,' he noted contentedly, 'one ceases to see any other part.'

Although the small force had come so far against the odds, not everything was going well. O'Connor smouldered at the escape of Babini, one of Graziani's remaining generals, and his resources were draining away. Abruptly Chink was plunged into events himself, and was present on 30 January with the advance Australian troops when they entered Derna, which barred the main road that looped around the headland to Benghazi. The knowledge that it was only a feint to make the Italians believe the main British attack was going to be along that route, instead of across the interior as O'Connor intended, made it no less momentous. Afterwards he warned O'Connor that Italian resistance was so demoralised that unless they moved fast their prey was going to slip away out of reach.

At Bomba HQ that evening, beside Harding and the commander of 7th Armoured Division, Michael Creagh, O'Connor brought him up to date. The situation was not that simple. Only fifty tanks remained runners, petrol was low and ammunition was limited. Interception of the retreating Italians would involve a 150-mile race across atrocious desert going and a greatly outnumbered battle at the far end. But the alternative was to limit themselves to following up enemy retirement, allowing the Axis threat in North Africa to remain unresolved. In the end the decision was made for them by enemy decrypts, when it became clear that the Italian command believed they would never risk the cross-country option. Chink was despatched at speed to obtain Wavell's necessary approval.

Shown into the Commander-in-Chief's office, he found Wavell at his most inscrutable. Sparse hair combed neatly back, blocky figure giving nothing away, he arranged and rearranged unsharpened pencils in parade ground drill on his desk as he listened, prompting him with 'Yes, Chink, I see,' at intervals. At the end he met Chink's gaze. 'Tell Dick he can go on, and wish him luck from me. He has done well.' Jubilant, Chink remembered to pass on O'Connor's apology for Babini's escape. 'Tell Dick not to fret. It is contretemps like those that add interest to that very dull business, war.' Chink felt more affection for him at that moment than ever before.

'Chink has returned with your heartening message,' O'Connor wired on 3 February. 'Thank you so much. The situation has now changed and I have determined to go forward with what we have at present, without waiting. . . .' Air reconnaissance had corroborated intercepts picked up during Chink's absence which revealed that Graziani's intention was to pull out of Benghazi in Cyrenaica to defend Tripolitania, the other half of Libya. If the Italians reached the bottleneck of Agheila first they would be able to slam that door behind them. At 0830 hours on 4 February the tanks of 7th Armoured Division roared off, and Wavell flew up briefly, signalling to Dill in

London on his return that if all went well they would be at the gates of Benghazi within the next few days. Chink was ordered to cover events, and O'Connor turned to him as Hemingway and Auchinleck had done.

The staff car with its two passengers bounced and jarred as it accelerated after 7th Armoured Division, and O'Connor's tenacity reminded Chink of a terrier ratting. They were following a grim paperchase of broken-down British tanks, beaten by the rough ground, and O'Connor swore quietly as they came upon each one, at one point wondering aloud if they could possibly succeed. They spent the night inland at Mechili and were off again shortly after dawn in a convoy of three vehicles. An armoured car doubled as escort and wireless contact behind O'Connor, and Chink now brought up the rear. 'Unfortunately,' as O'Connor wrote later with his customary restraint, 'both the armoured car and the second car broke down in the stretch of bad going.... As it was essential I should get to the Armoured Division as soon as possible, I was forced to leave Captain Dent, my a.d.c., behind with the breakdowns while Brigadier Dorman-Smith and I continued on our way in my car.'

Cut off from developments, monosyllabic, they drove through an interminable day. Their greatest worries were whether 7th Armoured Division would beat the Italians to the coast road, and whether their present car, too, would break down. 'Most exciting,' Chink said subsequently. At 7 p.m. they caught up with 7th Armoured Division HQ at Wazi Aziz, where their anxiety was puckered further by nearby rifle fire. It turned out to be nothing more than Free French troops making safe the Italian container bombs that were strewn like maiming thermos flasks along the way, and Creagh came out to meet them, smiling broadly. The Italians had been trumped with only half an hour to spare, and a safety net was strung out in the form of a second ambush at Antelat, further down the cross-country road. At Beda Fomm, beyond Benghazi, Italian columns and trucks were pinned down, and over 5000 prisoners had already been taken.

In the night 7th Armoured Division HQ moved up to Antelat, and O'Connor and Chink went with it, catnapping there in the car. At daylight drenching rain slowed the track as they zigzagged back to Mechili to find Corps HQ, and then forward again as far as Msus. 'No woman counted,' he wrote shortly afterwards. 'It was a stark world where men were happy being themselves, monosexual. Kipling has it in "The Passionless Passion for Slaughter." ' Benghazi surrendered in the afternoon. They slept again in the car without rugs, cold and stiff, and before dawn O'Connor was on the road again.

'The dawns over the Libyan desert over these last hectic days have been incredibly beautiful,' Chink scribbled for Eve's benefit. 'Lovelier because of the storms they carried with them.' Breakfast, after a breathtaking sunrise, was a cold sausage eaten absently as they monitored the fighting in the distance at Beda Fomm, parked beside 7th Armoured Division's command vehicle. At 9 a.m. a signaller handed a message to O'Connor which he scanned and passed to Chink, saying that they should inform Wavell. The entire Italian Tenth Army had surrendered.

'He took the message pad from me,' he wrote later. ' "How do we start this very unusual message?" "How about 'Fox killed in the open'?" I said. In his neat handwriting he started to write. . . . He turned to me. "By the way, is Mussolini a hunting man? If not, he'll need an interpreter after all." "I don't know," I said. "But he won't need any diagrams to know what's happened to him." ' The extent of the triumph was incredible. The tiny Western Desert Force had swept forward over 400 miles, taken 130,000 prisoners and destroyed an army of ten divisions poised to take Egypt and the vital oilfields. Their tactics had been unorthodox and daring, and their casualties low. Never, as Foreign Secretary Anthony Eden remarked in London when Bardia fell, had so much been surrendered by so many to so few.

The two men drove on to inspect their prize, bumping twenty miles over uneven ruts. 'It was bright clear daylight,' Chink wrote afterwards, 'with the air full of sea smells across a veldt just flowering with asphodel and covered with herds of gazelles and flocks of great slow-flying bustards.' O'Connor drove in silence, and Chink's curiosity freewheeled. He longed to know what it felt like to be a successful commander, and eventually could not keep the question to himself. 'Dick rubbed his ear silently. "Chink, I would never consider any commander entirely successful until he had restored the situation after a serious defeat and a long retreat." '

Turning on to the main Via Balbia, 'the Fascist autostrada of North Africa', they passed hundreds of abandoned vehicles and overtook an unending convoy of lorries, bonnet to tailboard, taking troops and Italian prisoners north to Benghazi. Buses of weeping women and children were in the line, and a priest bowed as they drew level with him. The poignancy and transience of their success hit Chink. 'One knew this was ephemeral, and that the same dawn and the same quiet antelope owned plains had seen the passage and end of other armies.' O'Connor broke into his reverie to ask what they should do next, a rhetorical question as both knew they were of the same mind. 'I knew what he wanted me to reply – go all out for as far as we can get.'

When they reached the scene of the surrender at Beda Fomm they found that the last Italian tank had been knocked out within a few feet of the Rifle Brigade officers' mess tent. It was still there, like a collapsed elephant. Inside the tent's flimsy canvas walls a hive of makeshift catering sustained a party around hastily erected trestle tables; they had one celebration drink and drove on. The captured Italian officers had been taken to two villas at Solluch, where O'Connor intended to enquire about their comfort. Watching him as he did so, Chink told himself that he had not been wrong about the resemblance to King Arthur at Maximilian's tomb.

At Ghenimes later that afternoon, halfway between Beda Fomm and Benghazi, both agreed that Tripoli – Tunis too, given luck – was now theirs for the taking with the extra Italian transport if they could send off quick pursuit via Sirte. But O'Connor was unable to act independently because Wilson's appointment as Governor-General of Cyrenaica took effect from that day. And Wilson's whereabouts were vague. On the off-chance that he might be making for Barce on the far side of Benghazi, Chink was despatched on his second diplomatic mission of the week with instructions to drive to Tobruk and get a message through to Wavell from there if he failed to locate him. Pausing only to wish O'Connor luck – 'and thank him for the hunt' – he was off.

Barce was partially demolished when he reached it the following morning, and there were no British troops to be seen. He combed the town for a second time, and found Wilson pulling up in a borrowed armoured car, having outstripped his signals. Dishevelled and mud-died to the eyes, Wilson gave permission at once but pointed out that Wavell's agreement was necessary too, and until the signals caught up they were out of contact with Cairo. Impelled by the need to get troops through the bottleneck of El Agheila while it was still possible, and so on to Tripoli, Chink did not hesitate. The 160 miles to Tobruk along wrecked roads took him fourteen hours, and he signalled Wavell and was on the Cairo road again as soon as it was light enough to drive the following morning. At 4 a.m. on 11 February, having covered 570 miles in eighteen hours and within five minutes of his usual hotel, the back right-hand tyre punctured. He switched off the engine and sat in the dark, stone tired.

Restored, spruce and expectant, he reported to Wavell's map room at 10 a.m. The greeting was warm, but Wavell's attention was elsewhere. 'You find me busy,' he told Chink, 'with my spring campaign.' He had to look twice at the maps Wavell was indicating before the truth sank in. Libya's familiar outline was gone; in its place he recognised Greece and the Balkans. He did not need to be told that Compass had ground to a halt, and that political needs had taken the decision out of Wavell's hands. In due course he would learn that Churchill had ordered troops to be sent to the aid of Greece, against the advice of the CIGS, in the hope of uniting the Balkan countries against Germany and Italy, and that only the uplift to home morale from Tobruk's capture had gained O'Connor the breathing space to reach Benghazi. The stupidity of the decision, when Mussolini's power in North Africa was so near to being broken, restored all his scorn for Churchill. At the time, infinitely depressed, all he could think about was O'Connor, waiting in the desert and confident of going on. There was no question of being allowed to tell him in person.

Weatherbeaten and half a stone lighter, he flew straight back to Haifa on 13 February. Superstitiously he noted the date; he had left for the First World War on 13 August 1914, docked in Dublin on 13 June 1921, and sailed for Germany on 13 July 1922. The sand in his hair and skin was hard to get out, and tingling under a cold shower next morning the impact of what he had seen struck home. The casualty could have been any army which had allowed itself to become rigid and obsolete, not just the Italians. 'There, but for the grace of God, went the King's Army in India,' he wrote at once. 'And I have no regrets that I made myself disagreeable.' Privately he dared to hope that O'Connor would include him permanently in his team. He had, after all, been wanted as BGS earlier, and there was more likelihood of being called upon now.

For two weeks he honed his operational analysis with its lessons for the future, and added to the report – 'for good measure' – a breakdown of his ideal army, the proportion of weapons and arms readjusted. He took it down to Cairo in person on 1 March, where he met O'Connor and spent two hours with him going over it. O'Connor approved it without alteration. 'I am well on the way to becoming a first-grade Cyrenaian bore,' he wrote cheerfully before going out to dine with the Wavells. 'We gambled magnificently and we pulled it off.'

(*Left*) Chink on leaving Sandhurst, 1913.
(*Above right*) His father, Edward.
(*Below*)1st Bttn, Northumberland Fusiliers
after St Eloi, 27 March 1916. Chink (*in cap,
arrowed*) putting on a good face one week after
hearing of his friend Lindsay Barrett's death.

(*Left*) Hemingway, on crutches, at the time of his first meeting with Chink in Milan, 1918.
(*Above right*) 'Bobbing' at Chamby: Chink steering, Hemingway at rear.

(*Above*) The godson: John Hadley Nicanor – soon to be known as 'Bumby' – on his father's knee. Note the Basque beret.
(*Opposite*) Chink, elegant even for tennis, on leave in Paris to stand as godfather to the Hemingways' son, 1924.

'Chink' – Major-General Eric Dorman-Smith – shortly after his spell as Auchinleck's unofficial Chief of Staff during the First Battle of Alamein, cap defiantly tilted, Cairo, August 1942.

(*Above*) Bellamont Forest,
Chink's family home.
(*Centre*) His mother, Amy.
(*Below*) The three brothers:
Chink (*centre*), Reggie (*left*)
Victor (*right*).

(*Above left*) Wavell, on right, and O'Connor.
(*Above right*) Horrocks.
(*Centre*) Penney.
(*Below left*) Montgomery.
(*Below right*) Sir Alan Brooke.

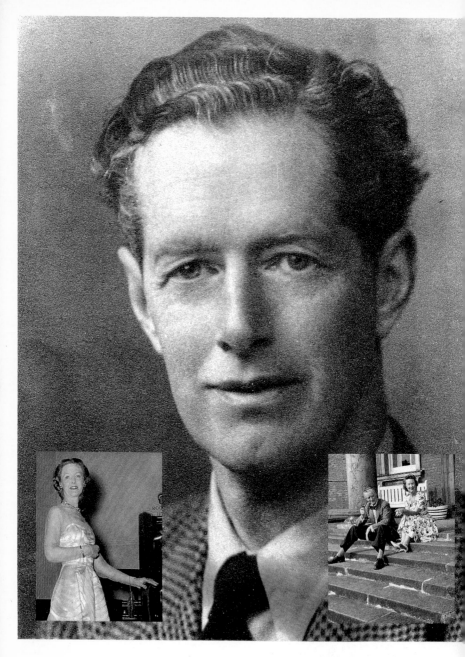

No longer Dorman-Smith but now head of the Irish clan O'Gowan.
In Hemingway's imagination he had evolved into Robert Cantwell,
the hero of *Across the River and Into the Trees*.
(*Inset left*) Eve during those years.
(*Inset right*) Chink and Eve on the steps of Bellamont Forest.

(*Left*) Estelle, the perfect officer's wife.
(*Above right*) Chink, rising high.

ow) Seeds of trouble: in this 1928 Staff College photograph can be seen many of the men who
ld play a decisive role in Chink's future. *From the left, top row:* Angus Collier (4th), Ronald
ney (7th), Oliver Leese (12th), 'Jock' Whiteley (16th), Chink (17th). *Second row down:* Richard
Creery (3rd), John Harding (6th), Robert Bridgeman (11th). *Third row down:* Philip Christison
d), 'Ginger' Hawkesworth (12th). *Fifth row down:* 'Sandy' Galloway (5th), Gerald Templer
th). *Front row:* Bernard Paget (8th), Bernard Montgomery (15th), 'Dick' O'Connor (17th).

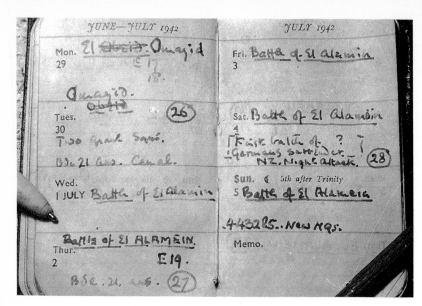

(*Above*) Chink's diary for the crucial week.
(*Below*) Confrontation at Eighth Army TAC HQ. Churchill, hands on
hips, faces Auchinleck (*front right*), Gott (*centre*) and Chink (*at rear*).

But the exaltation did not last. His report was not circulated, and it infuriated him that commanders who would have found it useful did not know of its existence. 'It makes me a little cross,' he wrote, letting off steam to Eve that June, as he brought the report up to date after Battleaxe, a subsequent operation, 'with so much happening since which bears out what I say.' And by that time there was a more personal disappointment which he hugged to himself and blamed on Churchill's poor judgement. The chain of events seemed indisputable. On the day he had failed to get permission to press on to Tripoli a tough, German disciple of the writings of Liddell Hart disembarked in that port, aware that no real resistance could be put up in time if the British came on. Erwin Rommel had been sent for by Hitler after the Beda Fomm surrender to rally the Italians with his own troops, and at first he attacked back cautiously. Finding that the British were concentrating on Greece, Rommel accelerated his counter-attack, and pushed the token Western Desert Force back along the route they had seized such a short time earlier. Appalled at the reverses, Wavell sent O'Connor back to advise his successor, the inexperienced Neame, and on 6 April both British commanders were captured behind enemy lines, as a result of Neame's faulty map-reading.

O'Connor's removal from the skilful, mobile fighting that was beginning in North Africa was a calamity for the British, and it was also a calamity for Chink's career. He would have been valued and fulfilled on O'Connor's staff, and it is fascinating to speculate about results if their partnership had continued. Writing twenty years later, the military historian Ronald Lewin likened their rapid advance to a classic example of the domino effect. What was still not brought out with sufficient clarity, Lewin pointed out, was the extent to which the long chain of successes depended on imaginative daring. 'We have to ask, in fact,' he summed up, 'how things might have been if through caution at the top, the first phase of Compass had failed or – no less disastrous – proved indecisive.'

The same thought had exhilarated Chink once in the braying Windsor dining room. And in that same room, under-utilised and tense in the depressing climate after O'Connor's capture, he was to float even further away from the mainstream. Every time he was about to give up, however, hope tormented him again.

9

Outsider – Insider

'If only I could get a foot in the jamb of the door,' he complained in a typical outburst to Eve, as news of the collapse in Cyrenaica built up.

> But I'm damned if I'm going to be a yes man or toady, or pretend to like men whom I think are crooks just because they might give me promotion or go in on their mutual admiration groups. And I am never, never going to ask anyone for anything. Grand merci NON!!! I wish I wasn't so damned uncompromising. Why did I choose this frustrating profession where all you need to be able to say is Yes Sir, No Sir, Sorry Sir, with an air of optimistic hero-worship, like a schoolgirl with a crush on the games mistress? Ugh! Brains? We just haven't damn well got any. We have personalities and prejudices and pomposities and politics.

So when a telegram – 'Brigadier Dorman-Smith report forthwith Mid East temp duty BGS' – brought unexpected release on the day after his fourth course assembled, he was gone before the directing staff could find adequate language to express their annoyance.

Cairo was humming with servicemen on leave from Libya. His fourth-floor flat overlooked the Gezira polo grounds and tennis courts, and that image of leisure tended to wipe out his pleasure at being able to pick out a distant pyramid at Giza. But apart from the red-and-blue armband he had to wear labelled BGS, which amused him by its similarity to the railway uniform worn by Amy's real father, the job of Brigadier General Staff was the next best thing to being in action. 'I tread like Agag, delicately,' he wrote the day after he arrived; it was the day Mechili fell, Salonika was captured by the Germans, and Churchill commanded that Tobruk be held to the death.

At GHQ ME, he walked straight into a tense atmosphere. On his first day Wavell failed to return from Tobruk on time, where he had flown in response to the news of O'Connor's capture, and it was not till after midnight that a call came through to say the Commander-in-Chief had had to make a forced landing on the far side of the border. Chink's inactivity was over. He was simultaneously detailed to take up instructions for the defence of Tobruk in the morning, a command which brought on the familiar jealousy of other men's success. At the side of Leslie Morshead of 1st Australian Division, the general in charge of the fortress, was John Harding, and in the desert Beresford Peirse was commanding 15th Corps. Both were jobs he longed to have.

The tactics of the indirect approach, as he analysed them in the army Lysander on the noisy three-and-a-half-hour flight, were now being used by Rommel against them; holding Tobruk ought to overstretch German resources and wrest the initiative back. It was impossible to remain envious when exhilarated by the drama of the moment. Not only was the operation order typed on nylon in an acetone container, which he was to break in an emergency to enable the acetone to destroy the order, but the situation waiting for him on the far side of the border was unknown. Touching down briefly at the rear of 13th Corps HQ at Sidi Barrani, the pilot reported back that the RAF were believed to be still holding the Libyan airfield at El Adem, but when they landed there at noon they found it deserted. Taking off again at speed, Tobruk was pointed out to him as an opaque dust storm billowing in the distance.

'I gave that pilot full marks for finding the landing ground,' he wrote later. 'We got down and had to taxi around in the darkness until our wing practically touched a hangar. From the airfield I was taken to Morshead's HQ. He and Harding seemed to have things well in hand.' He went through the orders in detail with both men in the commotion from accurate Luftwaffe dive-bombing, and buzzed back to Cairo at telegraph-pole height, happier than he had been for some time. The tin Lizzie was following the Via Balbia he knew so well, and as it passed over a large group of troops on the road beneath him, many looked up and waved. With a shock he realised they were the enemy, last seen face to face in 1917.

'Lord knows where our next struggle will begin,' he wrote that night. 'It is hell having lost our little Dick, and he really *is* a loss because his particular qualities are difficult to reproduce. Well, thank goodness he is alive and we may get him back someday. No good glooming. What we have to do is get on with the job.' Wavell signalled Dill shortly afterwards to suggest that any six captured Italian generals should be offered in exchange for O'Connor, a scheme with all the hallmarks of Chink's thinking; London declined, on the grounds of precedence.

On the morning after his flight, Rommel's assault on Tobruk opened. The fortress was to hold out through successive assaults for 240 days, supplied by a navy lifeline, and was to fall before Rommel's resources snapped because of British military mistakes in the meantime. And those 240 days were to be an exact measure of Chink's personal frustrations. The length of the siege mirrored his own isolation.

The trouble with the present was that he knew he was only standing in as BGS during Galloway's absence. The past continued to infuriate him, and the future looked as blocked as ever. And it did not help that his immediate boss was Lieutenant-General Sir Arthur Smith, whom he had disliked and provoked at Sandhurst in 1924. Then Smith had been Browning's predecessor as Adjutant and they had not had to work together; now he was Wavell's Chief of Staff, and in Chink's opinion a disastrous one. He soon came to the conclusion that he was running the office inefficiently and giving Wavell the wrong advice. In every letter out he complained to Eve, and she promptly told him to give up and join her. 'How could I turn my back?' he reproved, surprised to be misunderstood and loath to go down in her estimation. 'I am beginning to see daylight through some of our most pressing problems. Just a little time to breathe is what we need. This is rather a sticky baby to have handed to one, all ends wrong at the same moment. There must be skill and vision.'

But it was difficult to concentrate in the office, and in his flat, which he shared with two other GHQ staff, there was little peace either. 'Consequently a whole train of thought which I had saved up during lunchtime went to blazes,' he thundered after one such interruption. 'And now after a long afternoon and evening's work I'll find it difficult to resurrect, which is a *curse* for I know it to be valuable.' In Wavell's absence the overstretched team at GHQ ME had little sympathy for a creative personality who worked on self-imposed deadlines and the need to dominate. No one had guessed his insecurity before, and so no one made allowances now for this having increased. A good deal of Chink's tension actually came from trying to cope with the realisation that the higher up the army he climbed, the less suited he was emotionally to the community he had to work within.

Though he could privately dismiss supercilious generals like Smith as bulls in the Pamplona arena – 'and as likely to be towed out by a team of mules' – he was no closer to hiding his feelings in public. Snobs exasperated him more than ever, most conventional men continued to bore him, and Amateurs were an added torment because they now had a licence to kill. But there was no longer any comfort in feeling superior. Looking at himself through their eyes, as he could not stop doing, he despised himself, too. 'I felt shy and small and shrinking before his powerful presence,' he wrote after one such encounter. 'He takes about 90% of this world for granted and I can't even take 10%. If one doubts and questions everything, one becomes a sort of ghost in the presence of solid red-faced people. Whenever I look at his like I can perfectly well realise why I am not employed on anything worthwhile. I just don't exist for them. Incidentally,' he added on that occasion, 'I'd win their B. battles for them if only they'd let me, but unless you look as if you are 100% at home on a London club bumwarmer there is no hope for you.' Eve fanned the flames.

In the meantime the speed of events distracted him. He had been indoctrinated for Ultra, the top-secret information decoded by MI6 at Bletchley Park in England from the intercepted signals of German Enigma machines, and he relished every glimpse of enemy intentions. And he was used regularly by Wavell, whom he continued to respect. On 15 April he was summoned to prepare a plan for the WPC, explained testily as the Worst Possible Case, which in the present circumstances meant making the best of it if the Allies were forced to quit Egypt. Such planning echoed his own approach, and study of the WPC confirmed their lack of military resources. As he became aware of the true pressure that Wavell was under from Churchill to produce a master-stroke, his indignation and protectiveness made him less tolerant still.

But one small aggressive scheme, Operation Brevity, was taking shape to exploit Rommel's own spiralling shortages, and on 19 April he unfolded himself from a cramped Proctor aircraft to initiate the planning at 'Strafer' Gott's HQ at Baggush, the scene of previous meetings with O'Connor. 'The war,' he wrote characteristically, 'is at an intensely interesting stage.' The recapture of Halfaya Pass, the narrow gangway into Egypt between Bardia and Mersa Matruh, was Brevity's chief objective, but the May operation failed after initial success when surprise was lost by bad security. (Chink was firmly opposed to Brevity's larger successor, Battleaxe, and was shut out of the planning; his proposal of an alternative to its frontal approach was not taken up.)

'Interesting' was a detached response to the relentless German thrust across North Africa but Chink saw each move as a mental contest, and his ideas fizzed out, despite Smith's frown. Why not defend the frontier with a mine marsh studded with infantry? Why not slant the railway line they were building west from Matruh down towards the Agheila bottleneck, to confuse Rommel by setting up danger from there as well as the coast road?

He was not deterred when the pace at GHQ ME was stepped up. On 17 April Yugoslavia capitulated, followed a week later by Greece with its recent – and now vulnerable – injection of Allied troops, and in the scramble to evacuate as many as possible 26,000 men were landed halfway across on the island of Crete. 'At least we've got 80% of the chaps back, though we have lost much useful gear,' he commented drily. 'The same old tale. Allies with obsolete armies utterly unprepared for modern war, and the Boche all out with every modern inconvenience. With luck we'll get around this rather awkward corner.' The following day Ultra picked up Hitler's directive ordering an airborne assault on Crete, and he remained outwardly laconic. 'I think if I ever write the history of war, its title will have to be Mother Hubbard's war,' he wrote to Eve. 'It would be so lovely to find a nice juicy bone for the poor dogs of war, in place of a few dry splinters carefully collected from the last dog's dinner. My heart is sore for my little master with his over-whelming responsibilities.' On 30 April came 'yet another crash of international crockery', and Rommel attacked Tobruk once more. On top of continuing ominous cyphers about Crete, warnings came in about Iraq, an ally Britain could not afford to lose. And on 2 May an uprising duly broke out there.

As the disasters mounted the temperature rose. Kites wheeled over the building and windows had to be closed all day to keep in the cool. Inside GHQ ME, Chink brought in the harrying telegrams from Churchill and laced empathy with humour. 'I wish we could have a real good crack at the Hun somewhere it hurts him,' he wrote. 'There is always a way of doing these things, given a reasonable amount of means, imagination and guts. I'll provide the imagination, at least.' But though his nonchalant optimism was invaluable to Wavell and he kept ready with his own response to tactical situations in the desert, he was no more than a senior go-between. His job was to deliver orders and ventilate the Commander's problems, not to give advice.

The island of **Crete** resembles a prehistoric monster swimming west across the Mediterranean, its spine rising to 7000 feet. In 1941 Suda Bay, which curves into its right shoulder, was a vital fuelling port for the British fleet, and the countryside around seethed with veterans of the Greek Dunkirk, minus their weapons and equipment. It was here, Ultra intelligence revealed, that a major German airborne assault was going to come, and by 6 May GHQ ME knew not only how, down to the last operational detail, but when – 17 May. On the island, General Bernard Freyberg VC, commander of the New Zealand Division, had the unenviable responsibility of mustering a defence that would give the Germans no clue about advance Ultra knowledge.

Chink first flew into Crete on 11 May, and he stepped out of the patched Blenheim to find Maleme airfield bristling with ack-ack guns and searchlights. Apprehensive about Freyberg's commitment, after being told that he had complained directly to his own government, he was there to assess his attitude as well as to bring the latest intelligence picture and Wavell's order, and with his head still ringing from the racket of the small plane he made his way straight to HQ Creforce in Canea, the administrative capital. Freyberg's strength of character impressed him, reminiscent as it was of the last-ditch stands he had loved reading about in childhood, but ruefully he put him in his 'Bear of Little Brain' category as far as tactical sense went; it was a rapidly expanding classification that he had made no secret of keeping since his time in India. 'Last night I stood in the moonlight in Crete,' he wrote at dawn to Eve. 'Most beautiful colours of sea and land. Mountains were still snowpatched with deep ridges and valleys and I could see through my glasses mountainsides which spelt rock-climbing. For half an hour I stood on a high unfrequented place and breathed in this scented coolness and felt the whole spirit of Greece and Minoa inspire my vision.' Menace was like a hallucinatory drug, refocusing perception.

Crete's peril stood out even more clearly on the maps in GHQ ME when he arrived back to find Cairo simmering at 110° next day, with Freyberg's staunch reply that he would do his utmost. There were five days left. The following morning Chink flew to Alexandria to liaise with the navy, who under cover of darkness were urgently shipping unusable troops off the island and ferrying guns and equipment in. 'Things are on the march,' he noted on 15 May. 'And I toddle after them like a small boy being towed along overfast by a forceful and grim nursemaid. Archie is quite wonderful. They unload all sorts of unnecessary burdens onto him – worrying things which need a delicate exercise of judgement, and he deals quietly and effectively with them all. But he is perhaps too accessible and too ready to handle burdens.' That day Ultra revealed that Göring had sanctioned a forty-eight-hour postponement, and on 17 May Chink flew into Maleme again. He never referred to the true purpose of his weekend visit, but a direct link with Ultra was extended to Crete simultaneously. Before leaving, he asked Freyberg to name a successor in case he became a casualty, and as they said goodbye on Sunday evening it was implicit that the massive assault was due at 8 a.m. next morning. On reaching GHQ ME, however, Chink found that a further twenty-four-hour postponement had been intercepted.

When the first German transport planes throbbed over Crete, Freyberg was seen to check his watch and stoically observe that they were on time. But in the intense fighting that ensued the insufficiently strongly defended airfield of Maleme was captured, and with the enemy able to fly in troop carriers at the rate of one a minute the eventual outcome was in no doubt. By 24 May 10,000 German troops were on the island, and Luftwaffe air ascendancy paralysed British naval action in daylight. 'Crete has gone through the hoop all day,' Chink noted on the first day, monitoring Wavell's mood. 'APW met me in the passage at 8.30 p.m. "Well, Eric, if there isn't anything else I can do to get a move on in this war, I think I'll go home."' The remarkable thing, he wrote after the war, was that its grimness was an anaesthetic. 'In a collapsing situation we had no time for fear or feeling. Tobruk, the desert, Crete, Iraq, Syria, wham, wham, wham! The naval losses, the internal threats, Turkey's ambiguity, pelions piled upon ossas, and always the same tired old team to make headway against the sea of troubles.' He thrived on living on the edge himself, but he had begun to worry about the effect on Wavell of Churchill's constant interference.

On 5 May Wavell had exploded, shouting 'He must face facts.' While reading a telegram from Churchill, and in the strain of Crete the phrase soon slipped out again. 'Archie told me to prepare a draft telegram to the PM precisely describing the real situation,' Chink recalled after the war. 'I began with "The base in Crete is now in the front line," and Archie snorted and then wrote in advance of my opening in his beautiful handwriting "You must face facts." Archie knew just why I gasped then. I felt in my bones that the PM would never forgive that jolt.' But in fact the damage was already done. It was as well for the tired old team that they could not know that Churchill had told Dill on 19 May that he intended to move Wavell to India and replace him with Claude Auchinleck. Dill's thoughtful letter preparing Wavell was on its way by sea.

So stretched was the team now that Chink considered himself lucky if he got three hours' sleep during the twenty-four hours. Liaising with the navy took him often to Alexandria, and on 23 May, a typical day, he was there and back by 3 p.m. and still in his office at 9.45 p.m. that night. By the time he reached his room at 11.30 p.m. he was exhausted enough to smoke one of the cheroots he had recently succeeded in giving up, but the phone rang continually during the night and 'a procession' of duty staff officers filed through his room. 'That lovely town I looked at only 14 days ago is now largely in ruins,' he wrote, unable to get back to sleep. 'One hates not being able to help more.' On 26 May, after Canae had been bombed heavily to break civilian morale, Freyberg finally radioed that the situation was hopeless. Chink was accompanying Wavell to the Commander-in-Chief's conference aboard Admiral Cunningham's flagship off Alexandria that day; even *Warspite* was damaged by a bomb. He pointed out to Wavell that the German losses could not possibly be sustained and would rule out repeat airborne operations.

British troops on the island had to be got out fast. On 27 May, linking naval and military organisation, Chink flew back to Cairo and returned to Alexandria by road, flew to Cairo again next day and back to Alexandria when evacuation got under way that evening. He spent the whole of 29 May at the port, appalled by the high sinking rate and aching to help more. 'A day of grim decisions,' he scribbled on 30 May. 'Poor Archie. I'm afraid our enemies are crowing this morning, blast them. I'm afraid there is going to be a considerable outcry over this unhappy business. We are doing our best to bring chaps back, but that isn't easy.' By 1 June the Via Dolorosa, as he thought of it, was consummated. Only 18,000 of the 32,000 troops had been got away, and these included a reluctant Freyberg on Wavell's direct order. 'I blame myself not a little,' Chink admitted. 'One should have been quicker on the uptake, less entangled in the muddle hereabouts.' It was not self-importance, but sensible military judgement. Wavell has been castigated by historians for failing to anticipate the German move on Crete.

During the hectic countdown there had been one less sombre errand for Chink to carry out. 'A little matter,' as he wrote tantalisingly to Eve, 'of a declaration to Syria.' On 22 May he flew to Jerusalem to see

'Jumbo' Wilson, whose current responsibility was the administration of measures against Vichy French Syria. The Declaration was a guarantee of British good faith drawn up to forestall a German take-over of Syria, and its existence would help to steady the country under British control until the end of the war. If he was too often being used as a messenger boy, as he resentfully believed, at least the messages were important ones. He also brought Wavell's orders for Exporter, a Syrian operation which took place the following month, and a small Allied advance on Baghdad.

And in the desert, approaching Cairo, the German threat had become greater. Although Tobruk still held out, Rommel's troops were across the Egyptian border and had regained the Halfaya Pass on 27 May. At such a crucial moment it was harder than ever for Chink to tear himself away, but his stand-in duty ended on 3 June, on Gallo-way's return. Operational instructions for Battleaxe, which he opposed, were already out and that added to his frustration. At his farewell interview Smith 'mumbled' gratitude and indicated that the General Staff was about to be put on a proper basis. 'Something, anyway,' Chink wrote scornfully, unable to meet him halfway, 'but it will never be admitted.' Switching his mind to the customary post-mortem, he began to look forward to analysing the disastrous pattern of events in detail and was preoccupied at his final meeting with Wavell. 'Looking very tired, he was,' he scribbled briefly afterwards. 'I wish he'd take some leave. This unending responsibility is so utterly wearing.'

On his last night in Cairo, at a loose end, he bumped into Ronald Playfair, who had been a fellow instructor at Chatham in 1929. Then Playfair had had almost as original a reputation as himself because he contributed regularly to *Punch* and was a radical thinker. Less outspoken and more conventional, however, Playfair had now been promoted over him, and standing him dinner at the Turf Club, Chink hid his hurt at the contrast. They talked late into the night in the cool of the roof restaurant, and as the street noises filtered up his hackles lowered, one by one. 'Charming,' he acknowledged next morning, ruefully aware that Playfair could not help possessing the 'gift of ease' he lacked so conspicuously himself. The period at GHQ ME had emphasised how separate he had become, and how impossible it was to change himself. 'I feel I'm not being employed to my full use,' he declared at once in a letter to Eve. 'And yet I quite see why. Although I'm basically constructive, in a group which is out of accord with my views I'm an awkward and destructive component. I cannot accept the repose of letting things go wrong for fear of upsetting people.' It had begun to dawn on him that Smith was in charge of his promotion.

Back in Haifa, still mentally absorbed by Crete, he felt especially close to Wavell on 16 June, the anniversary they both kept of their wounding at Bellevaarde Wood; disturbing reports of Battleaxe made the 'headmaster' role more constricting than ever, though the school was bigger now than peacetime Camberley. 'He may be reaching another crisis in his career,' he wrote of Wavell that evening. 'And I wish that I was nearer him.' Six days later, when news of Wavell's dismissal was made public, he pencilled a terse entry into his diary – 'Sic transit gloria mundi.' Within the month Wavell's letter from India reached him, and he opened it with sadness. 'I hope you will fulfil your ambition to become historian of the Middle East,' Wavell ended. 'You have full leave to criticise my shortcomings. Till then, yours ever APW.' He put it carefully away. 'Poor Archie,' he commented to Eve. 'Well, it comes to all of us, to some sooner than others, and the important thing is to have interests.' It did not occur to him that, with the exception of her, he had none but the army himself.

Six months later he sat warily on the best chair of the best room of a small bungalow in a suburb of Salisbury, South Africa. Neat, he noted approvingly, and Mrs Bell, the fortune teller he had come to see, was as comely as she was black. Everyone was talking about her, Eve had insisted, and he had been lucky to get an appointment before his leave ended. He hitched his chair forward and the session began. 'Most of it was the usual stock in trade,' he wrote straight afterwards. 'Then she said suddenly: "The war will end in August." "Which August?" "I don't know. I think next August." "But that's impossible." "Still, I see it so. It will end for you, anyway." ' He paid up and left, annoyed with himself for having been gullible enough to go in the first place.

At first the news of Auchinleck's command had promised so much, and he had counted on being included. Torn over how to make contact, he had veered from not wanting to appear keen to sponge off an old friend to telling himself it was silly to be aloof simply because Auchinleck was in high command. Deciding on compromise, he had suggested a meeting at the end of the Telsch House term, and a summons from the Military Secretary had crossed with his own letter and immediately raised his hopes. He was to lunch with the Commander-in-Chief on 17 July, and he read a great deal into the fact that it was within two weeks of Auchinleck's appointment. They met privately in

Cairo the night before and Auchinleck promptly handed him a letter from Estelle, continuing their relationship where it had left off. He pocketed it to read later. He was much more interested in hearing Auchinleck's opinion of the Cairo Amateurs – 'the old school noose, we'll all be strangled in it yet' – and the new intentions.

Over lunch at Mena he put two main points across. The forces in the Western Desert ought to become an army command, and in O'Connor's absence he recommended General Sir Alan Cunningham, brother of the naval commander and enjoying a high public profile after advancing far and fast through Italian Somaliland into Italian-occupied Abyssinia. Auchinleck agreed that mobility was Cunningham's forte, promised that his next offensive would be the biggest yet and discussed outlines, but no firm job offer was made. In August Cunningham took up the command and in September Chink heard that the Western Desert Force was about to be renamed the Eighth Army; more to the point, it was also said that the Commander-in-Chief was about to visit him in person.

Auchinleck arrived on 5 October. 'He is most affable and made me laugh, saying "But I've come here to see you," ' Chink wrote expectantly, convinced that he was 'bursting' to get something off his chest. He booked a table for two at Pross's, the best restaurant in town and a legacy of the large pre-war German colony there, but by the end of the evening was no wiser. 'With the greatest of difficulty he persuaded his four military police outriders to go home, two stuck to us as far as the door and then we were free,' he reported cheerfully to Eve before sleeping. 'Consternation of local bar supporters when they realised his rank as he sipped a sherry. We had a good dinner: prawns, chicken Maryland, mushrooms, coffee and a bottle of good Chablis. After we sat on the balcony of my room in the moonlight and talked. . . . He didn't say "Chink, you are the predestined defender of Tobruk," or "The Western Desert needs you!" But it was a good evening.'

Anti-climax was swift. Nothing came of the visit, and he concluded that he was to be used as an occasional sounding board and nothing more. The sensation of banishment was rubbed in by having to entertain two rivals who were riding high. In 1937 Chink had been running neck and neck for promotion with a colleague whom he respected, Archie Nye. Now Nye was a lieutenant-general, two ranks ahead. But it was the impact of Auchinleck's newly appointed Deputy Chief of the General Staff, Neil Ritchie, that rankled most. Ritchie was two years younger and the job was the one he had expected himself.

Chink found him patronising, limited and assured, and five minutes was enough to confirm his view that selectors were continuing to choose men they felt comfortable with. Ritchie was a type he recoiled from, too repellent to be classified in the fond 'Bear of Little Brain' category, and he reminded him instantly of the 'lovely' Major of the Greys he had spotted at breakfast only a few days earlier, 'Utterly satisfied that the whole work of creation from its beginning till now had been designed to create a world in which he could satisfy all his needs. True that he hadn't been given a brain capable of having any needs except those foisted on him by tradition and custom, but those suited him amply.'

That such a type should have the job he wanted brought on the blackest depression he had experienced. 'Up till now it has been my lot to be faced by men whom I have passed,' he wrote next morning. 'Last night, realising my professional life was over, I lay awake and mourned. Soldiering has been everything to me and now I have been weighed in some balance and found wanting. Soit! Last night I mourned the end of nearly 28 years of work, and this morning felt swept and garnished.' The mood stayed with him – 'when I feel like this I feel quite hollow – empty, vacant, laid aside, like a dress upon a chair' – and showed as bitterness. He had had as many passovers as a Jewish village, he wrote to Liddell Hart, who was feeling similarly hard done by in England. Reading Eve's letters that constantly urged him to resign and turn full-time to socialism with her, he no longer dismissed the idea out of hand. 'Would I be running out?' he pondered. 'I have men almost as old as I am as students. They must have given up much to come back. On the other hand, I have been working flat out during the lean prewar years.' He made enquiries and was told it was not allowed. A War Office visitor reawoke his professional pride, and he snapped out of self-pity.

On 20 October hope raced through him again. At noon a delayed cypher arrived from Wavell asking him to be at Lydda airport at 12.30 p.m. 'I pulled out one of our new Fords and made it to the second – forgot I'd been a fast driver once. Wavell looked well, walked about as usual and didn't say anything except to answer my queries about Russia. Then, as he was taking off again, he tried to say that he had been talking to the Auk about my future. I said I thought I'd become unemployable and anyway I rather fancied myself as an Embusqué, while Haifa was a considerable improvement on Limoges.' Wavell left with an appreciative laugh and nothing more definite. Meanwhile the operation, codenamed Crusader, which Auchinleck had mentioned at the first lunch in July, was clearly getting under way without him.

He was wasting his time, he told Tiarks, who dismissed him as an idealist. Dining with Freyberg, the conversation slipped towards dangerous waters. The army, Chink needled, was seldom short on physical courage but it lacked moral courage. Freyberg put down his knife and fork. 'Moral courage, Chink? What's that?' The sad thing was, he wrote before going to bed, that the poor chap genuinely didn't know. Yet Freyberg, too, was rising high. Harding and Galloway, both junior to himself, were well ahead, and to cap it all Horrocks was an acting major-general in command of 44th Division in England.

The pinpricks continued. A letter came from Estelle in October to say that Wavell had told her that Auchinleck was being brainwashed by 'anti-Chink propaganda' at GHQ ME. 'I'm pretty sure Arthur Smith is behind it,' he stormed,

> but they will never say these things to one's face. If they could say 'Chink is inefficient and we'll report badly on him and retire him,' I'd understand. But what they are saying is 'We cannot report badly on him, so we'll isolate him and keep him where his capacity for making us uncomfortable won't worry us.' I suppose it is a compliment. What a firstclass poison whisper, Chink is his own worst enemy. Then if he isn't used or promoted, nobody is to blame but Chink. Not us who pass the whisper on or us who cleverly invented it. I am rapidly becoming the Man in the Iron Mask of the Middle East.

But Auchinleck was less easily swayed than he gave him credit for, and on the 31st of that month Secret Cypher Message MUL 416 10091/155, Private for CIGS from Gen. Auchinleck, went out requesting him for the post of DMT. 'He has imagination and foresight beyond the ordinary,' Auchinleck argued, 'and plenty of drive as well as futuristic outlook which I think very necessary just now. I know him very well indeed, and realise his shortcomings but am sure his brain is too valuable to waste.' Permission, however, was refused.

By the time Auchinleck arrived in Haifa on 13 November for a three-day stay, Chink had few illusions left. He was aware that the real purpose of the trip up to Palestine was to decoy the Germans into believing that the preparations for Crusader going on in the Egyptian desert were nothing more than cover for the move of a larger Allied force north to protect the oilfields, and he was disgusted to see Ritchie at Auchinleck's side. 'The Auk was very interesting, mainly about the past,' he wrote swiftly next morning. 'Today is to be reserved for the future of the war. In the car yesterday he talked about postwar personal futures and I told him I had determined to retire. "We'll see about that," he said "I'm pretty sure you won't." He certainly is in great form and gives the impression of possessing great reserves of power in his personality.' Auchinleck's ability to cope with the pressure from Churchill surprised him – Crusader was continually being likened to Blenheim and Waterloo – but as he listened to the latest plans dismay took over.

It was intended to send the infantry corps up the coast road into Cyrenaica while the armoured corps swung inland towards Tobruk in the hope of bringing the German armour to battle and then relieving Tobruk, and his old doubts about the synchronisation of the separate commands of armour and infantry resurfaced. But it was the new decision to decentralise divisional artillery that alarmed him most. 'I opposed it strongly,' he noted. 'I was told it had been decided. I did NOT approve.' 'It was nonsense,' he explained many years later, 'to atomise that powerful thing, a divisional artillery, by allotting its field brigades permanently to infantry brigades and then stick these groups into boxes miles apart.' Divisional control of the concentration of artillery was crucial, he argued, and if they had to have brigade groups these should be used for special operations only, like the Afrika Korps. He was overruled. Before Auchinleck left Chink wrote out a memorandum for him on effective reorganisation of tanks and infantry – 'cold, sustained calculation' – but judged it was not the moment to press it home.

Deliberately excluding Ritchie, he booked a table at the Piccadilly, a nightclub on the lower slopes of Mount Carmel famous for its Palestinian wines, cabaret and hostesses. 'We did not get to bed till after midnight,' he reported to Eve. 'And Lord knows how many indiscretions passed, mellowed by gin, chablis, brandy.' What he did not tell her was the revelation brought about by teasing Auchinleck, harmlessly as he had thought, about his wife Jessie's pleasure at being married to a commander-in-chief. Visibly upset, Auchinleck had confided that Jessie was determined to leave him and that he was trying to save the marriage at long distance. The ambivalence Chink had always felt towards her erupted into fury that she would – 'typically' – pull out at the time of Auchinleck's greatest personal pressure. It was a feeling he knew Estelle would share – but then Estelle was the cause of his own guilt, a confidence he had not felt able to give in return. There was one consolation: Ritchie knew nothing of that side of Auchinleck's life, which meant he still had one advantage over him. But next morning, impersonal once more, Auchinleck swept off with Ritchie, outriders geometrically on cue.

Three days later, on 18 November, Crusader was launched. British armour swept through the desert towards Tobruk and a battle developed in the waste of gravel around Sidi Rezagh, an obscure sheikh's tomb. Galloway, Harding, Freyberg, Gatehouse, Messervy, Gott . . . they were all involved. 'Wish I were with the chaps – in fact it is hard to think of anything else,' he wrote excitedly to Eve, doubts forgotten. 'The West is awake again and the Eighth Army on the move. I drink a glass to its success. I went through the outline with the Auk, which brings us back to a luncheon party at Mena in July and the fruits thereof. Of course there is a gamble in it. On the other hand I think everything has been done to minimise the dangers of the unforeseen and to leave a margin for mishap.'

At first he discounted doubts about the relief of Tobruk as press rumours. Compromises to the original plan were not yet clear, and the dangers of the unforeseen had not included the unthinkable, which was that Cunningham would lose his nerve when the battle turned against Eighth Army after 23 November. With news of Cunningham's replacement still secret, another change was causing him anxiety. In London, from 1 December, the CIGS was no longer Dill, who had worked himself into chronic ill-health, but General Sir Alan Brooke. And Brooke was the man with whom he had disagreed most sharply at the War Office only six years before; not only had Brooke condemned his mechanisation proposals but they had disliked each other on a personal basis. On hearing that Crusader had allowed Rommel to slip away into the desert with Tobruk still beleaguered, however, the worries about Brooke were pushed to the back of his mind.

On 7 December Pearl Harbour was attacked, and the following day Britain joined America in declaring war on Japan. Burma and Malaya were bombed in retaliation, which meant that Reggie was nearer the war than he was himself – 'so odd' – while all he could do was lecture on as much of the recent campaign as he was able to piece together from long distance. 'Tantamount to finding a couple of rib bones and a foot and thigh of some obscure prehistoric mammal,' he mocked savagely, 'and proceeding to build a plaster likeness.' Putting his pride in his pocket he wrote off to Smith and asked for copies of the orders for the students' benefit. Euphoria at persuading the RAF to send officers to Telsch House too – 'as great a feat as inducing woodcock to perch on one's gunbarrels' – evaporated almost at once.

His depression was persistent, and dining an army psychiatrist at Pross's one evening he raised the subject of the male menopause. 'I said "At what age does that occur, for I don't feel any particular difference yet I am officially middle-aged," ' he noted afterwards. ' "Oh, you aren't an ageing type," he said. "It mayn't happen to you till well after 60." ' But feeling young for his age made his inactivity worse, and his mood was as bleak as usual when he switched on the wireless for the London news on the evening of 11 December. At the report of Churchill's announcement in the Commons that day about the change of command during Crusader, he froze. Neil Ritchie was at the head of Eighth Army, appointed in the emergency by Auchinleck. It was the last straw. 'I dreamed at great length that my military life was ended,' he wrote after a terrible night. 'A bitter, infuriating dream of frustration.'

That evening he dug out his corduroy battledress and tried it on in front of the mirror. By 14 December he had made up his mind. He sent in a formal complaint to GHQ ME about his treatment since September, and ended by requesting to retire. 'They can't deny,' he informed Eve, aware of how triumphant she would be, 'that I am holding a less important job than when the war began, or that since I came numerous people junior have been promoted, also that I see no hope of change and that to be so treated is not conducive to efficiency.' Within four days the new Military Secretary for the Middle East arrived in response, and turned out gallingly to be Angus Collier, his close Staff College friend. Collier shook his hand warmly. Everyone was aching to promote him, he was assured – as soon as they could find a job where he would fit in. 'Nobody can find a job as remote as that,' Chink sneered, escaping to his room. 'I must go on being passed over because I am too brilliantly disturbing.' He repeated his retirement demand when they met up again and Collier refused to listen, explaining that Cairo had had a 'wonderful' job for him but the War Office had refused to authorise it and soon there would be something else. Over dinner Chink glared at his military executioner, as he perceived Collier, and ignored gossip about their contemporaries. Another night of gusty anger followed.

Pity from Collier was intolerable. Unable to sleep, he wrote compulsively to Eve.

I know more about warfare in its theory and principle than 95% of British soldiers. I am an infinitely hard worker in good health, never disobey an order, and because I stirred up a nest of torpid kraits in India and showed up Arthur Smith here, at 46½ I can only look forward to remaining mum in this tin pot establishment watching things happen disastrously in the world beyond my bars, because the men who manage things have neither the brains nor the vision to see further than the nearest corpse or the next battlefield. So I go to join Fuller and Mackesy and a few other intellectual misfits in a system which has no use for intellect. The joke is they are right. Brain in an army is like a nail in one's shoe, out of place if it is too sharp or hasn't been properly turned down.

In the morning he turned on Collier and refused a major-general's job in England – 'I want no charity and know exactly the sort of job that will be offered' – and then hated himself, remembering Collier's genuine affection. They spent a quiet afternoon walking in the hills and he calmed down. By mutual consent the matter was not broached again and they talked about rock-gardening, Collier's passion, and sought out flowers. A flock of chickor suddenly scattered, evoking shoots of fourteen years before. He was almost sorry to see Collier go. The respite was short, however. Almost immediately a signal came through, ordering him to report to GHQ ME as a liaison officer without increase in salary, and when he phoned straightaway to ask if it was a joke he was told the job had been devised especially for him by the Commander-in-Chief. He 'let fly' at the staff officer, shouting that big men shouldn't go slumming, and slammed down the phone, determined to tackle Auchinleck in person.

There was no air passage to Cairo. At 6 a.m. next morning he was off by car, following another bad night. 'I know I am useless to my country in a routine sherry-swilling job,' he had written at one point, unable to relax. 'If I can really be of value as myself I'd willingly give my life, but if somebody is playing at charity better for me to leave the Service.' Making faster time than he expected, he reached Cairo at 4 p.m.

'Roared into GHQ,' he recorded that evening. 'Seeking whom I might devour and of course ran into everyone, all delighted to see me. Arthur S produced a letter which I had not received promising me the earth, which I said I did not want. I was then ushered into the Auk's sanctum and we began a showdown. He was damn nice about it all and said I couldn't retire in wartime. To which I answered that I was technically a member of a neutral state and could do what I liked. Fast ball! We had the devil of a scrap and great fun it was. Of course he is a juggernauter and rides roughshod over one. They want me to do a perfectly poisonous job co-ordinating Armageddon between Wavell and the Auk.' What he could not admit was that to commute between India and Cairo would confront him regularly with Estelle, and he could not bear to be outranked back there by men who had been his juniors.

What to do with him? Auchinleck took him out to dinner and went through the proposal diplomatically until he was won over. 'I am satisfied that everyone is out to make full use of my talents but gingerly,' he allowed. 'A spate of work for three months and much travelling between Cairo, Aleppo, Iran and Baghdad. I am reluctant to hurt Estelle . . . but it is churlish and small-minded now to worry about rank.' He was finished with Telsch House, except for the end-of-term speech.

But examination of the job more closely led to a second confrontation with Auchinleck, because the title of Liaison Officer for Persia and Iraq dressed up the familiar messenger-boy role. 'He is so disarmingly friendly and genuinely sympathetic that I cannot support my own point of view without feeling smallminded and selfish,' he confessed. 'He said he wanted the use of my brain and that I must be tolerant and learn to suffer fools gladly. Why keep fools? They only get men killed! I am too proud and stubborn to ask what is to become of me, and at the moment I am a sort of internee, a stooge between Wavell and the Auk.' The nation, he had actually retorted, could not afford the luxury of fools in high places, and he intended to go on being as intolerant as ever.

He kept his word. There was almost nothing for him to do, as the two countries he was officially liaising between had that month reverted from Wavell's India command back to the Middle East, making him superfluous. Smith was still CGS and did not disguise his disapproval, and the relationship with Galloway held a grudge at Chink's end now, the same jealousy he felt for Harding, who was about to be put in charge of training. De Guingand remained a good friend, and he was glad to see him awarded an OBE in the New Year Honours List, but then annoyed to realise that 'virtually everybody else' had got something too. Smith – 'that Anglican faquir' – had been knighted, and he dashed off a verse that few appreciated:

They knighted him because, forsooth
He cheered us up at GHQ.
But that is not the total truth,
He helped to cheer up Rommel, too.

Auchinleck had persuaded him to restart their early-morning walks, to the disquiet of less favoured GHQ staff officers, and in the grounds of Gezira they stepped up their pace to a run; he thought of it irreverently as the Dawn Patrol. No equivalent mental exercise was forthcoming. On 2 January 1942, bored and functionless, he used the opportunity to ask for a holiday. Permission was given.

Chink spent a month in South Africa with Eve, had his fortune told by Mrs Bell, and returned on 8 February to find Eighth Army in a more dangerous position than ever. Smith called him straight in to say his job had dissolved, something Chink had tried to get him to see before going on leave, and gave him a lecture on accepting reverses. 'The man is a child, a clever nursery politician whose nanny is his idea of God.' The following evening he strode furiously in to see Auchinleck. 'The same old stuff, to the effect that I was a brilliant mind with twice the vision and speed of everyone else, but because of these qualities I was difficult to place because I make my seniors feel small. He could not give me a command appropriate to my status, and hoped this would not affect our friendship. I said I hoped he would stop feeling responsible for me and get on with the war. Finale was a reference to my bolshevik state of mind in December and a hope that I didn't take all this too badly. We then had a whiskey and soda and got down to his plans of campaign for which he sought my approval.' Analysis of the current situation had to be put into operational instructions for Ritchie, who still commanded Eighth Army, and the work was a relief.

But whatever Auchinleck might have in mind, Chink realised that he remained blocked because the Selection Board was made up of Smith, Ritchie, Wilson and Beresford Peirse. 'The whole body of my contemporaries and seniors have formed a tight ring like buffalo when a tiger is about and are standing horns down to keep me out,' he exploded to Eve. 'Just like the old General Medical Council when some unorthodox medico propounds a dangerously new theory which may damage their practices.' Wilson took him aside to say he thought he was being disgracefully treated, causing him a moment's shame. His irritability now was nearer the surface than it had been during Crete. Teased by Auchinleck one day that he was a mad Irishman, he snapped that he was certainly mad at the handling of the war and stormed out. He took every chance to intrigue against Smith and canvassed to have de Guingand put in charge of Intelligence, which was being poorly handled. Otherwise there was nothing for him to do.

When Auchinleck first suggested that he should visit Eighth Army to investigate command and control, but actually to take the pulse about Ritchie, his reaction was that spying would only add to his unpopularity. But soon, particularly after a talk with one of Ritchie's former commanders, Major-General Godwin-Austen, who had asked to be relieved, he changed his mind. 'The ferret goes into the burrow on Monday next with luck,' he relished, still angry that Godwin-Austen had had his orders countermanded. The burrow was along the Gazala–Bir Hachim front.

'I have given Dorman-Smith,' Auchinleck cabled Ritchie on 10 February, 'the job of enquiring into our present system. . . . I feel we are still too rigid and hidebound and that we must modernise ourselves in this respect. He is excellent at this sort of thing . . . and I am sure you will give him the benefit of your advice and ensure that he gets all the facilities he needs. It must be made clear that he is NOT snooping! Will you do this for me?' On 15 February, as Singapore fell to the Japanese, Chink arrived at Eighth Army HQ. The Western Desert, he mused on the way, ought to have its own tie by now – jerboas in white on a sand background.

'18 February: Useful talk with Ritchie in the morning and even more useful with a couple of contemporaries of like mind later without collusion.' By 20 February, within the sound of gunfire from Tobruk, he had reached Gott, who had taken over 13th Corps from Godwin-Austen. 'I begin to see the form here and as usual it fills me with keen interest because of its stupidity.' Gott, he estimated, had far more to him than Ritchie. '21 February: I am more than ever convinced that there must be radical and sweeping changes.' '23rd: I've heard a great deal which I came out to hear and I have been talked to very frankly. I do see now why many things have gone wrong and I have my ideas how they can be put right.' One of his confidants had been Willoughby Norrie, Commander of 30th Corps, and on 23 February he took the chance to sound out the legendary Jock Campbell, whose daringly pugnacious 'Jock Columns' had earlier reminded Chink of Hemingway's For Whom The Bell Tolls, which he had read in Haifa. Jock Campbell had taken over 7th Armoured Division on Gott's promotion and was larger than life, as he had expected.

Watching him drive off after their talk, 'hellbent for Cairo', Chink wondered how long his luck could hold. News reached them next day that Campbell had been killed within the hour, when his car overturned on a hairpin bend of Halfaya Pass.

Campbell, and every divisional commander he spoke to, lacked confidence in Ritchie, and Chink left Eighth Army HQ on 28 February with his own opinion vindicated. He longed to report to Auchinleck at once but his first day back was a Sunday and the Dawn Patrol was too conspicuous. They arranged a lunchtime picnic at Lake Fayum, where there was no chance of being overheard. 'The lake was sluggish-looking, unhealthy, large – like a typical tycoon,' he wrote later. 'There was a desert cliff all along the distance northwards, appropriate background to an unattractive sheet of water. The surroundings on the south bank where we stopped the cars to talk and eat were dreary, still wintry. It was cold and depressing, one of those glum Egyptian days. . . . I did not like what I had to say. I felt it would not go down well – nor did it.'

Auchinleck objected to his conclusion that Ritchie must be replaced. He could not go on sacking Eighth Army commanders, he explained, but even if he did the War Office would send out Montgomery as a replacement. Aware of the mutual antipathy when the two had worked together in England two years earlier, Chink gave advice he could never take himself and insisted that personal feelings should have no bearing on getting the right man for the job. When Auchinleck remained adamant, Chink volunteered to go up as Ritchie's BGS himself, although the idea affronted him, and was told he was 'too emphatic'. They agreed on 'Jock' Whiteley eventually; Whiteley had been a sound Staff College contemporary, and one of his whippers-in on the Drag.

Chink began his written report on 4 March, and it included condemnation of the use of amateur Jock Columns and the widespread desert jargon and old-boy familiarities. Eighth Army was 'more of a club than a strictly disciplined entity', he cautioned, and recommended immediate action. 'Chink was not the most tactful of men,' de Guingand would agree later, 'but from the talks he had with me on his return I can say without any doubt that he had arrived at some extremely sound deductions. He was particularly critical of the way the Army was being handled, which of course reflected on some of the commanders concerned.'

But with the report finished and a spurt of socialising over –

'amusingly subversive dinner with sundry pressmen, talking over world futures, good conversation' – he dropped back into suspicious introspection. 'I have become a piece of cuttlefish in the canary's care on which the bird sharpens its beak,' he complained to Eve, whose contribution was: 'Do *something*! Anything!!' He dropped into the Military Secretary's office to tell Collier that he could not justify his brigadier's pay, explaining that since 21 December he had spent a total of fourteen hours in discussion with Auchinleck, talked once to Field Marshal Smuts when in South Africa, done a two-week tour of Eighth Army and written up his report. Collier was sympathetic. On 11 March Chink dined with Whiteley, who wanted to discuss the imminent job with Ritchie and, that out of the way, was ready to listen to his own problems. Whiteley, as he expected, robustly prescribed getting drunk every evening and having a woman as well. On 16 March, 'unrepentant', he formally asked permission to retire, and Auchinleck tore his request up. Smith stopped him on the way out to say he was his own worst enemy and that he must learn to suffer fools gladly. 'I replied that I had no use for fools who got men killed unnecessarily and swept out.' He pounded around the Gezira grounds, a personal treadmill.

It would have been some comfort to know that in England Liddell Hart was drawing up a third list on which Chink featured, and that the incoming Secretary of State for War who had called for it was the ex-civil servant, P.J. Grigg, whose career had been enhanced in India. But as a friend at court, the Secretary of State would have little influence compared to the Chief of the Imperial General Staff, and here Chink's anxiety was fully justified. Late in January, during Chink's month-long absence in South Africa, Brooke had finished a late dinner in his hard-working week and reached for the army reorganisation proposals which Auchinleck had sent. He frowned over remarks like 'diluting' armour with infantry and the 'rigidity' of divisions, recognising the tone. Before becoming CIGS, Brooke had been Commander-in-Chief Home Forces and he had established the tactical doctrine for 1st Armoured Division, which was now in the Middle East and would be involved in any changes. Chink's runaway War Office tongue – 'the bankruptcy of the cavalry concept of armoured fighting' had been a favourite taunt – was as offensive to Brooke as ever.

'I was at that time,' Brooke elaborated after the war, when hindsight rounded out so much, 'beginning to be upset by many messages that emanated from Auchinleck's office. I was beginning to be suspicious that Dorman-Smith, one of his staff officers, was beginning to exercise far too much influence on him.' ('The Auk was too stubborn a type for me to claim any eminence grise status,' Chink would snarl when Brooke's diaries were published. 'I wish I could have done so – lots of things would have gone differently.') And on 2 March Brooke despatched Richard McCreery, an armour commander of the same mind, to counter Chink's influence. At the Staff College in 1928 Chink had scornfully referred to him as Dreary McCreery.

But he was not there when McCreery arrived because he was – yet again – in South Africa. The threat of resignation had caused Auchinleck to take seriously an idea Chink had been promoting since Crete for the formation of a Higher Command School there for new officers of general's rank. Informing Smuts that something like the Staff College for higher ranks was long overdue, Auchinleck packed Chink off to work it out in detail, and explained to Smuts in his letter of introduction that experience of the last few months had convinced him that most incoming commanders lacked training in modern warfare. Six days after the retirement row Chink flew down, and stayed openly with Eve. He threw himself into the project possessively, negotiating with Smuts and the General Staff, finding a building and working out the course syllabus. He got on well with the dapper, steely-eyed Smuts and persuaded him to close down the Pretoria staff course and use Haifa instead. Soon he had it all on paper. He drew up an eleven-week course for sixteen men of all services that included war games, a visit to GHQ ME to interview the Commander-in-Chief and examine the latest developments, and a tour of the battlefield, followed by under-study attachment to GHQ ME on graduation. He named it 'Tara', and counted on being put in charge of it himself.

The scheme could go ahead, Auchinleck was informed by Brooke, but not with Chink as Commandant, not on the same scale and not in South Africa, as Palestine was more accessible due to air shortages. 'Sorry about Dorman-Smith too,' cabled back Auchinleck, 'as I feel he has the brains, imagination, originality and energy to give the course a good start. He has it all in his head already. As to experience in command, I am afraid I do not place such a great premium on it as you do. . . .'

Chink was recalled on 8 May. The choice now, explained Auchinleck, was between two major-general jobs: Ritchie's old job of Deputy Chief of the General Staff in Cairo, or an unspecified role under Wavell in India. Chink did not hesitate. 'I said, stay here, naturally, because I know all about the ME,' he recounted to Eve. 'I will do my best to escape India and stay with the Auk. I am sure I can do better work here. Besides, it is easier for us to find each other after the war.' Wavell's reaction came on 12 May while they were breakfasting together after their run, and 'reluctantly' Auchinleck was allowed prior claim. 'A narrow squeak,' Chink added in a postscript, and set off euphorically to meet de Guingand with the latest *Harpers* magazine, in which there was an article by John Dos Passos that he wanted Freddie to read.

Irritation at McCreery's presence fell away. Red tabs and a useful job transformed everything and he 'basked like an Assyrian cohort in scarlet and gold', although he had to wait till 16 June for the appointment to be confirmed by the War Office. He began at once. The maps showed that in his absence Rommel had taken Benghazi and that Eighth Army was falling back fast, strung out down a vulnerable forty-mile line south of Gazala, but Smith was conspicuous by his absence in GHQ ME and in his place was an unexpected face. 'I am delighted to see Smith go but less delighted to see Corbett,' he wrote that night. 'A sound little nut of a man, but emotional and humourless and at sea in a big HQ, sharing the Auk's Indian Army inferiority complex.' In India Tom Corbett had been Inspector of Cavalry and one of the first names on his 'Bear of Little Brain' list, but he was an improvement on Smith and would be a useful channel to Auchinleck. Improving matters further, de Guingand was installed as Director of Military Intelligence.

'*14 May*: Without a doubt this is a much more efficient show than it was last year.' '*15th*: Yesterday I more or less swooped about the building looking at the layout and finding where chaps live.' '*20th*: Usually I go in at 8 a.m. I like a few quiet minutes to collect my thoughts in before the morning conference with the general Staff directors. I feel very inadequate. So much is going on and I've not got my data in my head. My mind should be free to think ahead and it won't be until I know my facts.' Auchinleck's resilience, after almost a year in the job, impressed him.

But Chink's proprietorial air offended people, and he came across as manipulative and arrogant. Harding, who was in charge of training, was incensed at being excluded from sessions that had previously been open to all the top staff planners, and Harding and McCreery were old friends. Chink's sense of humour grated too. A Gilbert and Sullivan production was on at the Opera House, and he laughed at British 'backs to the wall' predictability. He resigned from the rowdy Turf

Club, ridiculing it as a bear garden, for the less fashionable Mohammid Ali. Meeting his old Haifa student John Hackett again, he murmured that the only thing wrong with Eighth Army was an 'embarras de Ritchies'. 'I can't look upon this war business,' he was confiding to Eve meanwhile, 'as anything but a ghastly game played with gusto by two groups of underdeveloped children with dreadful potenties [*sic*] as toys. I cannot avoid the feeling of unreality. I, too, can play the game as it should be played, but with the sense that I am playing in a nursery as an adult.' He was reminded of his last fight with Victor in the Bellamont drawing room, and how enjoyable it had been. 'The same sort of business is going on now,' he added, 'only I seem to have grown up and can look at it all with an angry detachment.'

On 27 May he arranged a dinner at Mena for his Staff College pupil Prince Henry, Duke of Gloucester, who was touring the Middle East, and invited the other ex-students in Cairo. 'I laughed at our fantastic system,' he wrote to her afterwards, 'that he, who is created to exist in a vacuum by an intensive process of selective breeding, is a Lieutenant General, while one student, a good hardworking chap, is a brigadier, another a full colonel and the rest Lieut. Cols. He looks not unlike a dinosaur – same uncomprehending blank look, little brain in big skeleton. The world must shed its monarchs, just as it shed its dinosaurs.' As the dinner droned on his exasperation mounted. 'HRH had been told pretty clearly that most of us were busy men who got off to bed early, but didn't leave the table till 12.15. Was I angry!' So much was amateur.

The static Gazala Line horrified him, because it was fortified by minefields and defensive 'boxes' which he considered unsound, and which in turn were garrisoned by the brigade groups he had criticised earlier over the fragmentation of artillery. British Intelligence expected a frontal attack, but Chink believed that Rommel would take the greater risk of coming up obliquely from the desert, around the box of Bir Hachim. Setting both routes out on paper ten days earlier, he had advised Auchinleck to concentrate Eighth Army on the central ridge of the Trigh Capuzzo and to make sure that the armoured divisions did not operate under separate command. The expected attack had begun shortly before the dinner party.

'The German problem is how to disintegrate our layout and I think he is trying to do it by a combined feint round the south of Bir Hachim and a breakthrough south of Gazala,' he wrote impatiently early next morning. 'I'll know in two hours' time.' The judgement proved correct, and excited by anticipating Rommel's thinking, he worked through till late in the busy war room without strain. Information coming in indicated that the Germans were running into trouble and there was an opportunity for counter-attack. Auchinleck drew up a letter of advice detailing how this might be done, and told him to take it up to Ritchie in the morning.

'29 *May: Noon.* Trying to write in the flippant tail of a Boston bomber. Feet on the parachute exit, body wrapped in a not uncomfortable harness. Behind me sits the rear gunner and I hope he knows his job! Air and land situation vague, but from all we've heard today, most reassuring.' At Eighth Army HQ he was told that Ritchie was forward, and he waited. Contrary to expectation, the atmosphere was efficient and optimistic, and as soon as he reached Cairo again on 31 May Chink reported straight to Auchinleck and Prince Henry and then rushed off to join de Guingand and three other GHQ officers at the Mohammid Ali. 'We lifted our glasses to the first real resounding kick in the pants which the Boche has received,' he exulted afterwards. But before sleeping, he got out of bed again to add a significant fact. It was 'very interesting' that the Italian fleet was doing nothing to assist the German offensive, and two days later he returned to this apparent German Achilles heel. 'Enemy operations remarkably stupid,' he noted, 'especially in the way they left the *Italians* on one side of our front to attack us frontally while they came round the back. Did they really believe the Wops would attack? It is very reassuring for the future.'

By then reassurance was welcome. No Eighth Army offensive action had resulted from Auckinleck's letter, and Ultra decrypts, with their twenty-four-hour time-lag, showed up Ritchie's inability to anticipate Rommel's moves. The unchanged tone of confidence bore little relation to the danger revealing itself on GHQ ME maps, and Auchinleck's concern redoubled on 1 June when news came in of the loss of 150th Brigade, isolated in a box north of Bir Hachim, due to slow command reactions. With Bir Hachim now surrounded and Rommel's attack under way – 'Still consider the situation favourable to us' Ritchie signalled, 'and getting better daily' – a long conference was held and the resulting advice ignored again.

Chink was by now incredulous at Ritchie's underestimation of the opposition; although Rommel was strongly posted in the Cauldron, a bridgehead through the Gazala minefields, Eighth Army proposed to attack him head on there. Taking advantage of the early-morning run,

Chink urged Auchinleck to sack Ritchie and take over command, but to no avail. Meeting Francis Tuker, who had succeeded him as DMT in India and was passing through Cairo, he let rip. 'Chink was palpably anxious,' recalled Tuker in his memoirs. 'And took no pains to conceal his feelings when he discussed latest developments. He had no illusions.'

But surveying the tense faces that night at Evening Prayers, as the regular top staff meeting was called, he felt as set apart as always. Deriding them privately as the Gloom Club, his squibs about Bir Hachim still being a thorn in the enemy's backside drew perfunctory smiles as reports came in of the incompetence of the Eighth Army counter-stroke against the Cauldron position, codenamed Aberdeen. The extent of the failure was hard to gauge because of Ritchie's prevarication, as when he described the loss of 110 British tanks as 'not wholly successful' for Rommel. But it would later be apparent that co-operation between armour and infantry had fallen apart during Messervy's disastrous frontal attack, and Chink's anger then was hard to contain. 'There is a tendency to justify Bull in A China Shop behaviour,' he had written savagely of such actions, 'by the apology that after all, toughness counts in war and it's tough to run violently on the enemy from in front. Yes, but only tough on one's troops. I have never liked Soldiers' Battles, letting the soldiers retrieve the mistakes of High Command. It may be magnificent, but it *isn't* war.' His criticism of Ritchie's generalship became more vocal, but ironically he himself would be the one blamed for the losses of Aberdeen, after it had been refought over the bar at Shepheard's Hotel.

'*5 June*: The end will be favourable if Ritchie is even 50% competent. If he isn't then that's that and anything may happen.' '*8th*: There is no brilliance in our management. Courage, tenacity, obstinacy, but not the science. There are so few men in our army who make war their profession; such as there are are rebels, and rebels aren't employed till orthodoxy is emptied. I'm sorry for the Auk. He has stuck to NR and NR hasn't the divine spark. It's been going on now for 14 days and is nowhere near ended yet. I think I could have finished it in a week – but then I always do.' '*12th*: One has to rely on Ritchie's judgement. We have made mistakes, and when you make mistakes you're liable to lose points, and points in war are men and guns, tanks and vehicles. We'd have paid for "Tara" 100% already, had that school been in existence two years ago. Too damn late.' '*13th*: For two weeks now victory has been within our grasp, yet we haven't achieved it. The fault lies in ourselves. Auk may have to pay a high price for his loyalty to a man who behind an imposing façade is a very ordinary occupational soldier. . . . I regret that my glowing vision of the possibilities arising out of the original Axis failure should have temporarily obscured my judgement about the personalities concerned. If I can drive any consolation about being right, it is that one learns to back one's judgement in big things.' That day Bir Hachim fell to the Germans.

The Gloom Club was still in session after midnight in 'filthy' heat, with fans revolving slowly overhead, when Chink put his point that there was an opportunity to regroup and form a new front further back, between Tobruk and El Adem. He had come straight to the War Room from dining with the British Ambassador and Reggie, who was stopping briefly in Cairo on his way to a London meeting ('We were in pretty good form,' Reggie revealed subsequently, 'a damn good evening') – and left exhilarated that he had managed to convince them. But the move was based on false information, as Eighth Army dispositions had been inaccurately radioed back.

Churchill's insistence that isolated Tobruk had to be held to the death for the sake of morale in England added to their difficulties, because it was tying up troops that might tip the balance elsewhere. Militarily it made sense to refuse, and at the luncheon which Auchinleck gave for Reggie next day the dilemma was still unresolved. Meanwhile Chink was detailed to put his brother in the picture, and after explaining the tactical situation facing Eighth Army, he begged Reggie to put their case for reinforcements to Whitehall in person as soon as he reached London. 'I asked him bluntly – whether he thought that Rommel would get to Cairo,' Reggie recalled later. 'He considered his answer and, after a pause, said: "Provided the Auk accepts the plan which I am putting up to him, we can tie Rommel up into knots." . . . I suggested some of their fighting men must be pretty tired. . . . He agreed but said "Their tails will get right up once they know that we can defeat Rommel, which we will do if the Auk listens to me." ' It was a long way from the Heir gesturing towards his trees at Bellamont Forest, but attitudes remained the same.

Towards midnight in the War Room that night another imperative signal about Tobruk was brought in from Churchill, and Chink watched sympathetically as Auchinleck crossed to a desk at one side of the room and wrote out the order for the fortress to be held, detailing him to take it up in the morning. At 7.30 a.m. Corbett phoned to say that Auchinleck had decided to send him instead, as someone of equal seniority was needed. When Corbett returned, still flushed, Chink's anger at Ritchie's culpability showed how wise the substitution had been. Told that Ritchie had shouted, 'I'm damned if I will,' he snapped that he would have put him under arrest on the spot. Ritchie's reaction stood out as something more than Amateur panic. It was now clear that the bulk of Eighth Army, contrary to the information radioed back, had retired eastwards and left Tobruk, under the command of a youthful South African, the newly promoted Major General Klopper, dangerously exposed. It could no longer realistically be defended.

Chink tried to force the issue about Ritchie again on the Dawn Patrol next day, but failed. 'You ask me how much influence I have on events,' he had replied to Eve before setting off at 5.30 a.m., relieved to be officially confirmed as DCGS at last. 'The answer is that at present I have very considerable influence, but unfortunately I can't influence past decisions, and these are having their effect on the present battle.' Visiting the front with Auchinleck the following day, he was encouraged by a new impatience with Ritchie's assurances that Rommel would take his time over Tobruk. On the flight back he teased Auchinleck about the tourism potential of the coastline beneath them, pointing out that after the war a site near Gazala, where there was sweet water, could be very profitable. They could start with a hotel, a fleet of cars and a concession against competition from the local government; old soldiers would make excellent guides, and arrangements with the airlines would be simple. 'Very well,' Auchinleck responded. 'We'll start in partnership. Of course, the women will all want to shop in Cairo.' Pleased with his ruse, Chink dined with Wilson on arrival, and said what he really thought.

He had identified four main reasons for the run of disasters – Ritchie's poor judgement, the dispersal of artillery, the 'separatism' of the cavalry, and reliance on 'boxes' which the enemy could bypass. 'Here I am,' he wrote next morning,

> with a head running wild with ideas for reshaping this Army, because we have got to reshuffle it and its weapons before we find the right tactical combination. I honestly believe that half the Army are delighted to be settled down in fortifications again because they understand that. But we've got to dominate the desert for 500 miles. Wrong leadership, organisation and technique. . . . But it's hard to tell practical men to think big when the Army they are given is a scattered dust of minor units dispersed about a commercial institu-

tion called the British Empire. The only thing to do then is to shoot or fish or hunt or play polo, make love and die like a gentleman. Well the business now is to rectify this in the hot heart of a war in which the enemy still has the initiative. I start again today with the theories I held this time last year, and we'll see what can be done.

He lunched on sandwiches with Auchinleck at the Gezira Club among members relaxing in beachwear, and they discussed the general situation cagily over American iced tea, a drink neither had had before. 'The Auk didn't want to be alone and wished something constructive for the future,' he wrote afterwards. 'We had much the same conversation as eleven months ago only then he was still full of illusions and today he is a very different person. I greatly doubt that he'll be allowed to survive long enough to stage a comeback. I feel that he'll be made a scapegoat for the failure of a system, and even though he cannot escape a certain measure of responsibility for the choice of subordinates, yet his removal would be disastrous. He has so many of the qualities of a really great man.'

But in the dust of Tobruk Rommel's bombardment had already begun and that night the symbol of British resistance fell, yielding 25,000 men and vital stores. 'Klopper I met and liked,' Chink promptly wrote of the young successor to Morshead. 'Very inexperienced, absolutely loyal and I am certain did his best. I did query his suitability purely on experience, but it was too late.' Meeting Klopper during his leave in January had, in fact, been the spur for insisting on the urgent need for a Higher Command school.

Corbett shrank from the clamouring war correspondents, and Chink stood in for him with alacrity. On 21 June he gave an hour-long press conference, facing criticism which he subscribed to himself but could not admit. Determined to emphasise the need for Auchinleck to remain, he fenced adroitly and his phrases were widely taken up. 'The disappointment may be tempered,' quoted The Times on 22 June, 'by the consideration that in the see-saw of desert warfare . . . always the most mobile and hard-hitting force wins. . . . Tobruk was practically indefensible. . . . Our commanders . . . are not despondent. . . . They are convinced that the next time the pendulum swings it will go in our favour, and the swing will be deeper.' But the confidence was not an act put on to fool the press. He was still sure that losing Cyrenaica did not necessarily mean losing Egypt too.

'Oh, but it's hot, sweat pouring off me,' he wrote in his hotel room.

'How can one think clearly in such a climate? Only one *must*, and I believe my brain is working well.' The scenario of Wavell's Worst Possible Case haunted him, and now there was the added danger of German troops on the Eastern Front reaching the Caucasus by September. Ultra revealed that Rommel's intention was to outflank Egypt's frontier defences, and Eighth Army had 70,000 troops fewer after the losses at Gazala. To complicate matters further, it contained a high proportion of Commonwealth divisions, who had the right to appeal to their own governments against unwelcome orders.

Still Auchinleck supported Ritchie. Chink flew up with him again on 22 June, by which time Eighth Army HQ was nearer still, at Sidi Barrani. 'Auk taking the rear gunner's seat and I the bomb aimer's in the glass covered nose,' he scribbled en route. 'I know what frying in one's own juice feels like. What would the gallant befeathered major generals of old times on prancing chargers say of their modern equivalent, sweating like a basted quail in a glass casserole?' On arrival they found Whiteley evidently worn out, and Ritchie making preparations to fight at Mersa Matruh. Chink listened to the plans in disbelief. It was the area he had studied so closely himself, and when analysing it with O'Connor they had always agreed that only a token force should be put there, and strength concentrated instead on the higher ground inland. He had two words for Ritchie's stand – 'fatuously numb' – and gave him no points for bravery. Once more Auchinleck made no change of command.

On 23 June Ultra indicated that Rommel was poised to drive deep into Egypt, and air reconnaissance reported German troops sweeping towards Sidi Barrani. On 24 June Afrika Korps approached the now derelict Mersa Matruh defences where Ritchie was waiting to take them on. In German minds the battle was as good as won. Egyptian stamps with the joint profiles of Hitler and Mussolini were printed, and Rommel's appointment as Military Governor of Cairo negotiated in full. Mussolini had been so gratified by Hitler's telegram – 'British Eighth Army practically destroyed. . . . Historic hour . . . will not be repeated' – that he replied with an equal sense of occasion, declaring that 'The historic moment for the conquest of Egypt has come.' And to be ready for the triumphal entrance into Cairo he had already flown to Derna, equipped with a selection of full-dress uniforms and his favourite white horse. Aghast at the threat to the crucial oilfields, the Allies held their breath. 'We are at this moment,' intoned Churchill in

London, 'in the presence of a recession from hopes and prospects in the Middle East and the Mediterranean unequalled since the fall of France.'

In Chink's noisy, stuffy room at the Continental, with three-quarters of an hour to go before the dance band overhead packed up, his phone rang while he was writing to Eve. '*24 June: 11.30 p.m.* Just been told guardedly on the open that I must go to the WD tomorrow and be prepared to stay there for several days. Worse situations have been retrieved by bold and courageous action. We'll see what can be done, but it won't be very orthodox! You think I'm an incurable optimist. I do look on the bright side – one must. But I try to look at things objectively, as a military scientist.'

Glancing around his room one last time at 6.15 a.m. next morning, he took down Liddell Hart's *The Strategy of the Indirect Approach* from his row of books and slid it into his despatch box. 'One hot helter-skelter,' he wrote hastily at the foot of his letter. 'I've no idea as to my mission. But it's bound to be exciting.'

10

The First Battle
of
Alamein

Rommel had no doubt at all. 'The fall of Tobruk and the collapse of the Eighth Army', he pointed out subsequently, 'was the one moment in the African war when the road to Alexandria lay open and virtually undefended. . . . There [were] only a few days during which we could hope to conquer Alamein and take the Suez Canal area.' Egypt was the cornerstone of a strategic system of defence, because its loss risked not only the oilfields but a German–Japanese link-up, and that would cut Allied contact with India, south Russia and Turkey, ending all prospect of a counter-offensive in the Mediterranean. 'I took Dorman-Smith with me,' Auchlineck said for his part, 'because I knew he had a most fertile, active and a very good brain. I wanted him because I knew he was a man I could talk to – a fresh mind.'

That fresh mind studied the Commander-in-Chief as they perched on suitcases on the Boston's floor for the engines to reach full throttle at the 2 p.m. take-off. Wavell's dictum about the last ounce of optimism being more useful than many men had prompted him to begin as he intended to go on, and with the firm announcement that even condemned men had a last good meal, he had made sure of an excellent lunch first at the Mohammid Ali. Now he detected more uncertainty in Auchinleck than he had seen before, and cursed Jessie for unsettling him at such a moment.

But in concentrating upon Auchinleck, the anomaly of his own role escaped him. 'Major-General E. E. Dorman-Smith, my Deputy Chief of the General Staff', Auchinleck would explain in his official despatches, 'accompanied me as my principal staff officer, but no change was made in the staff officers . . . of Eighth Army.' But one function of high command is to establish a clear subordinate chain, and

Whiteley was already the Eighth Army's principal staff officer. Confusion was inherent in the decision to split that role and use Chink for GHQ ME staff work and Whiteley for Eighth Army business. It crossed the wires.

And the relationship was to generate rancour and suspicion because of its added unorthodoxy. In Chink's view, subordinate politenesses hampered decision-making. To work with the greatest effectiveness, he believed that a commander and a chief of staff should be as interdependent and equal as the Hindenburg–Ludendorff partnership during the First World War, in which the German commander contributed the authority and his chief of staff the creative thinking, working in tandem. Chink's view of himself as a chief of staff in the German system flew in the face of tradition, and tradition becomes more precious in a crisis, never less. Instead of seeing the personal ramifications and pointing them out for his own protection, he did not think beyond the urgent decisions facing them. He decided to sign himself DCGS in-the-field – 'like a London church' – and turned his mind to rallying Auchinleck and designing traps for Rommel. There was no need to say anything more about Ritchie, because he would be sacked on arrival.

Liddell Hart's theories were at the front of his mind because Basil had sent the latest edition of *The Strategy of the Indirect Approach* out to Haifa, and every débâcle had driven the reasoning further home. He took the book out now but Auchinleck spurned it, saying he did not expect to have much time for reading. Undeterred Chink, switched to direct recommendations.

Control of the artillery had to be centralised, he began, as they had less artillery than ever following Aberdeen, where four artillery regiments had been lost in the Cauldron. Auchinleck nodded, motioning him to go on. They were in agreement that Ritchie's dispositions at Matruh were unsound, with such a dangerously weak centre, and he pointed out that a co-ordinated retreat to El Alamein would buy valuable time and the opportunity to redeploy. They could count on 13th and 30th Corps and separate components of Dominion troops, but weakness in armour was a major problem. He advised regrouping the sixty heavy Grant tanks together and weeding out lighter vehicles for a Light Armoured Division, for mobile use on the flanks. Eighth Army had to be pruned down to essentials if it was to be flexible, and he suggested composite battle groups on the German model to make maximum use of what was left. Isolated 'boxes', he repeated, were a handicap. Above all, the Italians were Rommel's weak spot. If Eighth Army concentrated its attack on the Italian divisions, the Afrika Korps would have to be deployed in their support, which would dilute Rommel's striking power. Auchinleck approved each point, and they went over the essentials thoroughly before landing.

A yellow staff car was drawn up to meet them at Maarten Baggush, and Chink fielded glances from the staff at Eighth Army HQ while Auchinleck was in Ritchie's caravan. He intended to see Ritchie leave for himself. By 7 p.m., when Auchinleck came down into the familiar concrete underground operations room, Chink was in place with the rest to hear instructions he already knew. Memories of the planning there in 1940 brought back O'Connor's assessment of a successful commander. Would Auchinleck, he wondered, be able to restore the situation after a serious defeat and a deep retreat?

By midnight, when he set off ahead for Daba under a German air attack, he was satisfied with progress. Auchinleck had spoken well, and had been well received. The opportunity now to think without interruption was welcome, because he had always taught that achieving a cerebral rapport was part of dominating the enemy. 'From the moment we suppressed Ritchie,' he would be telling Liddell Hart within the year, 'I had the strangest feeling of certainty about all I did or advised. The certainty that I could see what the enemy was about to do and how one could damage him. It seemed as if all I'd read or thought about war came to my aid. I didn't feel I could go wrong.'

Since the late-night phone call he had been in his element, and he did not disguise it. Charles Richardson, summoned to take up the post of Lieutenant-Colonel Future Plans, had been stunned to be greeted with 'Oh Charles, we're having a *marvellous* time!' when he arrived by Lysander before the meeting ended. In his junior-staff capacity at Eighth Army Richardson wanted clarity and leadership, not debonair enthusiasm, and since his hostile opinions about Chink are on record it should be mentioned that he was not then indoctrinated for Ultra and so was only partially in the know. The team of six who would be meeting from the second night onwards for the regular Evening Prayers consisted of Auchinleck, Chink, Whiteley and Richardson, as well as 'Spud' Murphy and Hugh Mainwaring of Eighth Army Intelligence; Murphy gave the enemy picture and Mainwaring briefed on the preceding twenty-four-hour operations. By that time the enemy had raced 300 miles from Tobruk already, and was clearly ramming on to Alexandria.

Very quickly Richardson's hackles rose. He resented the fact that discussions which should have been led by Auchinleck tended to be led by Chink, and that his fellow sapper Whiteley was in the shade. 'It was clear to us that Auchinleck thought highly of Chink and admired him,' he said in 1985, 'because when he came up against the next problem the first thing he did was send for him. Auchinleck was dominated by him. Whiteley was at Evening Prayers as well, and it was difficult for him. He was advised that something would happen and then Chink would chip in. It was difficult to know who was right – I certainly couldn't make those judgements then.' Evening Prayers became increasingly grim to Richardson as ideas 'floated around' and impatience at Chink's 'mercurial' mind obscured the lack of ideas from the rest of the team. Whiteley was worn out, Mainwaring dour and humourless and Richardson himself did not feel he could give much advice. Chink's optimism was irritating, his energy wearing and his strong will set teeth on edge, and he had become too academic and arbitrary to bother with diplomacy.

The custodian of the incoming Ultra decrypts, E. T. 'Bill' Williams, was soon equally distrustful. Williams was an Oxford history don who had joined up in 1939, and he bridled at Chink's arrogance without comprehending his military expertise. The officers in charge of Ultra intelligence were in continual dread of it being misinterpreted or used so freely that its existence got out, and many commanders gave them good cause for worry. But Chink's ability to interpret the often random information was about to be crucial in the change of thrust and improvisation of the fighting ahead of them, and the nearest he would ever come in post-war years to hinting at its existence was when he boasted that it had been uncanny to know what Rommel was about to do next – a remark attributed to flight of fancy. Knowledge of the input of Ultra, which was admitted in 1974, and his understanding of it throws fresh light on bizarre contemporary impressions. One unindoctrinated junior officer recoiled as Chink tapped the map in the operations caravan one morning 'with his long fingers, declaring with frighteningly unreal afflatus "I think we'll attack here, tonight."'

One emotion shared by all the observers at Evening Prayers was apprehension, which distorts impressions; and the introduction of mixed-brigade groups heightened this. At that early stage of the war regiments were so independent that it was said no two units would co-operate unless their commanding officers had already slept with each other's wives, and Chink did not bother to explain that he was against battle groups too – in principle. In his post-mortem on Crusader he had recommended that regiments which trained together should operate together. 'To change the composition of brigades or to detach them without good reason destroys all team work,' he had written then. 'It should be done in exceptional circumstances only, and then only for a short duration.' But these were exceptional circumstances and the duration was going to be short and sharp, so he wasted no time on conciliation. Disquiet filtered downwards as groups were patched hastily together without explanation and Matruh appeared to be given up without a proper fight.

In contrast, Chink's confidence increased. 'The wheel has turned full circle,' he was writing elatedly to Eve. 'Our job now is to remember that as late as March 1918 we faced a similar disaster in France, only on a larger scale, and weathered the storm. We just need time and he'll give us damn little. We must make the most of split seconds.'

On the night of 27 June Eighth Army began to fall back to the Alamein position. This was a fifty-mile bottleneck where both flanks would be secure, bounded on the south by the quicksand of the Quattara Depression, impassable even to camels, and on the north by the sea. Alamein, Arabic for Twin Cairns, was a railway halt, with a short platform and a hut. The gap between the Mediterranean and the Depression was protected by four infantry boxes roughly fifteen miles apart, and dominated by two low ridges, the Miteiriya and the Ruweisat. 'You need have no doubt as to the ultimate result,' Chink promised Eve on 28 June. 'We've got a reasonable grip on the situation, and though we may have to give ground for a little, it's the power to fight the last round which counts. We have now straightened out our plans and I remain an optimist. We haven't begun with the Wop Hun yet, but we will.'

He concentrated his considerable charm on relieving the lonely strain which Auchinleck was bound to be feeling, careless of how that might appear. In the daytime they were rarely apart and at night they slept beside one another on the sand, in a lean-to tent attached to one side of Auchinleck's caravan. He understood why Auchinleck sometimes reached for his hand in the dark, and went to sleep without letting go. 'I think what sticks most clearly and vividly in my head,' Auchinleck would write as late as 1967, 'is that drive back along the dark and deserted road after we had taken over from Ritchie, and the next morning when we were very much alone in the desert. Also I remember often our tent at our HQ and our bedding rolls in the sand. I have always liked your outlook on life. . . . I do not think I could have stuck it out anywhere else, or without you to advise and plan ahead.'

In his GHQ ME staff capacity it was his job to keep Auchinleck up to date with the developing international picture and the Joint Planning Staff's timetable. He spent the afternoon of 28 June assessing the situation from the Commander-in-Chief's angle, so much more complex than the narrower view of the army commander, and concluded that to preserve Eighth Army, the sole shield of the Middle East, if necessary they would have to be prepared to fall back as far as the Delta where they would be able to halt Rommel by holding Cairo and Alexandria, which could not be attacked simultaneously. Unlike Wavell's Worst Possible Case, however, this conclusion did not stay in a drawer. Corbett was told when he called up, and meeting the two Corps commanders, Corbett alarmed them with the unnecessary comment 'The Chief has decided to save Eighth Army,' before returning to Cairo to work openly on provisional orders, encouraged by a cable from Churchill on 3 July. 'The whole idea', Churchill stressed then, after wondering how Rommel's tanks would get on among the Delta canals, 'is that Egypt should be defended just as drastically as if it were Kent or Sussex.' Chink, meanwhile, had moved on to something else.

'A bit sudden to be dropped into this very good imitation of a débâcle,' he wrote on 29 June, snatching a moment from planning with the staff. 'But I think I'm competing. We are still sorting ourselves out prior to giving battle again under more advantageous conditions which will cramp his armour and give our better artillery a chance. He has got Matruh but that means nothing provided he does not get us inside it, and he hasn't done so. Eighth Army is free to fight again. We'll make out somehow, and already the party seems to be sorting out fairly neatly. The Boche is flat out for victory, and if he doesn't get a decisive one he is going to experience a tremendous reaction. So we'll see how it goes. I'd sooner be here as a man than anywhere else in the world.' He had no more qualms about Auchinleck's aggressiveness after hearing him castigate 'these damn English' for being taught to be good losers for too long. 'I have never been one,' Auchinleck had rounded on him, seeing his expression, 'and I am going to win.'

And that priority justified the bruising of Whiteley's feelings on 30 June when Chink was asked to take over all the staff work, both GHQ and Eighth Army, and accepted without question. Dealing with two people on overlapping matters had been unworkable for Auchinleck in practice, and Chink saw the decision as a gain, because Whiteley's tiredness was undoing much of his own encouragement. 'The Auk detected a strong strain of defeatism in Whiteley and insulated himself from that through myself,' he would explain after Whiteley's death. 'I issued nothing to Eighth Army that was not approved by and directed by the Auk, and it was at the Auk's express orders that I behaved as I did. Personally I did not give a damn what I was. I had no staff, no servant, but I was at the Auk's elbow. He listened to me, argued with me and we made joint decisions. Perhaps he would have done better to send Whiteley away, but he did not want me to become tied down to general staff administration.' To compound his misreading of the human element, he requested that Whiteley should stay on as he knew the Eighth Army staff and had a good liaison with the RAF. Whiteley did his best in an awkward situation. He continued to put out all the written messages, although it was no secret that his job had been usurped by Chink. The classic command structure was fracturing, leading to order, counter-order and disorder. Had Chink been a man of sensitivity at all, Richardson and the others thought, he would have pointed out to Auchinleck that it would be impossible for Whiteley, and asked him to choose between them.

At Eighth Army TAC HQ, now behind Ruweisat Ridge, the twenty sandy-coloured vehicles were drawn up in a dispersed group. Auchinleck's caravan, containing a desk and a divan, was guarded by his Indian servant. Beside it the operational caravan was parked, its interior walls papered by Chink with large- and small-scale maps faced with talc, to make them erasable for the grease pencils. Within a few hundred yards was the general staff lorry, and nearby the intercept lorry, the communications vehicle and the mess lorry. With the exception of Chink, all senior staff officers, including Whiteley, had their own caravan, car and servant. 'I had my sleeping kit, and change of uniform and washing gear,' he said later. 'I looked after myself and Auk's old man did the tidying up of our sleeping gear. I have never worried much about such matters – why does one mountaineer?' His unofficial, rule-breaking status could not have been more starkly underlined.

By Tuesday, 30 June, Eighth Army was installed in the Alamein position. It mustered four infantry divisions, two with 30th Corps under the command of Major-General Ramsden to the north and two with 13th Corps, commanded by Gott, to the south. Preoccupied, Chink noticed little about him. Afterwards he would recall only the huge desert snails climbing in slow motion up shrubs of camel thorn, a sandstorm or two, a sudden plague of mosquitoes blown across from the Quattara swamp, the distorting haze of hot air just above the sand, a group of Arabs who drifted in from the west during heavy fighting to watch from the Alam Halfa ridge, and the widespread Eighth Army hobby of scorpion-fighting. 'The scorps were like armies psychologically,' he observed sharply. 'Prepared to sting but reluctant to take the risk of attacking.' At first the emaciated appearance of desert soldiers shocked him, but soon he was to be down to eleven stone himself. Alamein has inspired more descriptional imagery than any other battlefield, but Chink went through with the concentration of a candidate in a top scholarship exam.

He used Eve as a sounding board, rather than a diary, and under conditions when most men had trouble managing a postcard he wrote several times a day, covering as many as twenty pages at a time. A remark like 'We have just finished a conference during which you leaned on my shoulder and listened quietly with your hair against my cheek and your hand in mine' could lead to the less romantic comment 'The Germans seem to be hard, efficient blighters. We are too slow and idle. Cromwell found the same thing in his day and he had to remake an army before he got a proper instrument for war. I always have known the sort of army I want, and if we get away with this party I'll damn well see I get it.' To disguise names he used a code based on characters in *Jurgen*.

But, absorbed though he was, he deliberately kept up a relaxed, light-hearted front for Auchinleck. Tactfully waiting in the shade of the operations caravan the following morning, to allow him solitude, he was approached by a Telsch House graduate with an intercept in which Rommel instructed the 'ladies' of Alexandria to 'make ready to receive the Afrika Korps tonight'. He thought it ideal as a distraction and recorded his exchange with Auchinleck afterwards. 'Sir, I regret to report that Eighth Army is now attempting the impossible.' 'What the hell do you mean? Do you suggest we can't stop these buggers? I brought you with me because you're an optimist.' Lamely he read the intercept out and explained that Alexandrian whores had no honour to defend. 'Don't be a damn fool, Chink.' Chink never could take situations with the ultimate seriousness demanded by the army, he admitted once, and he tended to think of Auchinleck as a roundhead and himself as a cavalier. But one of Rommel's signals picked up the night before – to the Italian troops this time – had touched a deeper chord. 'Trust your Corps,' Rommel had exhorted, 'will now find itself able to cope with so contemptible an enemy,' and Chink recalled the Kaiser's dismissal of the British Expeditionary Force as 'that contemptible little army' in 1914. As he promptly told Auchinleck, it was a splendid omen.

And Auchinleck needed a fund of optimism to draw upon. After the run of disasters, self-preservation had become the priority of many of his commanders. De Larminat of the Free French had already protested that they were mad to stand at Alamein when they could be behind the waterline of the Nile. Dan Pienaar, who commanded 1st South African Division, was even more outspoken in an interview with the incoming BBC war correspondent Denis Johnstone. 'If Alamein goes, Egypt goes,' Pienaar warned. 'If Egypt goes, the Middle East goes, and what about the British Empire?' The gloomy observation was the culmination of three days of alarming impressions that Johnstone took good care not to broadcast, and instead recorded in his diary. '27 June: No one knows where we are going or where anything is. Germans through Mersa with 100 tanks. . . . Advanced HQ has been lost. No communications. Wires down and wireless largely jammed. . . . All looking for Eighth Army rear. . . .' '30 June: Tank officer says Germans laugh at our cavalry tank tactics – Whip up the brute and charge! – but not at our artillery fire. . . . Army HQ moved at 6 a.m. this morning . . . probably preparatory to abandoning Alex. . . . Navy gone already. . . . Rumour in Cairo today that Alex is lost already.'

As that rumour about Alexandria was being written down, Auchinleck was issuing the order to stand and fight the following morning. 'The Auk has been sleeping soundly for three hours now,' Chink noted during the night. 'He'll need his rest, poor man. This is a damn critical business and the highest commander's responsibilities are quite endless. I will be very glad when I can get him away from direct command of this party. I expect we are in for a busy two days. The Boche are faced with having to go on. They've come a devil of a long way in a very short time. We stand between them and the Delta, and it's a question now as to who can stick it in the battle which will begin in a few hours.' There was no sleep for him. At noon he had gone to the mess lorry for a drink of water and drained the glass filled for him from a jerrycan, only to realise too late that it was neat paraffin. He was full of inner cleanliness, he assured Auchinleck, but his mouth and throat burned.

212

On 1 July 1942, the anniversary of 19,000 deaths on the Somme, *The Times* spelled out the emergency for readers at home. 'This is the most serious moment for the Middle East since the beginning of the war, and unless we can hold Rommel's forces for a few more days, there is no kowing what may happen.... Eighth Army has been fighting a dogged rearguard action, allowing the enemy to press forward slowly until he is in a position where our commanders thought they could best hit him a hard knock.... A grim gigantic game of chess is being played out on those hot, white desert sands.' In Cairo panic was incandescent. The streets were clogged as people rushed to leave, and the hasty burning of official papers inside the main Allied Military HQ was to give the day its name: Ash Wednesday.

Out in the desert Chink took out his small pocket book to jot down 'Battle of El Alamin [*sic*]' in the heat of a gathering duststorm. The artillery had been concentrated, the guns had been going full blast since dawn, and the sound of massed gunfire thrilled him. 'The battle seems to be on and the enemy is again attacking away to the NW,' he wrote more fully when he had a chance. 'But at least we had yesterday to sort ourselves out. The Auk is in great fettle. This is a decisive fight for him and he revels in it. He is far happier in the field than in the office. He is proving himself to be a fine commander, full of decision and grip and determination.... I find myself doing a sort of brigade major to him with a great deal less staff than a BM would actually have. The Auk takes a big chance when he tries to handle a decisive show through one staff officer. Nevertheless if everyone does his duty during the next 48 hours we'll lick the blighters properly. We seem to be holding them well, and if they're licked here they are lost. It's going to be a close run thing.' Rommel's main thrust to the sea behind the Alamein box was halted by the artillery concentration, one of the first of Chink's measures to take effect.

At the late-night conference the day was judged to have gone well, but afterwards Chink slept badly. He was disgusted by the one setback of the day, the loss of the Deir el Shein box with almost an entire battalion due to the failure of armour to come up in time. A flaw in Staff College teaching, it occurred to him, was the insufficient attention paid to defeat and retreat, a psychological experience few soldiers escaped. But it was a worry about the future that kept him awake. His anxiety about the high proportion of Dominion troops in Eighth Army, with their ability to slow overall planning by appealing to their own governments, had been deepened by Pienaar's intention that morning to pull out the South African Division to forestall a second national disaster like Tobruk, an intention which Auchinleck had in this case been able to overrule. On a personal level he was concerned about Estelle. She was staying with the Wavell's in Delhi, and he wished she was safely out of India.

'It can be said emphatically that feeling is far and away better than it has been for some time', *The Times* reported on 2 July. 'Our tactics recently have been to harry the enemy without respite, never joining full battle but luring him on to receive hard knocks and then withdrawing to make him come on further. Whatever faults can be found with the handling of our troops in the opening weeks of the battle, extremely skilful use is now being made of formations smaller in numbers and inferior in material.' But German command propaganda was simultaneously being broadcast in Egypt claiming that Rommel's divisions had broken through with the support of dive bombers, and that Eighth Army was on the retreat. The population of Cairo, faced with the evidence of contingency planning, stampeded for the second day running.

Chink was up early to stretch and rub away sand. 'This is going to be a heavy fate-filled day, and by tonight we'll know the answer to a great many questions about the future of this local war,' he noted. 'A victory here today would solve so many problems. I'm equally prepared for every sort of ending, for this is a sort of Crécy.' He was in good spirits. The fresh 9th Australian Division was on the way up to reinforce 30th Corps, and he was sure that Rommel would soon have to employ his vulnerable Italian divisions. He advised Auchinleck that the heavy Grant tanks should be concentrated together on Ruweisat Ridge, the key to the Alamein position, and a directive from Churchill on Auchinleck's desk promising that fame awaited the commander who used his artillery properly caught his eye. At last they were doing that, he commented wryly, but fame was debatable. A routine had already taken shape in which he checked the operations map for overnight developments and occupied himself with forward thinking or current operational items, and everything too minor to concern the army commander. As the day cooled they walked about the encampment together. Their relationship – 'with a difference of scale' – reminded him of the partnership with Wavell at Blackdown.

He lived for the moment, snatching sleep and drawing on his reserves of energy. Two hours catnapping on the floor of the lorry that afternoon was enough to restore alertness. 'What a thoroughly muddled affair a modern battle is', he explained for Eve's benefit during one lull. 'The desert is so large that it is possible for large forces to weave in and out of each other like battleships at sea. Control is immensely difficult, for wireless is still untrustworthy and entirely unsecret. Speak in clear and you give the enemy your plans. Speak in code and you slow everything down. Use cypher and it takes hours encoding and decoding. You pay your penny and you choose your inconvenience. Our relatively tiny army is fighting in an area 50×50 miles, 2500 square miles of country, and in that vast space small mechanised forces churn round each other bewilderingly unless you hold the key to their movement.'

Hold the key to their movement. . . . When British tanks met German troops on Ruweisat Ridge that afternoon, instead of the expected gallant charge they were seen to hold off at long range, artillery support well co-ordinated. 'German forces', groaned the war diary of Rommel's 90th Light Panzer Division, 'seem unable to take this last English fortress before the Nile Delta with the forces available.' In the afternoon – 'along the lines I wanted', Chink recorded – Auchinleck ordered 13th Corps to move up towards the coast road, bringing Rommel's army under the combined fire of both corps as well as RAF bombers. Later it would be learned that Rommel changed his plans that night and accepted that his offensive would be able to continue, at most, for one more day. As he would acknowledge in due course, 'General Auchinleck, who had meanwhile taken over command himself at El Alamein, was handling his forces with very considerable skill and tactically better than Ritchie had done. He seemed to view the situation with decided coolness, for he was not allowing himself to be rushed into accepting a second-best solution by any moves we made.'

TAC HQ was under intermittent fighter fire on 3 July, and at one point a shell knifed through the operations caravan, causing Chink to dive with Auchinleck for the shallow slit trench beside the door. But his concentration remained on Ruweisat Ridge, where Rommel had attacked early, using armour of the Afrika Korps and – at last – two Italian divisions, Ariete and Trieste. Ariete was under counter-attack by Gott's 13th Corps, and by noon was reported to have lost all its artillery and to be down to five usable tanks. Chink took time during the afternoon to brief *The Times* correspondent and indicate where Rommel's next strike was expected. 'I asked him how we proposed to meet the attack,' ran the printed account. 'He smiled and said: "We've prepared our plans – whether the enemy attacks or not. . . . You can say the Eighth Army is no longer on the run".'

In this he was correct. On the night of 3 July Rommel ordered his men to dig in at 22.56, having signalled his master, General Kesselring, that as further attack on a large scale was no longer possible he was going to regroup to face a British counter-offensive. In Cairo, however, the shift in power was not apparent. Floating bridges were still being put into place over the Nile and inundations prepared, outdated and misleading signs of an emergency that had passed.

At 7a.m. on 4 July Chink had already been up for three hours, and he was thoroughly content. 'Such a beautiful dawn this morning,' he noted.

Quiet with a low whispering desert wind and the Eastern sky one great streak of gold and crimson, while above in the clear darkness was the morning star and its little follower. Just the desert horizon, that incredible band of colours. The sky deepening from light blue to sepia at the zenith and two glorious day stars. Like one clear high note of music. This is the fourth day of the Battle of El Alamein and we have at least gained indispensable time. More than that, we have administered a severe check to the enemy at a moment when I feel certain that he thought us down and out. We're full of fight, and may yet stage a decisive comeback. We are fighting to that end. The tide is surely turning.

That morning he inspected the first German prisoners, satisfying proof of the turn of events. 'Numbers of tired and demoralised Boche', he noted at 20.30 hours. 'But though we can claim a second good day, the battle of El Alamein is not over yet.' But in his optimistic way he refused to look at the negative side. 'We are a good deal stronger than we were four days ago,' he wrote. 'More guns, more tanks, more troops. The enemy will have to make a supreme effort to reverse the situation and regain the initiative. Things look very much better than I ever imagined when we started out on this adventure 11 days ago. It looked then as if we might be bundled out of Egypt altogether, unless some miracle stopped the rot.' To add to his pleasure he had been able to wash his face and shave that afternoon, for the first time since leaving Cairo.

In spare moments he was working on his customary post-mortem of the previous fighting, which made him even more disdainful of Ritchie.

'I go so far as to say', he concluded that night, 'that had the battle in front of Tobruk been fought on the same lines as this, Rommel would have been signally defeated after his first rush. It was a sad story and an unnecessary one, for what we can do now in the teeth of disaster could far more easily have been done then. The last four days have shown that the technique used here could equally well have been employed in the Tobruk fighting.' At 03.30 new Ultra information prompted him to work out a counter-stroke for the following day.

But in the morning the infantry–armour rift threatened to disrupt the all-out effort. German troops were still clinging to the west side of Ruweisat Ridge, where British tanks were hesitant to take them on as planned. Chink was at 30th Corps HQ early when the highly strung Commander of 1st Armoured Division, Major-General Lumsden, burst in to demand that his men be relieved, and he reported the confrontation at once to Auchinleck. The scene strengthened his opinion that the problem had to be ironed out quickly through combining armour and infantry under single divisional commands. In Eighth Army tribalism was adding to the mutual contempt, as Great Britain supplied the armour that never seemed to be where it was needed and Dominion and Commonwealth countries provided the majority of the infantry. But he kept his anger hidden in front of Auchinleck, and tried to consider the situation objectively.

'Today may well be decisive,' he wrote when he was alone. 'I doubt if Rommel's troops can stand the strain. Ours, too, are tired, but they've got water, rations and petrol and they've stopped going back. . . . Too hectic for anything except sleeping and eating, and very little sleeping at that. We are abreast of events as far as regards plans, anyhow, and nothing the enemy does can come as very much of a surprise or find us unprepared with a riposte.'

The strain and bustle of those days threw Chink and Auchinleck into their closest working relationship to date, and, demanding as it was, Chink was sufficiently detached and curious to ponder on the reasons for their affinity. He observed Auchinleck closely, and his contemporary letters refute later slurs that Eighth Army was being led by a defeatist commander. 'He really seems to enjoy his return to active campaigning,' an early extract runs. 'And he is, I feel, one of those rare birds, a real general officer with a mind and a will of his own which he is determined to impose on the enemy.' 'We lead pretty laborious lives because the Auk won't let up on things – quite properly,' he wrote another day. 'I think that habit of accepting the enemy's acts as acts of

God has done us much harm, so we intend to the best of our capacity to mould his will to ours. He's there to be defeated and fought at till he is defeated. This check here is significant. If the momentum is stopped it's not so easily started again.' At every opportunity he conserved Auchinleck's energy – 'it's late and he is already asleep, so I must try not to waken him when I go in' – and the shortcomings he also detected made him more protective.

'The Auk keeps me as a sort of third gear brain into which he changes when the situation is too uphill for his gears,' he wrote affectionately at one point.

He is a commander and a fighter but definitely *not* a deep thinker, though he has the power to grasp a new idea and the energy to put it into practice. He is besides a very good soldier and a very good manager of men, though less good as a judge of men. He is quite ruthless now and full of offensive spirit and energy. In some ways I am more forthright and uncompromising, and I'm a quicker thinker with perhaps a deeper grasp of basic principles. He relies considerably on my judgement which so far has not, I think, been false. We go over all possible developments of the situation together and then I interpret his views into policy memoranda on which the staff proper prepare orders. My duties I devise for myself in, I almost said, altercation with him, for discussion is frank and forthright and if I have carte blanche to speak my mind, he doesn't feel it necessary to spare my feelings if he disagrees. But between us we roll out the plans and policies and on the whole they're worked, though there have been anxious moments. Naturally we both watch our enemy like hawks and we study his mind and his ideas of our mind.

He came to see their working relationship in terms of two characters from Kipling's 'On the Wall', one of the stories in *Puck of Pook's Hill*, in which Parnesius and Pertinax defend Britain from the Winged Hats. 'Parnesius saw very clearly what had to be done,' he wrote of himself, 'but it was Pertinax who realised that things had to be done through men and knew how to manage that.'

TAC HQ kept sun hours. They rose at 06.00, breakfasted at 07.30 and worked through until supper at 19.30 followed by Evening Prayers with the team of six, and bed, side by side; whenever possible Auchinleck liked to be asleep by 22.00. But Chink had become used to living alone and the lack of privacy got on his nerves. To Eve he now complained that he had as little liberty as a paid female companion. 'And collect just about as much abuse, for whenever I suggest a new thing his first instinct is to force me to justify it by oaths. He usually says No and then goes off and does it. He's curious. I find him watching me as if for my approval and even borrowing my words.' Chink's fastidiousness jibbed at the 'hateful' blankets on hard sand, while the flies revolted him so much that he soon found the perpetual fried food inedible. He longed for a haircut – 'the electric light in the lorry casts the shadow of a very woolly head. . . . Haven't been able to wash properly for 14 days' – a bath and a change of clothes.

Sometimes Auchinleck glanced quizzically across as Chink bent over his latest letter to Eve and asked him to send his love to Estelle; Chink was not sure how much he guessed. His leg was incessantly pulled – 'I don't enlighten him' – about South Africa, and that began to grate. And their closeness was not lessened by the arrival of more Eighth Army staff on 7 July, which relieved him of the phone vigil and other chores but left him more time to brood on the twenty-four-hour proximity. He found he worked best when Auchinleck was asleep, and on 9 July, after 'wallowing' in sleep for two nights running, he changed his pattern to working late. That night he was tensed for the expected outcome of his stroke against the Italians, and conscious of feeling 'pretty exposed' on the Alam Halfa Ridge, where TAC HQ had followed the battle. 'Another day gained', he recorded cautiously when the results began to come in on 10 July. 'And we are worrying our enemy a little to stop him getting over-complacent. Morning news pleasing, but it's only morning and it's a long day.'

He concentrated on finishing a design he had worked out the night before, based on the Worst Possible Case thinking of 28 June. It was a defence plan stretching a tactically deft safety net in front of the cities of Cairo and Alexandria, so that if Rommel bypassed one trap he would be angled into the other. Three sectors five miles apart converged as bait, and minefields, radiating like a spider's web from each, stretched to British fortifications on the Alam Halfa ridge. He had been planning in conjunction with the Eighth Army Chief Engineer, Brigadier Kisch, a man he found stimulating to work with, and in due course the BBC war correspondent Denis Johnstone came across their work. 'Some genius', Johnstone recounted then, 'had planned our principal minefields and defence areas lengthways along the slope of the Ridge, rather like a ship with its bows facing the incoming waves . . . and this left the Barrel Track to Cairo wide open. If Rommel had driven straight ahead ... he would have been in the clear ... but without communications, for the Eighth Army ... would still be dominating the bottleneck between the ridge and the Quattara depression. ... A nice weighing of risks and possibilities. ... Here for the first time we had the spectacle of an ace German general not only being outfought, but outfoxed.' On the morning of 10 July Chink was already writing that the long-term Eighth Army defence plan envisaged a defensive battle in depth in the area El Alamein, and specifying Alam Halfa as the future battle area.

The more immediate riposte he had devised in the middle of the night of 4 July was a counter-stroke using the fresh 9th Australian Division against the Italian Sabratha Division, as Sabratha was revealed by Ultra to be holding the enemy front west of Alamein on the coastal sector. Embodying the principles of the indirect approach, the riposte began shortly and went according to plan. First, to deflect Rommel's attention elsewhere 13th Corps was pulled back and the Bab el Quattara box further south was evacuated, which successfully deluded Rommel into believing that the road to Cairo was open. Then, after an intense bombardment by massed artillery, 9th Australian Division attacked the Sabratha on 9 July and routed it. Rommel was forced to abandon his own planned offensive, and hasten north with 15th Panzer Division to stop the Australians breaking right through. On 13 and 14 July Rommel made a last attempt to force through with 21st Panzer Division, only to founder under massed gunfire.

And Ultra, with its up-to-date picture of enemy dispositions and intentions, also enabled Chink and Auchinleck to locate a counter-stroke against the Brescia and Pavia Divisions along the Ruweisat Ridge on the night of the 14th. Again the Italians broke, and Rommel, aware that his whole centre was in danger of progressive collapse, averted the danger by abandoning 21st Panzer's offensive near Alamein and moving that division to shore up the Italians. Further accurate Ultra information during the next two days led to the destruction of the Trieste and Trentino divisions on the 17th.

Chink charted his reactions day by day as the fighting continued. '*11 July*: I felt the Wop would behave badly once we got him in the open, especially now the vision of juicy brothels in Alex has faded and been replaced by the gleam of bayonets.' '*12th*: Were it not for his very good tanks, the enemy would be definitely badly placed. We'll find a way to deal with them, I hope.' '*13th*: 7.45 a.m. The situation shows no change. We are not complacent about that; it is now our business to *make* changes, and we'll do so according to our plans, not his. He does not seem inclined to do more than rest and reorganise and meanwhile he lies on a very wide front in close contact with us. Tempting, very! So we plan and hope for even 50% success.'

'*14th*: We have definitely stopped Triumphant Procession Number One. In due course we hope to reverse it. We just aren't quite ready yet. Tonight we'll try at him again. One must keep on and not let him settle down. *Later*: He is cracking at us again now – I hope without success, because if so we've scored heavily.' In the morning the attack against the Brescia and Pavia divisions was cramped by the failure of 1st Armoured Division to come up on time – 'the usual defective amalgam of armour/infantry' – and a Panzer counter-stroke took back some of the gains. Chink found the time-lag between details reaching TAC HQ and the true causes for them becoming apparent immensely frustrating, but by evening his optimism had reasserted itself. Although Eighth Army had not achieved the extent of success he had hoped for, four Italian divisions were now out of action.

'*15th*: We woke, Auk and I, to dubious news of results which gradually expanded with the sunrise into something more warming. The big thing now is to keep at him, give him no rest, wear him down until we are strong enough to act decisively. One can't tell in war where the breaking point is and we have to be penurious for a little yet. Small profits, quick returns. *Later*: Today has so far been more successful than we hoped. . . . *6 p.m.*: The clouds part. There is a little blue. Then they close again but each time the blue is larger and tonight there is a good showing. The tally of prisoners mounts but the Auk refuses to believe any story until and unless it has been actually verified, but any sort of bag is an agreeable change from our own losses which were heavy before the Auk took over. The enemy dances to our tune, not we to his, at present anyway.' The effect of his continual reassurance is easy to trace. In a signal Auchinleck sent to Smuts the following day to allay anxiety about the South African Division he relied, as so often, upon Chink's latest phrase. 'I am not saying we have won the battle,' Auchinleck signalled then, 'but the enemy is not making us dance to his tune.'

Chink kept up the moral support. At 11 p.m. on 16 July, the day of Rommel's counter-attack on Ruweisat Ridge, he allowed that it had been a long and anxious day but stressed that 'all the Boche attacks today have been beaten back with loss to him. We are well up on the balance of the three days' fighting.' On 17 July, with six Italian divisions knocked out, he summed up the British gains in a single gleeful sentence: 'We have dealt a number of shrewd blows where they are most apt to be painful.' He cut out a press photo of the Commander-in-Chief inspecting the front from a jeep, with himself just visible behind, and headed it 'I was Auchinleck's back seat driver.'

By now Rommel was fully thrown on the defensive, and in a letter that night to his wife he paid unconscious tribute to Chink and the effectiveness of Ultra. 'The enemy is using his superiority, especially in infantry,' he confided, 'to destroy the Italian formations one by one and the German formations are too weak to stand alone. It's enough to make one weep.'

Chink, meanwhile, was concerning himself with future planning. '[Rommel] has been butting his head against a stone wall in his effort to regain lost ground,' he wrote warily on the 17th. 'Gradually we are wearing him down and wresting the initiative from him. A prudent man might decide to clear out – not Rommel, he's a persistent beast.' The international implications fascinated him, a perspective kept in mind by his continued work on Auchinleck's commander-in-chief responsibilities. If they were able to beat Rommel, he often reflected, the effect on Allied morale would be far greater than the size of the contending armies warranted. 'We strive for total victory and our only aim is to attack and destroy because this is one of the world's decisive battles,' he also wrote that evening. 'To some extent it is already won since we have gained the time we needed to gather new strength and to organise positions in rear and make new plans. But that isn't enough. If Musso crashed a great many other plaster statues would fall too. It's a big vista and we are well aware of the importance of what we are doing. The question now is, which of us tires of the game first? If he hopes we will, he's wrong.'

Egypt was safe, unless 'the persistent beast' was given a massive injection of strength, because the Afrika Korps had been dispersed to stiffen the remaining Italians in the attempt to hold the line. The aim now was to force retreat. 'I think I can safely say that the enemy's impetus has gone,' he noted.

His offensive when it begins again – *if* we let it begin again – will be a new effort and not part of the rush we stemmed here 18 days ago. That is over. He must now stage a new campaign for the autumn – that is, again, *if* we let him. That is how I feel at the moment. We are far from the hunted days when we thought more of preserving our army than of using it against him. Now I plot the enemy's destruction, a much pleasanter form of reverie. . . . If I knew of a proper incantation to the old gods, Osiris, Set, I'd get going to marshal their assistance.

But at Evening Prayers the majority view was that one more early try would be made to get through to Cairo, and Chink's influence was lessening. On 18 July, in response to Churchill's demands for attack before the German threat evident in the Caucasus drew Eighth Army troops eastwards for the defence of Persia, planning for an immediate offensive, Operation Splendour, began. Its successive left and right blows were to be delivered by 13th Corps in the south and 30th Corps in the north, and hinged on adroit co-operation between infantry and armour with only four days to perfect co-ordination. Chink's heated arguments that Eighth Army was being pushed beyond its capability were ignored. Instructions for the first stage of Splendour were issued on 20 July, timed to reach a conclusion on his birthday, and his misgivings were confirmed almost at once.

On the afternoon of 21 July, when the critical first stage of Splendour was due to start within twenty-four hours, Ramsden of 30th Corps informed Auchinleck that Morshead, whose 1st Australian Division had borne the brunt of the fighting following Pienaar's earlier refusal, was now insisting on referring to his government before committing his men again. Without the Australians there would have to be a delay, and Auchinleck personally invited Morshead to tea in his caravan, detailing Chink to take notes. He sat in with interest, sardonically aware of the flattery that would be used.

'What are leaders and what sort of people like being led?' he pondered afterwards.

People who only do the right thing because they are told to do it by someone else seem to me infantile. People who know how to make the infantile do the right thing have a sort of nursery maid genius. Perhaps to be a successful nursery maid is to display considerable genius, but then the maid knows she is dealing with minds which lack the facts on which to base right action and the mental strength to apply what facts they do possess. To be leadable seems to me to betray mental weakness. To lead the leadable seems merely to exploit a weakness which one possesses in some degree oneself.

There was no escaping the fact that powers of command were far more important than tactical brilliance at this height.

He watched as the compromise was reached in which a British infantry brigade would lead the manoeuvre instead, and exploded as soon as Morshead left. Bringing the British brigade up would entail a forty-eight-hour delay, he pointed out, so the attack ought to be halted and replanned because Rommel would use the two-day advantage to regroup, dig in guns and sow further mines. Auchinleck overruled him. 'I sit here,' Chink fumed afterwards, endeavouring to look on the bright side, 'attempting to project myself into the mind of the enemy's higher command to see how we would face the situation. I think we'd not care for it at all. Exasperatingly slowly the reports come into Army HQ, but one must guard against curiosity.' But disillusioned though he was with Auchinleck, he put the ultimate blame on Churchill for insisting on a premature attack. 'Poor Auk,' he wrote at 6.30 p.m. on 22 July, after the bombardment of Splendour had opened. 'I wish I could take some of the pain from him. A big battle *is* a painful thing for a commander – the issue is so long drawn. Rather disappointed by the events, but not disheartened and we haven't yet played all our trumps.'

Alamein had slipped out of the news, but now it was back in the headlines. 'I saw British tanks rolling across the desert with dust flowing away behind them in tawny boiling wakes,' enthused *The Times* correspondent that day. 'The muzzles of slim guns protruding from their turrets were swathed to protect them against the dust. Their crews rode with handkerchiefs bound round their mouths to keep out the grit.' The same sight touched Chink on a raw nerve. Tanks reminded him of the urgent need for reorganisation, and his proposals for mobile divisions containing a mixture of armour, trucked infantry and guns, as in the NATO pattern today, were on paper and agreed by Auchinleck. Brooke's emissary McCreery was arriving up at TAC HQ that day to be informed of the intended radical change, and duly reported on time. As Chink looked on, however, McCreery refused point-blank to end the traditional separation of armour and infantry into their own divisions. Scorning 'Dreary' McCreery, whose stammer was always exaggerated when he lost his temper, Chink suddenly realised the extent of Auchinleck's stress when instead of placating him, as he had Morshead, he sacked McCreery in blazing fury and sent him away. The confrontation ironically took place just as the campaign's most tragic – 'Amateur' – frontal attack was getting under way, in which the inexperienced 23rd Armoured Brigade was to be wiped out.

Chink's estimate of a forty-eight-hour delay in Splendour was proving to be conservative, and on 23 July, when the Germans regained the initiative temporarily by counter-attacking, he disguised a 'certain inward agitation' and used the lull for the stocktaking he had got into the habit of doing on the eve of every birthday. The past year stood out as the most vivid of his life, mixing greater happiness and greater distress than he had felt before, and later as he lay trying to sleep he thought back to the birthday in the trenches twenty-seven years earlier. But Auchinleck, unusually, wanted to talk. He had made up his mind to send Corbett back to India, Chink now heard with surprise, but was unsure about who to replace him with. 'What,' Auchinleck asked, 'do you want to do next?' Disbelievingly he said he would have a crack at Chief of Staff 'if that was what was wanted' and Auchinleck grunted and turned over to sleep. It was getting colder overnight, calling for a second blanket, and Chink tossed and turned uncomfortably till dawn, sick to think he might have jumped to the wrong conclusion and exhilarated at the prospect of Smith's old job. But the matter was not mentioned again.

His birthday was doubly depressing. Not only was he 'the perfectly ghastly age of 47', but the date emphasised the dangerous hold-up in Splendour. The outgoing American Military Attaché to Egypt called at TAC HQ, enabling Chink to dabble in political intrigue directed against the Pentagon by telling him that as Rommel was 'fixed' the United States should intervene in French North Africa or Italy. He discussed the angle with Auchinleck too, who told Brooke on 25 July, 'We feel you already have a second front . . . here. Northern Africa and the whole of the Mediterranean basin is . . . really Europe for strategical purposes.' On the afternoon of his birthday they walked about in the old manner, and he tried to lift Auchinleck's mood by repeating that they had stopped Rommel, the priority all along. Privately he knew they should have been capturing Miteiriya Ridge at that moment, instead of handing Rommel extra time in which to consolidate.

But optimism was all he could offer, since his tactical advice was no longer being taken. 'I'm beginning to get a trifle bored with this battle,' he unburdened himself to Eve. 'The brave days are over now it's stable, and there is little scope for my bright ideas. I have to listen to advice being given which I'd not give myself. I'd be more use in Cairo. I'd like to leave this business to the heroes and go where in the shortest time I can remake an army fit for this sort of war, and re-organise and modernise it properly.' Twenty-sixth July, when the delayed Splendour attack went in, was a 'rotten' day, spent 'trying to convince people with vested interests that they must sacrifice those to principle', which meant dealing with the conflicting pressure groups of cavalry and infantry. Stifling sandstorms brought the sensation of breathing and eating sand, and all the news coming in was bad. He tried to believe that the allied counter-offensive might still prove as decisive as the Marne in 1914, but it was an effort. A corner of Miteiriya Ridge was gained, but minefields held up the attacking infantry and once more tanks failed to be in the right place at the right time. In *The Times* it was reported that fighting had taken on a more conventional form.

Chafing at his superfluousness, Chink envied the incoming de Guingand – he had persuaded Auchinleck to take on de Guingand in Whiteley's place – his 'normal' post. The change-over took place on 27 July. On the surface de Guingand appeared as friendly as ever but Chink sensed an underlying tension which he misread as the self-consciousness of a man learning his job in front of someone who knew it already. 'You'd laugh at Freddie,' he wrote at once to Eve. 'He bemoans his fate at being jerked out of Cairo and the comfortable unrealities of high strategy. At present he doesn't think he'll hold his job down for a fortnight, so as long as I'm here I can see that he makes no bloomers.' In reality de Guingand disapproved so strongly of the irregularity of Chink's close association with Auchinleck that one of his first requests was for Chink to be despatched straight back to Cairo.

But mentally Chink had moved on already, and his Cairo appointment was about to be confirmed. 'If the Auk remains,' he had speculated after the unsettling mention of Corbett's removal, 'he might consider me for his Chief of Staff, but an appointment of that nature is a compromise and I wasn't made of compromise material. I'm likely to remain agreeably beyond the limelight. I'm a retiring violet and I like to get my effect from the shade of big leaves. Also I haven't yet recovered from the bad time professionally which has left its mark on my assurance.' In Cairo his deputy Messervy was about to leave for India, which made convenient room again at GHQ ME, and he was delighted when his posting as Deputy Chief of the General Staff, Operations, Plans and Intelligence came through, to be taken up as soon as he could be spared. 'There is little more that I can do here,' he enthused at once. 'I anticipate our marking time for a while and in that period I can be more use in Cairo where I can get on with bigger things. I think the Auk would be better back for that matter. I know he hates

the idea of going back to GHQ. . . . He is getting very odd and I begin
to wonder if he is tiring. I think it's only reaction after last month's
fighting and strain, added to the shock of the earlier collapse.'

He had suspected for some time that Auchinleck was likely to
'temporise in the desert' to avoid the political pressures waiting in
Cairo, going so far as to warn bluntly that it was time for a public
appearance, because the loss of Tobruk would otherwise be remembered longer than the July successes. Now he was also worried about
his judgement, a worry exacerbated by the short time left to give
advice. After calling off Splendour the night before de Guingand's
arrival, Auchinleck had at once started to talk about a renewed
offensive, which Chink considered unrealistic because Eighth Army
was in no fit condition to deliver the *coup de grâce*. 'Failure at
Miteiriya,' he had noted severely in his pocket book on the last day of
Splendour. 'There must be no more failures.' Convinced that a
breathing space was necessary to train and reinforce, he kept his letter
to Eve short on the morning of 27 July. 'Now I feel it's time to turn to
the wider picture,' he signed off. 'I must stop to write an Appreciation,
for the time has come to reconsider our policy and plans.'

He knew logical argument on paper was the best way to convince
Auchinleck of a point, and with sweat sticking his arm to the page in
the stifling operations caravan, maps within glancing distance, he
began the analysis he preferred above everything else. The Appreciation was more complex than usual, as it had to keep in mind the wider
perspective of the commander-in-chief as well as the priorities of
Eighth Army's commander. 'I've been writing redhot for some two
hours,' he jotted at one point, 'and can only come to one conclusion,
which I regret because I am not a prudent person. On the other hand, a
counsellor must be objective and impersonal, and I hope I'm both. The
difficulty is to give proper value to all the factors.'

They led to three main conclusions. Shortages and lack of training
prevented Eighth Army from resuming the offensive until mid-
September. Rommel was bound to attack again, probably in the
southern sector about mid-August. When Eighth Army was ready it
should try to break through in the north, near Alamein, and therefore
train for this exclusively. Destroying the original after making two
signed copies, he handed them to Auchinleck to digest, 'after a brief
explanation', with a finished version of the reorganisation proposals
that he was more determined than ever to push through after
McCreery's opposition. Coming back after an hour, he found

Auchinleck in sharp disagreement with most of the conclusions on the grounds that they were insufficiently aggressive. After 'an altercation', he challenged Auchinleck to read it through again and list the military mistakes, and on his subsequent return Auchinleck conceded with a good grace and initialled the Appreciation. That evening Whitehall was informed that Eighth Army was going to remain temporarily on the defensive and recruit for a decisive effort.

'*10 p.m. 27 July*: The Auk has just scrambled out of the lorry office into the moonlight saying "Bedtime. Blast the PM." We do lead a queer life. Tiny battles and the highest policy all muddled up as only Lewis Carroll could imagine it.' The telegram in question from Churchill had had an ominous glint – 'I have not bothered you with messages while you and your Army have been so fiercely engaged but you and your Army have never been out of our thoughts for an hour. . . . CIGS is coming out to you early next week.' Chink shared Auchinleck's dread. Both men would have been more horrified still if they had known that Churchill was that same evening over a glass of port confiding his intention to his son Randolph and Eden, the Foreign Secretary, to extract permission from the King to accompany Brooke. Eden remarked that he would be in the way. 'You mean like a great bluebottle?' the Prime Minister was teasing, 'buzzing over a huge cowpat?' Exactly, said Eden firmly.

The unfinished business resulting from Auchinleck's acceptance of the Appreciation did not take long. At a brief noon conference on 28 July with both corps commanders it was agreed that one further meeting was necessary to study the points in detail, but for security reasons no other members of Evening Prayers were yet informed of the long-term decisions. Only de Guingand, still a puzzled newcomer, was present on 30 July when the holding instructions were confirmed, and at that meeting the situation map was brought up to date to reflect the forthcoming moves which were to culminate in the battle area at Alam Halfa. 'We haven't shifted Rommel, nor he us,' Chink estimated immediately afterwards. 'But his tone is very different. Everything has changed for the better.'

Chink's desert sojourn was almost over. On 31 July Auchinleck took him aside to tell him in confidence that Churchill was now coming out with Brooke, and added that as the crisis had passed Chink could take up his post and travel to Cairo in the plane he himself would be taking to meet them. His quip in reply that the party was over was automatic. At once he suffered his usual depression after intense mental effort, and he escaped to write to Eve for the last time at the oilcloth-covered camp table in the map lorry. 'I feel that the Auk's time is numbered,' he wrote anxiously. 'If only you knew the damaging gossip and backbiting that ordinary chaps indulge in and love. Normally it does very little harm, but in high places it is devastating. Human beings are really cannibals. We've given up eating each other physically but we feed on each other in every other sort of way, and when everything concentrates on war and military personalities the feeding becomes particularly foul.'

First Alamein, as it would come to be known, was a defensive battle that saved the allied cause in North Africa, and the cities of Cairo and Alexandria. But at the time and in all the years ahead Chink made no connection with the Cairo palmist's remark in 1941 about giving him a city to defend. His tactics and capacity to plan ahead and adapt in a rapidly changing emergency situation, however, can now be seen as crucial to its success, as was the blithe support he gave Auchinleck, who faced the bleakness of high command at a time when the marriage he depended upon was breaking up. 'It was the most difficult time I ever had in the war,' Auchinleck would testify much later. 'It was largely due to Chink's knowledge and flair and active mind that we were able to defend the Alamein position.'

And the enemy never denied that they had been out-thought at the last minute. 'We had succeeded in wearing down the British forces,' Rommel would write before his suicide on Hitler's orders later in the war.

After the fall of . . . Gazala we had stormed Tobruk. The British had retired first to Mersa Matruh and then to El Alamein. It was essential to do everything possible to bring about a British collapse. . . . Their leading men had clearly realised that the next battle in Africa would determine the situation . . . and were looking at things very coolheadedly. . . . Every time I was on the point of forcing a breakthrough with my German motorised formations [they] launched an attack on the Italians elsewhere [and] on each occasion I was forced to break off my own attack in order to hurry to the help of the threatened sector. . . . The British command was in its element . . . showing considerable enterprise and audacity. We were forced to conclude that the Italians were no longer capable of holding their line. . . . The one thing that mattered to [Auchinleck] was to halt our advance, and that unfortunately he had done.

Mussolini, before his violent death by lynching in 1945, credited Auchinleck and Chink with the turning point of both his own career and the war. 'The wheel of fortune', his memoirs stated, 'turned on 28 June 1942 when we halted before Alamein. . . . I told [Hitler] that we had lost the initiative . . . and that a nation which had lost the initiative had lost the war.' His translator explained that Mussolini looked upon himself as a gambler favoured by fortune up to the black day when she abandoned him, never to return, and that he blamed 28 June 1942 as the fatal day. His luck had stretched back as far as the cheering crowds in La Scala Opera House celebrating the Armistice in 1918, and a uniformed figure in the distance taking the salute in the Royal Box.

But for the allies the spin of the wheel of fortune went unnoticed. The sensation of being involved in First Alamein on the Eighth Army side was like that of sitting helplessly in the passenger seat of a car locked in a high-speed skid. None of the driver's subsequent skill in mastering it allays the fear, and as the kindly Gort had said at the Staff College in 1936, 'You're taking us too far, too fast, Dorman-Smith.' He was not going to be thanked for the experience.

11

A
Universal
Blackball

Brooke had made up his mind to intervene before the key moment at Alamein, as the intention to change the traditional organisation of armour and infantry alarmed him as much as the baffling Eighth Army picture. 'For some time I had become more and more uneasy,' as he explained in a post-war addition to his diary entry for 28–30 June 1942, 'at the situation prevailing in the Middle East. It was quite clear that something was radically wrong.... I mistrusted the influence of Dorman-Smith on the Auk. The crisis had now come and it was evident that I should go out and see what was wrong.' Coincidentally, the turning point of the crisis in the desert on 2 July synchronised with political confrontation at Westminster, when a censure motion on the handling of the war came up. Brooke had taken advantage of Churchill's presence in the House of Commons that day to do his tropical shopping in secret; he wanted to tackle the situation alone, without Churchill's interference.

But within twenty-four hours his hope of a private trip was dashed by an ironic chance encounter. As a small boy, Julian Amery had been helped up his first Swiss mountain by Chink, and for some time Amery had been serving in a junior capacity in the Middle East. On leave in London, with the familiarity of someone who had grown up at the centre of politics, he called unannounced at Brooke's office on 3 July, and Churchill happened to be in the room with Brooke at the time. Two things were necessary to save Egypt, Amery announced dramatically, ignoring Brooke's frown: more equipment and a personal visit from the Prime Minister. When he had gone Churchill purringly brushed aside Brooke's furious dismissal of the young officer as a bar lounger bearing gossip from Shepheard's. As far as the CIGS was concerned, the damage was done.

Shortly afterwards he heard Ritchie's version of events. Ritchie was one of Brooke's own protégés, after being his Brigadier General Staff during the retreat of the British Expeditionary Force two years earlier, and Brooke approached the meeting sympathetically. 'Neil Ritchie had done me so wonderfully well in France during the fighting leading to Dunkirk,' he wrote in his diary, 'and I had grown so fond of him that I hated seeing him subjected to this serious reverse. I told him I considered he had been pushed on much too fast by Auchinleck.' Loyalty excuses; antipathy condemns. He invited Ritchie to dinner the following evening and he stayed till 1.15 a.m. 'It was great value seeing him,' Brooke noted, 'and hearing full details of all the fighting in the Middle East.'

Misgivings concealed, Brooke met Churchill on 1 August at 8.55 p.m. on Number 4 Platform of Paddington Station. A special train had been laid on to Dauntsey in Wiltshire, from where the party were whisked by car to Lyneham aerodrome five minutes away, and driven into a hanger beside two waiting Liberator bombers to be measured for flying suits. Churchill's plane took off at 12.30 a.m., and the second an hour later. Both touched down for a breakfast and refuelling stop at Gibraltar, where Churchill regaled everyone at breakfast with an account of the cavalry charge at Omdurman, which he had taken part in as a young man. Recently Ernest Hemingway, the American writer whom he admired so much, had asked permission to include an earlier article about it in a forthcoming collection of inspirational pieces on war and courage. Kitchener, Churchill informed his audience, had also faced a stronger army when backed to the Nile. With an escort of four Beaufighters, Churchill's plane headed east at 7 p.m. and crossed the African coast to strike the Nile at Fayum. Here it dropped down to 300 feet as a precaution against enemy aircraft, and passed low by the pyramids, landing twenty-five miles from Cairo at 8.30 a.m. The road confronting the party was crowded with military transport, and lined with camps, depots and ammunition dumps. The heat struck them as oppressive.

Inured to the climate, Auchinleck and Chink were making prepara-tions to leave TAC HQ, and the thought of Kitchener crossed Chink's mind too – in a different context. He remembered his unexpected death in transit in 1916 and half-hoped that a similar fate might overtake

Churchill. 'The next week will be interesting,' he speculated as the Liberators drew near. 'Auk's fate will be in the balance. Had we won our battles at the end of July all would have been well, but through this and that hierarchical failure – particularly in the blue-blooded stratas, and very thin this blue blood – we did not pull off what in a more efficient party would have been a cinch. . . . The Auk may well fall under the bane of a mile long shadow. Sad if he does.' Cabell's allegory of Jurgen did not fail him even now. 'And from afar Jurgen could see two figures coming out of the east,' he had copied out for Eve's benefit the night before. 'So tall that their heads rose above the encircling hills. . . . One was a white pasty-looking giant, with a crusty expression. . . . "This place must be altered a great deal before it meets with our requirements," the other grumbled. . . . Then as the giants turned dull and harsh faces towards the garden, the sun came above the circle of blue hills so that the mingled shadows of these two giants fell across the garden. For an instant Jurgen saw the place oppressed by that attenuated mile-long shadow, as in heraldry you may see a black bar painted sheer across some brightly emblazoned shield.' Reporting straight to Corbett later that morning, in the hope of starting his new job at once, he realised by Corbett's jumpy behaviour that the shadow had already fallen.

In tackling 'the situation', Brooke had investigated Corbett straight-away and rated him 'a very small man'. Next he caught the gregarious Messervy just in time, who gave a summary of the tank commanders' point of view, relayed by contemporaries on leave; he also gave details of McCreery's sacking. Brooke's own allegiance, as he freely admitted, was to his 'many old friends in tanks', and these men he systematically approached. By 6 August he reached Lumsden of 1st Armoured Division (whom Chink had watched refusing to obey Auchinleck's corps commander) and Major-General Briggs, joint commander – with Messervy – of the disastrously planned attack on Rommel in the Cauldron. By now Brooke had also seen Freyberg, who had been badly wounded in the confused fighting at Matruh, and had lunched alone with the new Australian Minister of State, Richard Casey; Casey had only been in Cairo since the height of the Gazala losses, but all he had heard pointed to the fault lying squarely with the Commander-in-Chief's closest advisers.

As early as the evening of 4 August, however, Brooke was sure that he was on the right lines. 'I had not yet had a chance of seeing one of the worst offenders, Dorman-Smith,' he wrote under that day's date subsequently, 'and had not yet decided whether the Auk should go.' In conversation with Smuts, both men had agreed that Auchinleck suffered an inability to choose the right people. That Smuts might gain political ground in South Africa if a new face distanced the memory of Tobruk – particularly as his country had been against entering the war in the first place – was neither here nor there. Air Marshal Tedder put the competitive RAF view forcibly, and Wavell (who had been flown in) and Wilson were also sounded out.

Soundings were taking place at another level, too. The Military Assistant Secretary to the Cabinet, a key member of Brooke's team, was Colonel Ian Jacob, a politically minded soldier who would come to be be known as the personification of tact. And Jacob interviewed his own friends, so that if he were asked for an opinion, as he expected to be, he would be ready with one. He was not in the know about Ultra, and he was still shocked and puzzled by the carnage at Gazala. Equally to the point, he had disliked Chink since meeting him at the time of the 1000 marks out of 1000 Staff College coup, and it had been Jacob who, as organiser of the three-day Canal Brigade exercise in Egypt, had rejected Chink's complaint about the use of aircraft and had added 'a bad loser' to his mental picture of a vain man.

Over dinner in Cairo with 'four or five good fellows', all guardsmen who had been serving in the Middle East for some time, it became clear to Jacob that Gazala need never have been lost – if it had been properly organised in the first place. And that led to Chink, who was distrusted by one and all. He was seen as 'the fifth wheel of a coach' and 'a menace', Jacob recorded. It came as no surprise. Earlier he had talked to another old friend, Major-General 'Pete' Rees, wrongly sacked at the height of the Tobruk fighting and latterly in charge of the apparently defeatist Cairo defences. 'I felt very sorry for him,' Jacob wrote afterwards, 'knowing him so well and realising what a tiger of a chap he is.' On 5 August Jacob heard Whiteley's story, the most detailed indictment of all. 'He gave me a most interesting account of Tobruk,' he noted. 'When General Auchinleck came up and took personal command of the Eighth Army he brought with him his DCGS Dorman-Smith. The object of this was that Chink should deal with all the Middle East work. . . . Chink being the sort of chap he is, however, it was not long before he started issuing all kinds of fantastic things to the Eighth Army, and generally making Jock's position as BGS intolerable.' (When Jacob's diary was published after the war,

Chink was succinct. 'It was a pity,' he retorted, 'that these fantastic things had not been followed in May and June 1942.') Gossip spread like wildfire. On 4 August, for instance, McCreery dined privately at Shepheard's Hotel with Lumsden, Briggs and two other cavalrymen. All had just seen, or were about to see, Brooke.

Chink checked into GHQ early that morning. He was frustrated at not being able to get cracking on his reorganisation planning, but he was stimulated by events. 'We all go off tomorrow at 5.30 a.m. by air back to the sand,' he informed Eve, 'taking our distinguished visitors with us. I'm booked to motor most of tomorrow in the same car as the very top soldier of our Imperial Army. Rather a joke considering he and his cavalry have been patently side-tracking my poor self for so long. I met him this morning. He looks fit and active, though feeling the heat, and seems to be carrying his burden well.'

Brooke came across as more of a threat to Auchinleck, however, and knowing that an official investigation was about to begin into the loss of Tobruk, he had advised a return to the commander-in-chief's role as soon as Churchill's inspection was over. 'He seeks a moral refuge in the sand very much as the monks of old sought refuge from the snares of Cairo in the monasteries of the Wadi Natrun,' he wrote impatiently.

> I'm worried about the Auk. He'll have a breakdown – not a collapse but he is getting desperately irritable and all on edge. Rather unreasonable, too, and difficult to deal with. Corbett is equally on edge and in fact it's all very uncomfortable and it's up to the Auk to put it right if he can. . . . But he looks like death. He has lost weight, aged, stoops. I don't know what to make of him. He's quite unapproachable. Snaps and growls and is rapidly losing his two great assets, the power of making men want to work for him and also his level-headed grasp of essentials.

On 5 August he was up at 4.30 a.m., intrigued by the day out ahead at TAC HQ. 'The glass nose of a Boston bomber is a wonderful viewpoint for a desert dawn,' he scribbled. 'Behind me the sky is gold. In front it is still night and overhead to frighten me passed a large squadron of aircraft – our own. For a moment I thought they were Boche. A cloudy morning and we are flying low across the Delta, the Nile just behind. And here is the sand. Auk seems happier today. I had a short talk before we took off and I think the very great have been sympathetic.' Landing at Burg el Arab, he made conversation as they waited for Churchill's plane, and Auchinleck did not confide that he had already agreed with Brooke over the appointment of Montgomery to command Eighth Army.

The Prime Minister's plane arrived on time. Chink was amused by the look of the entourage, pale and plump in their tropical suits. Churchill shook hands with him on Auchinleck's introduction, but the politician he had waited so long to meet glanced away and said nothing. Then Brooke deliberately chose to travel with Tedder and Conyngham of the RAF instead. Widely spaced, the small procession of cars drove west along the coast road towards Alamein and paused at HQ 9th Australian Division, where Churchill was introduced to Morshead and Pienaar and pointedly talked alone with them.

It was a small, instinctive political gesture that snuffed out Chink's optimism once and for all. Churchill was travelling ahead in Auchinleck's official car, with Auchinleck relegated to a jeep behind the double line of troops who were lining the road. Stopping the car now, the Prime Minister climbed out and walked down between the cheering men, shaking hands, beaming, handing out cigars and giving his celebrated V-sign. To Chink the effect he was having was a sickening revelation. The cavalcade turned into a funeral cortège and he mourned for Auchinleck, the trusting sacrifice. He saw TAC HQ as it must appear to outsiders, squalid and spartan; breakfast was the usual greasy sausage, bacon and fried bread inside the makeshift dining cage designed by Kitsch, and Churchill did not disguise his irritation. 'Breakfast in a wire-netted cage', he remembered long afterwards in his memoirs. 'Full of flies and important military personages.'

For a briefing on the up-to-date military situation, the Prime Minister was taken afterwards to the operations caravan, a formality which Auchinleck had asked Chink to attend too, for moral support. As the door shut behind them, de Guingand, Williams and Mainwaring gathered around to listen. Inside, Chink's worst forebodings were being realised. Churchill interrupted Auchinleck to insist repeatedly that they must attack again, at once. 'He thrust stubby fingers against the talc of the wallmaps,' he recalled later.

Here, he said, or here. . . . We were alone with him, as Brooke had gone up the line. It was a little like being caged with a gorilla. Eventually the Auk said 'No, Sir, we cannot attack again yet.' Churchill swung around to me. 'Do you say that too? Why don't you use the 44th Division?' 'Because, Sir, that division isn't ready and anyhow a one division attack would not get us anywhere.' Churchill rose, grunted, stumped down from the caravan and stood alone in the sand, back turned to us. I wondered if he was thinking himself into Lincoln's shoes, when Lincoln dismissed McClellan at Harrison's Landing.

In the fifty minutes they had, the defence plan and the Appreciation's long-term points stood no chance of being accepted, and Chink knew they were not handling with sufficient adroitness a strong-willed politician of limited military experience. The eavesdroppers faded away, Williams sad and de Guingand, worldly wise, shaking his head. Before going on to the RAF, Churchill was introduced to Auchinleck's commanders and at the last moment he asked Gott to drive him to the plane. This would interfere with Auchinleck's intention to use the opportunity of having all his commanders together to go through the plans with them, and Chink was annoyed enough to object. Churchill swept off with Gott as if he had not heard him.

Later Brooke returned. He had visited both Indian divisions, where he had lunched with Briggs and interviewed Gott, Churchill's personal choice to head Eighth Army. At TAC HQ he took tea with Auchinleck and Chink and they explained their plans in more detail. Brooke appeared to approve, making no criticism. '2.15 p.m. Well, we've had a tremendous do,' Chink wrote to Eve, disguising his extreme pessimism, which now extended to his own career, '. . . and now they're gone off back. The great WC looked well. He's an old man, nevertheless. Brooke, too, has aged a lot, is now shrunken and potbellied, but quick, alert and intelligent. It must be the hell of a job and I don't envy him one little bit. Apparently he is prepared to give us a free hand as to reorganisation etc. All this I gather from remarks dropped by the Auk.' The RAF had been more astute, providing Churchill with an excellent packed lunch out of baskets sent up by Shepheard's Hotel, after which they were strongly critical of TAC HQ's siting so far from the RAF HQ, a necessary temporary measure during the fighting.

By evening Brooke's mind was made up. 'This had been a useful day and the process of clearing my brain and forming my opinions had continued,' he would disclose. 'I had now seen Eighth Army HQ and did not like the atmosphere that prevailed there. The Dorman-Smith influence on Auchinleck was, as I had feared, far too strong. Their sleeping caravans were even now pitched close together, and Dorman-Smith seemed to be continually at the Auk's elbow.' Churchill, too, had formed his conclusions. No fault lay with the troops, he was sure, and 'only to a minor extent' with their equipment. As in politics, a new team at the very top would bring fresh impetus, and long experience in the House taught how this was best achieved.

On 6 August Churchill sent for Brooke, and a telegram to the War Cabinet in London followed. It recommended splitting the Middle East command into two, Near East and Middle East. 'Auchinleck to vacate former and take over the latter,' Brooke's diary entry recorded, approvingly. 'Alexander to take over the Near East . . . Gott to take over Eighth Army . . . Corbett and Dorman-Smith also to go. Considering everything, this is perhaps the best solution.' Brooke, for his part, was preoccupied by Churchill's morning suggestion that he ought to take over command of the Near East himself, something he longed to do because he loved active soldiering, but reluctantly turned down in order to keep Churchill's military interference in check. 'One of the most difficult days of my life', he added, 'with momentous decisions to take as far as my own future and the war was concerned.' The telegram that would have such a momentous effect on Chink's future was despatched at 8.15 p.m.

At precisely that time he was having a farewell drink with Richardson up at TAC HQ. He had expected to be allowed to return the day before, and suspected now that his new job at GHQ was under threat. But as he handed Richardson a sherry he announced with his usual debonair bravado, 'Charles, I'm for the Star Chamber tomorrow.' He was about to be sacked, he explained nonchalantly, as he had an appointment with Brooke the following day; for the first time Richardson discerned that he was putting on an act.

The mood of fatalism had been touched off by an unexpected visit from Wavell that afternoon. They had sat together in the old companionable way in front of the war map, and Wavell had listened without interruption as he went through the July fighting and their future plans. 'I stressed the desirability of Rommel attacking prematurely via the 13th Corps southern flank,' Chink wrote, describing the agreeable interval later. 'And at last he said "Eric, you are very strongly posted here. Have you considered making a feint withdrawal to entice Rommel into the net?" I replied that I had thought of it, but anything tricky of that sort might be too much for Eighth Army and anyway there was only one direction a new Rommel óffensive could take – Alam Halfa – and we were catering for that. Archie agreed.' To a trained military mind the war map showed at a glance what was intended, and it would remain pinned up in place.

'6.10 p.m. Wavell turned up looking very well,' Chink wrote at the time. 'He never says much but we walked about for a while with his arm in mine. Queer, dour yet charming person. He made one or two shrewd comments about the campaign. Went round the front and returned covered with dust.' And after Wavell's departure Gott had called, transformed from his previously weary self. Attributing the high spirits to Gott's imminent Cairo leave, Chink asked if he was going to drive down, as a car was so useful in Cairo, or would like a lift on his own early flight. Gott said he was 'heartily sick' of his desert car and planned to fly from Burg el Arab later the next day, taking the daily RAF passenger plane; subsequently Chink realised that he already knew of his appointment as Army Commander.

The meeting with Brooke was for Chink to put across orally the proposed reorganisation, already submitted in written outline, and it had been arranged by Auchinleck. At daybreak Chink set out, glad to be on the move at least. '8.30 a.m. *7 August*. Now we've forcelanded with engine trouble, luckily at a landing ground, and I'm stranded here for half an hour at the Wadi Natrun. Very hot it is. There's no breeze. I will stay in Cairo tonight and go back to the Chief tomorrow. Incidentally, he seems a lot happier and certainly more reasonable. . . . Things seem to be working out for me to spend part of the time in the desert and part in Cairo. Better than before.' 'Got off in another Lizzie almost equally decrepit,' he added when he arrived. 'Made a very spectacular landing at Heliopolis right side up. I've telephoned the CGS and we meet at 3.30 p.m. for business.' Corbett's strained behaviour, however, was a barometer of GHQ tension.

At 6 p.m. he was shown in to Brooke and recognised at once that the CIGS was in a bad temper. The room was the one where Wavell had first received him in 1940 and lately, on so many occasions, Auchinleck. Brooke's discomfort in the 95-degree heat brought forth his scorn, and when Chink launched into the proposals to divide divisions into formations of two motorised infantry brigades and one armoured brigade, he was not surprised to see Brooke's face tighten. But there were no questions, and neither was he told that he was sacked. All the same, he stalked back to his hotel in a rage, sensing that the interview had been a farce. The man waiting for the next appointment had been 'Dreary' McCreery, an implication he understood only too well. 'I had no trouble turning his ideas inside out,' Brooke annotated in his diary unapologetically after the war. By that time the same mixing of arms within a division at brigade level had gradually evolved, under his authority.

But the sad news that Gott had been killed that afternoon, when the RAF plane had been shot down and machine-gunned on the ground, momentarily distracted Chink. 'Strafer Gott's death has got to me,' he confessed to Eve. 'It is almost as great a loss as Dick's capture. Loss to the Army, I mean. For he was a great man and would have gone far. It happened over the landing place from which I wrote to you.' And, too upset to sleep, he reviewed the day's developments. Auchinleck appeared doomed, and there was no indication of his own future. His request to return to the desert had been turned down, and there was nothing for him to do in GHQ ME.

He spent Sunday, 9 August, studying the Caucasus threat, but his old depression had returned in full. '2.10 p.m.: By the time you get this,' he warned Eve, 'the Auk will, I think, have gone into limbo and in that case anyone who has been intimately associated with him will go too. He hasn't told me personally, but he is in from the Western Desert with all his kit. . . . 7.30 p.m.: Nothing is public yet but the brokers are busy in the background, Wavell among them. Poor Auk. . . . The appearance of Alex is interesting. Everything is so uncertain and unsettled.' General Sir Harold Alexander, a guardsman, was another of Brooke's men, since he had commanded a division under him in the British Expeditionary Force in 1940. He was also an old friend of Estelle's and was bound to know about Eve. Chink had recoiled from him as an Amateur since overlapping with him at the Staff College, and at their last meeting in India he had told him to his face that all he ever did was sit on the fence. 'This', he now sneered, 'will make Europe safe for mediocre aristocracy. . . . He really isn't intelligent – able in a narrow way.' He felt even more angry when he found out that Alexander was spared the conflicting responsibilities that had bedevilled the job for Wavell and Auchinleck, by having the destruction of Rommel as his priority.

Auchinleck phoned early next morning. Chink was glad to be asked to lunch, over which his views were sought on the political compromise of splitting the Middle East command. Egypt, Palestine and Syria would be given to Alexander, which left Iraq and Persia, but they seemed likely to come under the ultimate command of the Commander-in-Chief India, which would make Auchinleck subordinate to a command he had once held himself. 'The Auk has been tentatively offered a pig in a poke,' Chink wrote afterwards. 'If he took it I'd go with him, for it would be almost as odd a venture as stopping Rommel, but I'm pretty certain he won't look at it.' Pragmatically he advised that it was always wisest to remain in harness.

Returning to the office, he was handed a document from Churchill instructing him to chair an inter-service committee to study the proposal of dividing the Middle East command into two. That, he informed Corbett, was putting the cart before the horse as the problems ought to have been assessed first. The brief was to examine the administrative difficulties of the separate commands, and members comprised senior representatives from the RAF, the navy and the Minister of State's Department. The deadline for acceptance was 15 August, and he set up a meeting for 5 p.m. on 11 August, in the Minister of State's office. 'Today,' he wrote sardonically before setting forth, 'I am one of a committee to carve up this demesne a little like Solomon's threat to the baby, and incidental to the transaction my own employment may go.'

It quickly became clear that the committee was seen as a formality. The naval representative assessed no change in the naval position, and the RAF representative unfolded instructions which said there could be no separate air command, so both would be unified under Cairo, with a small liaison force for Iraq and Persia. Chink interrupted. He pointed out that if the Germans pushed down through north Persia, as was expected, air action could never be whistled up in time because, since the desert had priority, delaying London intervention would be necessary. The flaw far outweighed smaller predictable snags, and he suggested that they draw up a list of the administrative recommendations, with a rider emphasising military objections to the hole in air cover and requesting that the danger should be re-examined. The committee members disassociated themselves from the rider. Chink signed it himself without illusion, noting privately, 'If the High Ups accept the recommendations about this rump command, automatically one will become "for disposal".' On his way home he dropped in to see Corbett, who had just been informed of his dismissal. '10.40 p.m.: Poor little man. He was rather stunned in spite of the fact that he was so brave about the possibility. Rather tragic in the office this evening. By 7 p.m. nothing doing, shutters up, everyone gone. No forward events can be planned – tragic. I hope they make an end quickly.' With a reduced Middle East command a DCGS would be redundant, and he was not reassured when Auchinleck mentioned that he had requested Alexander to take him on in Corbett's place, and had been refused.

The offer of the Iraq–Persia command, he now advised Auchinleck, should not be accepted as it stood, and afterwards he wrote down their exchange. '"I must decline to have anything to do with the proposition then, in the hope of stopping it?" the Auk said, and paused. "But when I first asked, you said it was my duty to accept. You realise, of course, that your advice, if I take it, ruins you too, for I'd have taken you with me?"' He was painfully aware that the appointment of CGS, which would have been his, carried the rank of Lieutenant-General and a knighthood – bringing him level with Reggie at a stroke and very probably taking him beyond. But he stuck to the military priority.

'11 August: After a day's thought I have been forced to the conclusion that I *must* advise the Auk against accepting, not because of his personal feelings but for the inherent and fundamental unsoundness of the proposition,' he wrote in the middle of the dilemma. 'And that, I suppose, really will be the end of me. Nevertheless, I cannot have it said afterwards that nobody at the time protested. Even the top soldier who is being dragged about minus his advisers behind this juggernaut is mute.' Brooke was not exactly mute. He had approved the idea, been tempted by the job himself and, exasperated by Auchinleck's doubts, had written savagely in his diary that it would have been a more soldierly act to accept what he was offered in war instead of behaving like an offended filmstar.

The report of the committee, Auchinleck recounted in his despatches, was negative. 'Its conclusions . . . make it very obvious that [there is a] grave risk of breaking down under stress of active operations.' But in the event their scrupulousness was wasted, because Hitler inexplicably missed one of the great opportunities of the war. And in terms of internal politics it was Chink's greatest misjudgement. A man with less integrity would have reasoned that the jobs were an expeditious pay-off, which someone else would grab if they refused. So by accepting they would be in position to use their influence for the greater good, because if the Germans did come down the Caucasus, who better than themselves to defend the oilfields? It has also to be said that if he had counselled acceptance they would have been able to protect their July achievements in army mythology. 'I knew I was signing away my own career,' Chink would write theatrically in due course, aligning himself then with Michael Collins's deadly predicament over Irish partition. But the experience was, in a lesser way, destructive. It was to disillusion him forever, as he came to perceive that he was expected to save himself and his master at the ultimate price of other men's lives.

And there was further disillusionment to come. The press had been instructed to prepare the way for the change of command of Eighth Army – now, with Gott's death, to go to Brooke's choice, Montgomery – and the tone changed abruptly, as he had guessed it would. Negative phrases like 'partial victory' . . . 'misfortunes' . . . 'not seriously dimmed' . . . 'little of the blame' . . . coloured desert reports, and he was sick for Auchinleck's sake.

'He has made mistakes, but so has every other commander in this war,' Chink responded. 'He is painfully young at 58, so much younger than I because all this business of High Command thrilled him. He was great, but with the greatness of a magnified second lieutenant who had achieved his dreams. I suppose all good soldiers are like that, [unlike] bad soldiers like myself. . . . I tried to warn him, but I don't think he ever realised. . . . To know these campaigns backwards and yet to be powerless, unnoticed, disembodied – it's a little like being dead and watching one's family make a balls of things.' The news of Montgomery's inevitable appointment cut at Auchinleck too, and filled Chink with misgiving. Montgomery reached Cairo that day, and reported to Auchinleck at once, although he was not due to take over command until 15 August. Chink was in the corridor when Montgomery came out and he shook hands with him, a gesture he fiercely regretted when Montgomery later alleged that Auchinleck had told him at that interview that he had intended to withdraw from Alamein. That evening he dined with Auchinleck at Mena House, and did his best to deliver the expected optimism.

'It is more than ever clear to me that my career is drawing to a close,' he wrote next day. 'Yesterday I did not see this quite so distinctly. I thought it would be a question of them getting rid of me. Now I see that it is for me to say what I think of them in a way that can only result in me getting rid of them.' McCreery's appointment as CGS was common knowledge. And at Eighth Army TAC HQ Montgomery insolently seized command two days early and demonstrated 'The Registering of Personality', his favourite lecture at the Staff College which Chink had cut; soon aided by a black beret. In the private files he registered it more unpleasantly, by compiling a grotesque Situation Report in which he branded Auchinleck and Chink with having intended to retreat. The up-to-date war map in the operations caravan was inherited by the new regime.

On 15 August, when Montgomery's command ought to have begun and Alexander's appointment took effect from 3.30 p.m., Chink's suspense finally ended. He was summoned to the familiar commander-in-chief's office on the dot of 3.30 p.m., and was back in his hotel room three-quarters of an hour later. 'I have just had my Hail and Farewell interview', he informed Eve angrily. 'We fenced about for a while. [Alexander had] seen Estelle in Karachi and he tried to talk about Reg. However, I finally got him to face facts and said that I was sure he'd be happier to be rid of me. He replied with avidity, "Oh, but you're going to a command at home". . . . My final comment was that how they used me was all one to me, since what I would like most would be to go altogether. That, apparently, is unthinkable.' He chose not to tell her that he had requested a month's leave in South Africa, ostensibly to lecture on the recent fighting, and also asked for his present rank to be continued for as long as he remained in Alexander's command; her admiration was vital, and to qualify for permanent rank each level had to be held for a minimum of six months. He was told to stay in Cairo, and was then shown the door. 'Chink's bolo [bolshevik],' he heard Alexander exclaim irritably. It was a sour consolation.

Humiliated and proud, he avoided the Gezira Club, the Turf Club and the Mohammid Ali. After the cool of the desert nights he found it too hot and humid to sleep properly, and usually wrote to Eve around midnight, at his most cornered. At that hour Brooke appeared to be working on a grand plan to install his men in key positions so that he would be free to command the invasion of north-west Europe himself, and Alexander was transparently roping in old social friends. In the daytime Chink paced about GCE ME with Corbett, killing time, or solitarily brooded. One lunchtime he sat for a portrait photograph in the major-general's uniform he still wore, and tilted his cap defiantly at a non-regulation angle. He ordered copies for both Estelle and Eve. 'At least they'll be evidence', he sighed afterwards, 'that for a little while I was a general.' In spare moments he tried to concentrate on Charles Morgan's novel *Spartenbrook*.

'To be employed in something stable and then lose it again,' he wrote in despair late one night. 'To see the stupidest man in the Middle East – stupid, ignorant, obstinate and a snob – become CGS at the end of it. To see the Auk wrecked after he saved Egypt and to see how it's all been done. It's quite enough. There is nobody I want to serve now, not Wavell, not the High authorities at home, nor Churchill. The feet of clay are too apparent.'

Without warning Auchinleck called round on the night of the 17th to suggest dinner at his hotel, and he sat in the back of the flagged car wondering how passers-by would react if they knew how hollow it all was. On the forty-five-minute drive out to the Pyramids, where Mena House was situated, he let his bitterness rip. He spurned reassurance and was icily silent when Auchinleck admitted that he still wanted to go on. In his heightened emotional state the dining room appeared to glow, although it was cooler than usual. As he sipped the dry sherry they always began with, while Auchinleck studied the wine list, he thought to himself that everything was immutable. Two tables away a pretty nursing sister flirted with a young hussar, lean, brown and lecherous from the desert. The figure might so easily have been one of Rommel's Panzer heroes; the service would have been as obsequious, the food as good, the girl, perhaps, as acquiescent. But so unchanged was everything that perhaps the narrow squeak had never really happened? He was in bad form, and he despised himself for being unable to snap out of it. Auchinleck dropped him back at the Continental afterwards with nothing profound said.

In the morning, after a night of self-reproach, he called at Mena House in the hope of being of more positive use, but Auchinleck had checked out without leaving a forwarding address. The ground shifted again. 'He walked off without raising a finger to help me,' he wrote incredulously. 'Poor Auk, to some extent that's a measure of his distress.' All day he wandered aimlessly about Cairo, sightseeing. 'How much worse the oriental city behind this occidental façade,' he mused at one café table. 'One realises the beastliness of the Middle Ages. A world of stenches, dirt and corruption, yet from that squalor came the glory of architecture, music and poetry.' Was there a message in that? It was said that Auchinleck was still in Cairo. (In fact, with the changeover about to be made public the next day, the Minister of State had whisked Auchinleck off to stay with him.) 'Perhaps I misjudge him', he argued with himself. 'What *does* it matter?' But it mattered almost more than anything else. He made up his mind that if he was still in Cairo on Saturday he would go to the press lunch he had been scheduled to attend and put the record straight.

But the day of shocks was not over. Back at his hotel he heard that Brian Horrocks had been flown in the day before and would be commanding 13th Corps in Eighth Army. Horrocks was already installed up at TAC HQ, under Montgomery's wing. And, as he was writing obsessively to Eve, an orderly brought an official envelope. He tore it open. 'In consequence of the reorganisation of the general Staff at this Headquarters,' it ran, 'you will relinquish the appointment of DCGS and return to the United Kingdom. A passage by air will be arranged for you at an early date and on arrival you are requested to report in writing to the Military Secretary War Office, from whom you will in due course receive instructions as to future employment.' 'Well,' he added tersely, 'that is that.' On 21 August he learned that 'Jumbo' Wilson was being sounded out for the command of Iraq and Persia, and Wilson did not take long to accept; one of the inducements was that he was allowed to pick his own CGS.

Word came that Reggie was stopping over briefly in Cairo on his way back to Simla where – paths crossing yet again – he was living as Governor of Burma in exile. After weighing his kit on 23 August Chink called round to see him at Shepheard's Hotel, running the gauntlet of gossip only to be patronised further. Reggie greeted him with a smug run-down of the brighter young Tories, and loftily promised that Duff Cooper had not forgotten the lesson on modern war. He warned him not to get involved in moves against Churchill when he got to London and ended by recommending the RAC Club in Pall Mall, as everywhere else was full. Chink let fly, mortifyingly conscious of their previous meeting. Whatever was said, he retorted, they had halted Rommel, coshed the Italians and Eighth Army had been poised for advance. 'You were quite happy about that,' Reggie reminded him long afterwards. 'I can certainly testify to the fact that retreat was never for one moment on your mind. I saw you again later in the evening when you told me the astonishing news that you were off to London that very same night. You were pretty well knocked out by that – with every justification.' When Reggie flew on to India, the passenger in the seat beside him turned out to be Corbett.

Chink's own journey was postponed for twenty-four hours, not sufficient to include the press conference. He did the rounds of the Paymaster and the banks and raised £60 for London, with the rest to follow. At 5 p.m. his car came as ordered to take him to the Gezira Club for tea, a last look that he was not, in the end, able to resist. 'It might have been 1938,' he scoffed afterwards. 'The terrace crowded, cricket, and the only thing wrong being the men and women in uniform and the different look of the crowd. I suppose it's quite hopeless to expect our stock to walk about grinding its teeth and talking war shop if it can go and play. Saw Jumbo Wilson watching the cricket and backed up by his usual claque of black-buttoned riflemen. So the ME, cut off at Syria, will be made safe for cavalry and guardsmen, while the ME in Iraq will blossom with riflemen.' And as the Liberator began its dusk take-off for the four-day journey ahead, he tried to forget that it was the anniversary of his first battle, when holding the bridge at Mariette had been the only concern.

On the other side of the world, in Cuba, the typed introduction for *Men at War* was delivered to Hemingway for correction. Hemingway worked on it for two days while the plane was in flight, and posted it back to his publishers with the finished editing of Churchill's piece on Omdurman before Chink landed. 'I was very ignorant at nineteen and had read little,' the first page of the Introduction revealed. 'And I remember the sudden happiness and the feeling of having a permanent protecting talisman when a young British officer I met in the hospital first wrote out for me, so that I could remember them, these lines: "*By my troth, I care not: a man can die but once; we owe God a death . . . and let it go which way it will, he that dies this year is quit for the next.*" That is probably the best thing that is written in this book, and with nothing else a man can get along all right on that.'

Chink himself had no talisman, and he was badly in need of one. The conviction that had sustained him since long before that meeting with Hemingway had snapped in two, and the British officer, no longer young, had lost his faith. Mrs Bell's prophecy often came back to him during that protracted flight, because the war had ended for him in August as she had said it would. He was on his own and he owed nothing to anybody; even Auchinleck had melted away. The first thing he would do when he arrived back, he resolved, would be to go to the War Office. 'Then, if I can, straight to James Grigg, Secretary of State for War', he notified Eve. 'I want to tell him about the Auk, not myself. Also I propose to make certain contacts, including Leo Amery. I feel fine and offensive now, and utterly free to do my duty as I see it.'

12

Solitary Confinement

Grigg saw him at once. He was as friendly as ever, gave him all the time he needed, and then launched into a diatribe about Churchill in return. But Gott's obituary in the two-day-old copy of *The Times*, which Chink found in the RAC Club, was a better gauge of the home climate. It was blandly written by Ritchie – 'When General Gott was under my command . . .' – as if the losses of Tobruk and Gazala had been of no consequence, and the warmth of Grigg's reception congealed before he reached the end.

Reading *The Times* always guaranteed a bad reaction, and yet he could never resist picking it up. 'Under its new C-in-C and commanding general, Eighth Army is in great heart,' he saw with distaste on 2 September. 'Refreshed, reinforced and eager for action.' And the editorials were equally partisan, 'General Auchinleck', that day's leader stated, 'aimed at only limited objectives.' He braced himself whenever the Middle East was mentioned, and on 8 September the attack was a personal one. 'The leadership and staff work of the Eighth Army', he read, 'has been refreshingly excellent.' He resigned from his service club, judging the RAC to be suitably anonymous, and bitterness settled in for good.

'Chink walked in here a couple of days ago,' Galloway reported to Auchinleck from his temporary dull desk job in the War Office, 'but I have not got anything out of him which is not sarcastic and really rather silly.' He had reported to the Military Secretary, General Sir Colville Wemyss, in a similar frame of mind, only to be reminded that many other major-generals were in the same boat. On 11 September loss of his temporary rank took effect. He was back down to brigadier.

It scarcely impinged at first. He was in a fever of worry over Eve, who had promised to join him but was silent, and with nothing to hold him in London he went down to stay with Edward and Amy in

Bournemouth, where they had taken a comfortable flat. He found Amy's energy highlighted by the confines and Edward more effacing than ever. Both his parents were worried by his demotion and sudden appearance in England, and greeted him excitedly with Reggie's doings. They were transparently curious about Eve's photo in his room, but he refused to explain and strode up and down the sea-front as day after day went by without word from her. Victor suggested that he join Browning's new airborne troops, but though he lunched with Browning in London and was tempted – 'damn dangerous but very amusing and worthwhile' – it came to nothing. And his brigadier's appointment came through. It was to the Welsh 160th Brigade in 53rd Division, part of 12th Corps in Kent, and the War office letter read patronisingly. 'I sincerely hope,' Wemyss finished, pleased as he put it that the opportunity one step down the ladder had been taken, 'that you will settle down to the new conditions and catch up.'

Eve phoned in her provocative, dramatic voice from the docks to say she had arrived with her daughter Elizabeth and a paid companion. He carried her away for a fortnight at once, staving off Amy's questions and her own family's insistence that she must not break up her marriage. 'This tiny intersected parochial island', he warned her, relishing the prospect himself, 'is going to prove a hotbed of gossip for us.' And since he did nothing to dispel it, he was right. Her family continued to disapprove and she alternated between living tempestuously with them and staying in a small family-owned house near the brigade; later they took a flat together in Putney. 'Is there any truth,' Reggie soon probed salaciously, 'that you are more interested in the eternal Eve than anything else? I have heard rumours.' Chink never gave a thought to his own recoil from Hemingway's treatment of Hadley. Only Amy was prepared to understand, believing Eve to be more malleable than Estelle.

He had never done any fence-mending for himself because Estelle had always done it for him. When he now suggested – tentatively – meeting someone who might be useful, Eve threw a scene. After the heights of First Alamein she saw herself as his exclusive inspiration. How could he leave her and go up to a club or restaurant when she had given up everything for his sake – and even left South Africa for him? Didn't he realise there was a widespread vendetta? Couldn't he see they wanted him out of the way? How could he lower himself even to contemplate it, when they were mocking him behind his back? She was the only one who was on his side. Usually she gave him an ultimatum:

if he went he would not find her there when he came back. In other moods she said his selfishness was making her physically ill and pleaded for the doctor. He always gave way. Her hypochondria appeared a delicious frailty and her possessiveness a compliment. He was unconcerned that she quarrelled with her sisters, possessed no women friends and exploited her paid companion; none of them were in her league. He was a very brilliant older man, he overheard her remind her mother, and she adored brilliant older men. But Chink, himself, she hardly knew.

One of the first impressions his new brigade formed was that of a highly-sexed man; it was the most dangerous game left. On his regular Wednesday trips up to London he and Eve lunched openly at the Berkeley Hotel and booked a room above for the afternoon. They were at their happiest on show, defying stuffy convention. When she took his name by deed poll he dictated the letter informing the War Office and did not grudge the lost contacts; not at the time.

160th Brigade was preparing for the invasion of France. It was stationed three miles from Sittingbourne, with headquarters in Provender, a sprawling, high-chimneyed Tudor house. Supersensitive to atmosphere, he knew he was not welcome. It had been part of Montgomery's corps, and everyone Chink met seemed to know he had been sacked by Churchill before Montgomery went out to Eighth Army. He did not like that, nor did he enjoy the Rip Van Winkle sensation brought about by the youthfulness of his officers. Eating in the mess was like 'feeding in the nursery'. He dreaded the 'kindergarten life', and found pretending to be interested in the 'miniature' world of the brigade an effort. 'I suspect', he continued to Liddell Hart, 'I will be unable to take myself sufficiently seriously to be the sort of paternal demi-god, Jehovah, a brigadier should be. I would have thought it better to use people like myself on some sort of panel for planning, organisation and training, rather than a senior regimental appointment.' A brigadier, he smarted, needed only to be a cross between a good farmer and a good overseer. 'Fine qualities in a limited field in which any excessive imagination or creative ability is a real handicap.'

In no mood to adjust to the backbenches, his touchiness kept everyone at a distance. His brigade major, Rex Cohen, found him fascinating but soon concluded that his isolation was self-inflicted. The description of the elderly Mrs Patrick Campbell as a great galleon sinking and firing on its rescuers fitted Chink superbly, he often thought. And Cohen, being a civilised wartime soldier who hoped to return to the world of high finance, did his best to throw a lifeline. Off duty, he invited Chink to his house off Eaton Square ('first class sherry and burgundy and brandy', Chink noted wryly. 'I'm afraid I got both feet into the trough and wallowed – I'm getting middle-aged and greedy') and made a case for him with his parliamentary and newspaper contacts. In the mess Cohen persevered with sensible advice. The army was more like a business than a profession, he pointed out. It demanded the arts of compromise, obliquity, mutual flattery and concession because there was no leverage except through a propitiated hierarchy. 'Of course,' Chink commented after one session, 'the extent to which Rex is right is the extent to which I am inevitably doomed to failure.' His divisional commander, Major-General Ross, was a sound, unimaginative regimental soldier, and junior to boot; the two were, in Cohen's view, poles apart. No one there had a clear idea of Chink's previous work, and his habit of scrutinising all major international moves made him appear a dilettante.

If Haifa had felt like a backwater, the brigade was solitary confinement. The fall was lower than he had expected in his darkest moments, having jibbed at even a major-general's command in England, and he could not play the game necessary to catch up. But it looked as if he was sulking. Comparisons were soon made between his behaviour and that of Ritchie, who had been given a division in Scotland by Brooke and continued to mix affably. But as Chink's musings at the time of his July analysis of the loss of Tobruk revealed, the two men could not have been more different. 'Could one go back to England, go into the club, call officially at the War Office to seek new employment?' he had wondered then, projecting himself into Ritchie's shoes. 'Wouldn't one want never to be seen again, never to wear one's name again? I know I would. I could not bear the idea of facing my old world. I suppose he would not mind. What should that man have done to himself?' And Ritchie's steadily rising graph exacerbated the downward curve of his own despair now, leading to further adverse comment.

He did try to play the role expected of him. On one exercise 160th Brigade were billeted on an Essex village, and he made his appearance at the local dance feeling less important than he was clearly considered to be. Everything was very small and inaccessibly parochial. 'One girl amused me,' he noted afterwards. 'A strapping land worker with the figure of a Juno – would look marvellous stripped. The chaps were after that magnificent anatomy like flies after jam. She was quite uneducated. I talked to her for a little and then to the WAAF officer, about 28 and the typical head girl, captain of the hockey team. She'd like bed, but she'd never let herself go.' This new assessment was a priority now, but in other ways he had not changed. 'Behaved myself admirably,' he congratulated himself after a similar occasion. 'This soap shortage made participation in the Paul Jones a trifle risky. I can't do with a smelly woman. I left early, just as it was warming up, in effect.'

The social round bored him as much, left wing as he had become. 'I can't see myself going back to country conversation,' he reassured Eve after the first Kent cocktail party. 'One is expected to know everybody, however negative. I do find talking insincerities to people unnerving to a degree. Bless their hearts, they are still so certain of themselves and they little know how much I feel their necks need wringing.' But the numbers of elderly people about saddened him, and he was at his kindest with vulnerable older women, who were in the majority. Rather than seeking people out who might have helped him, he made for the lonely and the anxious, and tried to make them smile. He was very hurt by Auchinleck's silence, and far too proud to get in touch with Wavell.

One friend who remained constant was Liddell Hart. 'Begin at the beginning . . .' was Basil's phrase for friends in trouble, and the solace he provided of a comfortable chair, the right drink and a perceptive ear came as a surprise. Chink had thought it was an expedient friendship and he was touched to discover that he was liked for himself. 'I emphatically disagree,' was Basil's invariable reply to his lament that he was finished. '*Not* justified, even as a raft of others' views. For in my own range of contacts I have found that you have quite a number of warm supporters in fairly influential quarters.' And soldiers rash enough to tell Liddell Hart that Chink was unbalanced – the same criticism levelled at fellow intellectual Boney Fuller – were reminded of George III's riposte to claims that Wolfe was mad. 'If that is so,' Basil quoted coldly, 'I wish that Wolfe would bite a few of my other generals.'

In October Chink sent Liddell Hart his full account of the July fighting. Basil floated the idea back that Chink should write the foreward for the latest edition of *The Strategy of the Indirect Approach*, using O'Connor's campaign as an example of the theory in practice; it was as much to distract him as to add weight to the subject.

Chink's refusal was ungracious. 'I am a nobody under a cloud,' he replied self-pityingly. 'I'd rather take the limelight off myself and focus it on the justness of the principle. I can't believe that the extraction of my dampsquib self will affect the issue. I could not be more harshly dealt with than by Court Martial. I feel the injustice strongly. Self-effacement seems right and proper to me, and you will just have to accept that fact.'

Firmly Basil lunched him at the Park Lane Hotel with his new wife Kathleen and two visiting American war correspondents, and Chink rose to the occasion, arriving with a red carnation in his buttonhole. To Basil's amusement both reporters took him to be a guardsman and, stunned by his stream of wit and irony, exclaimed that they had never thought a British general could be like that. It was the effect he had had on Hemingway, so many years before. Kathleen, however, was more discerning. She grew very fond of him as she got to know him better, and saw that behind the Edwardian elegance he was shaky and bitter. Basil was equally under-utilised, but less devastated by rejection; his writing, of course, provided the release Chink lacked. Six months earlier Grigg's proposal of a body of military experts under Liddell Hart and Henry Tizard, to create similar operational research sectors to those already run by the RAF, had been overruled by the War Office, and Basil remained as unpopular as ever with the army hierarchy. Their bright pre-war planning was a joke.

Eventually Chink was talked into writing the preface, and hope surged back. Reggie wrote to say he had been stranded in bad weather with Smuts on a Cornish airfield. 'What he actually said', Reggie elaborated later, 'was "When we got to Cairo we found that Army morale was so low that changes had to be made, and for my part the man I would not have replaced would have been your brother. He has a brilliant military mind".' Next an invitation came to meet the Permanent Under-Secretary, Ministry of Aircraft Production, and Chink was delighted to find it was his old friend Archie Rowlands, resurfacing after India. 'Can't think what he wants of me,' he wrote hopefully to Eve, 'but he is in very close touch with Grigg.' The meeting was friendly, and when they met again the following day Rowlands turned out to be as unswayed by military fashion as ever; he believed Chink had been badly treated and said he was wasted in a brigade. Stafford Cripps was introduced at a lunch set up by Liddell Hart – 'that makes ex and present cabinet ministers since my return nine, including Amery' – and he had an encounter with Beaverbrook, disagreeing with him over Russia's infallibility. Grigg continued to be welcoming. At a drinks party he met Cripps again, this time with Joad as well as Hore-Belisha, and Cripps said he was about to come down to Provender.

War Office permission for the Cripps visit was refused. Word came back on Cohen's grapevine that Brooke was implacably opposed to him, so it was no use approaching Churchill because Brooke had his confidence. Montgomery, also, was known to be opposed. Amery reported back to Reggie that it was impossible to do anything in the way of righting wrongs.

'It is a very bright and lovely November day,' Chink wrote that morning, determined to be positive. 'Automatically I had a very British reflex when I found myself trying the lawn with my heel to reassure myself that it was not too hard for hunting. Do wish I was on horseback. Instead, I'm going to exert all my store of tact and persuasion to get across a new tactical concept.' The concept was to use light armour-plated troop carriers for mechanical probing, like cavalry, and would have involved people from three sections; to Cohen's relief, Ross turned it down. The old house leaked draughts, the wood fires smoked, and winter was 'beastly' after so long abroad. Deliberately Chink acclimatised himself through regular runs and two cold sponge-downs daily, unsure what he was bothering to harden himself for. He went to the dentist, as he had been meaning to do since Haifa, and was told his front teeth had to be extracted; the new ones, to his surprise, made him better looking. He went to the occulist, who recommended glasses. He decided to think about that.

The Battle of Alam Halfa had been fought at the end of August and beginning of September, and he was able to dismiss it wittily in public after all. 'A brief encounter between British 13th Corps and Afrika Korps,' he pronounced, 'with the rest of Eighth Army and PAA (Panzer Armee Afrika) keeping the ring.' That Horrocks should have been the commander for a battle which Chink was sure Montgomery had pinched by looking at the clear dispositions Auchinleck and he had left behind on the war map was too painful to be faced directly. But Rowlands opened the wounds with the remark that Montgomery had operated their defence plan and it had gone like a charm, and only after one of his old sleepless nights was he able to write that it was good news. (Montgomery had made one major change, bringing the raw 44th Division near enough to use its guns as artillery.) And when the Second Battle of Alamein was obviously under way at last that October he read between the lines of newspaper reports jealously, finding comfort only in its delay, which proved the correctness of their own refusal to be rushed. 'That fact will perhaps be my justification', he told Liddell Hart, 'for saying that in my opinion the High Command have a totally unreal attitude to war.' He and Basil always referred to the High Command as they would to an elderly board of directors.

Chink occupied himself with paperwork during the long winter evenings, writing a criticism of the British system of command, unchanged since the previous war, and slating the failure to assimilate useful lessons. His report on Sidi Barrani, for instance, had still not been circulated. Montgomery's handling of the Second Battle of Alamein struck him as heavy-handed and uninspired. It had been too slow and too rigid, although Eighth Army was now gloriously swelled with reinforcements of troops and equipment. He saw no need for the bludgeon when the rapier would have done.

On 20 November his introspective routine somersaulted. 'I have just heard that the super panjandrum, Minister of Defence, Auk sacker, is coming to visit one of my battalions today,' he informed Eve hastily. 'And I am to meet the bloated creature at midday. There ought to be an element of comedy about this encounter – blast and damn!' Churchill was visiting 53rd Division, and as they paced along the inspection lines of his battalion together a small olivebranch was extended in the form of lunch on Churchill's train at Faversham station. He forgot all Cohen's good advice. Churchill and he sat at the centre table, with Brooke, Bernard Paget, who was now Commander-in-Chief Home Forces and had earlier taught him at the Staff College, and 'Pug' Ismay of the Chiefs of Staff at the table beside them. It was an ideal opportunity, and doubtless intended as one.

'Winston inspected bits of my parish last week,' he told Liddell Hart cagily in due course. 'He was affable, and discussed the summer campaign without due rancour. He never forgave the Auk for not taking over direct command of Eighth Army in May, and I agree with him over that. I couldn't go too deeply into things in the presence of Paget, who is, I think, jealous of Auchinleck.' All well and good, although he misread Paget's embarrassment. Reality, however, was rather different.

Act One centred around the fall of Tobruk. When Churchill announced that he had been the most discomfited Briton in America since Burgoyne – he had been staying with Roosevelt in the White House at the time – Chink was unimpressed. Tobruk was indefensible once Rommel had gained the plateau, he observed, so it should never have been left in isolation. If Rommel had assaulted it the previous November, he continued, it would have been taken then, so the South Africans had had a raw deal. 'What do any of you know about it?' he countered to the chorus of protests about fighting to the last. 'None of you have been there, let alone studied the problem. I have done both.'

Act Two featured a villain, the Vichy French collaborator Darlan, who was rumoured to be about to co-operate in Operation Torch, the allied invasion of North Africa. Chink had always found de Gaulle impossible to take seriously – 'he looks like and is a camel, but then he has to carry all the burdens of a hopeless caravan through pretty arid places' – but he had respected his courage. Darlan he did take seriously, and despised. Was it Churchill's intention to uphold such a seedy two-timer? Churchill glared back. 'Dorman-Smith, I'd do a deal with the devil himself if he helped me to kill Germans.' Not even the Prime Minister, Chink retorted, had a long enough spoon for such transactions.

The curtain was about to come down. Now that the Axis could no longer hope to win, he lectured Churchill, the trick was to help them lose neatly by issuing a manifesto to Europe – the Italians in particular – encouraging them to throw off the yoke. Churchill, restraining himself, said he did not wish to cause chaos. 'What do you think you're going to get anyway? Better it should be inspired by us.' His prickliest point was always the squandering of troops, and when Churchill stated that it was best to put the finest in first and attack, Chink took him up on it as if the Prime Minister was a dim Haifa student. 'All right. You put your best troops forward, they attack and they get killed. Suppose they are New Zealanders – there are now no trained New Zealanders . . . and soon no British Commonwealth. So then you put in your Indians. . . .' Exit, stage left. Paget's recollection was that Chink was so outspoken that it almost amounted to disloyalty to Auchinleck, the last impression Chink would have wanted to give.

Why did he do it? This luncheon, like the Iraq–Persia offer, was an opportunity to rebuild his career. He could have charmed an amusing lunch out of Churchill, none better, so was it impulsive disdain for the obvious – and dishonest – way back? Or did he see the lunch as his only chance to educate Churchill and so save lives? The Royal Northumberland Fusiliers' code, after all, was that they were good enough to talk to a Prime Minister.

Back at Provender the façade clipped straight back into place. 'WSC was in the best of moods,' he declared to Eve. 'Discussed old battles, the fall of Tobruk, El Alamein!! and the present campaigns. He said of Darlan, if the devil himself wanted to shoot at Hitler I'd encourage him to do so. One can't be too pernickety in war. Was most amusing over his talks with Stalin. Put down a couple of whiskeys and soda and a very good brandy and generally did the affable!!' Perhaps the explanation is that keeping pace with Churchill's drinking did away with caution. The Prime Minister's train sped on, and took Chink's reprieve with it.

By December Chink was seeing portents everywhere. A telegram came on New Year's Eve and he opened it expectantly: it was from Edward, dated June 1942, and congratulated him on his well-earned promotion. It had gone all the way out to Cairo and back again. 'A trifle ironical,' he commented. In January Eve told him she was pregnant and he was overjoyed, but in February she had a miscarriage. An exercise took him near his first prep school, which made him realise how differently life had turned out from his expectations. The success of others was constantly in the news. Going from stength to strength with the Eighth Army, Montgomery was being acclaimed as a hero and Horrocks was promoted to a lieutenant-general. Harding and Galloway had reached that rank too, noted the self-styled bottom brigadier of the British Army, while de Guingand had been awarded the OBE. 'It's odd to feel one is being punished,' he wrote, 'as only our class can punish anyone whom it thinks can be a disturbing influence.'

By the spring of 1943 he was even more remote. 'Having failed to keep pace,' he told Liddell Hart theatrically, 'I've left the world and become a hermit. I have no external contacts whatsoever and excluding matters of business I never speak to a fellow soldier. I think it's better for us returned empties to do this than sit around grousing in clubs. I have been squashed flat. I do not feel that I exist anymore, that is all. I am, in effect, dead.' He began to compare himself with Liddell Hart's other close friend, Lawrence of Arabia, and found much in common. 'I always thought he went to extremes about himself. Now, with my experience, I realise that it is the only thing to do. I do now understand that self-immolation is the proper gesture for heroes who have completed their tasks, vide Heracles.' Basil's patience was severely tested.

Chink was drifting further away, though he continued to carry out his job satisfactorily. In March the report went forward that he was fit to command a division, but he was beyond hope, in a personal hell. 'I'll write no more,' he told Eve desolately when she relayed the customary adverse gossip. 'I am too sad.' He felt he was skulking while everyone else risked their lives, and obsessively he looked back over his career to find how much of the spiral was his own fault. Army reform was the one thing any soldier would be wise to leave alone, he concluded after months of introspection. 'The blimps are bound to win in the end. If I'd been nice to seniors and their often deplorable wives, kept mute, I'd not have aroused opposition and dislike. But I'd probably behave in exactly the same way if I had my way again. To have done otherwise would have been dishonest.'

Dishonest . . . like dissembling on the train? He heard about Ezra Pound's Axis broadcasts, and remembered Paris in the early 1920s and Pound's kindly authority then. The Mob took menacing shape. When unable to sleep he punished himself by counting incidents of regimental bullying, or numbering the contemporaries who were advancing because they had characteristics he lacked, rather than abilities he knew he possessed. His own accountability grew more clear, but the role of brigadier came no easier with practice and his letters seethed with frustration.

'I, with my head already full of clearly the proper answers, had to listen to a contemporary holding very high rank gibber and grope towards the proper way by trial and error.' 'Military audience today: beef and no brain whatever. Guts, endurance, wasteful stupidity and yet a sort of inevitable steamroller strength.' 'The High Authorities seem to rely on some C of E god of battle to rescue them from their tactical errors on the day of fate.' 'What is one's duty? Is it to go blindly on with the mob or say "No, this is wrong," and take what's coming? I struggle with this question all the time.' 'I've a sinking feeling that I'm tilting against windmills. This little study office seems so remote from the places where things get done, and I feel so helpless against the mass of wellmeaning complacent quasi-efficient inertia which towers above me.'

In April an embossed 'Mentioned in Despatches' certificate arrived for his contribution in November 1940, and Cohen was stunned to see him tear it up and throw it in the ante-room wastepaper basket. As soon as Cohen left, however, he picked the tatters out and pieced them together to find out who had signed it; then he snorted and threw them on the fire, where they burned up as brightly as he had dreamed they would a few nights earlier. He thought back continuously to the losses of Mons and the Somme – 'the disasters can repeat themselves, and so narrow is our margin of superiority that we cannot afford defeat' – and the falling British birthrate was obvious in Kent, as it had never been from abroad. 'Safety first orthodoxy,' he raged. 'The orthodoxy of Singapore. The orthodoxy of Hong Kong. The orthodoxy of Burma. The orthodoxy of where next?'

And then Cohen, at his own request, was posted away and there was no one to prevent him looking into the military abyss as the months merged seamlessly into one another. It had been directly intimated to him, he informed Liddell Hart with black humour, that unless he relapsed into Blimpery he could not expect better employment, but since he grew daily more obsolete, Blimpery was bound to result. One evening he switched on his wireless for the news and heard a speech by Göring, who claimed that Germany was Europe's spiritual keeper against Bolshevism. 'It is usually in failure that one's ego tries to idealise one's stupidity,' he wrote in torment afterwards. 'I know that too well. I do it myself, and Göring's speech might have been made by EDS.'

Unexpectedly a phone call came from the Military Secretary to say that a VIP was demanding to see him. Did the name begin with A or a letter at the other end of the alphabet, he ventured? 'Well, it's not A,' came the cautious reply. Agog with curiosity, he arranged to meet Wavell at the War Office at 11 a.m. on 3 May, which allowed too much time for second thoughts, and by the time he crossed Whitehall to keep the appointment he was ramrod-straight with self-consciousness at the contrast with their previous meeting at TAC HQ. The Commander-in-Chief India and South-east Asia sat alone in a small, borrowed room. He was in bad form, Chink detected beneath the passivity, but as matter of fact as ever; Wavell did not mention Estelle or confide his continuing difficulties with Churchill. Like Chink, he too was in disgrace and uprooted from family security, but unlike Chink he was not reacting as if the end of the world had come. Stoicism separated them.

Wavell wanted to talk about his recent campaign against the Japanese in Burma, the reverses of which – compared to the lustre of Montgomery's Eighth Army triumphs – lay behind Churchill's latest animosity. But as Arakan had had little newspaper coverage, Chink felt more out of touch and thin-skinned than ever. 'Wavell looked up sharply and gave his familiar short laugh,' he recorded afterwards. '"If you had been there, Eric, it would have been different. My generals were too orthodox."' This was too much. He forgot that he had wanted to avoid Wavell in India and forgot his pride in the race of emotion. He snapped that he had been rotting away for nearly a year, available at short notice, so it was a pity that that had not been thought of before. They would not meet again, and he would always regret parting on that note.

Distressed, he went on to lunch with Rowlands, conscious that he had behaved poorly, and polished a version for Liddell Hart. 'Saw the great Archie in London,' went that account. 'He seemed a little piano. In his usual direct approach he hinted that I might be of use in India but avoided any concrete offer. So I, too, was oblique and politely unenthusiastic.' 'Queenie' Wavell's disapproval of his love life, it occurred to him, was probably a stumbling block – 'she would also have ruled out Napoleon and Nelson' – and Eve had to face the realisation that he would have accepted a definite Delhi job this time had he been offered one.

But was such an offer considered? Wavell wondered in his own diary why Churchill had taken such a strong dislike to Chink, but he also noted Chink's 'sour resentment', and Wavell had no time for pique. In any event, the timing was against them both. Within a month Wavell was moved aside to succeed Linlithgow as Viceroy, and Auchinleck took his place as Commander-in-Chief, stepping back from the wilderness he had been in since August 1942. Rowlands had implied as much over lunch that day, when he leaned forward to disclose that 'Buddah' was finished, and unknowingly extinguished Chink's last flickering hope as he did so. 'I think it is a very good thing,' he wrote dispassionately when the change was made public. 'APW is too used now to making war in a small way with restricted resources, and has got into the habit of averting defeat rather than organising victory. He knows much more of the philosophy and history of war than A will ever know, but I think A is more of a man of action if they give him a first-rate staff and really good commanders. He will purge some of the Delhi GHQ limpets pretty drastically, but he won't ask for me because he will only call me when he is in extremis.' He had no hope of rescue any more. When Horrocks was badly wounded that summer and sent back for a long series of operations, he castigated himself for his previous envy and was too humiliated to visit him.

Meanwhile he kept on working. In his evening solitude he listened to Yehudi Menuhin's broadcast concerts, indulged himself in the wide range of Penguin paperbacks, and avoided clubland. He wrote only to Liddell Hart and Rowlands, apart from his family. His London visits were spent in a Berkeley bedroom with Eve and later in the Putney flat, and, though they often quarrelled these days, the good days were more than enough. Journeying up and down to her by train, he studied people at his leisure, and the charm he had once been able to dazzle with was not as dead as he supposed. Long-legged and spruce, shoes gleaming and brown suit pressed, his buttonhole fresh and so obviously a soldier, he kept extensive notes on his fellow travellers, deploying his monocle strung on a black cord; it had been the only possible solution to the eyesight problem.

'Travelling solo with a red girl and a black dog, she so smart that the very powder on her says "Rendezvous". Not a very long rendezvous, the grip is too small. Hair to my eyes quite excellent – Venetian red – and some more powder, then to lean out of the window till a man comes in – a commander RN. Falls over dog and into her arms, and then almost sits on her in one side of the carriage. He is now shaking all over. She is sweet with him. Her rather spoilt face softens and grows gentle in anticipation. Phew! I almost howl.' Other couples touched other nerves. 'Opposite me are a couple I try hard not to dislike. He aged 60, say, actively fat, well dressed, wealthy, full of selfish, acquisitive, aggressive moments. She dark, brown eyed, tall, Spanish type. Shaded moustache on upper lip, male conscious, say about 28. Large diamond naval crown and a quite lovely Kerry Blue terrier. These two monopolise one side of the first class compartment emphatically, with the Kerry Blue on the seat too. The plutocrats are glorious, everything I am fighting against, though brown eyes is prepared to recognise that I might from my appearance be a tolerable member of a world they consider suitable to live in.'

None of his personal disillusionment showed. Only an old friend would have noticed his new front teeth, no longer bucked, and the loss of his moustache which he had shaved off as a badge of the conventional; with the resulting sense of exposure had come the realisation that his hair was going grey. Concentration on other people made a change from the tedium of thinking constantly about himself, and his focus changed in this secluded year. 'There is a very tired grey woman, with a boy aged about 11 and a girl. She seems to be alone, poor person, and so utterly clogged with children. Hair anyhow, hands gone to pot, just a woman without any more hope. So sad. Her children are restless and noisy and uncontrolled. I feel so sorry for her.' But sometimes the journeys up to London were buoyant. Liddell Hart continued to canvass on his behalf, and in July 1943 Herbert Morrison was the target. Mussolini's fall came as excellent news.

At brigade HQ the try-out for the invasion of the continent, Exercise Spartan, promised some personal satisfaction, and though he disliked the format of a bridgehead – 'tactically unwise' – and forecast a succession of command flaws, he threw himself wholeheartedly into teaching along modernised Blackdown lines. Rowlands came down in his official capacity to observe the result. '*12.5.43*: I spent Saturday night and Sunday morning with Eric DS,' Rowlands informed Liddell Hart, 'watching his brigade doing an exercise which involved the clearing of an anti-tank field for the passage of tanks. I was very impressed with the spirit and keenness of the troops who had been at this sort of thing for three years. I expected to find them browned off.'

160th Brigade was judged outstanding, but the limitations Chink had predicted showed up generally and when the tactical criticisms of Spartan were put on the desk of the Secretary of State for War, Rowlands called round to Grigg's office to remind him that Chink had prophesied each one. For some time he had been sending Grigg a copy of Chink's correspondence with him, because he and Grigg were in agreement about the waste of his talent, and for a while Grigg had not replied, which Rowlands put down to overwork. But now Grigg lost his temper at once. He did not want to see anything further from Dorman-Smith, he shouted without looking up, and the reaction was so extreme and so unexpected that Rowlands was taken aback. The reason for it was very simple. The murmurs about Eve had reached Grigg at last, and he had been so very fond of Estelle in India. From now on Chink was finished as far as he was concerned. There could be no excuse for anything immoral and so no further communication – most certainly no support.

Recognition for Chink's work on Spartan was not forthcoming, and despite his recommendation for a division, no posting came. Is is coincidental that Grigg and Brooke were becoming close in a support- ive relationship forged in the turmoil of working beneath Churchill? 'Brooke's work', as Grigg felt free to disclose in 1946, 'covered . . . the choice of individuals for senior military appointments. In it I was associated with him for more than three years. I do not recall any important matter on which we were unable to accommodate our views. He has, too, a delicious faculty for mimicry which I have often seen exercised to caricature the highest and mightiest . . . and a very warm heart for friends and colleagues.' And beyond Brooke soared Churchill. 'I know of no major matter', confirmed Grigg, 'in which Mr. Churchill decided to take a line that was opposed to Brooke's advice.' Grigg could have been the most valuable of friends, superbly placed to help Chink, and instead he had switched round to being vehemently against him. The mimicry is readily imagined.

Rowlands, whose ability to harness talent was to become legendary behind the scenes, remained staunch. But he was not to be around for long, because towards the end of 1943, when India was being prepared as a base for the offensive against Japan, he was appointed Adviser on War Administration to the Viceroy, and went straight out to Wavell. Liddell Hart would claim that before Rowlands left he urged that Chink should be given a major-general's appointment and that Grigg put him forward for one, but a decisive shake of the head from the old guard in India put a stop to the promotion. Certainly one of Rowlands' last loose ends was concerned with Chink. 'It is a pity', he wrote in November, 'that he is not higher up in the counsels of the War Office . . . but he has offended against the light and I am not very hopeful that he will go very much further. . . .'

On 11 November Chink was told the name of his new corps commander, and his first reaction was that it would be comic if it didn't hurt so very much. 'I have just heard,' he notified Eve, 'that Ritchie is coming to be two above me. That makes a nice layer of inefficients. I said that if the news were true, Ritchie would be very uncomfortable with me under his command and that I'd better go elsewhere. Clearly that is necessary in view of what happened in June 1942. That remark is being passed to Ross tonight and I hope he'll get cracking. To think that they would ever re-employ the man who by his ignorance and stupidity lost us Tobruk defeats me.' He was currently reading Pitt's *History of Human Stupidity* and there were diplomatic lessons to be learned from Pitt. Carefully he put his note to Ross on an exalted basis – 'So unfortunate for General Ritchie' – and sat back, reawakened.

'Better to be kicked downhill than to stagnate,' he noted, 'but to most people nothing is more stupid than to offer oneself for crucifixion on a point of principle.' The principle concerned was that his contempt for the Corps Commander would be impossible to cover up because his men knew of their previous confrontation, and so it would be bad for command, like a cancer. He ran his usual four miles in record time that day and the weather was as keen as a knife and crystal clear. 'You know', he warned Eve, as he had so often warned Estelle, 'that I have perhaps been unwise again, but for better or for worse I have written personally asking to be moved away.' Ritchie was due to take over 12th Corps on 27 November, and now the days stood out sharply, one after the other. On 14 November word came that he was going to be moved, without the date being specified.

He travelled up to see Eve in London on 19 November, keyed up, and a family got into his carriage at the next station. 'The daughter is a pretty, under-developed brown eyed little mouse, and she asked what I did,' he jotted down. 'So I said "Soldier." And had I been fighting? "A little." "How long had I been a soldier?" 'Much longer than you've been alive." "Oh, but that's impossible. I'm nineteen." Rather sweet.' Unfolding himself from the seat at Victoria, he decided to stir things up even more by requesting to depart before Ritchie took over, and the response was swift. The Assistant Military Secretary phoned on 21 November to tell him to go. On Paget's direct order he was to vacate his command and stay on leave of absence until further notice.

A Confidential Report was placed on the files by Ross that afternoon. '*C/182/27/A. 21st November 12 Corps A.* 1) Brigadier E. E. Dorman-Smith MC has been in command of 160 Brigade since 17 September 1942. 2) He has held Brigadier and acting Major General appointment since 1938. 3) I recommend that he now be allowed to go on full pay pending re-employment in the rank of Major General. 4) I request that a replacement in command of 160 Brigade be made as soon as possible. 5) This is in no sense whatever an adverse report.' On 22 November Chink requested confirmation that his removal had been no reflection on his efficiency. The uncomfortable impression was beginning to dawn that he had played into somebody else's hands.

'Dear Dorman-Smith', wrote Paget obliquely but kindly. 'The reason why I agreed to the request of General Ross . . . is as stated in his letter. . . . Neither he nor I intended any reflection on your efficiency as a brigade commander. I am sorry that a misunderstanding has occurred.' And Wemyss – 'My dear Chink' – promised to hasten matters. 'In the meantime there is nothing for you to do,' Wemyss counselled, 'but be patient.' December came, and the brigade was still without a commander, although Chink had recommended his second in command. The void worried him professionally. On 19 December he approached the Under-Secretary of State for War, having been previously tipped off by Rowlands about Grigg's *volte face*. 'Trust not considered impatient,' he badgered the Under-Secretary, 'if point out . . . increasingly difficult to explain suspension from duty.' He was now living with Eve in London and being prompted daily about the vendetta; he requested a formal explanation 'to protect myself from possible calumny'. At the pre-Christmas lunch with the Liddell Harts there was still nothing to report. On Christmas Day, pulsing with anger, he discussed legal advice. Little was suggested.

By the end of January he was in a nightmare that was made no easier for being mostly of his own making. Ritchie held every card – 'I heard [Dorman-Smith's] removal', the new corps commander was sneering, 'was because he was stale' – while he himself was reduced to half pay. Eve was rich but he was not, and now the gap mattered. There were few friends in high places to help him. He contacted Hore-Belisha and wrote on the off-chance to Dick O'Connor, who had just escaped from German custody. He lunched with Grigg's intelligent plain wife and she was sympathetic, but she knew when to protect her husband. Nothing happened.

In the New Year Honours List he read that Brooke had been made a field marshal, and out in Burma, according to the newspapers, Slim and Christison, his contemporaries at the Staff College, were visibly adding to their laurels. Paget was succeeded on the Selection Board by Montgomery; Grigg and Brooke were said to be imploring Alexander to take him on in Italy. 'Alex naturally wants to run his own patronage and brigadiers are part of his perks,' he wrote furiously. 'So it's unlikely they'll succeed in getting me there.' He was told by Paget that his foreword to *The Strategy of the Indirect Approach*, upon which he had spent much time, could not be published under his name because Auchinleck's despatches were not yet out, and he began to see himself in company with Fuller and Hobart – 'dropped down an oubliette'. As if to show how high contemporaries were going, a fellow Sandhurst instructor, the ardent cricketer General 'Bimbo' Dempsey, was appointed head of the Second Army. 'I expect Bimbo has developed into a ritualist with a façade of pseudo-originality but with a cricketer's flair for man-management,' he sniped. A very different communication was on its way to him. 'Dear Sir,' it announced, 'I have the honour to inform you that you will relinquish the temporary rank of Brigadier with effect from 28th January...' He had plunged down to colonel's rank because he was out of work. The oubliette yawned.

He asked for a court of enquiry into his case and itemised grievances, and in February a feeler was put out by Ralph Glynn, an MP on the Services Select Committee. Glynn invited him to stay for the weekend and, in a gentlemanly way, leaned on him to take back his request for a formal explanation. Chink declined. Lecturing Glynn about mistakes in the current Anzio campaign in Italy, a beach-head operation like Spartan, he pressed on him a copy of the criticisms he had sent to Rowlands, and left early. A few people approached him, off the record, to say he was doing himself no good by insisting on an explanation and he brushed them away, continuing to write too many letters and pester too many senior people. He felt he was being treated as if he was Oswald Mosley, whom he loathed; he remained as anti-German, anti-Fascist, as ever. 'In this country we have professionals who aren't allowed to play and players who have never been professionals,' he told Liddell Hart. 'I amuse myself by a fortnightly letter of insults to the Military Secretary in which I say what I think of the Army Council. Doesn't get me anywhere, of course.' He turned down the offer of a junior command in Northern Ireland – 'a noncombatant vacuum' – by return post.

On 3 March 1944, reduced to begging, he wrote to Wemyss to say he was prepared to serve in any rank anywhere, as long as it was in active service. On 30 March, having been unused for four months, he was taken up on his word. 'You have been selected', the telegram informed him, 'for the appointment of commander of an infantry brigade, Allied Armies in Italy.' It was to be under Alexander, in the beachhead of Anzio.

'I interviewed Colonel Dorman-Smith on 30 March,' wrote Wemyss, 'and told him of the decision. . . . I explained that there had been considerable delay in settling his case owing to a variety of cumulative factors. . . . I explained that it had been previously decided that he should get command of a brigade in the field before he gave up command at home, and his removal was handled unfortunately in that his subsequent placing had not been arranged. The fact that General Ritchie had assumed command of 12th Corps clearly caused General Paget to remove [him] without proper consideration. . . . No doubt . . . harshly treated . . . Colonel Dorman-Smith has clearly been penalised for his enforced idleness and lack of recent opportunity, and this is fully recognised.'

The likelihood is that no one bothered to look at the brigadiers' names when Ritchie's appointment was made, and that it was not the finely honed vendetta Chink took it to be. Such reverses do happen, and they can even be turned to good advantage; one of Ritchie's chief qualifications for reinstatement had been the uncomplaining way he worked his passage back. But that was never Chink's way, as might have been expected. Wemyss's letter – Chink had had to stand over him to get him to write in the end – was intended to draw a line under the episode and it finished encouragingly: 'Colonel Dorman-Smith goes out to the Mediterranean to qualify for advancement.' He took his copy, left the War Office swiftly, and was on his way.

13

The
Mincing
Machine

Major-General W. R. C. Penney, Diligens the head neophyte in the Staff College pantomime of 1928 and commander of 1st Division at Anzio in 1944, protested as soon as the cable came through. Everything he had heard about Chink in Cairo during his period as Chief Signals Officer to Auchinleck and Alexander confirmed how right he had been to dislike him earlier. Clearly it had been his fault that so much went wrong in the desert, and now that they had a good team running things, with Penney's Staff College model Oliver Leese in charge of Eighth Army since January, it was typical of Chink to think that he could walk back in just because he felt like it.

Penney had climbed higher than he had expected in the days when he used to taunt Chink about being doomed for the staff. Although alarm had been his first reaction when Alexander asked him to take a division the previous autumn, a talk with the man he admired most, Montgomery, had reassured him and not only was he now in charge of a fighting division, but he was having to cope with an abrasive Anglo-American working relationship. Old for a divisional commander and known to be a man who did everything by the book, he had put up with the relayed sneer of the US General Mark Clark (that he was 'not too formidable a general but a good telephone operator') in the interests of co-operation, since the British were in a secondary role in the joint operation at Anzio. But tolerance had its limits, and Chink was not writing this script.

'I once sent a personal signal to C-in-C that I would NOT have Dorman-Smith,' he wrote later. 'Alex riposted with a personal signal to me saying it was apparent I did not realise this was an order. So there we were, and the stage was set. The next time I met Alex he apologised for his rude reply and added with his wellknown smile: "You see, that is what I got back from the CIGS when I sent HIM a telegram like the one you sent me."' John Harding, Chief of Staff to the Commander-in-Chief, had been standing beside Alexander when Brooke's signal came through, and was asked for his opinion. Harding, recalling the tensions at GHQ ME, advised him to refuse. Chink, he explained, made difficult men more difficult. 'I have discussed the question of Dorman-Smith with Leese,' Alexander had replied to Brooke. 'He is strongly opposed to having him as a brigade commander in his Army and I agree. [He] is a disturbing influence, and I could not afford at this time when we are faced with many other difficulties to add to them by accepting this officer.' But the overruling had been prompt. 'Leaves by air with orders on highest, I repeat highest, level that he is to command an Infantry Brigade. Most important that this should be carried out expeditiously.'

Penney, reading Harding's tactful letter in April, realised that he had been lumbered with Chink because the other divisional commanders in Italy were too junior. 'The C-in-C is very sorry', Harding wrote apologetically, 'to have to give you extra responsibilities, but he knows that you will make the best of it, particularly in scrupulously giving Chink a good run for his money.' It meant that one of Penney's best brigadiers would have to be moved sideways to make room for him, and as he waited for Chink to arrive the last sentence of that day's communication from Harding beamed a sympathetic wink. 'I do hope', Harding signed off, 'you won't find him a trial.'

Penney had had enough trials already. The major Anzio operation had gone wrong from the start, although it was no more than a decoy to a decoy. The joint Anglo-American advance up the mainland of Italy of the Fifteenth Army Group, incorporating Eighth Army, under Alexander, from which Anzio was supposed to divert attention, was itself going ahead to distract Hitler from preparations for the intended *coup de grâce* of the Normandy landings in France. The seaside town of Anzio had been chosen as the beachhead because it was within thirty miles of Rome and on the far side of the German Gustav Line that blocked Fifteenth Army's path, and though British planners had advised using four divisions, the Americans had halved the force by supplying only sufficient landing craft for two. And when the landing force waded ashore on 22 January 1944 towards a clear road to Rome, they had been ordered to dig in for twenty-four hours by General Lucas, the elderly US commander, and consequently both divisions had been cordoned off there by the Germans and pinned down. Penney's 1st Division had drawn the worst of the subsequent fighting, and the brigade he would have to give Chink had been driven up into the German cordon with horrific casualties. Anzio was recognised as being the worst shambles of the war, and the press correspondents on the beachhead were referring to it graphically as a mincing machine.

Chink approached Anzio briskly. He made a new will bequeathing his War Office correspondence and military papers to Liddell Hart, and left him with the mischievous admonition: 'Continue to be a signpost to good sense and a warning to tactical roadhogs. They also serve who only point and wait.' He thought of the Biblical precedent of Uriah, sent off to be conveniently killed in battle. 'Only the Army Council has no Bathsheba and wouldn't know what to do with her if it had.' Rommel, he estimated, would have had his men in Rome within twelve hours of landing, so the tactical roadhogs were undoubtedly in charge.

But he set out on 28 April in good form. After command of an operational brigade came a division, if all went well, and he intended that it would. He recognised the passenger in the next seat on the BOAC flight to Algiers as the politician Harold Nicolson, and the centre of the war came close again. 'Very good company,' he wrote approvingly. 'A curious type – national Labour representative but not genuine Labour in mind.' So well did they get on that Nicolson pressed a book on him from his bulging briefcase and said he could return it when he got back to England. It was McCurdy's *Structure of Morale*, and had caught Chink's eye because of War Office rumours about the low Anzio morale awaiting him. 'Won't agree with all of it, of course,' he noted, 'but intensely interesting psychological stuff.'

At Algiers he melted into the background, book in hand, as soon as he realised that Nicolson was being met by Duff Cooper, who had been appointed British representative there with the French Committee of National Liberation; despite Reggie's encouragement, he was too shy to introduce himself. Flinching from the tumult of Algiers, he bought a raincoat, thick boots, two blankets and a beret, as advised, and on the spur of the moment waited to see Jumbo Wilson, who had succeeded Eisenhower as Supreme Commander of the Mediterranean. Speculating whether Auchinleck and he might have been there instead, he had to leave for the five-hour flight to Naples before Wilson's meeting ended. And in Naples there was no time to call on Alexander and Harding, as he had intended, because a fast American launch was waiting to whisk him to Anzio. Stepping ashore he found his divisional commander waiting, and he did his best to hide his shock. He had not thought of Penney for years.

Too late, he deduced that Ronnie, as he instinctively called him, was 'a tinderbox beneath a damped down exterior', because as soon as he mentioned the Whitehall line about morale in 1st Division being non-existent, Penney's icy manner changed. 'I did not want you at first,' Penney stormed, though others could hear, 'and I do not want you now.' And Chink's usual charm, which he took care to exercise by ringing to apologise as soon as he realised the rumours had been inflated, only made things worse. 'I was NOT', Penney wrote later, still bridling at the thought that a politician had taken Chink seriously, 'prepared to take him at his own – or Winston's – estimation.'

Was Chink, as so often, exaggerating the animosity? According to the BBC war correspondent at Anzio, Wynford Vaughan Thomas, if anything he did not realise its extent. There were a dozen senior officers there at Chink's level and above, and Vaughan Thomas studied 'Eton in Uniform', as he privately called them, closely. 'Chink came to Anzio with a lot of poison about him,' he observed later. 'It seemed to me to date from the desert, *violently* anti him. My feeling was that they didn't welcome him coming and they thought he was planted on them. They all feared at senior level that he would do the same thing at Anzio as in the desert, with that report on Ritchie, and they assumed he was sending reports on them to High Command. He most definitely arrived on hostile ground.'

Busy at once, Chink tried to put Penney out of his mind. 'Rather attractive here except for lethal noises', he noted cheerfully the first night. 'I can't escape from the impression that it is a Pilgrim Father's affair, with the harbour full of assorted Mayflowers. The natives on our frontier are definitely hostile and we are colonising under difficulties.' Flowers bloomed in the churned up earth and Rome was a short jeep ride away, behind large red signs warning DANGER, SHELLING, MAKE NO DUST and NO TRAFFIC IN DAYLIGHT PAST THIS POINT. In the distance the ruined Factory had been pointed out, once Mussolini's model village but wrecked in fighting eight weeks earlier, and near the Factory was the Flyover, a shelled bridge. It was nauseating country to fight in, he was informed. Everywhere the ground was bisected by ravines chiselled out of the soft sandstone by rain, and christened wadis by Eighth Army veterans. Entire brigades had been wiped out in them as the five and a half German divisions surrounding them held the upper slope. The countryside beyond appeared intact and in the Alban foothills villages gleamed in the sunlight. But nothing out there moved.

As colonists, they were cramped. The perimeter at one point was only three miles deep, and by now 72,000 men with all the paraphernalia of corps and army headquarters were compressed into the small space. 3rd Infantry Brigade's three battalions were in an olive grove, and as soon as he was introduced he saw them in romantic terms as a circumscribed semicircle of young men. The face of one of his colonels was familiar and then he placed 'Bunny' Careless, Cassells's prickly Controller of the Household in India and a close friend of Elaine's husband, Kenneth Bols. Careless commanded the King's Shropshire Light Infantry and with the other two battalion commanders, Brian Webb-Carter of the Duke of Wellingtons and James Hackett of the Sherwood Foresters, had been through the recent fierce fighting; the Sherwood Foresters, Chink learned, had the unenviable record of the heaviest losses on the beachhead.

He was shown around their sector by his young brigade major, Henry Leask. 'A good lad,' he estimated with relief. 'Very regular army and a first class staff officer.' Their defences, he judged, were wide open to the shelling and deep trenches were long overdue. It was standing-room only, Leask explained, and furious fighting because if the Germans cracked the crust they would all be in the sea. Everyone was suffering from strain. Cigarettes were in unlimited supply and official exhaustion centres had become necessary. At once England was infinitely remote.

Guns spat as he bent over the first letter to Eve, conscious that his sandbag hut was too shallow to be effective. In the olive grove noise was distorted by the trees, and it felt more exposed than London during the mini-Blitz the previous winter. 'Rambles, whams, great lightning c-rrumps', he noted for her benefit. 'Then the little vickers and spandaus go stammer, stutter, and the Long Tom's roar drowns everything.' The likeable extrovert vigour of the outgoing brigadier, 'Jimmy' James, would make his own job more difficult, as James had been with the brigade since the landings, but he did not tell Eve this. 'He is going off to say goodbye to Brigade HQ personnel as I write,' he hinted. 'He seems a particularly fine type, pleasant and efficient. They have just given him three cheers and I feel a bit of a beast. He has undoubtedly got them with him.' Sensitive as always, he could tell he was resented as an intruder.

'As you so rightly say,' Careless would agree many years later with Penney, '3rd Brigade was a bit of a law unto itself. We were a very close knit brigade . . . very much part of a family. . . . Jimmy James was one of us – as, for that matter, was our Divisional Commander! – and we did not take kindly to an imported brigade commander.' But the brigade's hackles were also up for a reason that never occurred to Chink. At Anzio it was known, as everywhere else, that he had once been high on Auchinleck's staff. But here it was believed that his brother, as Governor of Burma, had pulled strings to get him a second chance. From being a meddling politico at DIV HQ, he was seen as a failure with connections at brigade level, and the separate assumptions were set to buzz towards one another.

It was a young man's war by now, after the attrition of five years of fighting, and at Anzio the routine was especially wearing. Troops stood to half an hour before dawn and remained in battle stations in the line for as long as it was light. Chink was roused at 05.30 for the night reports, and 'visited downwards' all morning, going around subsidiary headquarters and forward companies. If an attack was planned that day, details had to be worked out in between. At any moment shelling was liable to freeze the frame. In the evening he went forward to places too dangerous to visit earlier, and after supper out of a tepid dixie, he worked on in the operations room till 23.30. 'A longish day,' he observed. Penney appeared to be ostracising him, which struck him as petty because the priority was surely the good of the brigade, but it came as a relief to be spared sanctimonious lectures.

The order he ached to give was effected as soon as James left, and on 1 May the digging of trenches began. Soon communication trenches linked up all the posts; there was even a tunnel at one point that he could jeep along. Sometimes he felt the years had peeled away to 1915. 'Dull and dangerous position warfare', he noted, 'each side can hear the other talking in places. It's monotonous and wearing for the troops, much what their fathers underwent, and psychologically they find it more trying. They've got to learn to dig like beavers and wire like spiders – a whole host of new tricks of the siege trade. At present they don't know how to make bullet proof posts or realise that the art of survival lies in digging while suppressing the Boche by sniping and mortaring. I want to get the sniping effort better organised, too.' Seventy-five per cent of wounds at Casualty Clearing Stations at Anzio were from fragmentation missiles, and when 3rd Infantry Brigade's casualties dropped other brigades copied them. The parallel with Ypres was so evident that Chink could not understand how Penney had missed it. Interviewing Chink at this time, Vaughan Thomas was impressed.

Diagnosing a distinct lack of smartness, and being of the school which thought high battle endurance stemmed from discipline and good administration, as well as determination, courage, and physical fitness, he ordered spit and polish tightened up all round. Steel helmets were no longer to be left on graves, but were to be used again. A higher standard of saluting was expected. Litter was an offence, and smoking forbidden during demonstrations. For camouflage reasons, white vests could no longer be worn in the open. He had never understood the art of encouragement *en masse*, and it came across as an unnecessarily fussy staff approach. Word went round all sectors that he considered them incompetent and sloppy, and at DIV HQ, where Penney presided that first week, the implication from a newcomer that things might be improved was fiercely resented.

Chink knew goodwill depended on the attitude of his three battalion commanders, and learning that Webb-Carter had deputised for James in the past, he expected him to bear a grudge for being superseded now. But Webb-Carter, elegant and laconic, supported him. And Hackett, who was the epitome of a sound, regimental soldier, was clearly prepared to give him a chance. Careless, however, was a different proposition. There was an atmosphere from the beginning, as both retained memories of the clashes in India, and an incident soon took place that polarised them further. Hearing that Bols had been killed in action, Careless put his pride in his pocket and went at once to give his condolences to Chink. 'He gave me the impression', Careless wrote incredulously later, 'that he hadn't heard he was dead and that he couldn't care less.' Chink sent him away without disclosing that the marriage had collapsed, and that he held Bols responsible for Elaine's unhappiness.

All three colonels were much younger than their counterparts in England, and in letters home Chink took to signing himself 'Mr Bultitude'. He could see the response when he mentioned the first war – history now – or Hemingway – whose books had been on their school English Literature course, on a par with Dickens. He missed none of the incredulity at his monocle and Edwardian courtesy, or the smothered laughter at his own design of battledress with its unfashionable wide trousers and puttees. He knew he came across as a stage character and he could do nothing about it. Nor could he do anything about his lack of recent battle experience. It was over twenty-five years since he had last been under direct fire, and that put a glass pane between him and the rest of the brigade which he was more conscious of than they were. 'I hope people won't think I am chucking my weight about,' he wrote privately, 'because I'm ambitious or anxious to rebuild my fallen fortunes. That is not the case at all. I'm happy to be here and content to have my career go the hard way.' He handled fear in his habitual manner. As at Mons, Ypres and First Alamein, he used a mental trick to maintain judgement: he viewed all his soldiers as actors in a Shakespearean play. He took a part himself, applied stage directions aloud in his mind and simultaneously watched the performance from afar.

He was having to face up to more, in fact, than the young men around him could comprehend. Only a soldier of similar rank would have understood, and as Henry Leask rose high through the army in his turn, much that was inexplicable about Chink at Anzio came to make sense to him. Russia and the Balkans are all very well in theory, Leask was tempted to shout in 1944, but they're not the priority if bullets are whistling through your hair. Getting up the guns by evening was more than enough for other brigadiers, but his brigadier wanted to discuss why they were bottled in and how they could be fighting the entire battle more intelligently. It was possible to adjust upwards, Leask learned in due course, but not downwards to such an extent; to switch from forecasting moves six months ahead to the small-level decisions facing a brigade within several hours was too great a difference of scale. But as always Chink asked for no quarter and gave none.

When he had been there for a week he was glad to hear that Penney was going on sick leave, due to a neck injury sustained in February when his caravan had been hit. And the temporary replacement was 'Ginger' Hawkesworth, who had whipped in with the Staff College drag in 1927, and who soon revealed that he thought alike about Arthur Smith, Ritchie and Auchinleck. 'The nights are London 1940, the population London and New York 1944, the tactics Ypres 1915 and the wild flowers are beautiful,' Chink wrote brightly to Eve, revitalised. 'I am reading Tartarin de Tarascon, it seems appropriate.' He was as fit as anyone else – certainly fitter than Penney – and he did not feel his age. Visiting a brigadier on his flank one day, he was asked if he was any relation to the Chink Dorman-Smith at Cairo, and instead of the usual sly dig it turned out to be a compliment when the man exclaimed that he looked too young.

Inland brooded the Colli Laziali – 'the hills like beasts at their hunting lay,' he liked to quote, 'Chins upon paws to await their prey' – and astride those hills were the Germans, looking back down at them. The thought tantalised him as he went about his sector. 'They can see all the beachhead,' he wrote, projecting himself late one night. 'The busy mine sweepers, the destroyers out beyond and the balloon barrage floating nostalgically over the Porto. To take the sharp edge off their observation we make smoke continually across our back areas, and the two little towns hide their scars in drifting veils of chemical clouds.' The olive grove was summer green and sandy underfoot, making his mac and boots superfluous and reminding him of a Camberley wood, and the Uppingham quadrangle might have been carved from the sandstone of the wadis. He allowed himself to hope. As a matter of routine he was bound to be under scrutiny, and when he proved himself, by September, he would get a division. 'I would rather be here', he wrote to Eve as he had written before First Alamein, 'than anywhere else.'

The nightingale singing outside his dugout reminded him of the poetry of Wilfred Owen as he savoured backnumbers of the *New Statesman*, winced at the day's sunburn, and re-read *Jurgen*. 'Always fresh.' He remembered to write to Auchinleck in time to reach him on the second anniversary of their flight up to Eighth Army on 25 June, and he kept his image of the Big Picture adjusted to sharp focus. That vigil began on 12 May. 'Last night Alex began his big effort to break through to Rome,' he wrote at night, employing the familiar tone he could never use with the brigade.

I wish him luck, but there can be little or no finesse. It must inevitably be a slogging match. Rome has become a symbol of this war, as Baghdad and Jerusalem were in the last war. Well, after many tribulations we entered both. I understand acutely how the Afrika Korps must have felt when halted only 60 miles from Cairo. I am told North Africa and the Middle East have become sleepy hollows in the trough of war. I can visualise old Jumbo slumbering like Chronos in the Garden of the Hesperides.

He had no idea that behind his own back he was called Old Chink.

But his earlier liking for Americans was in abeyance. The Pamplona brotherhood of 1924 bore little relation to the crewcut, gum-chewing army that was twice the size of their own, four divisions to two by then, and taking less than a fair share of the dangerous troglodyte life. Resentment of the Americans was endemic among 1st Division, and even the tolerant Webb-Carter leaned forward one day to murmur that America was the only country to pass from barbarism to decadence without an interval of civilisation in between. The dandy in Chink recoiled from the unshaven chins, the buttons undone, the creased olive-green uniform and general lack of discipline. He found wisecracks irresistible in the long joint conferences, and his dry humour did not translate. Tension was mounting higher as the likelihood of breakout drew near.

Lucas had been replaced for some time by the younger General Truscott, and it was the American's plan by the middle of May to break out through the key town of Cisterna. 3rd Infantry Brigade were put in the spearhead of a British diversion along the west flank of the beachhead, and given the objectives of Green Bush Hill and the village of Pantoni. Chink deployed Webb-Carter's Duke of Wellingtons and two companies of Hackett's Sherwood Foresters on the right, and one company of Careless's King's Shropshire Light Infantry on the left, with an artillery bombardment to precede the attack.

'I have just been speaking to the CO of my assaulting battalion who at this moment is sitting in a ravine only 400 yards from the unsuspecting Hun,' he scribbled on 22 May.

A little like telephoning from the café de Paris to a chap in the condemned cell at Dartmoor. *Later*: We have dined well, a normal dinner, people formally dressed, flowers on the table, jokes, laughter, and not a word about the battle about to begin in 18 minutes. The liaison boys have fitted up a spare loudspeaking R/T set in the Mess dugout. They will listen to that and BBC or Rome music simultaneously. It's a calm, beautiful evening among the trees. Nightingales sing. Far clouds float overhead. One smells the evening breeze. What is about to happen seems unbelievable. It has begun. The first guns have been fired. My first offensive battle.

Operation Ant and Aphis, as it was codenamed, surged out under cover of darkness. Gaps were cut in enemy wire and lanes made through minefields, and though the attack ran into more stubborn resistance than had been expected, Pantoni was secured at the cost of ten killed and ninety-seven wounded. 'I would like all officers and

NCOs who have led patrols', Chink instructed next day, 'to see the ground they covered in darkness and ask themselves whether they really got where they thought they did. . . .' The German positions were as professional as he had expected, but the severity of the defence that Careless's men, in particular, had met was accounted for by the desertion of one of their own corporals in time to warn the enemy. No longer feeling his youthful anger at death, Chink now felt sad and fatalistic. He could not go as far as Rupert Brooke, he reflected that evening, as there were no rich dead or poor dead – just dead men. 'Very still, lumpy and tumbled, and covered with foul, shiny bluebottles.'

The Germans had taken the bait and left Cisterna vulnerable to successful American attack, and on 25 May, when the breakout was a *fait accompli*, he was as exultant as those half his age. 'Today the beachhead lost its virginity and merged into the Fifth Army,' he crowed. 'I think Kesselring has lost the battle for central Italy. The question is, can he now stand in front of Rome?'

He was quickly brought down to earth. A new brigadier called round whom he had taught at Camberley, and the ex-student hesitated over whether to call him Sir or Chink. 'One does get one's nose rubbed in it.' As they were moving up past the Alban Hills towards Rome, Hawkesworth was replaced by a young Canadian, Charles Loewen, and Loewen's lack of seniority compared to himself emphasised as nothing else could the apparent determination of higher command to humiliate him in front of his officers. When they met, however, he liked him – 'forthright, foul-mouthed, tactless, efficient, no Yes-man, we'll get on' – and he could not see that Loewen's modern four-letter-word style made him appear more of an anachronism than ever.

By 2 June the 4000 men of 3rd Infantry Brigade had advanced to a shell-pitted wheatfield near Rome, and orders came to take Aquebona Ridge next day, a prominent feature behind a ravine that lay ahead of them. Intelligence revealed that it was held by crack units of 4th German Parachute Division, and Chink had little time to shape up the attack as he was due on the American front at Velletri that afternoon, where a British brigade was about to be needed.

Planning on the morning of 2 June was urgent. The attack could take place from first light onwards, so embodying his law of seizing the psychological advantage Chink selected midday as the enemy's weak spot: no assault would be expected at lunchtime, and it would probably coincide with a relief change-over, flustering German reaction further. Leaving the lesser details to his battalion commanders, as was the practice in England, he kept his appointment with the Americans. It was an approach in direct contrast to his predecessor's total involvement, and Careless watched him go with misgivings. When 3rd Infantry Brigade moved up that evening, Careless took the precaution of reconnoitring by himself to within a stone's throw of their objective, determined not to attack over unseen ground again, as at Pantoni. It left him very little time for sleep. At 11.55 hours on 3 June the bombardment began, to be lifted two minutes later for the assault to go in. By 13.30 tanks and reinforcements were across the ravine, and by 16.30 it was clear they had driven the Germans off the ridge. At dusk, when a second brigade passed through to take up the fighting, Aquebona Ridge had been gained, 3rd Infantry Brigade was dug in, and patrols roaming forward reported that the enemy had pulled out. Prisoners admitted that they had been caught out between reliefs, and British casualties were low at eighteen killed and wounded. It had gone off like a copybook exercise.

It was at this point, however, that an incident took place that was to have a catastrophic effect on Chink's career. On edge in anti-climax in the dark, with a minimum of sleep and keyed up by having to lose contact with the Germans, Careless lost his temper with Chink. 'I got pretty desperate with him during the night,' Careless wrote later, 'and told him it was imperative that he should come forward to see for himself; it was impossible for him to command where he was.' Chink did not come forward, and the exchange took place over the R/T. Webb-Carter listened in.

Traditionally the brigadier, as commander of a brigade operation, stays back at his headquarters to control his three forward battalions by radio. When communications are so vital the brigadier must balance his duty to all three battalions equally, and risking himself for one puts all three in jeopardy. That is the classic position, as taught at the Staff College in 1927, used in command at Crete and Alamein and in exercises like Spartan. But at Anzio a new custom had evolved of more human contact. With the sharp drop in age and experience at every rank, it had become the practice there for brigadiers to reassure battalion commanders personally, because of the claustrophobic nature of the fighting and the added danger of hysteria. At the first sign of nerves they would go briefly forward to radiate normality and leadership, despite the risk. James had commanded like this instinctively. Chink was of the old school. 'I am a great believer', as he wrote once, 'in each level of command being coldly just where it can function effectively and not sitting in the next below's pocket.' There was no military need at all to go forward that night, but there was an emotional one because Careless was known to be highly-strung. But then nobody had told Chink of the change. He missed the formative experiences, Penney had left him to sink or swim, and Hawkesworth and Loewen took him at face value as an Anzio veteran.

'The attack was a great success,' Careless would recall selectively many years afterwards. 'But who was responsible for its original planning, I don't know.' Sitting next day in a pretty part of the golden *campagna*, fifteen miles nearer Rome and proud of his planning, Chink was unaware of trouble brewing. 'Really a model operation and its planning and launching has given me great confidence in my tactical ability,' he noted instead. 'Reads a bit like Monty, that one! I was given the job of cracking this position at very short notice. Enemy position neither wired or mined but his posts most cleverly sited and built by Italian labour; deep dugouts in each section post and deep connecting trenches, a formidable proposition but, more serious still, held by a very tough battalion of para boys. . . . I shall sleep well in my tent under a full moon.' The bodies of two Italian officers of the Folgore parachutists, attached to the Germans, had been found shot in the back, which underlined the ruthlessness of the troops they had dislodged.

Glad that Careless appeared to have settled down, Chink made a point of going to give him the news that he was putting him up for the DSO, which Webb-Carter and Hackett had already won; their names were going forward for a bar. But Careless had been teased over the R/T during the fighting about getting his DSO at last, and he expected it. Chink was taken in by the guarded politeness, and saw no link with Penney's return set for two days' time.

With Rome taken, 1st Division were detailed to stay on the outskirts, with the exception of Webb-Carter's battalion, which would be representing Great Britain in the victory parade. 'I hate the idea of good troops getting all softened up in the pubs and brothels,' Chink wrote approvingly. 'And, besides, aren't we getting on with this war? I want to get into Germany without delay.' But he turned down the offer of troop-lifting transport – 'rattling along in filthy lorries on roads in a perpetual fog of choking dust' – in favour of building up extra marching fitness after the inactivity of Anzio. It was an unpopular decision. On 6 June he slipped into Rome on his own. Officially he had to make arrangements for his battalion's part in the parade, but unofficially his destination was the Grand Hotel, which he had last visited in 1919, and where he intended to carry out a private rite.

Elbowing his way between drunken GIs, he reached the peace of a side table and ordered a drink. 'Here we are in June,' he wrote, blocking out the clamour,

> and it is 24 months after Ritchie's disasters and the Auk's subsequent retrieval of them and now, at last, after incredible delays and disappointments, we are in Rome with our enemy in disorganised retreat. It has been a long dusty road and I deeply regret that the men who began it, Archie Wavell, Dick O'Connor, Strafer Gott, Jock Campbell and others like the Auk who carried on their work, are not here to see its climax. New men who never knew the bitter years in the desert will reap the reward. Curious how I seem destined to be a spectator, but because the road from Cairo to Rome is a connected journey I am glad to have seen the end of it, as I saw its beginning and the depressing middle parts. . . . All the big shots will come rumbling in to fortify their egos with the dust of antiquity now. Depressing thought. I expect we'll have Churchill along any day with zip-fastened toga and utility bag wreath.

And he raised his glass and drank a toast to the men who ought to have been there instead.

The spell was broken. A GI pawed a young Italian girl, and when a prostitute solicited Chink in the street outside he pushed her away, repelled by the thought that two days earlier she had been in bed with Germans. The Borghese Gardens were dried up and unplanted and the maps on the wall of the Victor Emmanuel Memorial charted the growth of the Fascist empire. Pushing down longings to see Milan and the northern Alps, he met the American organisers of the parade and convinced them that his battalion ought to march with fixed bayonets and that detachments from his other regiments should line their route. On the day he watched from the crowds around the saluting base at the Porta Pia and the change from the brave days of Eighth Army's solitary stand was vividly demonstrated when Loewen was made to step down from taking the salute. 'Mark Clark', he fumed afterwards, 'spoiled what should have been an all-British party by turning up with a bunch of thugs and taking the salute himself.'

D-Day, the successful Normandy landings, had already pushed Rome into second place and information on the fighting in Brittany was scattered and unsettling. 'So Monty has got Brest,' he wrote lightly to Liddell Hart within the month, 'nippled Rommel in the bud, so to speak.' (Montgomery would not capture Brest, however, until 19 September.) His old depression was back. The fighting in Normandy reminded him of Ritchie's corps command, and Penney's return disheartened him. Billeted in the *castello* that had been the head-quarters of the German division routed at Aquebona, he looked out at the Canaletto vista and fought the sense of hopelessness. 'One thing is clear,' he concluded after the habitual post-mortem was done, 'the whole business at Anzio was seriously mishandled. But mistakes show up in retrospect and reveal ignorance, misplaced optimism and inertia. History will not flatter the conceivers, the planners or the senior executants.' Penney had not come well out of the scrutiny, and Diligens struck him as a most apt name, since there had been no imagination there. But above all the complexities of a sea landing strengthened his view that military formations had to be reorganised from the top. Lack of synchronisation remained a flaw, and he had no expectations any longer about raising professionalism. 'We are incorrigible half cock shotters,' he noted wryly. 'The inhibited English public school mind suffers badly from ejaculatio praecox even in its military tactics. We cannot learn to hold our fire.' The familiar conclusions added to his melancholy and he kept himself to himself more, as he had done at Provender. Meanwhile the constant paperwork fuelled the rumour that he was reporting back to high command.

On 13 June he treated his three colonels to dinner in Rome, ordering asparagus, steak and 'very passable' chianti in advance, and thanked them for their support. Over the cheeseboard, amused by their surprise, he proposed a training exercise over the place names of Macaulay's *Lays of Ancient Rome* and assured them it was an opportunity Wavell would not have missed. 'I do feel I'm getting the confidence of these men,' he wrote afterwards, misreading Careless's good manners. 'Certainly they know that I'll never put them in battle on the wrong foot.' But his next outing was a less pleasant prospect. On 22 June he was scheduled to take Penney along the breakout line, and bring him up to date with the brigade's movements in his absence. 'I will do showman as best I can,' he groaned beforehand to Eve. 'He still maintains Anzio was a success – magnificent English quality not to admit mistakes but liable to be misleading historically.'

The meeting got off on a bad footing at once. Penney was not alone, but had Loewen with him, and disparaged his deputy's efforts at every turn. Chink, for his part, was determined to show both sides of the breakout line, to demonstrate the German efficiency they would continue to be up against; it had the added appeal of testing Penney's nerve. 'It was most interesting and instructive,' Penney wrote later, 'but for me very frightening as Chink tried – unsuccessfully, I might admit – to make me accompany him over ground where I knew there were plenty of mines!' Chink's dare backfired, and anger at Loewen's treatment made him throw away his minor advantage. Penney's possessiveness about 1st Division so sickened him that he made no effort to be conciliatory.

By the time Penney left, Chink's mood was black. 'On the way back,' he recorded that night,

> alone in my car, the cat emerged from the bag. I had done myself 'no good' in the six weeks with the Auk at Alamein. Because, I suppose, the Auk having been reinstated as C in C in India they have still got to have a whipping post for all the rude things we said about the cavalry. If they can't destroy me physically they will give me the *coup de grâce* professionally. I felt in my bones today that I am the preordained scapegoat. Just have to wait till I see how they do their dirty work: they are certainly not going to let me gain any military reputation. All through this conversation ran a bogus morality. A and B were 'no good' because they had affairs – he considers me immoral as well as intransigent.

Touchiness sealed him off once again, and he was deeply offended to find his name left off Penney's list of Catholics for an audience with the Pope. When a new corps commander, Lieutenant-General Sir Charles Allfrey, who inevitably had taught with him at the Staff College, came to inspect the brigade, even the kindly Allfrey was snubbed. Chink had had a raw deal, he began awkwardly, but he hoped all would forgive and forget. 'I replied that I knew of nothing for which people had to forgive me,' Chink wrote, still hurt, 'so he answered that he meant I would forgive them. I told him that I was damned if I would. He seemed pleased to see me, but I saw by his expression that he found me very changed.' Allfrey was cut short when he said it was not too late to regain lost ground. The war, Chink corrected him, was too near its end.

Four days later news came that James had been killed while forward, encouraging one of his new colonels at the height of attack, and to Chink the brigade's grief was as palpable as heavy black crêpe. If James had not been moved for his sake, he blamed himself, he would still be alive; it was understandable that the men would now resent him even more. But he did not cancel his mountain-warfare course reconnaissance, scheduled for the following day, in order to attend James's memorial service. Careless noted this and hated it.

In the long interval for training Chink had too much time to brood. A caravan was delivered and he took it over superstitiously, remembering that when he had eventually been given one at Alamein he had been sacked almost immediately. Work on the Macaulay exercise reminded him of Wavell, making him lonelier still. His letters chart an increasing detachment. 'Something in this life is narcotic to contemplation, the boredom of it, perhaps, and living with Englishmen twenty years my junior, having nothing mental in common.' 'Without the possibility of professional development it is difficult to maintain interest or enthusiasm.' 'I admit these troops defeat me. They are so lethally stupid – can't or won't think tactically.' 'I've never been less use to anyone in my life. I'd be more use in England. Besides, I'm not wanted here. I'm merely keeping somebody's boyfriend, 10 to 1 some young guardsman, out of a brigade command.' 'Professionally I seem to have lost that active interest in novel methods and techniques. I suppose that at last something inside me realises that never again will my ideas be of any use in the Service.' His brigade major watched sympathetically. 'He withdrew mentally,' Leask remarked in due course. 'He allowed the machine to carry on by letting the chaps at the lower level apply their good sense. In the end we ran things without Chink really being at the controls, but it wasn't disastrous because the command set up was so good that things ran.'

At long distance Liddell Hart tried to keep up Chink's spirits, sending on praise from Tuker ('a warm reference'), Rowlands ('clearly a very high opinion of you') and Auchinleck who, he assured him, was trying hard to get Chink sent out to India when the Italian campaign was over. And a mutual friend at the War Office had recently tried to have him appointed Director of Tactical Investigation, 'for which job you are clearly the best fitted of all'. 'No, Basil,' Chink growled back. 'It wouldn't have done for me to have become DT at the War Office until I'd satisfied the critics that I'd been cleansed of my sins of criticism and unorthodoxy. There really is no place for me in our Army. Analytical, critical, tactless – I have never been able to accept cricket as a cosmology with a rectangle or oval, finite and bounded, in which life in peace and war is played to rules laid down by an MCC representing court, stock exchange, county and church.' And his letters were no longer sealed in envelopes, but were on open view in airgraphs which were photographed and reduced to postcard size for the new airmail lift-out.

The summer of impotence drifted along, and his four-monthly report was due. After the many changes of command he began to worry about who would be making it out. 'I don't know,' he speculated gloomily. 'Ronnie Penney was away in England practically since I arrived. He is, however, well in with the powers that be. He is a narrow, jealous type who has been jealous of me ever since Staff College days and is even now, in my downfall, jealous.' But on 21 July Penney came up to inspect the King's Shropshire Light Infantry ahead of rumours that Loewen was about to take over 1st Division permanently, as Penney's neck needed further treatment. Chink kept well out of his way, and Penney spent most of the visit talking alone with Careless.

But on his birthday, 24 July, he could not avoid him. Penney came again, all smiles, to say goodbye formally and thank him for his work. Chink was unable to respond in kind. 'He said the Military Secretary was coming here and did I wish to see him,' he noted afterwards. 'Replied I, "No, why?" That is what they cannot understand, these toadies and lickspitters. No, I've finished with the regular Army as the right wing of a conservative party.' The dynamic reappearance of Loewen was a distraction, but two days later he heard that Leese had been knighted, kneeling on a hassock in a field near Rome, and the thought of Penney's satisfaction and Leese' triumph overcame the comic aspect. When Liddell Hart wrote to say that a third member of his 1927 Staff College syndicate, Robert Bridgeman, was on the warpath in the House of Lords about his treatment, he snapped that it was like being in perpetual immersion in a bad public school. 'You're not to worry', he assured Eve, 'that I won't get free of the Army at the first opportunity. I am coming back to you the very day I can do so with honour and without letting the other chaps down. I must see this business through now, though. The Hun is kaput and I only regret that I had so little hand in his downfall. At the end of the war I will send in my papers.'

He threw himself into the stiff four-day training exercise Rupture, mordantly amused by the appropriateness of its name. As expected, the multi-dimensional concentration proved draining. 'The troops refuse to be interested in something which hasn't got real death and real

Jerries,' he scribbled on the final day, 'but I notice they make all the usual blunders which get them killed when we are fighting. They would rather die than think – literally the junior ranks let themselves get killed because of their tactical inadaptability. It breaks my heart to see them. But they don't mind.' A VIP car roared past as he was making his way back to the *castello* and splashed him with mud, conjuring up a wet Flanders road in the Great War. Trudging up the stairs, he found Loewen waiting for him in his room. And Loewen was clearly upset.

'He talked for an hour about myself,' he wrote next morning, too tired to write till then. 'Theme: I had lots of friends anxious to help but why did I feel bitter, others were in the same boat. I really tried to be polite. I did point out that anyone who'd been the recipient of special high up malice without redress and so consequently had forfeited his career had a good reason for bitterness. That is the tale – Chink's bitter. Wish I had some bitter pints of it to wash away bitterness. But I did make him realise that the day we stop fighting I'm off, if it's humanly possible.'

What had brought Loewen so late at night? Chink agonised about it during the official lunch he had to attend for King George VI, who was visiting the area. During his absence on leave, which was starting the next day, the brigade would be moving up to Assisi, which was the stage before Florence and the next major obstacle, the German Gothic Line. Did that explain Loewen's urgency? Reaching Rome, Chink heard that Penney had not gone straight back to England for treatment, as he had said he would be doing at their farewell meeting, but was staying on there in a hotel. It struck him as curious, but he put it out of his mind.

On 8 August, refreshed, he flew back to the brigade in a small observation Taylorcraft. Gazing down at the pretty pink roofs and palazzos beneath, everything felt timeless. 'Andromache waiting for Perseus or some beautiful Umbrian courtesan attending her next client,' he imagined happily as the plane was in flight. 'Pity I haven't brought my gorgon's head, but no room for one in a Taylorcraft.' Abruptly his mood was shattered by the man who was waiting to meet him. General Sir Sidney Kirkman introduced himself as his new corps commander, and Kirkman had been his junior in 1940. Then Kirkman had called him Sir; now he did not use his nickname and commented enigmatically on fate's reversals. 'To which I replied', Chink noted afterwards, 'that in the senior ranks of the Army there had to be either knights or knights errant, and anyway, I'd sooner finish the hunt on a bad horse than on none at all. Well, the hunt is almost over.'

Within three days they were in line within sight of the German forward positions. Florence had fallen, and the hunt was gathering pace. 'I was tired last night,' he confessed to Eve. 'I am consistently attending conferences, the results of which are cancelled almost before I can cover the ten slow miles back to my own temporary HQs. I then return on crowded skiddy roads to a fresh meeting. However, who am I to comment on military restlessness? It is such a rare quality.' He spent 12 August in forward posts among vineyards full of laughing girls harvesting the grapes, and was rejuvenated. 'How consistently the heroic evades me,' he mocked himself as he rested momentarily in the sun. 'And I'm aching to be brave, if only to confound the Army Council!'

A message was waiting for him, asking him to meet Loewen at once at a specified grid reference. It turned out to be a clearing in a wood, and Loewen was already there in his jeep. As Chink heard him say that Penney had got away with murder, a sense of *déjà vu* suspended him. An investigation had been carried out, Loewen explained unhappily, on complaints made by Chink's three battalion commanders who no longer had confidence in him. He brushed that aside. They would never have gone behind his back, he protested, because it was contrary to King's Regulations. Loewen's face was enough. The orders were to report directly to Rome, leaving at 05.00 hours next morning, and Webb-Carter would resume command. Chink was excessively polite, the only defence left. Alone in the clearing he took out his revolver and thought about suicide, but after a while felt histrionic and put it away. He drove back to face the Mob. 'Only one more night to get through,' he wrote when he reached his room.

To borrow Penney's phrase, the stage had indeed been set, but Chink would never learn the real plot. 'Many years before,' Penney disclosed in 1953, 'I and many others of my and Chink's contemporaries had decided that brilliant as he undoubtedly was, Dorman-Smith should be kept a long way away from active command of troops in war.' And to achieve this Penney did not go by the book. He left three records, and the two written at the time contain significant discrepancies.

'Soon after my return in mid-June,' Penney wrote to Leese on 3 August 1944 while Chink was in the same city, unwinding,

I had my suspicions all was not well ... particularly between Dorman-Smith and his commanders and also between him and his

HQ staff. I decided that as long as I remained in command I would do nothing except keep my eyes open. I knew [all of] them very well and was confident of . . . intervening when necessary and exercising supervision. After I relinquished command, however, I felt I could not leave it at that; I therefore spoke privately to each CO in turn. They unanimously expressed their anxiety about going back into battle under [his] command. . . . None of them knew Dorman-Smith before. . . . I personally feel that he has aged considerably and that he still feels somewhat bitterly towards life. My own opinion is that he should not be in command of troops.

In the paper he wrote at the end of July, under the luminously revealing heading 'Colonel (T/Brig) E. E. Dorman-Smith', he was more specific.

Early in July my GSO 1, Lt Col. Thubron, spoke to me of an uneasy feeling developing . . . partly personality and partly incidents during the [Aquebona] battle. . . . When I left Division on 24 July I decided I could not let the matter rest. Directly and separately I asked each CO between 24th and 29th if there was any trouble, and if so what it was. . . . I pointed out . . . that I was taking this course because I had relinquished command and could not pass on to my successor mere suspicions. . . . I would decide what action to take in the interests of all concerned. . . . *Webb-Carter* (DSO and bar) told me categorically that down to Coy Cmds going back into battle was . . . viewed with apprehension. . . . *Careless* (DSO) when I told him originally I was leaving Division said it is a frightening change in view of our early return to battle. I assumed and confirmed he referred to the prospect of battle under Dorman-Smith but had felt as long as I commanded the Division I would be able to deal with the situation. . . . At a later interview he said substantially the same as Webb-Carter. . . . He had not received the direction, support and assistance which he should have. *Hackett* (DSO and bar) confirmed what the other two alleged, viz. lack of direction, close contact and support in battle. He states the feeling is spreading. . . . In view of the state of affairs . . . I consider he should be relieved forthwith. . . . I have so far not said anything to Loewen or DS because [it would] . . . a) only make things worse and b) I have been able to go fully into the matter only since relinquishing command. I consider, therefore, that I should now be failing in my duty to all concerned if I did not bring the above to the notice of the C-in-C.

But interfering in Loewen's division and going behind his back and that of the corps commander to Alexander – despite Penney's claim that the cross-examination was entirely for Loewen's benefit – was breaking the strict army code. Penney made a point subsequently of clearing his motives. 'I would make it plain', he wrote disarmingly, 'that Dorman-Smith and I were always personal friends, though different temperamentally. There was on my part no backlash of feeling over anything that may have happened or not previously, e.g. in the desert.' But that does not tally with his contemporary statement: 'From my previous knowledge of him and his history I considered that [he] was unsuited for command of troops in the field. I voiced my misgivings.'

In 1984, shortly before his death, the battalion commander of the Sherwood Foresters, James Hackett, wrote about his side of the transaction for the first time. 'I remember I was hopping mad', he revealed, 'when I was summoned to DIV and asked by the G1 to give my opinion of my bde comd. To me this was blasphemy, there being such a thing in those days anyhow as loyalty to one's commander, whatever one might think of him. I told the G1 that exactly and left in a dudgeon! After all these years I still feel angry about it.' The G1 at a divisional headquarters is chief of staff to the divisional commander. Penney's statement about Hackett, therefore, is not true. All three commanders did not complain. They were also summoned instead of going of their own free will.

What about the rest? Webb-Carter left no record before his death. Careless had known Chink before, as Penney must have been aware, and had disliked him heartily since their regular altercations in Simla and Delhi, where they had met only on a social basis. And at no time at all had Penney, despite his protestations, advised Chink or reassured Careless. Rather than exercising constructive supervision, in fact, he had blown on the flames. The documentary evidence is convincingly presented down to the use of decorations as character references, although it was Chink who recommended the majority of awards. The brigade major, the staff officer mentioned, was never consulted and remains unconvinced that his colonels would have been disloyal enough to go behind their brigadier's back. 'British commanders', in Leask's opinion, 'do not do this.' At no time was there any direct criticism of Chink's professionalism. 'After he arrived,' even Penney conceded, 'he did some first class work in improving his sector. . . . His brigade did a successful breakout attack and his troops are in high fettle. His organisation of subsequent training left little to be desired.'

Dates in the documents conflict. In one contemporary account Penney stated that his suspicions were raised by Thubron at the beginning of July. In another he wrote that he was in his hotel in Rome. Loewen having already taken over command, 'and this time for good', when Thubron came to see him to say the three commanding officers wanted to talk to him. Examining the second, this must have been from 24 July onwards, so how was he able to interview the colonels elsewhere separately between the 25th and 29th without prior arrangement?

'The Military Secretary', he also wrote, 'happened to be in Rome and he was an old friend and brother officer of mine. So I sought his advice. He advised me to consult the Army Commander Oliver Leese with whom I was about to spend a day or two on a farewell visit. I told Charles Loewen what I was about to do and his only comment was "Don't be too hard on Chink." I replied that Oliver and I knew all about Chink and we would take whatever action we considered necessary.' But Loewen was now divisional commander. Penney had no authority to act, or to block Loewan from decisions that affected his command. Even so, he stayed with Leese at the beginning of August, by which time his irretrievable interviews were completed, as well as the first extensive document stating that Chink should be relieved of command. Only then was it decided that a letter could be sent to Loewen asking if he considered Chink was fit to continue in command – a question that had to be answered by an unqualified yes or no. And after talking to battalion commanders who had been unsettled by questions and promises, only one unqualified reply could be given. The kindest interpretation is that Penney was not as 'scrupulously' fair as Alexander had trusted him to be.

Kirkman took over as corps commander on 6 August. He was curt at the landing strip at Greve on 8 August because he was embarrassed. 'Saw Charles Loewen, Dorman-Smith and Brigadier Firth,' his diary entry for that day runs. 'The last two were to be there anyhow. Object of visit was really to meet again DS in view of the fact that he is likely to be adversely reported on.' And on 14 August it was to Kirkman that Chink went to protest. 'A long interview,' wrote Kirkman. 'Situation is that Penney, after he had given up command, wrote a letter saying that he had consulted DS's company commanders and found as he expected that they lacked confidence in him. To have done this after he had gone and without having confronted DS with the accusation is to my mind quite wrong. He also said he was tired and too old, which is probably nonsense. Dorman-Smith was, of course, forced on us out here and forced onto Penney, but the whole procedure is wrong. It gives him a great grievance and may lead to trouble.'

The situation in 3rd Infantry Brigade was far from ideal. But the machinery had been there all along to correct it, and had been ignored. Penney imparted no constructive advice when Chink took over, despite his concern for the brigade's welfare. Subsequently, he did not tell him of his suspicions, and so gave him no chance to clear the matter up. And later he went behind his back, in contravention of the system, and interfered with a direct chain of command. The subjective approach was so incorrect that it was disbelieved at higher levels. However it had been done, Paget speculated when he heard, it must have been irregular. Archie Nye wondered how a divisional commander could possibly have consented to meet a soviet of officers to discuss their brigade commander. Hackett's outrage mirrored conventional reaction. And Loewen found a way to make his feelings plain. When Careless was posted away from 1st Division shortly afterwards and asked if he might call to say goodbye, there was no reply. Unrebuffed, Careless drove over anyway, but Loewen was out and nobody would see him. 'So I got into my jeep,' Careless wrote, 'and drove to Fifth Army. I felt a little hurt about this and it seemed that the same friendliness no longer existed.'

Chink's writing on 15 August is practically illegible, the most striking sign of his distress. 'You must now find somewhere for us until we can leave England,' he wrote to Eve from Rome. 'In many ways I am not sorry, the position here was, as you predicted, impossible. The war seems nearly over. I must wait in Rome for a few days until, of their generosity, they find me an air passage.' It struck him that Mrs Bell's prophecy that the fighting would be over for him in August had referred not to 1942, as he had thought, but to 1944. She had also said there was little promise professionally. 'There is nothing more for me anywhere in the Army. I don't care. I have done my best. But I still hate failure for whatever reason, and I still feel ashamed.'

Unaware of Leese's part in the transaction – and from both Alexander's and Penney's testimony he would seem to be one of those who vowed at the Staff College to keep Chink from command of troops –

Chink asked him for an informal meeting. He prepared a six-and-a-half page defence in advance, and the twenty-three points covered his disgust that an adverse report had been canvassed behind both his back and that of the commander of 1st Division, his acknowledgement of the difficulty his arrival had caused, and his regret that James should have been moved. He drew attention to Penney's possessiveness about 1st Division, and his ill health, strain, lack of assistance and long absence. Pointing out that he had made no technical mistakes, but conversely had strengthened the sector at Anzio and had carried out two successful assaults, he went on to describe the contrast of his style of command with that of James. 'He centralised, I decentralised, he spoonfed (probably knowing his commanders); I (not knowing them) expected them not to look for assistance from me in their own sphere. . . .' It was a lengthy document, packed with emotional undertones. 'To sum up,' he concluded, 'I have been placed by good intentions and mismanagement, bad luck and ill-intentioned malignity, in an impossible position with a most unfair result. I therefore appeal to the Army Council for the annulment of the [adverse] report. I request instead permission to rid the Army of my difficult presence by immediate retirement. I make no more demands than that.'

Ironically Leese arranged to meet him on the evening of 17 August in the lounge of the Grand Hotel, where Chink had toasted his Eighth Army predecessors. 'An amusing sequel to our last meeting in Delhi,' Chink wrote bitterly the following day,

> when I was the senior. Now he held all the cards except the joker. That was my report on the incidents of this neurotic institution. He was a little shocked by that and more by my request to quit, unbelievable in wartime. 'But', I demurred, 'this isn't my war, you've not let me have any of it. Can't I even go and make a shell or put out a fire?' No, I mustn't even do that if it can be avoided. He has declined any staff work in this present rank. I have declared myself quite disinterested not only in my service future but also in nationalism per se. Both shocking statements. The situation now is that I am to wait here for 7 days. I'm given special telephone facilities – such a joke. I've kept my car, driver, servant. But I must not trust these guys at all.

Leese had skimmed the document, said he would have copies made for the Army Council, and left without another word. Chink regretted the retirement threat almost at once. 'Of one thing I am certain,' he had written only a fortnight earlier. 'The German military power must be overrun and killed in the open. At the end of this fighting every German soldier must experience physical defeat.' But the obsessive diatribe was irretrievable now he had handed it to Leese. Charon in the Camberley pantomime had become Charon in real life, with the power to take him to the underworld.

'The nombre de dios expedition failed,' he wrote to Eve when he was more composed. 'Partly I blame myself as being insufficiently adapt-able to the part I was expected to play. It's over now, but the climax was the smartest and least principled frame-up I've yet seen in this pretty tricky service jungle.' Convinced that Ritchie had been placed above him as a ploy to manoeuvre him out to Italy, he suspected the long arm of Brooke and was sure that Churchill had directed that he must never go higher. Penney appeared no more than an instrument, and Jumbo Wilson's signature on the order dated 19 August which directed him to be despatched to the UK filled in the final twist. To cap the humiliation, Horrocks had two weeks earlier been given command of 30th Corps in Normandy, and it was said that Montgomery had sent his own plane to England for him. Even sports-mad Horrocks, despite his bad year of hospitalisation, was going to end the war at the top.

Chink's final Liberator journey was to St Mawgan's airfield in Cornwall, where he landed in drenching rain. As the last train to London had gone, he waited out the night on a bench in a row with others, and for once nobody else impinged. He was cured of his military dreams, he wrote bleakly. 'Grown up perhaps, at last.'

As soon as he could, on 11 October 1944, he retracted the retirement request. 'I wish nobody to think', he wrote to the War Office, 'that I would apply to leave the Service in wartime, except as a protest against gross injustice.' Later that month his appeal came up. It was heard by the Number One Selection Board chaired by Grigg, and members included Brooke, Wemyss and Nye. Two weeks after the broadcast news of Rommel's death, which Chink listened to with considerable regret, the result arrived.

It was addressed to Colonel Dorman-Smith MC, and was dated 1 November 1944. 'Sir . . . The Council have now given careful con-sideration to your case . . . and have decided that as no further suitable employment can be found your retirement will be carried out. . . . You will be placed on retired pay with effect from 14 December 1944 when you will be granted the honorary rank of Brigadier.... I am to conclude by saying that the Secretary of State has it in command of the King to convey to you on leaving the Active List of the Army the thanks of his Majesty for your services.' They had taken him at his word. Against his will he was hurt that there was no personal note from Grigg, and the use of the King's name sickened him.

'The Army Council have come to the conclusion that I must either run or leave the Service,' he informed Liddell Hart. 'And naturally enough refuse to abdicate. So I am forcibly retired on 14 December. Soit, I've had it. I'll go quietly. At 49 I begin where I was at 19, only this time without a calling. Meanwhile the orothodox aristos triumph, Leese to Burma and Dreary McCreery to [head] Eighth Army. No wonder it's me for the hemlock.' On 14 December, in civilian clothes, he bumped into 'Boney' Fuller in the street, and thought it a suitable finale. One thousand marks out of 1000 seemed an eternity ago.

After the war a story about Chink spread among the military clubs. Theory broke down in practice, the punchline sneered. One afternoon Jacob met Brooke in the Rag, as the Army and Navy Club was known, and during a break in conversation enquired about Chink. Jacob had come to the fount of the story. 'Well,' Brooke began expansively, 'I gave orders to put him in command of a brigade in England after Cairo, and if he was successful after three months he would be sent out to a brigade in Italy. And after three months he was reported favourably on, so I signalled Alex and even Alex didn't want him. But I persisted, and so he was put in charge of a brigade there. After a month the commanders formed up to a man and said "You can do what you want with us, but for God's sake get rid of Dorman-Smith!"' Brooke's mimicry made the story come alive.

Dick O'Connor was sad when the tale reached him, but he did not forget it. 'Later Brookie gave him a brigade under Alex,' he recalled in old age, 'and I am told that his three COs lined up and said they would not stand him and he was sacked finally.' It was a popular story because it always got a laugh, and it came up often. Penney was now Assistant Controller at the Ministry of Supply, just around the corner from clubland. He made no correction.

In fact, the shutters had slammed down at once. Wynford Vaughan Thomas asked questions in Italy when he learned that Chink had gone, journalistic instincts pricking. But Vaughan Thomas was parried with suave Establishment ease. 'He's left.' 'Why?' 'Oh, for other worlds . . .'

14

Across
the
River . . .

A new world, a new start . . . a new identity. In 1949, after four years of
silence, a brief notice appeared on the Court Circular page of *The
Times*. Brigadier Eric Dorman-Smith, it announced, had taken the
surname of O'Gowan, as head of the Irish clan of O'Gowan. And the
man behind that distant squib of bitterness, as it was perceived, was
equally changed. By 1949 Chink had become scholarly and in the main
introspectively sombre. He was gentle, instead of sarcastic, sympathetic, instead of critical, and he was profoundly pessimistic at heart.

At first his hurt was not as evident. Still very much the soldier,
stereotyped and caustic, he stood in the 1945 general election as a
Liberal and contested the Tory stronghold of The Wirral in Cheshire;
his first instinct had been to side even more provocatively with Labour,
but genuine approval of the social welfare proposals of the senior
Liberal, Sir William Beveridge, swung the balance. Penning the predictable ex-military man's slogan 'Be British, Be Bold, Vote Liberal'
and railing against the bad map reading and poor man-management
skills of his agent, he drove himself on to shake hands, smile at babies
and empathise with demobilised soldiers and their families, wincing at
the self-projection involved. At night he took refuge in the novels of
J.B. Priestley and looked no farther ahead than polling day. Eve
remained in London, opposed to the whole idea and angrily denying
inconsistency, and Edward's dismay extended to the choice of party.
Amy, alone, had sent a cheque for £100.

The Wirral was the largest of all the constituencies, and a lost cause
from the beginning. Confident of the majority of the 110,200 votes was
another ex-army brigadier, the Conservative candidate John Selwyn
Lloyd. Labour was represented by a staunch county councillor, Miss

Bulley, and spurred on by her grasp of local controversies and the face of Churchill looming out of Tory posters, Chink tried to overcome his parade-ground manner and set out after the returning troops' vote. At Haifa he had often predicted the disillusion of conscripts with stay-at-home officialdom and suggested a post-war League of Angry Men as a rallying point. He resurrected the notion in The Wirral, and the League captured the front page of the the *Daily Mirror*, only to be ridiculed two days later by the *Daily Express*, whose reporter could find no members. He took the press comment in his stride. The energetic campaign delayed long-term questions and enabled him to score points off the Establishment and Tory philosophy in public, but it never entirely captured his emotions.

In the event he was relieved not to lose his deposit and to finish with 14,302 votes. The shock national result put Labour in power, decimated the Conservatives and almost wiped out the Liberals, making it a creditable enough showing, and Selwyn Lloyd's win was offset by Churchill's fall and the public humiliation at the West Cardiff polls of the ex-Secretary of State for War, P.J. Grigg. Slipping away early from the Liberal post-mortem on 8 September, Chink took the next ferry to Ireland and began the first stage of his metamorphosis. England, he informed Liddell Hart by post, was no longer for him.

Post-war Dublin was quiet, its beautifully proportioned Georgian squares and quays elephant grey and smaller than he remembered, and it was a city of contradictions. Barefoot boys sold newspapers and beggars implored, but dining at his favourite restaurant Jammets, or at the Russell or Shelbourne hotels, there was none of the rationing he had come to expect. Extra-generous measures of spirits were a prelude to menus proffering oysters and game in season, salmon, steak, beef or lamb, and a wealth of cream- and egg-rich puddings. Although the long, unpainted Georgian windows and over-crowding stood out to his newly observant eye, the great power of the Catholic Church seemed more concerned with censorship than with improving living conditions, and his religious ambivalence flooded back.

But squarely at the top of the Catholic hierarchy – so similar, in many ways, to the ascending British Army structure – was his old childhood friend, John Charles McQuaid. Gone were the days of knocking down conkers together with well-aimed sticks and fishing with worms as bait. Now McQuaid, spoken of as the most powerful Archbishop of Dublin for many years, was beset with more ceremony than Montgomery and Alexander – and was distanced, as they were, by achievement. Chink jibbed at trading on old acquaintance, as he had jibbed throughout his army career. Instead of making contact he speculated on their opposite paths, and enjoyed envisaging what McQuaid, who was known for strict application of church rules, would say about such an immoral private life. But McQuaid's eminence had one warming effect. It made the Catholic Church less formidable and Ireland instantly his own country again, in a way that England had never been. The new Gaelic lettering that he practised so diligently matched his expectations.

Eve joined him, with Elizabeth, in November and it seemed the best of omens when her pregnancy was confirmed and the likelihood of a second miscarriage receded. As Bellamont Forest belonged to Edward in his lifetime, they rented a house in Dublin at 11 Mespil Road, Ballsbridge, and on 10 May 1946 she gave birth to a son, Christopher, by caesarian section at the Portobello Nursing Home. Nineteen months later the prophecy Chink had counted on came true when Eve had a daughter, Rionagh. He bought a spaniel and a family estate car, but was as aloof a parent as Edward had been. A nanny was hired on Eve's insistence, and he faced the problem of how to fill his time.

After toying with the notion of backing a literary magazine, he decided to take a degree in archaeology at University College, Dublin, but much to his surprise was turned away for having insufficient qualifications. Undeterred, he attended every archaeological lecture that was open to the public, studied Saxon English, and spent most days in the university library, using a reader's ticket. He had hours to kill and he revelled in the freedom of undisturbed concentration. Finding that the routes from Europe of the tribes that had settled Ireland originally were unknown, he set himself to analysing names and legends and examining geological and trade factors, and used his mapping experience to chart the likely movement lines. Genealogical research also fascinated him. After delving into his own past as far as possible, he became engrossed in tracing back the Jacobean and Cromwellian strands of fellow Irish soldiers and began with the family trees of Brooke, Montgomery and Auchinleck. As in India, the friendships he was making were not those most brigadiers would have formed, and without the counter-balance of army life their influence was the stronger. Owen Sheehy Skeffington, an academic liberal whose passivist father had been shot during the Troubles, became one confidant, and the historian and intellectual Hubert Butler, brother-in-law of the theatrical director Tyrone Guthrie, another.

But in March 1948 the libraries, lecture halls and companionship were summarily removed when Edward died, and isolated Bellamont became Chink's responsibility. And the unexpected death, coming at a time when he was extra-sensitive, threw him back into bitterness. Edward had made no secret of his belief that Chink had let down the Crown and thrown away his army career wilfully, and had spent their last meeting reproaching him for not 'knuckling down'. With no chance now to win back his father's respect, Chink was curt and defensive at the English funeral. Reggie had recently returned with Doreen to live permanently nearby in Hampshire, and Amy's open preference for them added to the overwhelming sense of failure. Chink had set out for the funeral numbly; he returned with the old tension of anger.

He took over Bellamont defiantly. 'I don't see why we shouldn't ignore the whole shooting match,' he instructed Eve. 'We'll live as detached as we would in Surrey. I think we might defy convention.' In his diary he made a note of an apt quotation – 'It does not become Irishmen who boggle so little at murder to boggle so much at adultery' – and he closed up the house in Dublin without looking back. Eve's condescension towards other women and her explicit flirtatiousness with husbands, allied to Chink's fondness for shocking and his often savage wit, made them an uncomfortable couple to entertain, but though cut by many, because they were living together, they had fitted into a small circle in the city. Cootehill was not Dublin – let alone Surrey. Ignored by the families that had once come round to accepting Edward and Amy, they were thrown together without an invitation to break the monotony. He professed not to mind. The wider world filtered through via the wireless and day-old English newspapers, and the stars overhead as he walked the dog at night were old friends. Recognising Orion, Cassiopeia and the Bear in the first unsettling period was like catching sight of his own face in a mirror in a strange room. He turned increasingly to Irish newspapers, and kept himself to himself.

He knew he had become morose, but the old spark of fun had gone. He did not fool about with Elizabeth, who was the same age as Elaine had been in the same house, or tease her with the practical jokes he had loved before the war. Though they walked the grounds together and he often read her stories, he shut himself away in the library for the rest of the time, and was so withdrawn that she thought of him as gloomy. Lack of money was one anxiety. Death duties stretched ahead for seven years and the income that had sustained a pleasant Bournemouth lifestyle for Edward was insufficient to keep Bellamont in good order. He had no capital and the estate had run down in Edward's prolonged span as an absentee landlord, making Eve's large income an extra source of friction between them. A series of agents farmed the land and some took advantage of his inexperience. When he tried to run it himself, grudging the time spent away from his books, he was unable to make much profit.

The move to Bellamont showed up the false expectations of their relationship. As their quarrels escalated he took to being icily aloof, and Eve spent even more time in bed or escaped to London for weeks at a time. Her hypochondria became more marked, and the children were left behind at Bellamont, where the two younger ones were looked after by Elizabeth and a procession of nannies. The lack of domesticity that had attracted him in Haifa now infuriated him, and he felt cheated by her lack of interest in the children. When he protested at sending Christopher and Rionagh away to boarding school in England before they were four years old, she overruled him by coldly paying their fees.

Diagnosing insecurity as the reason for Eve's discontent, her mother traced Estelle and pleaded with her to divorce Chink. (Eve herself had been divorced, with Chink cited as co-respondent, as early as January 1947.) Estelle had come back from India and was living in a remote cottage in Hampshire, too hurt by the newspaper photographs of Eve around election time, in which she had always been captioned as Mrs Dorman-Smith, to want to see anyone from her previous life. She resisted Eve's mother at first because she clung to the hope that Chink would come back to her one day, despite their one taut conversation over the phone when he had told her to consider herself a war widow and had hung up after shouting 'The man you know is *dead*!' But on hearing that he had two children, she reluctantly let go. As bitter over the loss of her marriage as he was over the loss of his career, she lived on in seclusion. She considered herself still married to him, but for the sake of anonymity reverted to her maiden name. Although he sometimes spoke of her to Elizabeth, when they were alone, he did not get in touch. Their divorce, with no third party cited, became final in March 1949.

With Eve's mother as witness, the marriage took place at the City of Westminster Registry Office on 17 May 1949. Chink was fifty-three, Eve was thirty-six, and he gave his profession wryly as 'farmer'. But it solved none of their personal problems, and in Ireland the position was unchanged because divorce and registry office ceremonies were not recognised, so they were still considered to be living in sin. Eve spent even longer stretches in London, unable to understand why he chose to shut himself away at Bellamont, and at first he tried to explain. 'I have never recovered internally,' he began one tortuous letter to her, 'from the damage done between 1942 and 1944. That makes me resent people. I cannot ever again be at home in England. . . . That is why I am inclined to drink rather rapidly when I am among people in order to get past my own barrier of defence and to overcome aversion.' Alone so much with the children, he buried himself in genealogy and ancient migration routes. The outside world became less distinct.

Changing his name was something more than the bitter stunt it appeared to be. He had been nicknamed O'Gowan at the Staff College in 1927 and had toyed with the idea of a deed-poll switch on and off during 1941, after beginning his affair with Eve. Research showed that he was entitled to be the head of the small East Ulster clan of O'Gowan, which had originated in Ballygowan in County Down and had figured prominently in the census of 1659, and he compiled the proof needed by the Genealogical Office in Dublin Castle himself, retaining Dorman since that was also one of his Christian names. The English press, however, saw it in simple terms. 'Brigadier Eric Edward Dorman-Smith, who was chief of staff to Auchinleck at Alamein,' a gossip column item in the *Daily Express* promptly sniped, 'has renounced and abandoned his English surname. He is to be known in future as O'Gowan, the gaelic name of his fore-fathers. . . . The Brigadier, who lives at Bellamont Forest in the border county of Cavan . . . said last night 'My change of name has no political meaning.' But that was being equally tongue in cheek, as his provocative notice in *The Times* proved.

Rather than decreasing, Chink's resentments were building up. The publication of de Guingand's memoirs in 1947, in which he was named and belittled, had hurt, and the emerging general picture of the desert war as Montgomery's personal triumph was impossible for him to accept, extending as it did to the withholding of the '8' on the Desert Star from troops who had served under O'Connor, Wavell and Auchinleck. The sight of his Appreciation of 27 July 1942, which appeared unsigned in the *London Gazette*'s supplement of Auchinleck's Despatches in January 1948, had driven home the extent of his annihilation in contrast to the prestige of men he considered inferior.

Penney, Ritchie, Horrocks, Messervy, Norrie, Cunningham, Godwin Austen, Whiteley, Leese, Arthur Smith, Corbett and Jacob had all reached general's rank and were publicly acclaimed; everyone except Corbett had been knighted, including de Guingand. Changing his name was also cocking a snook at a system which rewarded Amateurs.

The invigorating effect did not last. 'This damn farm is a frightful life,' he soon complained to Liddell Hart, who remained a loyal prop. 'They ought to have given Napoleon ten cows and a few pigs, he'd never have found the time to leave Elba. The mistake was giving him a frigate and a battalion. No romantic should have anything to do with a farm. I miss my profession and I am bored to tears.' Sometimes he even turned against Liddell Hart and blamed his theories for his own exit from the army – 'I could too easily see that the clumsy crooked chaps were turning a science into a shambles. . . . I was a fool to quarrel with my bread and butter' – but Basil refused to take offence.

At the end of May 1950 Wavell died, and the news soon plunged Chink into a deep and lingering depression that was worse than anything he had gone through before. On the day of the funeral he shut himself away in the library where Wavell had sipped whiskey after shooting, and listened to the broadcast commentary. Brooke, long elevated to Lord Alanbrooke, Auchinleck, Smith, O'Connor and Montgomery were among the mourners in Westminster Abbey, but Churchill, who had only to walk across from the House of Commons, had contented himself with sending a representative. All Chink's hatred of Churchill came to the fore again and he drew no parallel with his own behaviour at the time of James's memorial service at Anzio. Wavell was the man who most of all had spelled integrity and security, and recollecting him, as he constantly did that long wet summer, was like taking the lid off a deep well. If he had gone to Wavell in India in May 1942, he came to acknowledge, he would have missed the débâcles of Cairo and Anzio and enhanced his career into the bargain. 'A quixotic decision,' he tortured himself. 'In a personal sense, unfortunate.' Almost clear now of Eve's spell, he began wishing he had never met her. In gusts of anguish he sorted through his boxed army papers, tearing up many and burning the shreds on the library fire. Often the past was too painful to be confronted directly; he flung in some without reading them.

Wavell's death stripped away pretence. He was sickened by the introspection, but unable to stop. 'I had a deep sense of injustice,' he wrote of the period later, 'and behind that a fear that some weakness in myself which I would not admit might well have brought that injustice upon me as a form of justice. I do not like admitting failure, and I hate to think that some fault in my make-up led me to let the Service, for which I lived, down.' That lost world had been his real home, after all.

But if one door closes, as he had maintained in happier days, another opens, and the new door was close to hand. The proximity of the border, eleven miles from Bellamont, had already aggravated his longstanding dislike of partition to the extent of joining Clann na Poblachta, which was a new anti-partition political party led by Sean MacBride and supported by a cross-section of liberals, idealists, socialists and hard-line republicans. 'Not being allowed to soldier,' he admitted to a close friend, 'I escape into national politics as the next alternative. Without, that is, being a politician. Does that make me an amateur, like Churchill?' De Valera had approached him to say that his expertise in defence would be appreciated by Fianna Fail, and so adroitly had this been done that he continued to believe that the Shadow Ministry of Defence might have been his. But he had stayed with the more radical Clann and now he was glad. Although not an elected member of the Dail, he savoured his little bit of influence.

MacBride, whose childhood French accent was untrammelled by the years in Ireland, liked Chink personally, and invited him to the Dail restaurant often to discuss military angles and anti-partition policy. Chink, in return, appreciated having his advice sought by the son of Maud Gonne. The outlooks of both men, ironically, were in direct contrast to their opinions of thirty years before, when they had nearly met in Carlow. Then Chink had been the conventional British Army adjutant, and MacBride the young IRA officer despatched behind his back from Dublin to tighten up discipline in the Carlow area. Now MacBride, who had moved from violence to politics, worried about Chink's growing interest in republicanism, and tried to prevent him getting a reputation for supporting an illegal organisation. He was having little or no effect. Articles against partition under Chink's name had already appeared in the *Republican Review*, and when Ireland left the Commonwealth the previous year his public approval – 'a sacred cow' – had been carried to the letters page of the *Irish Times*. He seemed to have something to say on most political topics, and had taken to measuring success by the haul of insulting letters back. So the new door had been ajar before Wavell's death. The timing of the jolt, however, was enough to push it open.

Chink had just got back from his first – and only – anti-partitionist tour of America when Wavell's funeral took place, and he was in the familiar mood of restless futility. He had suggested the trip to the Department of Foreign Affairs himself on reading of an impending propaganda visit to the United States by the Northern Ireland Unionist premier, Sir Basil Brooke, and costs had been paid by the American League for a United Ireland. Fervently against communism his latest target had been the strategical implications of partition which, as he argued in every speech and newspaper interview, created a vulnerable gap in the Atlantic Pact. Exhilarated by America, he had toured from coast to coast and got his point put on the Congressional Record, but Brooke's views had achieved much wider press coverage. By the time the Northern Ireland premier and his wife flew up to stay with Alexander in Canada, where the former Commander-in-Chief was the Governor-General, Chink's anger at such an extensive network of British power was only held in check by his equal dislike of the Irish–Americans he had met – 'the hyphen wreathed in faded shamrock' – whose aims he regretfully dismissed as 'nostalgic baloney with a sinister political background'. A skit on his efforts featured in a popular Jimmy O'Dea variety show in Dublin, diminishing his sympathies further.

The shock of Wavell's death and Churchill's bland indifference, coming so soon after his return, made up his mind for him about which side he was on. He contacted the American Ambassador to propose a trained Irish contingent for the US Army to fight in the Korean War, explaining to a friend that he would 'like to see the professional Irish soldier break with the British Army. That hasn't been done since Red Owen O'Neill came to Ulster in 1642. . . . The USA could resurrect the Irish Brigade which was the Afrika Korps of the 18th century. I just hung the idea onto the Korean War because one has to begin somewhere.' In due course the Pentagon turned the proposal down, pointing out that it was impossible for aliens to be accepted as members of the US military services.

In May 1951, feeling like 'a middle-aged prostitute who still has an L plate up', Chink stood for election again. This time the seat he was after was in the Dail, the constituency was Cavan, and he was an independent candidate standing for a United Ireland, the Clann seat being filled. He campaigned as energetically as ever against partition and on the dangers of neutrality, but his British Army background was anathema to local republicans and though he parried shouts of 'Where were you in 1916?' with acerbic zest he knew he would not get in. As in America, where because of his accent and manner he had often been met with the same distrust that had kept Sir Roger Casement at bay over forty years earlier, he came across as a caricature of the landowning Ascendancy gentleman. His slogan 'A Vote For O'Gowan is a Vote Against Partition' was naive in an area where many voters made their living from cross-border smuggling, and the fact that he had previously run for Parliament in England counted against him. 'Don't worry about me being a Celt,' he assured Eve, who as usual was away in London. 'What I really am is a chameleon. Just at the moment I am sitting, flyless, on a patch of green and saffron. I daresay I'd even match up with the Union Jack.' The poll was low, his votes lower still, and the vacuum continued. 'I still keep mucking about rather pointlessly on the outer fringes of the Irish political scene,' he wrote to a friend despondently, 'for no good reason except that I do not like untidy situations.'

It was in this frame of mind that he waited for the much publicised appearance of Churchill's account of the events of July 1942. 'That gross brute Winston Spencer Churchill is serialising his third volume and getting around to the part I know about, Tobruk and Auchinleck,' he fumed shortly beforehand. 'He is being so damn unjust and so bloody inaccurate about it all that I ache to weigh in to the discussion. I will when it begins.' He was concerned enough to travel to London to warn Auchinleck, whom he had not met since their final Cairo dinner, in person, only to be appalled at the fatalism with which Auchinleck responded. By now Chink was treating the War Office with contempt. He had sent back his reservists badge by return – 'Wonder whose damn fool idea that was?' – and as for reporting in writing on 1 January each year, he took aggressive pleasure in not doing so.

The Hinge of Fate, the fourth volume of Churchill's *History of the Second World War*, was published in July 1951. Flipping through to the pages that interested him, Chink learned that his name had been included in Cabinet despatches and that he had been sacked not by the military hierarchy, as he had always supposed, but on Churchill's recommendation. The personal revelation was less important, however, than the slur on Auchinleck's reputation, and an entry in a subsequent chapter steeled him to sue for libel. 'I am sure,' Churchill had written, 'we were heading for disaster under the former regime. The Army was reduced to bits and pieces and oppressed by a sense of bafflement and uncertainty. Apparently it was intended in the face of attack to retire eastwards to the Delta. . . . Many were looking over their shoulders to make sure of their seat in the lorry and no plain plan of battle or dominating willpower had reached the units.'

'Winston's factualism,' Chink snorted to Reggie, 'is historically packed with meat and botulism.' One example was Churchill's claim that before Alamein there had never been a victory, which ignored O'Connor's triumph over the Italian Tenth Army, and the deference to Rommel for superior skill also annoyed him. 'Had Rommel been serving Churchill, at what stage would Churchill have sacked him? My guess is after Crusader, about Christmas 1941. The Churchill system would have destroyed Nelson, Wellington, Clive, even Marlborough.'

At his favourite Dublin bookshop, Hodges Figgis, he bought two copies and insisted on a receipt, and soon his legal team consisted of Sir John Esmonde SC and junior counsel William Finlay, and his cautious solicitor cousin Philip Smith, who had a practice in Cavan and often advised him. The former Taoiseach John Costello SC was retained for the defence. 'You must realise my sense of injustice done to Auchinleck,' Chink stressed, quite undeterred by the fact that Churchill was currently Prime Minister and tipped to win that year's Nobel Prize.

He crossed over to see Auchinleck once more, and again permission to use the documents in Auchinleck's private files was withheld. He left in a temper, and a solicitor's letter caught up with him in Ireland to request the return of any relevant correspondence. So little of their former rapport appeared to remain that he took the trouble to work out that Auchinleck must have got to know Leese well when the latter began working in close partnership as Commander-in-Chief Allied Land Forces South-east Asia from December 1944 onwards; it also occurred to him that Auchinleck might think he had paid off all obligations by the offer of the Iraq–Persia job, or possibly blamed him for losing that opportunity. But nothing was going to deflect him from taking on the case alone. He threw himself into it as if it were a military campaign, and the slow months of preparation were eased by knowing that if it went to court Churchill would have to come to Dublin to defend himself. Preparations for the Coronation, relayed by television, kept him on the boil. On the day, he glared at the screen as the camera showed Alanbrooke, Alexander and Montgomery on the dais, and Churchill close at hand.

On 1 May 1953 a formal complaint was made on his behalf that, unless amendments were forthcoming, proceedings for libel would be instituted. Any settlement would have to produce a public apology and the withdrawal of that volume in its present form. Letters went out to Churchill as author, Cassells as publishers and Hodges Figgis as booksellers, claiming that readers would come to the conclusion that he was one of those primarily responsible for the disasters of Gazala and Tobruk, and had failed in his duties as Deputy Chief of Staff. Action was reserved against the American publishers and distributors.

In London Churchill was unimpressed. He showed the letter to his legal adviser, Sir Hartley Shawcross, only after he had had it for some time, shrugging that he did not think it necessary to do anything. On the face of it, Shawcross was an unusual choice as confidant, having been Attorney-General in the post-war Labour government which had put Churchill out of office, but on his return to the Bar after Labour's defeat in 1951 he had become a regular adviser, and reading the letter again he scented danger. Shawcross's personal admiration for Churchill dated from observing him in action during the bleakest point of the war in 1940, and he felt as protective about Churchill as Chink felt about Auchinleck. In his experienced view, it was never safe to fight libel actions because juries were unpredictable, and this letter held added threat.

It would be a sensational humiliation for England if the Prime Minister had to give evidence in a Dublin court, and damage to the British Army would also be unavoidable since the case could end with half the army in court on one side and half on the other. But there was a more humane reason for keeping the seventy-nine-year-old premier out of the witness box. Shawcross had been present at the dinner party earlier that month when Churchill suffered his second stroke and, through being in the confidence of Lord Moran, Churchill's doctor, he knew him to be on a knife-edge. The likelihood that the case could take as long as two years to reach court added to the health risk, and his predicament was exacerbated by the fact that news of the stroke had been kept secret from the public; even to the Cabinet Churchill's absence had been attributed to severe overstrain, and it had been kept out of the press through the co-operation of the newspaper owners Beaverbrook, Camrose and Bracken. The plaintiff did not know it, and could not be informed.

Keeping his letters to Churchill on a personal basis and all meetings informal, Shawcross began to make his case. Brooke was contacted first, followed by Montgomery, Alexander and Penney. In Germany, where he was commanding a brigade, Charles Richardson received a letter; from Suffolk Ian Jacob contributed his relevant 1942 diary extracts; and de Guingand was flattered to be invited to lunch alone at 10 Downing Street with Churchill and Shawcross. The Dublin solicitor Arthur Cox, whose long-established practice was in St Stephens Green, was engaged on Churchill's behalf. If the case went to court it would be heard in the rebuilt Four Courts, the prominent building that had been shelled in the Civil War, five months after the Northumberland Fusiliers pulled out in 1921.

That year on his birthday Chink reached the age limit for his rank and ceased to belong to the regular army reserve. The letter which anonymously regretted that the time had come for him to leave coincided with one from Churchill's solicitors stating that he had not been fit to be DCGS ME, that he had been re-employed in Italy and had proved unsuitable there too, and that documents to prove this would be publicly released if the case went to court. He said the Cairo issue alone was in question, and challenged them to go ahead.

Recognising the impasse, the dignified Shawcross flew to Dublin in the first week of November 1953 to mediate, paying for his own fare. Over lunch with Chink and Esmonde at the Shelbourne it was agreed that a writ would not be issued if an acceptable footnote were inserted, and Liddell Hart was agreed upon as a suitable interpreter of historical accuracy; drafts from Dublin would be submitted first. 'Sir Hartley Shawcross went to Dublin last week and came back to find a fine crop of rumours about his visit,' reported the *Daily Express*. 'Some said he had gone to see about the transfer of the remains of Sir Roger Casement, hanged for treason here in 1916, back to Ireland. Others said that he had an Irish grandmother. Sir Hartley has countered with the story that he went over to see if Irish girls are as beautiful and as charming as he had been led to believe.'

Behind the scenes, the first two drafts found no common ground. But Liddell Hart advised Chink to accept the third. 'The references to officers,' it ran, 'are factual only, and are not to be taken as imputing personal blame to any individual. . . . Major-General Dorman-Smith did not become Deputy Chief of Staff until after the fall of Tobruk and he had no responsibility there or at Gazala. He was subsequently appointed to a command in Italy.' Shawcross, too, advised that it was the most that could be expected. '[Winston] felt some doubt as to the last sentence . . . [about] Italy . . . in view of what happened,' he soothed. 'I am afraid there is no prospect of the PM feeling able to go beyond the substance of the present note.' And by 12 March 1954

Chink had accepted it, after an amendment to the second last sentence, after his name, to read: 'only became Deputy Chief of Staff on 16 June 1942. He thus bears no responsibility for the fall of Tobruk or the defeat of Gazala. From 25th June–4th August he acted as General Auchinleck's principal operations officer at HQ Eighth Army. . . .'

But a libel action still appeared unavoidable, because Chink was adamant about the need to rectify the 'retreat to the delta' slur, and here Liddell Hart, who had been translating Rommel's papers and knew the other side of the story, was wholeheartedly in agreement. 'The sentence *does* read like an imputation of funk,' he appealed to Shaw-cross. 'So his reaction is very natural and one that the PM of all men should be able to understand sympathetically.' The blandishment was wasted. On 29 March Churchill refused to alter a word, and Liddell Hart was prevailed upon to act as honest broker once more.

'I have restudied the Appreciation [of 27 July 1942] very carefully,' he responded. 'I cannot find the slightest sign of pessimism anywhere in it, or any shadow of doubt about holding on to the Alamein position.' Noting that the original information had come from Mont-gomery, he continued: 'Montgomery's tendency to paint everything black prior to his arrival on the scene has long been a joke among his fellow soldiers. Also his tendency to sweeping and unfounded assertions. I have known him 30 years and long wondered how a man so careful and thorough in his own work could indulge in sweeping assertions so easy to disprove.' The more he thought about the matter, Liddell Hart astutely added, the more concerned he became about the wider aspects, because research into the War Diaries confirmed that the design of operations in July 1942 had been well conceived but bungled by subordinate commanders. It would be very damaging to Commonwealth relations, he pointed out, if this came out in court.

Again Shawcross judged that the moment was ripe for personal intervention, and to prevent the press tracking him as before he arranged a seat over on a freight plane, travelling incognito. Chink had agreed to a private meeting in the home of Churchill's solicitor on Howth Head outside Dublin, and when Shawcross landed at the military airfield of Baldonnel on 2 May he was driven straight there. The two men went into the dining room, and closed the door.

'It became clear that he was not acting because he had been slighted, but on principle on behalf of Auchinleck,' Shawcross said sub-sequently, emphasising that he had made no notes at the time. 'I was feeling very distressed myself – in fact I was near to tears. I was fighting quite a battle for the old man. But I felt I must go on until we'd reached either an agreement or a decision. . . . I wasn't going to get very far playing on his heartstrings to win sympathy, and I thought he would insist on his pound of flesh whatever I said. I don't normally pace around the room. But I did feel unhappy about it, and I did feel it was going to be extremely hard to justify the paragraph in the book.' Anxious to finish the case once and for all, Shawcross was prepared to settle, but the frailty of Churchill's health had now become public knowledge, which strengthened his hand.

Admitting from the start that Chink had a complaint, he countered by asking if he was prepared to sully the reputation of the army and take the responsibility for Churchill having a fatal stroke in public. He had summed up his adversary well. Chink's code of chivalry won out, and after several hours he capitulated and they shook hands. Having given away his advantage, all he gained in correction of the insult to Auchinleck's generalship was one short sentence – 'My appreciation . . . of the handling of Eighth Army is supported by Rommel's remarkable tribute' – which was to appear beneath his other footnote, putting it out of context.

'We reached agreement on a form of words,' Shawcross informed Liddell Hart. 'I undertook to put this to the PM. . . . I liked him personally and had some sympathy with the position in which he found himself.' And grudgingly Churchill gave his consent, after consulting with Alexander. As he said in his letter of thanks to Liddell Hart, he had never wished to hurt Chink but nor had he considered him a factor of any importance in his narrative.

Tactfully, Liddell Hart did not show this letter to Chink, who very soon came to regret his compassion when The Hinge of Fate continued to appear without the footnote for many years. 'I fell for that,' he castigated himself. 'I would, of course, but I was a damn fool.' Wavell's death had hardened him again, but his last illusions about British power were wiped out by the outcome of the case. His young son was bullied over it at preparatory school, and Chink's stand had made him so unpopular at the traditionally-minded Kildare Street Club in Dublin that an acquaintance from the Genealogical Office who took him there to lunch had to guide him straight out again, shocked by the hostility to his guest. Paradoxically, the alternative of the Stephens Green Club, which was predominantly nationalist and Catholic, barred him also; this time his taint was immorality. But the clubs themselves were no loss to Chink. He was happiest in isolation at

Bellamont, and within seven weeks of the pivotal meeting with Shawcross the new door slammed back on its hinges.

The summer Saturday afternoon of 12 June 1954 drifted tediously along at Gough Barracks in Armagh, Northern Ireland. At the gate the Royal Irish Fusiliers sentry blinked back torpor and concentrated upon keeping his Sten at the correct angle, well aware that there was no magazine in it. When a car drew up and a man climbed out of the back seat and approached he thought it was one more unemployed local coming to ask about enlistment. But suddenly there was a Colt .45 in the man's hand. As the fusilier found himself being bundled along towards the armoury he had time to see a strange sentry in identical uniform in his place outside and a red three-ton lorry being waved through. Within half an hour seventeen other soldiers and one civilian were tied up alongside him, and the armoury was bare: 340 rifles, 50 Sten guns, 12 Brens and an assortment of .22 rifles were heading south with the nineteen men who had taken part in the raid and by 5 p.m., when a general alarm went out, all were on the far side of the border. In Northern Ireland police powers to stop and search were reactivated and the authorities' only consolation was that no ammunition had been stolen as well. In Southern Ireland public scorn about the capability of the IRA was being hastily revised.

Chink followed the details avidly. He was stunned by the resemblance to a 1943 raid in Haifa which he had been told about while languishing with 160th Brigade at Provender. Two military three-ton lorries with the expected quota of troops in British Army uniform had driven into a training school on Mount Carmel using the same ruse, and made off with the contents of the armoury. And those weapons, added to others taken through similar ploys, had enabled the Hagganah and Irgun terrorists eventually to win independence. Like many others serving in Haifa, he had discounted the Wanted posters for Abraham Stern and joined in the derision led by High Commissioner MacMichael but hindsight showed how wrong they had been. 'I am delighted by Armagh,' he enthused immediately. 'So neat, a really good job and it will put an end to this totally unprogressive ticking and tieing with the quite impossible Orange mind.' His first contact with the IRA took place shortly after the raid, and it was a simple matter to get in touch. He already knew Jim Lynch, the senior officer for Cavan/Monaghan, and word was passed down to Dublin HQ that 'the Brigadier' wished to meet the men responsible.

Chink's train of thought was well founded, because the genesis of the raid did lie in the Palestinian campaign, although inspired by a later operation. In March 1946 fourteen members of the Irgun Svai Leumi, red berets correctly topping off their khaki, had raided Sarafand, the camp which contained troops from 6th Airborne Division and a Hussar regiment, and driven away with the customary three-ton lorryload from the armoury, and it had been Menachim Begin's adventure-style account of it in *The Revolt*, published two years before Armagh, that gave the IRA the plan; Begin acknowledged studying earlier IRA lessons when formulating his own campaign.

The IRA of the time must be seen in context and more emotive judgements of the 1990s set aside. Then, it was a totally different organisation to the Provisional IRA of today; the group formed by the more militant following a split in the movement came into being after Chink's death. In 1954 official IRA policy was not to endanger civilian life, and a ruling was in force against bombing or sectarian acts. Wolfe Tone's dream of a country where to be Irish took precedence over individual religion was shared by many members as well as by a wide cross-section of sympathisers throughout the country who had not yet been exposed to the horrors of more recent campaigns. Chink's inspiration similarly looked backward before skipping, in a buccaneering way, excitedly forward.

'Ireland is never in danger until someone of their own kidney takes a hand,' he had exulted earlier. 'Witness Parnell and that tragic Erskine Childers.' Briefly he had played at IRA soldiers himself in New York in 1950, when he had accepted an invitation to march to the head of a parade of IRA veterans and rebutted Unionist criticism with the riposte that Smuts had worn Boer and British medals side by side. In a revealing letter even earlier to *Aiseiri*, a small nationalist newspaper, he had estimated that the Six Counties could be seized back with government backing, 'lots of money, say £10 million, and three years of planning and training at least', and added that he was the only man he knew expert enough to command it. But this was the real thing, in the footsteps of one of his childhood heroes, the eighteenth-century Irish patriot Lord Edward Fitzgerald, who had also been a British soldier in his day.

It is no coincidence that the final communication of *The Hinge of Fate* settlement was exchanged nineteen days after the Armagh Raid, and that almost at once Chink was writing that, as far as Britain was concerned, he had had enough. Always a stickler for correct procedures, he noted that he had been released from the army the year before, and that as he lived outside the Queen's dominions it was no longer his duty to act against her enemies. Fired by the unexpected professionalism of the Armagh raid, he thought back to India and Egypt, two other countries where he had lived under regimes that had subsequently handed over independence. His aim was the removal of the border, and his reasoning for that the strategical flaw it brought to the Atlantic Pact; the southern policy of neutrality would have to be dismantled afterwards. But his jibe to Liddell Hart about the North being a Protestant Tobruk held by the Brookes and Alexanders showed his subconscious feelings.

The IRA Chief of Staff Tony Magan and the Adjutant-General Charlie Murphy came to call at Bellamont, having taken the precaution of checking him out beforehand. Neither was in uniform or carried a gun, but they introduced themselves by office, not by name. Chink began by saying that he totally approved of Armagh and wanted more of the same, and Murphy, who had planned the raid and led it, was impressed. 'Here is a man, I thought,' he recalled thirty years later, 'an ex-British Army officer in the autumn of his years, telling me "I really am more Irish than I ever was. I want to help you people." I realised he was crossing a great divide. I also thought, here was a man who could be a real help to us – how many estates are there in such proximity to the North?'

A tall, twenty-four-year-old Dubliner with prematurely grey hair, Murphy worked as a clerk in Guinness's brewery and had grown up respecting the veterans of the Troubles who lived in his locality. Magan was a generation older, an austere man in continual pain from rheumatism and, unlike Murphy, with more enemies inside the movement than friends. Neither found any incompatibility between Chink's new dedication and his old career, and both were agreeably reminded of Erskine Childers. Chink, for his part, had disciples again. He responded with a fresh burst of energy.

'I do not believe in bloodshed unless it is totally unavoidable,' he was soon writing to Sheehy Skeffington. 'Unfortunately in dealing with Official Britain respecting the surrender of a possession, bloodshed is always unavoidable. Partition is not going to be kissed away. Certainly extend the hand of friendship which no Orangeman is going to take, assuredly see your problems in a world perspective, but realise that having done these things *ad infinitum* you will have got not one whit nearer reunification. Ultimately even Connelly had to arm, fight and die.' In July 1954 he crossed to Manchester for the sole purpose of speaking at a reunification rally and quoted from St Joan by George

Bernard Shaw about 'the Goddams on foreign soil'. He had nailed his colours to the mast. Ireland, he went round saying openly, was in the position of a patient with a broken leg which would have to be broken again before it could be set correctly.

But although he continued to see a great deal of Murphy, who soon thought of him as a mentor, he was frustrated at not being allowed into the decision-making of the IRA. When it came to the planning of the successor to Armagh, a raid on the Royal Inniskilling Fusiliers depot at Omagh to rectify the lack of ammunition, he was only consulted when Murphy came up against a problem he could not solve on his own. The British Army lorries the IRA intended to take this time had to be disposed of afterwards, and the original plan to empty them in the South and drive them back again into County Tyrone to be burned proved unworkable in the timing. 'Three British Army lorries in the 26 Counties would be a tremendous political problem,' Murphy said subsequently.

It was no use just burning the bloody things – it was absolutely vital that they had to disappear. The Brigadier suggested sinking them in the lake at Bellamont. He went down and surveyed it, and he was familiar with the lorries already. He had a great attachment to his lake, and he was tickled pink at the idea of them going down in it. We looked at the best places to put them in, and the important thing was that they wouldn't bog down on the way in. The location was ideal – they would be gone in an hour.

But the raid on Omagh went wrong when a sentry was not silenced, eight IRA members were captured, and there are no submerged British Army lorries in the town lake of Bellamont today. Chink heard the details on that evening's news with dismay, and although he at once wrote off to the papers in praise of the two 'salutary and antiseptic' actions, it was clear that the IRA could not be equated with the Stern Gang. Hoping to improve matters by training, he allegedly went through with becoming a member in Magan's presence.

During 1955 and 1956 Bellamont Forest was used twice a year as an IRA training ground at weekends, but instead of being in charge of it, as he had thought would be the case, Chink was shut out of the instruction. Gerry McCarthy, a hard taskmaster in his thirties who was the IRA Director of Training, arrived on his motorbike to take charge of each group of twenty-five men from North and South, and Chink took his walks elsewhere whenever a camp was in progress. Tents were erected out of view near the outhouses and each group brought in its own food.

The training carried out in the Bellamont grounds included engineering and battlecraft, all types of arms – rifles, machine guns, sub-machine guns, revolvers – and foot drill, explosives and field-craft. Recruits were taught how to attack a strongpoint, lay an ambush, move across country and withdraw, and were also given night training. Only once was Chink asked to take an inspection, and the incongruousness then of his British manner deterred McCarthy from a further invitation. Aware of his penchant for writing to the papers and anxious to have as little official attention as possible paid to him, Murphy muzzled him by providing an outlet to the headquarters in Dublin. The addresses of three contacts with no republican involvement were given, all of whom were prepared to forward letters on to Murphy in fresh envelopes, and soon an average of two or three a week reached him, containing comments and suggestions for future operations. None remain. Murphy kept them until he went on the run later, and the neighbour who looked after his papers, packed in a suitcase, believed she was about to be searched, and burned them.

But Chink yearned to be of more use. He fitted out his largest cellar as an operations room, pinning up maps of Northern Ireland, moving in a large mahogany table and chairs to go around it, and installing a telephone extension in case he was wanted while they were in session. All calls went through the local exchange, which made the line as insecure as if the Special Branch were tapping it. The room was rarely used. Magan and Murphy preferred to talk over sandwiches upstairs, and eventually he set up a sandtable in there and began giving simple lectures on tactical situations and map-reading to McCarthy's senior trainees. He was not yet sixty, and needed at least to talk the language of that lost world.

The years of teaching had been more fulfilling than he had realised at the time. As at Sandhurst, Chatham, the Staff College and Haifa, he liked winning over novices and revelled in debate. Murphy and McCarthy, young enough to be overawed, were touched to be treated as equals and provided the respect he missed. 'I would literally go off my route just to call in,' said Murphy later.

He was like a 19 year old, not his own age, full of enthusiasm. There was no doubt in my mind that if we'd said 'We want you to lead the group' any time, the minute he'd have been told he'd have been gone. He was like a coiled spring. Not that we'd have let him, I may say. We were very conscious about his loyalty to the British Army and didn't want to put him into any invidious position, or risk him losing his pension. I'd say 'We're only interested in three things – how to get there, what to do when we get there, and how to get the hell out of it.' He used to laugh and say 'Jolly good show.'

Chink was much taken by the ideal of the sacrifice of young men's lives and approved of the dedication, which extended to teetotalism – but he did not give up his own pink gins.

His relationship with them was one-dimensional. He never asked their names or enquired about their personal lives, and in return did not talk about his war experiences, though he sounded off about Churchill. Dublin headquarters remained in agreement about the use of the grounds being his most valuable contribution, and the raids on Territorial Army stations and cross-channel barracks were done without consultation. Informers were inside in every case; for Armagh the contact was Sean Garland, in Omagh, Patrick Webster, and in England the Corkman Frank Skuse would in due course be the one to send out information.

General tactics, however, were freely discussed, and the sessions confirmed his view that they lacked the necessary ruthlessness. In the mid-1950s the IRA ruled out attacks on the part-time Protestant B Special security force because of the sectarian ramifications, whereas in Chink's opinion they were facing a military situation in which the B Specials were the eyes and ears of the Northern Intelligence system, and so ought to be 'broken'. When he went on to point out that partially trained men could never be relied upon to use knives, and so crossbows would be more effective, they recoiled. For Chink it was a detached mental exercise, like the war games he had played with Hemingway. There was a strong element of make-believe, as the stage-set ops room and his insistence on addressing them as 'Sir' demonstrated. Bellamont, he had even let slip in the first heady days, would make a perfect headquarters.

When he proposed the capture of Finaghy Field, the twelve-acre symbol of Unionism, on the Northern Ireland public holiday of 12 July – to seize the psychological advantage of the indirect approach – it was turned down. He drew up detailed long-term plans of attack for the invasion of Belfast and Derry, and was told they had no reinforcements and insufficient resources. To McCarthy it was obvious that Chink was unable to change scale and see the IRA as it was, because a weapon lost was almost more important than a man lost, in contrast to British Army values. Paedar O'Donnell, a veteran IRA member, called at Bellamont to warn Chink that he could not afford to get mixed up in a fiasco. 'One of the things I liked most about him,' O'Donnell said once, 'was the way his mind came across the whole way to meet yours. His alertness to ideas was very quick. But there was no force to be tactically organised in the way he would expect, and even thinking the problem *could* be resolved that way was impractical.' There was no real place for Chink in the IRA, either. 'Wish I had been there,' he wrote after a minor scuffle in Armagh.

His children were unaware – and would remain so – but Eve was in Chink's confidence from the start. When not away, she usually sat in during meetings – making a great impression on Murphy, in particular – and through her excited hints many others found out. But Chink himself made no secret of his support. He peppered his conversation with phrases like 'homeopathic violence' and the 'Northern Ireland bridgehead', and as stories spread he came to be credited with running current operations. By now he did not take this as a compliment. When asked outright by one friend if it was true, he snapped that things would have been done much more efficiently if so.

His cross-channel correspondences were often equally indiscreet, horrifying Reggie who was a respected JP in Hampshire, and one of them would have unexpected consequences. His fascination with Boy Browning's wife Daphne du Maurier had survived his break with the army and deepened into a confessional penfriendship which Eve resented. After his death Daphne du Maurier would base a short story named 'A Border-Line Case' upon his IRA involvement, and here Chink makes his final fictional appearance as Nick Barry, who relishes his secret life of guerrilla tactics and historical research while ostensibly no more than a bitter recluse. (He inspired Daphne's imagination, as he had Hemingway's, and is also identifiable in the personality, style of speech and mannerisms of Sir Richard Grenvile, the cavalier hero of *The King's General*, published in 1946. 'Faults that I had caught glimpses of in youth were now increased tenfold. His pride, his arrogance, his contempt for anyone's opinion but his own – these were more glaring than they had ever been. His knowledge of military matters was great . . . but I doubted if he would ever work in harmony with the other leaders. . . .') With two other old friends, however,

Chink was always more cautious. Liddell Hart's regular contacts continued to overlap with the military establishment, and with him, as with Horrocks when they occasionally lunched together, Chink took care to be circumspect.

To the authorities, however, Chink's imprudence made him appear a harmless crank. He was generally written off as a bitter man who had lost his touch, and when rumours reached his old regiment they were sad but unsurprised. The General Officer commanding Northern Ireland, General Sir Ouvry Roberts, was an old colleague from Chatham and India days who had once been a great admirer of Chink's tactical originality. Hearing that he had changed his name and was campaigning for the end of partition, Roberts was convinced that he had gone off his head. Senior members of the Northern Ireland government, with whom Roberts worked closely, were equally unaware of the extent of Chink's involvement, and the Royal Ulster Constabulary dismissed him as a 'semi-fool'.

But in Dublin at least one member of the Special Branch had suspicions. When the campaign opened in 1957 most arrested IRA men were held in the Bridewell, a Dublin city-centre lock-up, for the forty-eight-hour detention period before they could be charged, and one member of Dublin headquarters was lying on his bunk there when a voice at the spy hole in the cell door began ranting at him about 'so-called republicans mixed up with the likes of Strickland and Percival'. Strickland and Percival, of course, were the two British Army officers whose pitilessness in Ireland had made them hated during the period when Chink was Adjutant in Carlow; Montgomery had then been Strickland's brigade major. But at no time were road blocks set up around Cootehill.

Looking at the situation in the round, Chink tried to convince himself that the pressure of small-scale raids might be stepped up to the point where Britain had to employ more troops than could be afforded over a long period; it was the factor that had eventually gained Egypt's independence. But during 1955 and 1956 he was kept even farther away from the formulation of IRA policy. Murphy became tense after his brother's life sentence in England, following an abortive cross-channel raid, and he quarrelled with Magan and visited Chink less often. Instead, Murphy turned increasingly to a new member who was nearer his own age, thirty-three-year-old Sean Cronin. Cronin had worked recently as a journalist in America but before that had trained in the Irish Army, and soon after joining the IRA was appointed director of operations, but significantly he was not brought up to Cootehill to meet Chink. When an internal split in the organisation necessitated the planning of a serious campaign to retain the Northern support, again Chink was told nothing more than the outline of Cronin's plan, which was codenamed Operation Harvest.

When Harvest opened on 11 December 1956, Chink had to content himself with following news items. Cronin had planned a four-pronged attack by columns of fifteen men on the nationalist counties of Fermanagh and Tyrone, and Monaghan hospital, within fourteen miles of Cootehill, was earmarked for casualties. At first the authorities were taken by surprise, but the IRA momentum was shortlived. On 14 December the Southern government reinforced police border patrols with army units, and in the North the 2800-strong RUC force was mobilised on an emergency basis. The Unionist population was outraged, and the British Prime Minister Anthony Eden, harassed by the Suez crisis and the Hungarian Revolution, chided Dublin, which stiffened the determination of the Dail to crack down. Meanwhile RUC barracks began sandbagging and checking their early-warning network, and along the 250 miles of border all but seventeen roads were closed, and the rest cratered and spiked. 1000 full-time and 11,600 part-time B Specials were redeployed. On 15 December the repressive Special Powers Act was reintroduced.

On that cold day Chink had two unexpected visitors. Murphy called, and with him was Cronin, the new Didirector of Operations. Chink promptly asked them both in. 'He was exceedingly friendly and intelligent, neither patronising nor pompous,' summed up Cronin later. 'He was tall and spare, wore an old tweed jacket and corduroys, and when we walked outside he put on a cap. We talked a great deal, and it was a stimulating evening. I did not think it odd that an ex-British general would be fiercely nationalistic. He was, after all, Irish.' Discussion was chiefly about Harvest, which Chink thought reasonably sound, although he pointed out that the IRA would need greater support in the North, and Eve brought in tea. But this was the formal breaking off of all contact, and not the casual call Chink took it to be. McCarthy had called on the same errand shortly before Harvest began. His usefulness was over.

Within a month Cronin, Murphy and Magan were arrested and later received what were the first of a string of six-month sentences; and in Dublin the Offences Against the State Act was reintroduced. 'In terms of Machiavelli,' Chink wrote, 'this is the time to step up the pressure.'

Instead of the British Minister for War becoming drawn in – his secret hope – only one extra battalion was being sent to Northern Ireland and that, he soon sniffed, was a converted artillery unit. He tried to interest Larry Solon, a freelance journalist he had met, in a scoop for *Picture Post* – 'if identities are rigorously respected, shots of boys training, border reconnaissance patrols and briefing sessions could probably be arranged' – but the story was deemed unnewsworthy. The Catholic Church, as represented by his old friend John Charles McQuaid, condemned support and he often thought how very far apart they had grown; McQuaid would have recognised the training camp area, as they had often played in the outhouses as boys. In a general election that summer Fianna Fail swept to power in the South, wiping out Clann na Poblachta in the process, and de Valera was known to deal harshly with the IRA.

Chink faced facts, as he always advocated, and occupied himself by mapping out designs for various all-Ireland political frameworks which would recognise two separate states. He floated the most workable as the basis for a Gentlemen of Ireland's initiative to his near neighbour Sir Shane Leslie that summer – Leslie was the eccentric cousin of Churchill who had sponsored the young Scott Fitzgerald – but between them they could whip up no wider support. Chink then proposed regular joint consultations between young delegates of every Irish party, from Unionist to Sinn Fein, which could take place at Bellamont. But these proposals, too, ended up in his burgeoning filing system. 'Perhaps this island of prudes and poseurs,' he admitted, 'is beginning to get me down.'

Thoroughly disillusioned by now about the IRA's grasp of strategy, quite apart from tactics, he reacted strongly in February 1958 when Reggie probed about the cross-channel raid at Blandford Camp. 'I am not in the secrets of the IRA, thank goodness,' he retorted. 'Some of their transactions defeat me, as do their politics. You ask me for the rationale – my reply is "Search me." I can only think that someone believes it worthwhile to spread the tensions, very unwisely in my view.' And although he would continue his public support as operations dwindled, both in speeches to university debating clubs and in letters to the newspapers as far afield as the *Scotsman* and the *Guardian*, his dream of being a latterday Lord Edward Fitzgerald was over.

By the time the campaign was finally called off on 26 February 1962, he had even become cautious. When Rory Brady, the chief of staff who succeeded Magan, called at Bellamont later that year in the hope of enlisting his support for an appeal to the House of Commons to release the remaining prisoners, Chink reacted quite differently from his unstinting acclaim of eight years earlier. The IRA, he stipulated caustically, must not cut the ground from under him by restarting activity near Christmas if he gave his word that they would not. Only if given such a pledge would he contact the leader of the Liberal Party, Jo Grimond, through his brother, who happened to know him well. Brady gave his word. Telling his mother, a staunch 1916 republican, about the encounter afterwards, much to Brady's surprise she remarked that it was a shame there were not more members like the Brigadier. In her time there had been Erskine Childers, the O'Rahilly, Constance Markewitz, Maud Gonne and Sir John French's sister, Madame Despard, and people like that could be very useful. It was an opinion Chink would once have endorsed with alacrity.

He did his stuff. Reggie, to his discomfort, put in a quiet political word and wrote back that the IRA were VUPs – Very Unpopular People. Whether or not the approach had any effect is debatable, but the releases did start and that, to use one of Chink's favourite phrases, was that. Brady did not return, and Murphy did not get in touch when, suffering from severe depression, he was released from prison. McCarthy returned to Cork, Cronin to America, and Magan had only ever seen Chink as a tool. The outbuildings gathered dust, and the training grounds reverted to rabbits and the occasional fox or deer. Chink never did change his opposition to partition and the status quo in the North, but he had mellowed to the point of being able to ridicule it. 'I now begin to favour its retention as a tourist attraction like the Beefeaters and the Horse Guards,' he teased one correspondent in 1963. 'One could sell it as genuine Victorian Toryism. Nothing could be funnier than the Twelfth of July and the wee men in bowler hats! I think the whole thing ought now to be consciously preserved as an imperial monument, and paid a subsidy as such.'

The experience of blending into the patch of green and saffron was cathartic. It brought the lost world a little nearer, satisfied a few old scores, introduced adventure and – more importantly – a cause, and for a few years was the ultimate self-deceptive game. There is an affinity with Hemingway's U-boat hunting off Cuba during the war, and more than an echo of Don Quixote. As for judgement, it is reminiscent of the poet Yeats's support for the Irish Blueshirts, Ludendorff's alignment with Hiter, and 'Boney' Fuller's espousal of fascism. Like them, he was a creative visionary, and his involvement underlines the breadth of his imagination and his lack of conventional restraints. There was no Wavell at his shoulder to sift the bubbling of ideas and say 'No, Chink, that one really won't do,' no O'Connor to raise an eyebrow, and no Estelle to inject common sense.

And in the euphoria of a fresh allegiance he had not sabotaged the old one. At no point did he betray the trust of Ultra by threatening to leak its existence, or exploit his military contacts at the top – John Harding was CIGS in London at the time, and Ouvry Roberts in charge in the North. He was also meticulous about not compromising an old friend like Brian Horrocks, whose role as Black Rod conflicted with his own choices so sharply. The memory of Smuts's rival set of medals was clear-cut. Above all, he had had the opportunity to inflict a measure of lasting international harm on England by pressing his watertight case against Churchill, and for honourable reasons had chosen not to do so. Approaching retirement age he remained a conundrum. He still watched what everyone else was going to do, and deliberately took the opposite direction.

Early one afternoon in the 1960s Colonel Henry Cramsie, Royal Northumberland Fusiliers, pulled into Dublin on a day's visit with his wife. Cramsie had been on the top Cairo polo team of 1937 and, retiring to his family home in Northern Ireland after the war, had found himself commanding a TA unit of the North Irish Horse on the border during the latest IRA campaign. After carrying out some business he took his wife as a treat to the Shelbourne Hotel for tea. Cramsie was wearing his regimental tie, his favourite for every smart occasion, and as the couple entered the tea room he made out Chink, wearing the same tie, sitting at a table inside. 'I said to my wife, "Hold on," ' Cramsie recalled subsequently. ' "My God, Chink's in there. I'm not going to have anything to do with him." And I walked straight past his table without looking. I felt he'd let the side down.' He was finally beyond the pale.

15

... And into
the
Trees

Hemingway's novel *Across the River and into the Trees* was being serialised in *Cosmopolitan* when Chink reached New York on his anti-partition tour of America in the spring of 1950. For twenty years he had had no contact with Hemingway, but browsing in Scribner's bookshop on 6 April, the day after his arrival, he called on impulse to the adjacent publishing house for the address of their most famous author. Erect and spare, pepper-and-salt hair combed neatly, the cord of a monocle leading from the lapel of his sports jacket into the top pocket behind his silk handkerchief, and his Burberry over his arm, he leaned forward to deploy his most old-world charm. Instinctively he exaggerated each English nuance.

Hemingway, he was informed, was visiting New York simultaneously and staying at the Sherry Netherland Hotel. He phoned from a nearby callbox but Hemingway was out, and on the spur of the moment he left a message with his own number at the Commodore Hotel on 42nd Street at Lexington Avenue. While he was cursing the sealed windows of his centrally heated room after breakfast the following morning, not yet adjusted to the time change but up and dressed since 6 a.m. and unsure what to do with the blank day, Hemingway phoned back. He was to come straight round to the Sherry Netherland because there wasn't much time, the unforgotten twang instructed. He did as he was told. 'Come in, Chink. I've some poetry to read to you. I think it's good. I can't talk poetry to anyone but you.'

'Hem was gross, lavish, champagne like water, young ardent, grey bearded, fat but hard,' he described the meeting later.

Writing poetry. Read me a damn good poem. . . . He's very interested in the Rommel story. Will help all out, recognised necessity of
telling story on principle. Very well informed on British layout,
including my past! Offered me Marlene Dietrich. I declined, feeling
that I wasn't yet up to the local Matterhorns; besides, all the really
steep places have already been fixed with ropes and pitons. . . . His
new wife, Miss Mary, was packing clothes and books, not young,
small, blonde, squaw-like female who seemed to regard me with
some distrust. She drifted in and out of the apartment suspiciously.

But after the first euphoria he found himself cataloguing the changes.
Fame did not appear to have altered Hemingway and his clothes were
as unselfconsciously practical as ever, but champagne was the wrong
substitute for the steins of beer, and he could not stop comparing the
plush hotel suite with the slapdash Paris apartments of his memory.
Unlike their previous casual routine, callers constantly interrupted
them. Hemingway's publisher brought in a contract; two lawyers, one
after the other, represented former wives Chink had not met – 'never
have anything to do with alimony, Chink, it kills you' – and two grown
sons came in, introduced to him as Gregory and Patrick, whose mother
disconcertingly was not Hadley, but her successor. He resented each
interruption. After being prompted to talk about Alamein he was
anxious to tell Hemingway everything before the couple left for Cuba
at noon and what he had to say was painful and urgent, the greatest
contrast of all with their earlier encounters. For the first time, too, he
had something to hide; he steered the conversation away each time
Hemingway asked about Anzio. The morning passed too quickly.
Finding Hemingway so knowledgeable enabled him to get straight to
the personality clashes, and as responsive to his audience as ever he let
in a few light touches. It had been Hemingway's original concept, he
reminded him, that all fronts were as diaphonous as a spider's web if
one had first-class intelligence and weak points were attacked first,
knocking out the spider at the centre. But his secret knowledge of
Ultra, too, came between them.

'[Hemingway] had so much to say and Miss Mary had so much to
pack that we got nowhere and everywhere simultaneously,' was his
summing-up of the disjointed morning. 'His exit shedding two dollar
bills to the staff was magnificent, even if his luggage did not live up to
it. . . . I went with them to their car at the hotel door, Hem carrying

two canvas buckets stuffed with new books. "Do you have to buy books, Chink? They're my ammunition." ' After their departure Chink found he was still clutching the large signed and framed portrait photograph that Hemingway had pressed upon him, and ignoring the supercilious hotel porter he took it with him to a small restaurant further down the street where he placed it on the table and consoled himself by ordering a dozen blue-point oysters. Two straws remained. Hemingway had promised to write an introduction to the book he hoped to bring out one day on the desert war, and he had been pressed to come down to Cuba as soon as he could get away.

'If it hadn't been inevitable it would have been extraordinary,' he wrote to Hemingway that night.

Destinies aren't extraordinary if one just lets them work. So this one has worked and what is 25 years or so? Nothing at all, or at best only something to bleach or bloat us – silly anatomical tricks which don't count. . . . In my opinion it's high time we united to take charge of the planet again. We've let it rip for too long, wherefore all sorts of indifferent exploiters have taken over at the point we left off, and I don't think they've made a very good job of it all. . . . I'll come down to Cuba as soon as I can. . . . Thanks for the bubbly. One day we'll drink beer again in buckets.

Had his façade, perhaps, been too convincing? 'Remember,' he added to a subsequent letter, 'that beneath this flippant exterior beats a broken heart, or damn near broken anyway. I no longer permit anyone else in the world to call me Chink, but you're too damn big to be stopped so I'll let it be.'

Buoyed up by the unexpected meeting and preoccupied by the years he had thought forgotten, he moved on to Washington. The busier schedule included addressing a Washington Press Club Luncheon and appearing on television, and the guide assigned to him was a twenty-eight-year-old freelance journalist, Elise Morrow. Her name began with an E, like Estelle and Eve, and she was the same age they had been when first met; a continuation, it appeared, of destiny at work. Taking advantage of the thirty-year age gap he played the mature general to the hilt, and soon she loved him in return. But though Elise was a rapt and intelligent disciple who brought out all the tenderness he no longer showed to Eve, he had no real intention of breaking up his marriage. The grievances intruded here, too. Elise was married to the assistant editor of the *Saturday Evening Post*, Hugh Morrow, and when Chink was introduced to him he saw him not as a rival but as a useful lever for putting across criticism of British wartime policy in North Africa. With Morrow's help he concentrated on setting up a series of future articles for the *Washington Post* and Elise was contracted to help him write them.

In each new hotel room as the tour progressed he placed his signed photograph of Hemingway in a prominent position, aware that a little window-dressing added to his impact. The serialisation of *Across the River and into the Trees* was being widely advertised, and swept by old and new emotions he caught up with the last two instalments. The central character is Robert Cantwell, an American senior soldier demoted from general to colonel who emerges as a resentful casualty of his own idealism, and so inward-looking and bitter have his wartime experiences made him that the devoted love of a young Italian girl of good family, Renata, is eclipsed. Elise saw similarities at once – principally between herself and Renata – but Chink believed that Cantwell was a projection of Hemingway's own longing to command in war. Taking heart from the realisation that Hemingway, too, must have gone through similar agonies of mind, he reproached him at once. 'How do you know things only I know? That was great writing. You understand sorrow. Why didn't you tell me?'

But Chink himself, as the Hemingway biographer Jeffrey Meyers has established, is the chief model for Cantwell. (The character is also drawn from three other military friends, as well as from personal disillusion. Charles Sweeny, a larger-than-life soldier of fortune; Gustavo Duran, an artistically-minded officer Hemingway got to know when covering the Spanish Civil War; and 'Buck' Lanham, a dynamic West Pointer first met in Normandy in 1944 who reflected General Patton's hatred of Montgomery.) Meyers points out that *Across the River and into the Trees* was the result of Hemingway's need to ventilate anger and grief at his old friend's treatment, after reading de Guingand's memoirs in 1947 before the novel was begun. From de Guingand's clue – 'There is no doubt that an unnecessary and vicious vendetta was waged against [Chink] by the Army hierarchy. From being on the point of being made a Lieut. General and VCGS in Cairo he was demoted overnight to a brigadier' – Hemingway had known him intimately enough to be able to envisage the long-term emotional consequences, no less harrowing for being self-inflicted. 'I have failed,' says Cantwell, 'and I speak badly of all who have succeeded.' 'Do you like Rommel?' asks Renata. 'Very much.' 'But he was your enemy.' 'I love my enemies, sometimes, more than my friends.'

In *Across the River and into the Trees* Cantwell regrets that he destroyed a regiment by following other people's orders, while in reality Auchinleck and Chink refused to use the untrained 44th Division before they were ready. But precise details, including the turning down of the Iraq–Persia offer, were not then public knowledge. Hemingway's accurate mental picture of Chink is most evident in the dialogue. 'If I had lied as others lied,' says Cantwell, 'I would have been a three-star general.' Elsewhere, in passage between Cantwell and Renata, she is told that 'Monty was a character who needed fifteen to one to move and then moved tardily.' 'I always supposed he was a great general.' 'He was not,' the Colonel said. 'But he beat General Rommel.' 'Yes, and don't you think anyone else had softened him up?' Even Chink's 1918 Shakespearean quotation makes its appearance once more, in the sentence: 'He and the Colonel both remembered the men who decided that they did not wish to die, not thinking that he who dies on Thursday does not have to die on Friday.' And although the American Cantwell speaks of his trade, instead of his profession as Chink usually did, as early as 1924 Hemingway had written a poem entitled 'To Chink, Whose Trade is Soldiering'.

Chink did notice the resemblances in the fall of rank, the disgust with Montgomery and the relationship with Elise. But he made no ultimate connection between himself and Cantwell, even when the complete galleys were forwarded to him in Ireland on his return. The ending, in which Cantwell dies from a terminal illness at the age of fifty, found no response in him at all. 'Angina, it reads like,' he analysed. 'But I suppose . . . nothing particular to live about. . . . Yet something always seems to turn up to start a new interest in life. At least, it does so with me.' He accused Hemingway of using death to sidestep more complex issues. Had Cantwell gone on living, he put it to him revealingly, and had to face retirement and the loss of Renata against a background of 'bigger and better Montgomeries', it would have been more poignant. But no amount of re-reading changed his firmly held opinion that the character's sole genesis was wish-fulfilment on Hemingway's part.

'It seems to me,' he observed eight years later, 'that Hem is still nostalgic about a military career, and for that reason enjoyed the last war not a little. Something of that reflects into *Over* [sic] *the River*, where he confronts his lost youth with his present decrepitude.' Did such a superior view allow him back some of the self-esteem quenched by their uneven meeting in New York? Was it too painful to suppose that the hollow failure Cantwell might be himself?

Across the River and into the Trees, which Chink was sardonically amused to note was promptly banned in Ireland under the aegis of his other old friend, McQuaid, is a much darker book than *Fiesta/The Sun Also Rises* where he made his first appearance. It takes on a tragic significance in the context of Hemingway's outrage and compassion for him and of their joint middle-age disillusion. As Chink was writing to him within seven months of their reunion, 'You and I have this in common, we belong to a defrauded generation; we have had the sticky end of two world wars and we have seen the crooks and slim boys get away with the spoil. We saw this coming as we talked in 1924 – we still see it. [Only] you had far fewer illusions than I.'

The visit to Cuba fell through, but they wrote regularly and rallied each other – 'How do you like it now, Gentlemen?' being a sure sign that reassurance was needed – and in Chink's bleakest years immediately following the death of Wavell it would be Hemingway who took over Liddell Hart's role of chief comforter. Chink's hurt was so near the surface that even a salacious joke about forming a Cantwell society for adulterous over-fifty-year-olds had a blacker side; appointing himself a founder member he put MCS after his name (Member Cantwell Society), to obliterate the MC that had once meant so much.

The mutual support continued after a break caused by Chink, who shut down all his private correspondence during his action over *The Hinge of Fate*. He got in touch again in 1954 to congratulate Hemingway on being awarded that year's Nobel Prize for Literature, and bringing him up to date about the Churchill case pointed out in unchanged tone that 'the Baron Munchausen of British Political Literature' had been the previous recipient. Hemingway was more taken by a third-party comment which Chink passed on to the effect that each had wished they were the other. 'I would like to have been you with my luck and your brains,' he agreed. 'If we could have mixed our lousy talents it might have made a fairly sinister and dangerous condottiere of some kind. And a better writer than me. . . .' But the encouragement was wasted. Chink had given up trying to complete his own account of the North African campaigns by then, and if his moods of despair were growing fewer, they were no less intense. 'We two relics,' he reached out to Hemingway during one, 'of the alleged lost generation. Aborted, really.'

Back came Hemingway's misspelled, warm letters on the opaque airmail paper with La Finca embossed in scarlet across the top, written with a broadnibbed pen in blue–grey ink or signed in thick pencil if typed. Invariably Chink replied too soon, in lonely contrast to the days when he excused a casual note with the words 'I know that if I don't write now I never will, for I surely am the laziest correspondent in the world.' But although Hemingway continued to urge him to visit Cuba and he toyed with the idea of moving there permanently with Eve and the children, he had become too wary on second thoughts to risk it. 'Somehow I feel,' he wrote privately in 1958, 'that my relationship with Hem is something of my youth that it might be unwise to renew in such altered circumstances. We have been apart too long for the atmosphere to be easily recaptured. The result might be just two old men trying to rediscover long lost territory futilely. . . . I think I will stay away for both our sakes.'

He continued to write to Elise too but covertly, through his solicitor. Eve had found out about his secret by coming into the library unexpectedly one afternoon and catching him in the act of penning a love letter. In the same way that he had denied her ten years earlier to Estelle, so he bluffed that it was only to make sure of the *Washington Post* commission, but the damage was done. Their row was searing and she took refuge in a nursing home in England, returning his letters unopened with taunts like 'So you're feeling randy again?' scrawled across the envelope. He filed each one away.

Eventually she returned, but now that she could no longer believe she was his unique inspiration their relationship was more fragile than ever behind the public façade. He had no patience with her hypochondria and intensified his solitary physical-fitness programme in retaliation. He began attending Mass again and after a while she followed his lead towards Catholicism, but as their marriage could not be recognised this caused additional stress and led to a bizarre predicament. His first marriage was considered invalid because it had been to a divorcee but an annulment was necessary before Eve would be free to marry, and one of the conditions laid down before that could be granted was an indefinite ban on sex; they were to inhabit separate bedrooms and sleep at different ends of the house. Chink gave his word and having done so moved down to another floor straightaway, deaf to Eve's widely broadcast complaints that she needed sex for her health's sake. No one would have found out if he had broken the trust and it had been imposed in the belief that they would refuse, but the Church, like the army, had underestimated his implacable sense of honour. And the Church, like the army, failed to live up to his expectations. Eve's ceremony of admission eventually took place in Dublin in 1957, but the annulment continued to be withheld. She rejected Catholicism and his weeks of belief were interspersed by months of cynical alienation. In some moods he argued that sexuality ought ideally to be suppressed; more often he suspected that they had been manipulated into the unnecessary sacrifice by a display of power for its own sake. He knew McQuaid too well to go behind the local bishop's back.

Bored, cornered and lonelier than he cared to admit, he did not look forward to the publication of Montgomery's *Memoirs*, which were due out in August 1958. Still raw from Alanbrooke's scathing diary extracts in *Turn of the Tide* the previous year, over which he had had to be dissuaded from legal action, he counted the days and then drove the 140 miles to Dublin and back for a copy, unable to wait for the post. The 'humourless egotism' of the account struck him as reptilian as he sat up all night reading it, and he was so incensed by the claim that Auchinleck had admitted intending to retreat to the Delta that he put through a call first thing next morning to ask Auchinleck what he intended to do about it. He had become so used to the fatalism that he was elated to find him 'hopping mad', and he dashed off a letter at once in response. 'Whatever attributes I still possess are as much at your service as they were on 25 June 1942,' he affirmed. 'To fight will also be to fight for the honour of the whole officer corps of the British Army. Monty had only to glance at the wall of your caravan to get all the clues. His memoirs make no reference to the map; his readers are invited to believe that he found Eighth Army in paralysed chaos.'

The resulting press controversy drew in so many of their old colleagues that soon Chink felt more alive than he had for sixteen years. 'Another battle of El Alamein is going strong,' summed up the *Manchester Guardian*. 'The argument, of course, will sway one way and another just as the fighting in the desert did. But there will surely be some fixed points. One is the Appreciation at the end of July . . . another the Hinge of Fate.' Out for blood, Chink was sure they had Montgomery over a barrel and would have been happy for the row to go on indefinitely, but privately and with far greater speed than in his own case a settlement was being reached over a footnote of withdrawal. 'I think I know what you have had to bear,' Auchinleck prepared him for the news in the sensitive, modest manner of old that Christmas Day. 'And I do feel for you deeply because I have failed you in a way, I fear. . . . I am due to fly to Pakistan tomorrow. Wish you were coming too. We could have fun walking once again before breakfast.' But Chink was not too downcast. Their reconciliation brought access to all the documents Auchinleck had withheld earlier, and he now had in his possession the despatches copy of their final Eighth Army situation map, which was proof of their veracity. The bleakest years, when at his most anguished he had boycotted his stepdaughter Elizabeth's wedding because it was taking place in England, had without his realising it come to an end.

Correlli Barnett, a young Oxford graduate who had read Military History and the Theory of War, put down *The Desert Fox*, a life of Rommel by Desmond Young, and thought it was high time somebody wrote about the pre-Montgomery era in North Africa. He was given Chink's name, among others, by the established military author Major John North, and took up the immediate invitation to Bellamont with alacrity, expecting a conventional retired senior officer. 'He was distinguished and enormously vivid,' he said later. 'Curly hair, tall and spare, and a springy step. He had a deep voice which seemed to move from an Irish accent to a British Army one easily. Very quickly he elicited what I knew and we talked hammer and tongs about the desert. He felt very deeply about the wreck of his career and he returned to the theme compulsively. His information was obviously coloured and one had to aim off for this, but sitting in the library that first morning, talking and getting answers, one had the feeling of equality. He was a mutual conversationalist.' The effect that Barnett, who was congenial, avid to learn and thirty years younger, had on Chink was the customary revitalising one that each new disciple brought, and under his questioning he began to ease back and survey the wider period. 'The subject is so distasteful to me that I rarely go back to it dispassionately,' he warned as Barnett continued his research in England. 'But 16 years has passed [sic] and one should be able to consider it without too much internal bleeding.' He found it helped to refer to himself sardonically as Dorman-Smith RIP whenever he figured in the anecdotes.

A second writer got in touch. John Connell was a well-known broadcaster and journalist in London who had taken up Desmond Young's suggestion that he write a biography of Auchinleck, and while interviewing him had been advised to talk to Chink. 'Your contribution,' Connell's letter urged, 'is uniquely valuable because you have been isolated from people . . . and think and feel about them without the patina of all the years.' Like Barnett, Connell was taken aback at first by the thoughts and feelings that poured out when Chink began to talk about Auchinleck, and finding him immensely likeable he did his best to persuade him to come out of isolation to acquire that patina for his own protection. Emboldened by the two new friendships, Chink gradually broke away from the monasticism of the past fifteen years. In March 1960 he accepted an invitation to attend a Military Commentators' Circle meeting in London at which Auchinleck was to be the guest speaker – 'Shall I wear a shroud or a goatskin?' – and here he met a third writer, R.W. 'Tommy' Thompson. Thompson was to become a more malleable disciple than Barnett and Connell, and identified with him closely.

In September 1960 Barnett's book *The Desert Generals* was published, with appendices containing Chink's Appreciation of 27 July 1942 in full and a defence of his abilities. It rapidly became a controversial bestseller with its criticism of Montgomery's generalship and the lack of credit for the inherited plan used at Alam Halfa, and Chink's only regret was that Amy was by now too ill with cancer to take it in. He found the press coverage exhilarating and protested to Barnett that he 'hedged' whenever he was contacted himself, but it was from this time onwards that a rumour began to spread about a map at Bellamont which could prove that Montgomery had lied about Alam Halfa; Chink had unpinned it personally before leaving Eighth Army TAC HQ, it was said. In due course some visitors had the map pointed out to them with its tell-tale marks of old drawing pins across the top, displayed on a large easel that stood in a shadowy corner of the library. As with the Hemingway portrait in America, Chink knew when window-dressing advanced his cause, and he had no qualms about transforming the more mundane despatches map into a lure to catch the public imagination after the wide circulation of Montgomery's slurs.

But in 1961 an opponent whom he had no wish to challenge personally broke silence. In response to Barnett's argument that the more famous Second Battle of Alamein had not been necessary, Alexander brought out his memoirs and, using the same Major John North who had recommended Chink to Barnett originally as editor, went on to deny that there had been an existing plan for Alam Halfa. His own despatches, however, had mentioned one, but that sentence was omitted from the truncated version which appeared in the memoirs. 'It is extraordinary,' Chink wrote in exasperation to

Connell, 'to think that this is the twentieth year since Alamein and most of the performers are still alive in very much the same attitudes.' He resolved to sue, but admitted to Liddell Hart that he was heartily tired of refighting the First Battle of Alamein and longed for an end to it. 'But since [Auchinleck will not] undertake the task, I remain the sole person who can make the challenge. I'm getting on in years. I'm lazy now and shy too, but I feel it is my duty. A queer way to go into a case, not much minding if one loses providing one challenges the big giant Bad History.'

Respecting Alexander as a gentlemanly soldier – 'if not for his military brain' – he swung his action against North, and assembled a legal team headed by Finlay with the literary-minded legal prodigy Ulick O'Connor as junior counsel and retaining the top Irish barrister Ernest Wood if it went to court. But after much preparation he was advised to stop. The point in contention was too specialised for a jury of laymen to comprehend, and he could not be said to have lost financially. His only consolation was that Liddell Hart resigned the presidency of the Military Circle in London, of which North was a member, and cited C.P. Scott's principle 'Comment is free but facts are sacred' in his resignation speech.

The sensation was that of taking one step forward and three back, but he was unable to let go. 'On 2 July Churchill told parliament that it was a crisis of Dunkirk dimensions, and no English channel between us and Rommel,' he corrected one reviewer. 'Now I believe the theory is that Rommel, who has become an honorary Englishman, stopped of his own accord at Alamein to pick desert flora. It is almost an insult to British sportsmanship to suggest that he was stopped against his wishes.' The military memoirs that appeared thick and fast testifying to the effectiveness of Montgomery's Registering of Personality kept him on the boil, and when Horrocks joined in and sent him an inscribed copy of *A Full Life* he retorted that he would clearly have to call his own memoirs *A Foul Life* as a companion volume. The patina Connell had wished for him showed no sign of beginning to form. 'If I had to write my book again tomorrow it would be the same,' Montgomery was reported as saying, despite his climbdown after Auchinleck's challenge. 'If other people think it is not true ... I suggest ... they write their own books.' To Chink's frustration Auchinleck would not entertain the idea, and so the rearguard action continued.

But bit by bit the myth was being amended. *The Desert Generals* marked the beginning of the process of re-evaluation, and that same year Chink was heartened to get a letter from Ronald Playfair, the *Punch* contributor at Chatham thirty years earlier who was now entrusted with writing *The Official History of the Second World War*. They had not met since the impromptu dinner in Cairo at the time of Crete, and the reason for Playfair's contact was to say that he had sent off the manuscript of the third volume which included Alamein, and that Chink would find it 'sympathetic'. Talking to Professor F.H. Hinsley, the historian who would bring out *The Official History of British Intelligence in the Second World War*, he found that Hinsley had independently reached the same conclusion about the decisiveness of First Alamein. And McCreery – Dreary McCreery, with whom he had never expected to have anything in common – criticised Montgomery in the *12th Lancers Regimental Journal*. He filed away that under a pencilled-in heading 'First Crack in the Armour'.

To his great surprise Bernard Paget, the instructor he had most respected at the Staff College and whom he had last encountered at the disastrous lunch on Churchill's train, got in touch. He fully agreed, wrote Paget, about the failure to exploit the German loss of initiative from July 1942 onwards, and he proposed that Chink should write a study on the co-ordination of the higher direction of war – 'including the political' – for students at the Imperial Defence College. In this Paget was no more successful than Hemingway, but they continued to correspond until Paget's death, and on one of Chink's rare visits to London they met for lunch, during which Paget confided that Churchill had taken the credit for his own invasion plan Skyscraper. By now Chink's kindness tended to take the form of a sombre aggressive protectiveness, and when Paget died in March 1961 he leaked the story to the press without consulting Paget's family, who were distressed. At sixty-six he was as self-willed and headstrong as ever.

But there was one approach that he kept to himself which would have been a most useful weapon in his continuous battle against Bad History, a term he had borrowed from Compton Mackenzie. In 1954, out of the blue, a telegram of good wishes had come from the Afrika Korps reunion at Heidelberg 'in memory of hard days near Alamein during July 1942'. Confirming the fidelity of Hemingway's reading of his character in *Across the River and into the Trees* he had cabled straight back, responding 'Hard times make strong ties.' In a letter of thanks, Rommel's son Manfred revealed it had been sent on to Kesselring, and continued: 'I have been present at many discussions during the last years. It was always pointed out that the North Africa was in the moment of greatest danger saved for the British by Field Marshal Auchinleck and his assistant leaders in 1942. Even my father, who really thought a lot of FM Auchinleck, did not believe at this time that he might be able to reorganise the British Army at El Alamein in the extent he really did. The German leaders – also my father (I remember that, and also my mother) – pointed out that they felt that they had been outmanoeuvred in July 1942 at Alamein.' Quixotically Chink made no attempt to get this into the papers too.

Despite their great difference in temperament, he was closer to Reggie in retirement than ever before, whereas Victor had settled in Malta and seldom communicated with either of them. Reggie followed his legal skirmishes and emotional upheavals sympathetically, and as the politician in the family made it his business to find out that the Secretary of State for War had the gift of restitution of rank. Encouraged by the changing tone of the war books and the support of John Connell, who had researched the background for his biography of Auchinleck and for the book on Wavell that he was about to commence, Reggie ignored Chink's protests and decided to go ahead with an appeal in the autumn of 1960. His aim was to have him gazetted as Major General Retired with the KCB, and grudgingly Chink gave permission, on condition that Auchinleck was awarded a suitable honour – there was a vacancy, he pointed out, in the Order of Merit – and that the proper Africa Star was awarded to all troops who had fought in the desert before the Montgomery era.

The Secretary of State for War was John Profumo, whom both Reggie and Connell knew slightly, and the interview took place at the War Office on 24 October; Chink stayed in Ireland. 'I do not think we let you down in any way,' Reggie reported.

Profumo was obviously both interested and moved. . . . I handed him your diary and [some War Office] documents. These shook him quite a lot. He was very puzzled about the 3rd Brigade incident at Anzio . . . so I served it to him straight. P finished: 'I appreciate your attitude. If my elder brother had been treated as on the face of it yours has been, and had I the power to do so I would threaten to pull down Buckingham Palace. . . . Of course in the War Office we have a number of cases where for some reason the events of the war left brilliant men high and dry. I myself know a number who, in my opinion, should have gone to the top.' I replied that that might be so, but it would be ruddy good for the morale of young officers if they could realise that the WO had a heart. For you, dear brother, I will pull down Buck House, but you will have to trust me to put up your arguments. I doubt whether justice will come your way, but the words are Box On.

The official reply took three months to come, and when it did arrive it was not signed by Profumo. 'I do not deny that Brigadier Dorman-Smith may well have been unlucky,' wrote the Parliamentary Under-Secretary of State for War. 'But it is another thing to accept that the changes of staff . . . were necessarily wrong in the circumstances of the time. . . . No doubt historians will continue to express different views. Nevertheless those immediately concerned . . . were satisfied that changes must be made. . . . Unquestionably they had the right to do so.' No qualification existed for the honorary rank as it had not been held for the necessary aggregate period of six months. While Reggie was livid, Chink expected it and he had become cynical enough not to be thrown back into depression. He took the law into his own hands and frequently used the rank of major general from then on, and remarked when the Profumo sex scandal hit the headlines that it proved the lack of judgement. As Reggie said, Box on.

Nineteen-sixty-one promised to be a less extreme year, but on 2 July the death of Hemingway was announced on the lunchtime news and his newfound equilibrium was shattered. He wept in front of his son Christopher, who had never seen him cry before, and shut himself away to work on an earlier memoir of their friendship all afternoon. Relations were due that evening and he read it aloud to them after dinner, but he left Hemingway's photograph in place on the grand piano in the unlighted ballroom beyond. Other deaths had plunged him into intense grief, but this was the hardest to come to terms with because he had no doubt at all that it had been suicide.

Over the following days he went through their letters, having kept carbons of many of his own, and found no comfort there. He had been the one to stop writing – yet again – and he had not even sent a card in reply to the one Hemingway had sent him that Christmas. 'I feel guilty,' he blamed himself, 'because on re-reading them it seems just possible that I could have helped Hem over that difficult stile into the sixties of a man's life.' Hemingway's last letters harked back ominously to their youth together in Switzerland and Paris and he had even signed the Christmas card 'Popplethwaite'. When *A Moveable Feast* was published posthumously with its public celebration of their climb over the St Bernard Pass, where he was portrayed as always a step ahead, secure and reassuring, he loathed himself all over again for staying at a distance out of a sense of touchy inferiority. The dialogue between the young Hemingway and Hadley wounded him particularly. 'He had always been my best friend and then our best friend for a long time. . . . "I hope Chink will come. He takes care of us." ' And his advice over the suitcase was back to haunt him. 'Chink had taught me never to discuss casualties,' he read with horror, and bitterly regretted not having made him talk about the more recent casualties before they became destructive.

He coped by taking his own advice. He did not discuss casualties, refused every request for an interview and responded positively to only one approach, that of Carlos Baker, the biographer chosen by Hemingway's family. But he paid an anonymous and he thought appropriate tribute. He took part in the BBC's Fiftieth Anniversary commemoration of the First World War and recited one of Hemingway's Mons Cameos from *In Our Time*. In his clipped voice, without introduction, he contributed the episode at the bridge of Le Cateau, and made his way back again to Ireland without realising that the inscribed copy in his pocket was now worth a great deal of money.

Hadley wrote to ask if she might visit him that September, and to their relief they found their liking for each other unimpaired; his godson, he was astounded to hear, had been told to follow his example and had joined the United States Army. They wrote regularly after that, and he confided his difficulties over summoning up information for Baker's thorough biography.

So damn easy to be sententious and to miss the lad we knew. Paris, Les Avants, St. Bernard, Milan (Milan before you!), fishing at the end of the lake. . . . How could I tell a professor about Milan 1918? We were all too young. . . . What happened to us all? I don't want to open old sores; you need not respond if this is what happens. But we shared such riches in Hem's innocence. On looking back, what full years they were. Surely the times when we were together were the best of them – for me, anyway. . . . You see, Hadley, the pundits who write about Hem seem to skip these important years, thinking that since Hem wasn't 'important' then, they weren't important either. Hem was even more important then, to ourselves and to himself too, perhaps, than he ever was afterwards.

No sooner had he suffered the shock of Hemingway's death than Amy died in England, having needed nobody except Reggie for a long time. 'It is just the full circle,' Reggie had confided recently. 'At school Mops would come down and take me out for the day – and then back I had to go to that other world. Now I take her out for the afternoon and she feels exactly as I did when I had to return. The joy of meeting hardly compensates for the sadness of parting and I feel completely inadequate.' Glad that he had not got that responsibility, Chink had ceased envying him for being the favourite, but though he had expected her death, unlike Edward's, he found it very hard to come to terms with the fact that she, too, had died without understanding what had happened to his career.

Eve's mother died shortly afterwards, but the shared experience brought them no closer to each other, and as he was becoming older and deafer the gap between them was widening even further. She enjoyed standing behind him in company where he could not see her and miming the winding up of an ancient piece of machinery, and he had got so used to her remark that he had been dead for some time that it no longer hurt him. Cerebral and self-contained, he worked through to peace of mind with the aid of a regime of stiff exercise and long hours in the library, his spaniel his constant companion. 'I rise at 5 a.m.,' he told one enquirer. 'Breakfast lightly, run from 6 a.m.–7 a.m. After a cold bath I lay the fires and get Eve's breakfast ready. A few more chores and I'm ready for the minor tiresomeness [of correspondence]. I admit to a siesta. I'm apt to doze over television. I read the *Irish Times*, the *Guardian, Telegraph* and *Observer* and find myself getting daily squarer. No theatre, cinema or racegoing. Antiquarianism and history, plus warfare and philosophy, form my reading.'

But the old man's outline was partly a pose; he had no intention of vegetating. International military developments continued to fascinate him and his distrust of communism, which he was convinced was a conspiracy devoted to world conquest, kept him constantly on the alert. He believed Western strategy to be inferior to the 'neatness' shown earlier in Korea, Indo-China and the Formosa Straits. He had followed the Congo War intently, having got to know and like Conor Cruise O'Brien, the representative of the United Nations Secretary

General in Katanga, and lambasted the United Nations Forces for being 'ad hoc national contingents flung together at a moment's notice'. But it was Western reliance on the H-bomb with its ultimate threat of nuclear war that alarmed him most; that was the 'utter negation' of good strategical practice, and he criticised it at every opportunity. He was reviewing regularly for the book pages of the *Guardian*, the *Scotsman* and the *Irish Times*, and relished the extra platform. Novelty intrigued him as much as ever, and his latest enthusiasm was dowsing. Friends he trusted and the pretty women he loved talking to were unable to relate the highly strung cantankerous staff officer portrayed in books to the youthful man for his age who was such fun to be with.

But as his seventieth birthday approached he was becoming very conscious of the march of time. On 24 January 1965 Churchill died; Brooke had died in 1963. A week after staying with Chink, John Connell had a fatal heart attack. 'Queenie' Wavell wrote to ask for papers that had long been returned, and addressed him as 'Dear General.' 'Very distant,' he noted sadly, 'for all we knew each other very well once.' An unexpected letter came from Francis Tuker, who had taken over from him in India, ending with the words 'I doubt if two worn out old hacks like us will ever meet again,' and soon Tuker was dead, followed by 'Boney' Fuller and Archie Nye. 'I am sorry Tedder has gone,' wrote Auchinleck. 'I liked him though he was not easy. . . . Arthur Smith and his wife came to lunch yesterday. He looks just the same, only grey instead of fair-haired.'

De Guingand sent his latest book *Generals at War* and time was evident here too: it was inscribed 'To Chink, in recognition of the part you played. With happy memories, Freddie.' 'Happy memories, blimey,' Chink exclaimed to Barnett with a grimace, but in his letter of thanks he was conciliatory. 'Was I ambitious?' he asked him, philosophically picking up a thread from de Guingand's book. 'I don't know about myself. Really ambitious people play their cards better than I did. I was ambitious for the success of our arms, of course, and I could not bear bunglers any more than you could – we had that in common. It was kind of you to write as you did.' It occurred to him that he was older now than Churchill had been at the time of the harrying and sacking, and that he, too, would automatically think he knew better than younger men. On visits to Dublin he often saw the Chief of the General Staff during his time in India, General Sir Eric de Burgh, reduced to aimless window-shopping in his late eighties.

Horrocks had never got his full health back after his wounds, and had given up the demanding role of Black Rod in 1963. 'I am conscious that physical energy is diminishing,' confided Liddell Hart, whom he had thought indestructible. 'I find it difficult to work such long hours as I did 10 years ago, and am more conscious of strain.'

But in May 1965, indomitably offering at eighty-one to find his own way up from the airport to save trouble, Auchinleck came to stay, and to Chink's intense pleasure they were as easy in each other's company as they had been in the desert. 'He is a remarkably good visitor,' he noted. 'No trouble and most appreciative. I motored him about a bit. He fairly eats topography, loving to ride with the map on his knees. He has changed but little, a slow, tenacious old badger of a man, shy but a fighter back, intelligent to a point and then numb. He talked about the past, still wondering about Ritchie. He certainly does not show his years.' Reassured, he hoped to be in equally good health at the same age. Montgomery, too, seemed imperishable.

But within six months that hope was gone. He began to suffer such severe spasms of stomach pain that he gave up his exercises and had to prop up the foot of his bed at night in an attempt to relieve them. He held out, fighting them alone, until his stepdaughter Elizabeth came to stay in April 1967 and was so shocked by his drawn appearance that she made him go to a doctor. He was admitted the same day to hospital in Dublin where he was given a blood transfusion and operated upon for suspected cancer of the caecum. A three-inch growth in the abdominal wall was removed but he was not told the surgeon's estimate that he had two years to live at most, and as soon as he was discharged – after a bout of malaria which he attributed to Anzio – he drove himself on again, irritable and perfectionist. By the end of June he was walking five miles a day and swimming in his favourite lake whatever the weather, but tests at his check-up indicated a shadow on his bladder. Against the odds he had developed a second primary cancer and underwent another major operation on 20 July, during which a malignant growth was excised from his left ureter.

Thin and weak, he welcomed visitors to his hospital room with his old charm, underplaying it lightly, and gave an approving interview for Radio Telefis Eireann on Israeli tactics – 'what a triumph for intelligent unorthodoxy' – in the Six Day War. 'Though no one will admit this growth is cancerous,' he confessed in a letter to Auchinleck, 'I suspect it was. Carcinoma is a nasty mistress.' Employing the last ounce of optimism, he transferred his estate to Eve through an *inter vivos* legal arrangement, and gambled on surviving five more years to forestall death duties.

Auchinleck was much in his thoughts. Between operations he had not forgotten the most significant of his anniversaries, a day more important to him now than his birthday which fell three weeks afterwards. 'This morning 25 years ago,' he noted in homage to Auchinleck,

I wrote in my pocket book 'Battle of El Alamin'. I got the spelling wrong but the fact right. Thanks to your indomitable guts and your tactical redisposing of the South Africans *outside* the El Alamein box, it was enough. Do you remember how hot it was, a khamsin hiding everything? I wonder whether you know that on that day Rommel announced he had broken through and was on his way to Alexandria? Anyway, if nobody else does, I salute you. You saved literally everything on that day. . . . How much the country owes you.

His great consolation was Auchinleck's friendship, and he wished they did not live so far apart. Auchinleck had settled in Marrakesh, opting for the sun after so many years in India and turning down his offer of the Steward's House at Bellamont. Chink kept all his letters in a special drawer of his desk, and more than anything they brought a solace that Cantwell never found in *Across the River and into the Trees.* 'I know what I owe to you,' Auchinleck had written on one occasion, 'and realise very clearly, as I have always done, that without your wise and indomitable thinking always at my side and in my head, we could never have saved Egypt . . . and all the rest. I am very glad the truth has at last been told about the decisive part you played in bringing about final victory in the Western Desert. The "voice" was certainly yours, even if the "hands" were mine.'

Facing facts, he resolved to leave his papers – including the well-known Eighth Army map, which he still claimed was the original – to Manchester University, where Auchinleck was placing his. He made one stipulation: Manchester was to initiate a study of the entire desert campaign in association with one German and one Italian university. He hated parting with his papers, but the interest of the historian M.R.D. Foot, sent by Manchester to collect them, made it less painful. Foot, in turn, was impressed by his grasp of the current Vietnam War and his forecast of the Tet offensive.

Shaving had become so exhausting that he grew a full set of Victorian whiskers, which were ginger, the colour of his old moustache, and had the bonus of disguising his hearing aid. The elder-statesman appearance which they bestowed amused him. Apart from his emaciation, which he disguised by dressing immaculately, he did not look ill, and he still glanced into every mirror he passed and smoothed his hair approvingly. He spent 1968 quietly and conserved his dwindling energy; to that end he gave up the three-monthly cystoscopes he had come to hate for their indignity since they took too much out of him. 'He has made a remarkable recovery and is enjoying life,' Tommy Thompson noted when he came to stay that September, 'knowing how fragile his basic hold may be upon it. So far from death to everyone but himself. Eve is free of nerves.' On his own again Chink soaked up the sun. A cousin calling unexpectedly found him with his shirt off and was shocked at his skin-and-bone appearance but Chink drew his shirt on at once and joked, refusing to discuss his illness. 'There is so *very* much to talk about,' he fenced.

As winter came on he remained indoors, reading and disinclined to write, saddened by the loss of his spaniel. 'Dogs remain a solace,' he had written to Barnett shortly before it went missing. 'Dogs and books.' But he looked forward to February. His son Christopher had joined the Royal Regiment of Fusiliers after studying law, and was coming on leave before joining the regiment in Hong Kong, and he put all his effort into appearing fit because he knew that Christopher worried about leaving him. To demonstrate his strength he accepted an invitation to lecture to the Commanding Class of the Curragh Military College, the Irish equivalent of the Staff College, and chose as his theme the constant need for an open mind, as typified by O'Connor's campaign. 'Odd,' he wrote to Liddell Hart afterwards, 'to be speaking to soldiers again after all these years.'

In the void after Christopher's departure he picked up his letter-writing habit again, and typed away in the library with a rug over his knees. 'This winter past I've been refreshing my World War Two thinking,' he challenged Thompson, 'having concluded that one cannot understand the vagaries of our warfare unless one returns to the study of Churchill himself. Wasn't he a bit like a headmaster of a public school? He took the Sixth Form, leaving administration to the bursar, matron in chief etc. War Cabinet as housemasters; chiefs of staff and field commanders as prefects – bad boys could be sacked. Did he unconsciously model himself on a Harrow School system? It's a thought. Also he had favourites, ultimately Alexander and Mountbatten. And

Monty as head boy!' Montgomery was no longer an ogre, but a plain middle-class Briton with his roots in Victorian convention and insecure for most of his life. A monkish quality, he decided. 'The Army was his monastery and by 1946 he had become the infallible father superior.' The lost world still took up most of his thoughts.

He was in continual pain by now and was resigned to losing his five-year tax gamble. But he refused to be sedated as he was determined to keep a clear mind, and his last comment on the army was characteristically wry. Putting it to Thompson that military technique had simply evolved too rapidly between the two wars to be comprehensible to most men, he could not resist a dig at Churchill. 'I doubt whether he understood the real implications of the Desert War,' he continued. 'And so the tapestry weaves, Winston as a purple thread among the golds and reds and blues of other men. . . . What he could never understand was the calibre of the top soldiers and sailors, how different they were from the earlier vintage – better trained, more experienced, more dedicated, less socially affected. The age of the great amateurs was past. Very well,' he had to leave it at that point, 'I'm going to stop here for the present.' Sustained effort was beyond him.

At the end of March Baker's long-awaited biography of Hemingway reached him, and he read it straight through, mustering his powers of concentration. Sad as the ending was, he wrote back to Baker on 2 April, he now realised that sadness had pervaded Hemingway's life throughout, something he had never seen at the time. 'The sort of sadness one feels for the bull blinking for a moment before hurling himself into the arena to do the only thing he knows how to do, to kill,' he explained. 'It was Hem's tragedy that his art necessitated an endless de capo until he couldn't anymore return to his beginnings; the circle became a spiral.'

His own spiral was almost completed. On being told that the latest symptoms were a return of the original cancer of the bowel he wrote to Elizabeth in England and asked if she could find the time to visit him; his daughter Rionagh was nursing in Dublin, near to hand, and he didn't want to alarm Reggie, who had had a heart attack. 'I saw a crocus yesterday among our snowdrops. A signal that one should shake off winter's lethargy,' he wrote to Liddell Hart, wanting to make contact but not mentioning his illness. 'Very glad to get your letter,' Basil wrote back by return. 'It would seem to be a case of telepathy, for only yesterday I turned up your letter of 16th October and made a note to write to you.'

Elizabeth arrived at the end of April, and was taken aback to find a taxi waiting for her at the airport instead of the familiar estate car. When she reached Bellamont towards evening she was frightened to see how ill he looked, and as she kissed him he whispered that she had come just in time. But he swept her off to have a drink straightaway and made amusing smalltalk; confused, she let him dictate the pace. During supper he excused himself suddenly and left the room, and when he failed to come back she went out after him in a panic. He was lying collapsed in the hall, haemorrhaging. 'Then I knew,' she said afterwards. 'And I realised he had been waiting for me. We put him on a sofa in the hall, propped up, and the doctor thought he was going to die there and then. Poor dear. He loved Bellamont so much he would have liked to die in the house, as he had been born in the room above, but he was given injections and though he nearly lost consciousness he was awake when he was put in the ambulance. My mother wouldn't go with him and I was very cross about that. Off he went without her, bless his heart.'

At Lisdarne Hospital in Cavan the haemorrhage could not be stopped. Rionagh drove up and Chink asked if Christopher could be sent for, but the long journey from Hong Kong was complicated by flight connections. He kept up with the radio news bulletins and asked for the papers to be read aloud to him but grew steadily weaker, and on 10 May, willing himself not to die on Christopher's birthday, he requested the Last Rites. At 8 a.m. next morning Elizabeth was woken by a phone call from the matron asking them to come urgently. 'And the extraordinary thing I can never forget is that my mother dressed up for ages. All I wanted was to be there, beside him. "I know he'd like me to look my best," she said, and went on choosing everything so slowly, down to her diamond regimental brooch. It was an eternity while she changed her mind about the right clothes, pinned and repinned the brooch, did her hair this way and that, and made herself up. Eventually we got there. He was just faintly conscious, because I remember giving him a kiss and he died almost at once.' Two hours later Christopher reached the hospital.

The Times obituary by Liddell Hart appeared on 13 May, the number which had dogged Chink throughout his life. 'He was not what the Army calls a "commander",' Basil began judiciously, 'in that he had not those qualities of patience, understanding and tolerance demanded of those who aspire to organise and train men.' The news had been broken to him by Correlli Barnett, stricken because he had not known how ill Chink was. 'A great shock,' Basil wrote privately. 'So many memories come back of him and his keen mind, charm and debonair manner,' and he composed an extra tribute which *The Times* printed as well. Barnett dedicated *Britain and Her Army*, the book he was working upon, to his memory.

And in Marrakesh Auchinleck was desolate. 'Two days before the cable I had said to myself that I must write to Chink. It is a long time since I had news of him. I owed him more than I could ever repay. Perhaps my dearest memories of him are from Simla in the year before the war, when we used to walk in the mountain air before breakfast and talk. He was tragically mistreated and betrayed in the end. Envy and malice pursued him but he never gave in. I am glad his end was peaceful, but I am very sad.'

Appendix A
Land Warfare

by Brigadier E. E. Dorman-Smith, M.C.

The simplicity of land warfare was, I believe, referred to by Napoleon, who said that in warfare everything is simple, but went on significantly to add that it was the simple which was difficult.

In the history of land warfare it is only on rare occasions that human communities have been equally prepared at any one time for aggressive action. Normally, the aggressor, a dissatisfied power of some sort, seeks gains in goods and territory, while the possessor of those goods endeavours to ward off attack. Accordingly, continental military thought sums up the basic elements of land warfare into Attack, Defence and Freedom of movement or action.

Of those three principles, Defence is common to aggression or anti-aggression since even the forces of aggression must make their home-land secure from any counter-attack before embarking on their enter-prise. In primitive communities, aggressors unless they happen to be nomads from distant lands protected by sea or mountains or great deserts, defend their own cities or villages with walls before they move to attack their more prosperous neighbours. Therefore, throughout history, the first business of communities having anything of spiritual or material value to defend, has been the protection of their property by fortifications. Fortifications are the earliest development in land warfare. But the ultimate object of the aggressor being the reduction of the victim's will to resist by cutting off his means of livelihood, necessitates his entry, with armed forces, into his victim's country. That introduces the second main element, in land warfare, the mobile field army. Now, to defeat the aggressor or to save his own life, the defender may retire within his own fortifications and wait for an opportunity to strike the invader as he moves into the depths of his country. To counter this the invading field army must reduce the strong places containing the defender's mobile forces. This brings us to the factor of siege, and because the overthrow of fortified places by siege cannot usually be undertaken solely by a field army, which is designed for mobile operations and requires means of warfare too heavy and cumbrous to keep pace with it, we get the third element of land armies. Therefore throughout the history of land warfare, you will find the following three elements in all land armies:

(a)   Fortress holders,
(b)   Field fighters and
(c)   Siege layers,

and though occasionally you will get homogeneous armies the units of which have been equally capable of carrying out these three functions, oftener you will have distinct and separate elements in an army for the three functions. The basic problem of land warfare is therefore to find the proper balance between fortifications, field armies and siege troops. From this brief review we see that the elements of land warfare fall in the end into two main groups – the first group being Fortification and Siege, the second being warfare 'in the Field'. Throughout history the balance of importance between these groups, the static and the mobile, has see-sawed. In the days when powerful field armies and their supplies could lie safe behind fortress walls ready to pounce on the rear of armies which left the fortress untaken, fortification and siege formed the primary branch of the science of land warfare. As field armies grew larger (and this awaited the development of the art of maintenance) they could afford to ignore the mobile troops in the fortified places and fortifications because they were of less importance than field armies. But the ultimate instrument of decision in land warfare has usually been the battle between the field armies; it is therefore important to understand the mechanism of battle, because this knowledge is the best guide in organizing a field army.

The first task of any army, whether it fights in a fortress or in the open, is to preserve its means of sustenance. Field armies draw their sustenance from their line of communications, or on occasions from the countryside over which they are fighting, so, broadly speaking, field armies are most vulnerable to an attack from the rear, and this attack is most effective when an army is immobilized by attack, or threat of attack, from the front or flanks. To this end, field armies which do not wish, or are unable, to attack, seek to form strong battle fronts which are too extensive to be turned by flank attacks without the attacker's army being broken into two unco-ordinated parts, each weaker than the defender's reserves. On the other hand the attacker by developing greater mobility, endeavours to out-manoeuvre the enemy on one or both of his flanks; either to deliver a decisive attack on them or alternatively by feinting against one hostile flank to make the enemy over-extend and then to break his original front by a direct and violent onslaught. The Defender* who awaits the attack may, if he decides to give battle, either resist and exhaust the enemy in preparation for a counter-stroke or he may by giving ground, draw the attacker into a situation in which he in turn exposes his flank and rear to counter-attack. That was the expedient of Hannibal at Cannae and a similar manoeuvre saved the allies at the Battle of the Marne in 1914. In each case, both the attacker and the defender strive at some stage of the battle to bring off the rear attack. A field army must therefore be designed for attack and defence and the ultimate delivery of the rear attack.

In the history of land warfare, the problem of organizing a field army for attack and defence has most commonly been resolved by dividing the army into three main elements:

(*i*)   A line of battle strong in defence and capable of attack if supported by

(*ii*) A fire element; and

(*iii*) A mobile assault element for the rear attack.

To make these elements manageable in large armies, they are first grouped into units by functions and those units in turn are grouped into higher formations, either unmixed as regiments or brigades, or into groups containing a mixture of the three elements.

Field armies require the highest possible mobility because mobility added to protected offensive power has throughout history been the secret of the rear attack. An army equal to its enemy in fighting power but 50 per cent more mobile can do what it pleases with its enemy. The ideal mobility is reached when the line of battle, fire and assault elements are all more mobile than the adversary. On rare occasions in history this ideal has been reached by having all elements in the army mounted, as with the Mongol armies, but normally the assault arm was

---

*In 1914 the Germans threw their whole weight against the Allies' left flank. In 1940 the Germans feinted against the Allies' left by attacking in Holland and north Belgium. The Allies reacted by leaving the frontier fortifications in north France and advancing to Dutch and Belgian assistance and the Germans then broke the Allied centre on the Meuse.

mounted, the fire element was horse-drawn and the line of battle walked on foot and set the real pace of the army. This was common to all European armies, but even so the army with the highest power of manoeuvre on the battlefield normally succeeded in developing a successful flank or rear attack. To-day, though the main elements of land armies remain, all, through mechanization, can be equally mobile, while wireless control has made possible dispersed manoeuvre in the approach and on the battlefield. But today a new arm for the rear attack has appeared in the air-borne land soldier.

Supply and the transport of supplies and impedimenta has been a constant preoccupation of armies. All means of supply have been essayed. From living on the country or foraging, living on magazines and supply by mobile wagon trains, down to the elaborate supply system of to-day. But be it realized that neither mobility nor fighting power can be achieved until the maintenance and transport problem has been solved.

The last great constant in war has been the human factor – the leader and the led. The led by training, given normal military virtues, can be shaped into whatever military mechanism we give the commander, but the real commander, although he may be matured by experience and guided by the severe principles of war, is unique, born, not made. It is the art of the commander which applies the principles of war to strike the enemy where, when and how the enemy likes it least.

Our studies of the mechanism and mobility of armies on land should not ignore the important part in land warfare played by sea mobility made possible by sea power. In ancient history the armies of the Mediterranean nations, Greeks, Persians, Carthaginians and Romans fought as armies at sea as well as on land. Sea fighting in fact did not become a specialized business till after the Spanish Armada. But it is rather with sea-carriage of armies than sea fighting that we are now concerned. The seaways have frequently turned the flank of the landways. A 'sea-mobile' army has a safe road to the rear attack.

This inconvenient truth is apt to be ignored by the soldiers of continental armies, but islanders whose livelihood depends on the sea and on sea power have no excuse for such ignorance, their armies without sea mobility are only half effective.

Now the history of land warfare has not by any means been one of steady and continuous advance towards the solution of these problems. The ancient Greeks and Romans brought fortification siege and field warfare to a proficiency which was then lost for over 1000 years;

and even in the best periods of the art of warfare it frequently occurs that armies have been raised and organized with more regard to custom and precedent than to basic principles, though there are many examples to the contrary. But whenever a mechanism of land warfare has been created and used in accordance with the basic principles of war and in the light of the best available experience, it has triumphed with ease over land forces which, through failing to watch the development of war and to modify their practices accordingly, were quite unable to understand the fate which was awaiting them or to avoid it when it arrived. That is the real meaning of modernization.

Modernization is not a thing of last year or this. It has been going on steadily throughout the centuries. Whenever there has been a really effective army, it has been a thoroughly modern one for the period in which it was built up. Modernization therefore seeks, first, to provide a General with the highest speed of movement; secondly, the best fighting power; and thirdly, an efficient service of maintenance in the field. The task of those who are responsible for the creation of land armies in any epoch is to build up a fighting machine with the most modern weapons and equipment, in the light of the principles of war and the best experiences of the day. The fulfilment of this task demands constant and continuous efforts towards the evolution of better methods and a readiness to scrap the outworn or obsolete, both during actual warfare and the intervals of peace between wars. It is fatal to begin the new war where the last one left off, and this can be clearly shown by the study of the history of land warfare in our own time since 1914.

Part II

It must be remembered that in 1914 air power was in its infancy. The armies of 1914 were the last in the history of warfare to operate only on the ground. In Western Europe, the field armies assembled behind frontiers protected by fortified places which guarded the main lines of approach. They were organized into infantry divisions which fought on foot and were considered capable of assaulting the enemy's line of battle. They were supported by artillery and they had cavalry divisions for the rear attack. Their weapon basis was the one-man weapon, with a certain amount of automatic firearms amongst the infantry. They were numerically the largest armies which had ever taken the field.

Their transport was, as always in the past, horse-drawn. Their tactical idea was based on the flank manoeuvre followed by a cavalry attack against their opponent's rear. They were armies in the tradition of Napoleon and Wellington modified by the experiences of 1870. But they had *modern* rifles and some modern artillery and no one realized the effect of this modern wine in the traditional bottles except a continental banker named Bloch, who prophesied their utter inability to apply their tactical ideas because of the effect of modern fire power. He was right.

At the outset the fortifications fell with surprising speed because the aggressor had produced secret siege weapons. Then the invasion passed the fortresses and the field armies met and, after a short period of manoeuvring, they were locked in a stalemate because unarmoured beings could not face the enormous fire power developed. Out of this evolved the paradox of a connected line of field fortifications which turned into something much more permanent, stretching for hundreds of miles from sea to Alps. The field armies went straight into siege conditions and became fortress troops and siege armies. Both sides then began to increase their own defensive fire power by adding more and more automatic weapons and their offensive element by producing a more numerous and powerful artillery. Each in turn assaulted the other, failed, and then settled down to think again. With the passage of time both sides evolved new weapons and methods – the Germans gas, the Allies the tank, the Germans hurricane bombardment and infiltration tactics by infantry which the Allies copied. On both sides there was the evolution of the Air Arm, and Land Warfare developed a new dimension. The result was that by 1918 both of these armies, which began as field armies, had succeeded in evolving a siege technique capable of carrying an assault through semi-permanent fortifications and so restoring field warfare, but even when field warfare was restored, neither side ever succeeded in breaking the other's front and developing the rear attack, because the horsed cavalry of the mobile arm was too vulnerable. Moreover, the demands on the production and supply system necessary to provide the armies with the immense quantities of warlike stores and particularly shell placed an intolerable strain on the maintenance system and the effort to turn a field army into a siege army had the inevitable result, that the armies on both sides had become almost powerless to move. Decision in land warfare still awaited the resuscitation of the rear attack to decisive depth. Realizing this the Allies, with the industrial resources of the world behind them, devised a new type of field army for the 1919 campaign – a war machine designed to reintroduce the rear attack, and, comprising some 20,000 armoured fighting vehicles. This new-model field army was to combine heavy tanks for the frontal assault, mobile tanks for the rear attack, armour-protected infantry for the follow-through, and fire support from the air to cover land movements when the penetration had passed beyond the range of the artillery and the original front; and there were to be armoured supply echelons fit for cross-country movement, and even air-supply. The old army would be left *in situ* to contain its adversary's front while the new moved to the decision. Owing to the German collapse in 1918 under the strain imposed by the blockade this project never eventuated, and the full development of modern Land Warfare was thereby postponed for 21 years.

Meanwhile, the war had spread from the congested battlefields of France into the open lands of Eastern Europe, the deserts, plains and hills of North Africa and Western Asia. In these areas, however large the armies, there was still sufficient room for tactical manoeuvre and therefore, for the flank or rear attack to develop. The British and Indian Cavalry exploited the rear attack in Mesopotamia and Palestine, but the war ended before mechanization of any sort really entered the Eastern theatres. There was, therefore, no real development of modern mobility in those regions and the easy victory of unmodernized forces did much to blind the eyes of those in power to the fact that the day of the horsed soldier in war had passed forever. Thus the Land Warfare of 1914–18 ended at the point when true modernization was about to make a new model army capable of restoring life to the stagnating field armies which had become siege armies. Then came anti-climax, for the collapse of the armies and air forces of Imperial Russia, Austria and Germany, left the allies in a sort of military vacuum, and they were too exhausted to realize that their own destruction at the hands of the Treasury officials of their countries was equally imminent. What survived of the Allied armies differed but little from the armies that took the field in 1914 and drifted into the four years' siege.

In the interval between 1919 and the return match of 1939 the stimulus which the first world war gave to civil industry had its reactions on military evolution. Aircraft evolved out of all recognition. Everywhere motor transport replaced the horse. Inventors were busy on the weapons of the last war, modernizing and improving the types of machine guns, mortars, tanks and artillery which made their first crude appearance in 1917–18. By 1934 a stage had been reached when the makeup of armies no longer depended on the limitations imposed over the whole of history by horse-and-foot mobility and one-man-one-weapon. New means for improvement on old methods were there for anyone who wanted them and was prepared to use them. A stage had in fact been reached when the authorities responsible for the maintenance of the machinery of land warfare had to choose between two alternatives – the first a rejuvenation of the existing or old model pattern of army, which in the case of the British and French armies were the 1914 models with a top-dressing of 1918 equipment, by eliminating horsed transport, improving the infantry armament, mechanizing and re-equipping the artillery with longer ranged and more powerful weapons, adding a proportion of assault tank units and modernizing the cavalry arm by the substitution of tanks for horses. This process apparently left the basic tactical idea unchanged; so much so in fact that after such a rejuvenation the British army was able, without mental discomfort, to keep in use a Field Service Regulation which had been written before the army had been 'Voronoffed'. The second alternative was to return to the conception of 1919 but with all the facilities of 1935 and create new model armies scientifically designed for their special tasks, adapting weapons, mobility, supply systems and so on to the strategical functions which the particular army might be called upon to perform. But to understand the events of 1939–40 it is necessary to see how the contending nations absorbed the new equipment and weapons of war into their military organisms in the interval between the two wars.

Curiously enough, Russia, in spite of her unenviable reputation for military ineffectiveness, was the first great power to remodel her army. By 1935, she was able to show visitors from the British Army that she had taken the lead both in mechanization and in air support for land operations. In fact she seemed to have developed two parallel armies – one the old-fashioned 1914 model of horse, foot and guns, and the other a very highly mechanized armoured and mobile force, air-supplied, air-supported and backed by a large force of air-borne troops whose advanced guard in landing was found by parachute battalions. The underlying tactical theory of the mechanized flank attack or the armoured break-through followed by the rear attack aided by the air arm, air landings and air support, had been very elaborately developed. We shall probably never know how much Russian development owes to German thought and assistance, though there is plenty of evidence that before the rise of the Nazis, the Germans were prepared to collaborate with Russia to defeat the Versailles Treaty. But this early development of Russia along lines afterwards adopted by Germany is very significant and it seems logical to believe that long before the Nazi revolution the German army was busy absorbing the lessons of the war in the hope of a comeback and working out the practical details in Russia. The Germans had, however, to be careful not to come too clearly into the open; but as early as 1927 the German High Command had formulated their tactical ideas about the next war and based them upon a violent offensive developed at speed, regardless of loss and of what was happening on either flank of the attacking unit or formation.

In General von Seckt's book, 'Thoughts of a Soldier', you find the idea of a highly trained and equipped army as the offensive spearhead of a 'follow-up' army less mobile and less elaborately equipped. At the same time the Germans resuscitated their air forces, and, when they did so, they went a very long way to harnessing their air power to the land offensive. It now appears that Hitler's offer to drop no bombs beyond 50 miles of the military front was entirely logical and a definite pointer to his intention in war. They also produced with considerable secrecy a tank powerful enough for a frontal break-through against any anti-tank resources of the French or Polish armies and yet sufficiently mobile for a campaign of movement against the rear of the enemy. To accompany these vehicles they had motor-cycle and light infantry divisions, and there is no question but that air supply had been prepared to maintain these spearhead forces. To make the rear attack more sure they had several airborne divisions with parachute-advanced guards, and as with the Russians, it appears that the bulk of the mechanized land force was created independently of the remainder of the army under a separate inspectorate. Quite logically they put a large portion of the anti-aircraft troops under the air arm. The rest of the army, which was by no means allowed to rot, was designed for holding, occupying and following-up. It was mainly infantry with horse-drawn pneumatic-tyred transport, strong in anti-tank and anti-aircraft weapons and amply provided with close support and medium artillery. The proportion of the mechanized and airborne forces to the remainder of the Army was 1 to 8. But though the German war machine was primarily designed for offensive warfare, they did not neglect defence. The design and layout of the 'West Wall' and the depth of its defensive zone seemed to indicate that they were aware of the connotations of a modern armoured break-through and were determined not to be taken that way themselves. Thus in Germany, the army and the air arm developed logically and thoroughly for modern land warfare with none of the vacillations and inconsistencies produced by political instability, financial sabotage and inter-service jealousy, which wrecked the armies of the western democracies before they reached the battlefield. Lastly, the Germans did not neglect seaborne mobility as a means of rear attack. They had considerable successes with combined operations in the Baltic in the First World War; the Baltic is ideal for combined sea, land and air training and Germans worked hard to perfect landing operations before war began.

Interestingly enough, Japan is the other modern exponent of the art of combined land, sea and air operations. The outstanding military feature of Japan's war in China – the only one which is new or genuinely modern – has been her highly developed organization for landing troops including a very wide range of motor landing craft launched at the points of landing from special transport ships designed to carry and release them.

At the end of the last war France was left with the largest army in Europe. She had 2500 tanks, 3600 aeroplanes and 12500 cannon, but France had suffered war casualties of over 2,300,000 killed or disabled, and these not only reduced her fighting strength for the future but in some way broke her offensive spirit. The fact that she might yet again have to face the Germans without the help of powerful allies led her to look for assistance from the chain of weak nations on the Eastern flank of Germany; and, when it became clear that these were unlikely to be of any real value, she started to build an expensive line of frontier defences behind which she would mobilize her Field Army. That, of course, was never finished. It stopped where the French, Belgian and German frontiers met. Had it been carried on to the sea, things might have been very different. The French Field Army, as far as one can see, was simply the army of 1918, with increased infantry fire power, a number of heavy tank brigades, a powerful artillery partially mechanized, and a weak mobile arm of some three light armoured divisions and some horsed formations. The tactical idea was based on the frontal battle, a rigid and inflexible line of infantry formations, maintaining a constantly intact front with marked disinclination for sudden or unsupported advances and flank movements. This was the 1918 idea of the wall of men which might become the trench of men if things went wrong. It does not seem to have occurred to the French that this slow-moving, cumbersome and rigid machine, forming under the protection of an incomplete frontier barrier lacking in depth, even if it were sufficiently large to fill any front which the Germans might attack, was an ideal target for the German army organized on the tactical idea of the unregulated violent offensive designed to drive a rear attack to great depths. Lastly, the French neglected to organize or defend the civilian population in the rear of their armies.

The Polish Army, as far as its field army went, was a bad imitation of the French army. Furthermore, Poland had no frontier fortifications, no modern mobile arm, and a very small air force.

Britain stood committed by the Locarno Pact to support France if attacked by Germany or vice versa. We had a land army which, though responsible for Home defence, the defence of Egypt, the British commitments in the Middle and Far East and the defence of the great naval bases, was the poor relation of the Defence Forces. The restrictions imposed by the rigidly interpreted Cardwell system which tied the home army to the notoriously conservative and obsolete army in India, the increasing age of the senior officers and their dislike of novelty, the dead hands of the Treasury and party politics in England combined to prevent any radical remodelling of the British army. In consequence two years before this war began there were in England four regular infantry divisions, one armoured division, all only partially equipped, and 12 to 14 Territorial Divisions untrained and unequipped. Equipment to arm our air and fortress defences was provided grudgingly. Furthermore, the Treasury obstinately refused to re-equip the small forces in the Middle East, and the army in India was only fit for tribal warfare. With such a hopelessly inadequate army it is not surprising that our tactical ideas were left over from 1918. We reckoned on employing the infantry divisions made more mobile by the substitution of motor transport for horses, supported by an armoured mobile arm in a war of movement in Western Europe. This was and remains the theme of Field Service Regulations, which still puts the infantry before the tank. Just before the war the army in the United Kingdom began an expansion on the lines described in order to fight alongside the French, although this expansion was mainly in the infantry element. There was, however, a strong but submerged feeling in official and non-official circles that if we had to send an army to France it should contain the elements lacked by the French, i.e., armoured and mobile formations. In the end we managed to place ten modernized infantry divisions alongside the French for the northern battle and we lost everything except the personnel. The armoured divisions did not take part in that fighting; they arrived in France too late. Our failure to produce a modern Field Army was to some extent offset by our care for fortresses such as Singapore. There our grasp of fundamental principles was right. But as soldiers we feel that by far the most noteworthy deficiency was the lack of military air support: the army had no air transport for troops or supplies. There was no possibility of an air-landed rear attack and no air-craft to deliver a tactical bombardment for a follow-up if we outstripped our land artillery.

So in northern France we had the pathetic spectacle of two indifferent armies: one obsolete, the other semi-modernized aligned against a Modern army which combined in its organization the best principles of the art of war and the most up-to-date equipment and technique.

In the circumstances, it is difficult to see how the Allies intended to fight the war on land. We know what happened in Poland. That campaign was finished perfectly logically in about three weeks, and we in the west did nothing to help Poland but awaited our turn for defeat. When it came, Germany, with 13 armoured, 7 mechanized, 3 air, and approximately 160 ordinary divisions struck the Allies, totalling some 2 armoured, 91 infantry and a few mechanized divisions at a moment when they had left the fortifications which they had been building for six months. The German armoured forces broke the Meuse Front, drove in behind the fortified belt in the north, developed the rear attack against the northern group of armies, turned south against another weakly-held and over-extended battle-front, pressed home the attack, broke through again, made another rear attack towards the Swiss frontier and that was the end. Still, it is interesting to note that, apart from the rear attack by parachutists, the Germans produced no new development beyond what was latent in the 1919 tactical idea. It is also very noteworthy that, whereas the victors of the first world war were content to relax their efforts, the nation whose armies had been completely demolished was not only foremost in building up its resources on really modern lines but made full use of the advantage of starting with a clean slate.

Before we close this lamentable chapter let a soldier say that the destruction of the land forces of the democratic powers arose inevitably from the abiding vices of democracy, pseudo-intellectualism, parsimony and a middle-class dislike of fighting men. It was a sound instinct which put the Cenotaph in Whitehall.

Part III

The destruction of the French Field and fortress armies and the ejection of the BEF from Europe has left the Axis and Russian land forces in control of Europe and Northern Asia. It also leaves the British Commonwealth, behind its sea and air defences, free to reorganize its land forces in the light of the war's lessons for whatever operations may be in store in the future. In this we are helped by the fact that we are no longer required to conform to the tactical and strategical ideas of a continental ally. Sir W. Robertson when he hoped that 'next war we'd have no bloody allies' was not far wrong.

2. The question now before the commonwealth is, 'What are we going to do with our new found freedom of action bought at a price of £100,000,000 and many valuable lives?' Our first action must be to review the lessons of the war up to date and co-relate the experience of Flanders, North Africa, Somaliland and East Africa to the fundamental principles of war and the new weapons and equipment which are now coming to hand. In doing so we must free our minds from all preconceived or residual tactical ideas and strive to remodel our land forces objectively, firstly for the immediate tasks in hand, and secondly, for the future. In so doing we land soldiers must recognise that just as in the past, success in seaborne operations derived from sea supremacy so henceforward, on land, success in land operations will derive from air supremacy.

The first necessity is to make certain that any of our vital bases which are liable to attack are sufficiently fortified. As things stand now the bases which may be in danger are England, Malaya, Egypt and India. But the forms of attack which these may receive differ. In the case of Egypt and India it takes the form of a land attack by modern armies, but armies separated from their objectives by great distances and deserts – supported by modern air forces. England and Malaya can only be attacked from the sea and the air. Where modern forces may approach us on land we must be prepared to meet them with modern defences. These defences must be so organized that wherever the terrain does not admit of our holding a continual fortified barrier we are in a position to meet deep thrusts against our L. of C. This dictates 'fortresses' in depth, a good example being Mersa Matruh in the Libyan Desert. Furthermore in populous areas wherever rear attacks from the sea and air are likely to develop they must be met by something akin to the *levée en masse* such as the HOMEGUARD. It is nowadays essential to organize and control the non-military population within striking distance of hostile air or land armies.

We must also create modern field armies, adequately equipped against air attack and armoured assault and yet capable of developing a rear attack in combination with a frontal attack. This requires a powerful armoured mobile arm and a line of battle element well supplied with armour and supported by modern assault tanks and modern artillery. Modern artillery now includes the bomb from the air. Incidentally the greater the mobility of the field army in comparison with its adversary the less need is there for fixing the enemy frontally before delivering the rear attack. Immobile armies are fixed by their very immobility. Hence our final aim in organizing a field army for mobile action in Africa or Asia is the 100 per cent mechanized force, air-supplied, operating in conjunction with forces landed from the sea and the air. In the course of our operations we may meet the strong places of the enemy. We must be prepared to destroy them scientifically by air and land attack without wasting our field armies in inadequately supported assaults.

The mobility of our new model field armies must be adequate to their tasks. so it is permissible to guess at some of these tasks.

First, there are the important channels of communication to keep clear. Among these are: the English Channel and the Red Sea. To clear the English Channel it may be necessary to reoccupy the area Calais–Boulogne; the Cherbourg peninsula; the Finnisterre peninsula; and the Channel isles. The mobility required for this task is amphibious. Land mobility need not in the first intance be high. Forces strong in local assault power will cross on wide fronts on an agreed plan and endeavour to form connected bridgeheads. Air supremacy will be an essential preliminary to this operation. This will be the real task of the Royal Air Force; but under the cover of this air supremacy the armies will require air support for bombardment, transport of troops and supplies, evacuation of wounded, etc. The provision of this support will largely free them from the incubus of cannon and land transport.

The capture of Massawa and Assab would clear the Italians from the Red Sea coast, thereby removing any threat to our sea traffic between the forces in India and Egypt and releasing our warships for other duties. This again is an amphibious operation requiring sea and air supremacy and air support to the landed force. This amphibious operation on the Red Sea coast is not, however, the main task of the Eastern group of armies: our armies in North Africa, Western Asia and India. Until the Eastern armies are ripe for the grand counter-offensives it is necessary to defend a strategical front stretching from Kashmir to the Western Desert of Egypt and the Ethiopian Frontiers of the Sudan.

Now the characteristics of this vast front are surprisingly uniform. From Quetta westwards there are thousands of miles of desert lands rarely broken by fertile river valleys or highlands. From the south the sea thrusts two great arms into this block – the Persian Gulf and the Red Sea. To the north-west is the Mediterranean. Railways and roads are few. The land is barren and waterless. The characteristics of this very extensive theatre dictate the characteristics which modern armies should have for operations within its borders. Field Armies operating anywhere from North Africa to India must be fully mechanized and must be supported and supplied by air. But given mechanization, armour and air supply, such armies will bring back to land warfare the technique of Ghengis Khan's army, which combined the line of battle, the artillery and the rear assault in an army of one mobility.

The main elements of modern armies will therefore be Armoured Divisions, Mechanized Infantry Formations, Army Air Forces and the Maintenance Element.

Anywhere in the Middle East such an army would become even more decisive if certain specially organized and equipped divisions of infantry were available when required to develop the rear attack from the sea, which in these areas is so conveniently placed for us. The final requirement for our modern army is one or more airborne divisions which can initially be modelled on the German or Russian formations but should eventually be modified for the special circumstances of eastern warfare.

The new model Eastern army we require should have defensive forces to hold areas in which it is not intended to operate offensively and also our main bases. In some places this defence will be mobile, in others fortifications will be possible. Our main defensive areas are Malaya, the Western Frontier of India and Palestine. Our offensive areas will in time become the Red Sea and the Sudan, the North African littoral, the coasts of south-east Europe and possibly the Balkans.

Now for the counter-offensive.

Assuming that our fortresses, seaways and land corridors are secure – what then? Consider the Germans' position; a large and efficient land army, a weak ally sitting on a peninsula in a sea in which he is not predominant, a doubtful Balkan situation and more doubtful Russia. Hitler is much in the position of Napoleon from 1808 to 1812; with much the same need to obtain a quick and final decision. Our business is to refuse him that decision and to stretch him to the limit of his resources. In Napoleon's day we chose Spain for a 'stretcher'. To-day we have the choice of the Balkans, South Italy, the Mediterranean islands and Libya. We may even eventually have Spain. We have also for the matter of that Norway and the French coast. Everywhere the sea lies between us and our enemy; we must make its shores an area of ever-present menace.

So the next task of our field forces is to become amphibious. We should, I feel, organize and train everywhere for combined operations and let the enemy know it too. The army has got to grow webfooted. But before we can develop an amphibious strategy in the Mediterranean it looks as if we ought to remove Libya from Italy. If so, that involves a desert campaign mainly of armoured divisions supported and sustained by aircraft and backed by motorized troops to hold the bases in rear. Given a properly organized army, say four Armoured Divisions and four Motor Divisions, the task should not be insuperable. And having involved Italians and Germans in that campaign for which they are, I feel, ill-equipped, the moment may come for the attack on South Italy. But since for some time to come initiative on land rests with the enemy, the trouble is to foretell from where the counter-attack on land will start. It may even start from Iraq, Southern Arabia or Central Africa.

Without venturing too deeply into conjecture we can, I think, see the broad lines of our return match taking shape into two main armies, west and east, both amphibious. The west to operate on the Atlantic coasts. The east to secure the Middle East, clear the North African coast and gradually mop up the northern Mediterranean coast until the Balkans, Italy and Spain detach themselves from Germany. For this we land fighters will need modern fortress-holders, a modern field army and perhaps modern siege troops. We may need all of the 4,000 tanks ordered from America and all that we can make ourselves. We will need our wings, something approximately to an army air arm, at least an air detachment, to serve the land battle, bomb where we need bombs, parachute where we need parchutists, transport where we need

360

to be transported. We soldiers must be prepared to help in the evolution of that arm. We must get forward with our own evolution towards speed and mobility on land and at sea. The marching soldier is an anachronism in open warfare in the vast distances of the Near East and North Africa.

We have got the cause, the time, the men, the money and a clear-cut target. We have world industry behind us. There is nothing in the world to stop us winning the third round in land warfare except the relics of that ignorance, timidity and financial turpitude which has cost us so dear in the last twenty years. And in organizing the army of the Eastern comeback, India must take the major part.

(Reproduced by kind permission from *Journal of the United Service Institition of India*, vol. LXXI, January 1941.)

Appendix B
Appreciation of the Situation in the Western Desert

El Alamein, 1445 hours,　　　27th July, 1942.

Object

1. The defence of Egypt by the defeat of the enemy forces in the Western Desert.

Factors

2. *Comparison of Strength.* Table A* shows a rough comparison on a brigade group basis, based on what we now know of the enemy's present strength and his reinforcement schedule. From this it seems that the enemy will hardly be able to secure a decisive superiority over us in the first half of August, provided we fight united, since the Germans would begin any offensive with an inferiority of about three infantry brigade groups and possibly 40 per cent superiority in armour. The enemy may also be inferior in artillery. It would seem that, though the Axis forces are strong enough for defensive action, they are hardly strong enough to attempt the conquest of the Delta except as a gamble and under very strong air cover. There remains for the Axis to use one German Air Landing Division, but this is taking over I.S. duties in Greece and Crete and seems unlikely to be an asset. It might, however, be used to redress the balance at a decisive moment.

*Not reproduced.

Throughout August the anticipated balance of strength hardly justifies a German offensive, unless we make a serious mistake and leave an opening. He may, however, be reinforced in the second part of August, though nothing is known to be scheduled. On the other hand the Axis may make great efforts to strengthen *Panzerarmee* in the shortest time.

3. *Land Forces – Numbers and Morale*. Broadly speaking, though all our forces have been through hard times, their morale is high. German morale is probably a little lower and Italian morale not more than 50 per cent. In view of the known inefficiency of the Italian forces, any offensive action taken by the Axis forces in August would have to be 80 per cent German.

4. *Material*. The Eighth Army has some 60 Grant tanks now and will receive another 60 Grant tanks early in August, but there will be no more coming until September. The deduction is that it is necessary to husband our armour carefully in view of the fact that during August the enemy may build up to between 150 and 200 German tanks.

Eighth Army's deficiencies in transport are mounting. A summary of the present state of equipment of the major formations of Eighth Army is attached as Appendix X.* It is also necessary to husband our ammunition resources. These stand at present as shown in Appendix B* attached. The enemy has, however, similar deficiencies and his reinforcing division is notably deficient in anti-tank weapons and transport.

5. *Training*. None of the formations in Eighth Army is now sufficiently well trained for offensive operations. The Army badly needs either a reinforcement of well-trained formations or a quiet period in which to train.

6. *Fighting value with reference to air forces*. At present we have such air superiority that, while our troops are relatively free from molestation, the enemy is continually attacked by night and day. Our land forces are considerably heartened by this, and a large measure of tactical freedom and security accrues from it. Unless the enemy is strongly reinforced and our air forces are correspondingly reduced, this superiority will assist our offensive or defensive and gravely impede the enemy. Our air superiority is a very considerable, if somewhat indefinable, asset.

7. *Vulnerable Points*. To us the two vulnerable points are Cairo and Alexandria. Occupation of the Cairo area by the enemy would

*Not reproduced.

363

eventually dry up the Sweet Water Canal besides securing an important area for air and land maintenance. Alexandria is useful as a naval base and port of ingress for supplies. The present position of Eighth Army at El Alamein denies direct access to either place by road and flanks any attempt to by-pass. The defences of Alexandria – Cairo – the Delta proper, east of the Nubariya canal and the Wadi Natrun area will be well forward by 14th August and should be complete, in so far as defences are ever complete, by the end of August. Bottlenecks exposed to air action are the Nile crossings at Cairo and northwards; these are being supplemented by two floating bridges south of Cairo and by improving the routes from these bridges eastwards. All arrangements for demolitions in the Delta are being made. The enemy has few really vulnerable points. There are bottlenecks at Sollum and about Matruh and Baggush, and his long L. of C. is vulnerable to attack by raids from the air or inland or from the sea. But otherwise the enemy is not physically vulnerable, except to direct assault. Morally his Italians are always vulnerable. The soft-sand areas of the country east of El Alamein, notably the 'Barrel Track' axis, the Wadi Natrun, the sand area to its north, are all added difficulties for the enemy's movement, particularly as they cannot be widely known to him.

8. *Ground.* The armies are now in close contact over a forty-mile front between the sea and the Quattara Depression. Most of the area is open and can be largely controlled by artillery fire.

The front divides into three main sectors:

A. From Tel Eisa to exclusive the Ruweisat Ridge. This area is held by two divisions (five infantry brigade groups). The Tel Eisa salient has considerable offensive value, but is not essential to its defence, unless the Miteiriya Ridge is also held by us. Most of the area is difficult for wheeled movement. It is on our side strongly defended by the fortified locality of El Alamein and the mined positions to the south. This area is well supported by strong prepared localities to a depth of twenty-five miles. The enemy lies in open flat country. His positions lack any well-defined features and are covered by extensive minefields. At El Daba he has dumps.

B. From inclusive the El Mreir depression to inclusive the Bab el Quattara Depression. This area is held by two divisions (four brigade groups) supported by the equivalent of one armoured brigade. We hold the high ground in this area at Pt. 63 on the Ruweisat Ridge. This position is naturally strong and has been fortified to considerable depth. The enemy holds strongly a series of depressions which give good cover. His front has been well mined and has some wire.

In sectors A and B both the enemy and ourselves have attacked in turn without success.

C. From exclusive the fortified locality in the Bab el Quattara depression to inclusive the complete obstacle of the great Qattara Depression. The enemy is well posted on strong ground at Kelat and Taqa in positions which he has prepared for defence. The object of these positions is to protect his southern flank from being turned by our mobile troops. We have no defences in depth opposite this sector, which is lightly covered by mobile troops.

9. *Time and Space*. Had the enemy the available resources, Italy and Germany are far nearer to El Alamein than is anywhere in the United Nations. The enemy should therefore be able to reinforce quicker than we. On the other hand, apart from distant Benghazi, he has only two serviceable sea ports, Tobruk and, much less useful, Matruh. He may also make use of the railway to a limited extent. He is faced with long road hauls and a sea passage vulnerable to air and submarine attack. This affects the building up of reserves for an offensive. We are nearer our bases. Our limitation is the rate that men and material can reach Egypt from overseas. His limitation is the rate at which it can reach his troops when it arrives. This indicates the necessity of blocking Tobruk and Matruh and attacking his road and rail transport and his shipping.

10. *Political Factors*. Hardly enter into this appreciation, except inasmuch as pressure may be put on the Axis command to press on to Egypt before their army is ready or has sufficient margin of force. Our danger lies in a politically unstable Egypt in our rear. So far this danger has not developed.

11. *The Russian Front*. The operations of Eighth Army are linked to the fate of Russia. Should the Axis penetrate the Caucasus, Eighth Army might be reduced to the lowest margin to provide reinforcements for the new front. Moreover a considerable Axis success in Russia would release air and land forces and equipment for the reinforcement of the Western Desert.

12. *Maintenance*. The enemy is experiencing great difficulty in maintaining his present forces at El Alamein. This condition may improve gradually when more heavy transport vehicles come from Italy. It is not likely to improve so much that he can maintain an

appreciably larger force than that envisaged in Appendix A.* Our maintenance presents no real difficulties, except that our stocks of 25-pounder shells are not inexhaustible, and we could certainly maintain forces of double the present size of Eighth Army in this area if they existed.

Courses open to ourselves and the enemy

13. *Ourselves.*

   A. To continue to attack the enemy in the hope that he will crack before his army is reinforced by fresh troops. The pros and cons of attacking are:

   In the northern and central sectors we have made two attempts to break the enemy's front without success. Failure has been due to lack of trained troops, rigidity of organisation and limited resources in armour and infantry and it seems that the enemy's positions are now too strongly held to be attacked with success with the resources available.

   We have also attacked in the southern sector, but weakly and largely as a diversion. Our attack failed, but the enemy though strongly posted is not numerous here, and this front might go if suddenly attacked. If it did go, it offers access for our mobile troops to the enemy's flanks and rear.

   The problems of attack on this front are, firstly how to find the supporting fire without unduly weakening the northern and central sectors. Secondly, how to find the troops. The only formation which might be used is the weak N.Z. Division supported by its own artillery, the artillery of 7th Armoured Division and some of 5th Indian Division's artillery. This would have to be deployed in secret and developed as a complete surprise. Failure would probably make the N.Z. Division unfit for further operations for a considerable time. Having in mind the weakness in numbers and training of this division the chances of success can only be rated as 60–40. Failure would seriously deplete our present resources. On the whole this attack hardly seems advisable at present.

   B. To adopt the tactical defensive until we are strong enough to attack, which, unless the enemy's position deteriorates, will not be

---

*Not reproduced.

till mid-September at the earliest. The obvious objection is that we give the initiative to the enemy if he is able to use it. It is very doubtful if he will be able to take the initiative till late in August with any hope of success. In fact if he attacks before, provided we have a reserve in hand including up to 100 Grant tanks, we have a good chance of defeating him seriously in the area El Alamein–Hammam. Moreover the critical period for the preparation and manning of the Delta and Cairo defences is now over. There is little danger of the enemy getting any value out of by-passing the Eighth Army on its present ground. There may be a critical period late in August before the new divisions (two of armour, two of infantry) are ready, but this might be tided over by preparing their artillery battle groups in advance of the rest of the divisions and so reinforcing Eighth Army. (This project requires further examination.) This defensive could also be mitigated by enterprises against Siwa and the southern section of his front and by seaborne attacks.

14. *Courses open to the enemy*. The enemy must resume the offensive without delay, but he is unlikely to be able to do so before mid-August and even then no real margin of superiority except in A.F.V.s, is apparent. He will certainly try to attack before the end of August and as Eighth Army defences gain in strength and depth he will be more than ever tempted to avoid them and seek success in manoeuvre. This may well land him into serious difficulties in the soft desert.

Alternatively, he may have to adopt the strategical defensive because our forces are too strong and too well placed for attack. If he does, he may either stand his ground or withdraw to an intermediate position covering Matruh, which will eventually be to our advantage for he will still be in striking distance when we are again fit to attack. If he goes back to the Egyptian frontier, it is questionable whether he should not be left undisturbed.

15. *Course recommended*. Seeing that we are hardly fit at present to do any more attacks, our best course is the defensive combined with offensive gestures from time to time, including raiding. The cover plan should be such as would induce the enemy to strike prematurely, i.e., mid-August, say, between 10th and 20th August. Meanwhile the Army front should be strengthened, and so held that at least one formation could come into reserve and train. At the same time the command of Eighth Army should be put on a permanent footing.

16. *Plan recommended*.

Intention. Eighth Army will defeat any attempt to the enemy to pass through or round it.

17. *Method*.

(a) *Forward troops* –
30 Corps: 1 South African Division, 9 Australian Division.
13 Corps: 1 New Zealand Division, 7 Armoured Division.

(b) *Reserve* –
5 Indian Division (4 Indian Division eventually): 1 Armoured Division.

(c) *General line of* F.D.L's El Alamein defences –
Pt. 63 (eastern) on Ruweisat Ridge – vicinity of Alam Nayal. South of Alam Nayal the flank will be covered by 7 Armoured Division.

(d) *General line of reserve positions* –
For forward bodies, the most western line of the new rearward position.

Should it be desired to avoid the full effect of an enemy attack in great strength the above F.D.Ls can become the outpost line and the main front can be withdrawn accordingly.

(e) *Matruh*. Should be blocked by the Navy without delay.

Tactical Technique and Future Organisation

18. In the light of the course recommended it will be necessary to adjust our tactical technique. This should be based on three facts:

A. We have to be prepared to fight a modern defensive battle in the area El Alamein–Hammam. The troops detailed for this must be trained and exercised so as to get the maximum value from the ground and the prepared positions.

B. Eighth Army may have to meet an enemy's sortie developing into manoeuvre by the southern flank from his firm front on the general line Bab el Qattara–Taqa Plateau. We must therefore organise and train a strong mobile wing, based on 7th Armoured Division, comprising a divisional artillery, 7th Motor Brigade, 4th Light Armoured Brigade, and possibly extra Crusader units. This mobile wing must be well trained in harassing defensive technique.

C. Eventually we will have to renew the offensive and this will probably mean a break-through the enemy positions about El

Alamein. The newly-arrived infantry divisions and the armoured divisions must be trained for this and for pursuit.

19. From the point of view of GHQ, the organisation of our available forces in August and September might take the form, as shown on following page.

This goes further than the present appreciation, but can hardly be separated from it because, should this idea be adopted, it means that the formations now in Eighth Army will not be relieved and the new formations will be built up and reorganised irrespective of the immediate needs of Eighth Army.

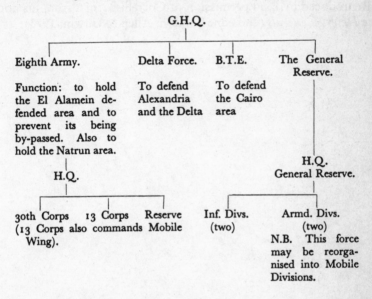

G.H.Q.

Eighth Army.

Function: to hold the El Alamein defended area and to prevent its being by-passed. Also to hold the Natrun area.

Delta Force.

To defend Alexandria and the Delta

B.T.E.

To defend the Cairo area

The General Reserve.

H.Q.

30th Corps   13 Corps   Reserve
(13 Corps also commands Mobile Wing).

H.Q.
General Reserve.

Inf. Divs. (two)

Armd. Divs. (two)

N.B. This force may be reorganised into Mobile Divisions.

20. *Summary.* The enemy now holds in sufficient strength for his purpose a front from which he cannot be dislodged by manoeuvre or any attack Eighth Army can at present deliver. We are strongly posted for a defensive battle. The enemy is attempting to build up his strength and renew his attack on Egypt. Eighth Army requires re-equipment and training before it will be fit for offensive operations. During August it is unlikely that either ourselves or the enemy will be strongly reinforced on land; a successful offensive by either side is therefore unlikely. Provided the land and air situation does not change, Eighth Army can be reinforced about mid-September by two armoured

divisions and two infantry divisions. This may give us a superiority sufficient to justify a direct attack on what may be by then a strongly organised front. Alternatively, we may develop a threat to the enemy's rear via Siwa. The immediate need is to reorganise present forces with Eighth Army and to rearrange the front so as to provide an army reserve. The longer-term policy is to train the newly-arrived divisions for the counter-offensive which it is hoped might begin in the latter part of September.

E. Dorman-Smith, Major-General.
[Accepted by General Auchinleck, C-in-C, ME]

Reproduced by kind permission of Correlli Barnett from his book *The Desert Generals* (2nd edn, London, Allen & Unwin, 1973)

List of Sources

All quotations by Chink are taken from his personal letters, many in private hands, and his papers – which include military correspondence relating to his career and his account of the war – at the John Rylands Library, Manchester University. Throughout, these are also drawn from extensively for fact and detail. In each chapter the other main sources used are set out briefly below.

The following abbreviations are used: JFK=John Fitzgerald Kennedy Library, Columbia Point, Boston, USA; M=Manchester University, John Rylands Library; LHC=Liddell Hart Centre for Military Archives, King's College, London; ONT=MacMaster University, Hamilton, Ontario, Canada; PRO=Public Record Office, London.

Introduction

Newspapers: *AngloCelt*, May 1969; *Daily Telegraph*, May 1985. *Archives*: Uppingham.

Chapter 1: Inheritance

Books: *Burke's Irish Family Records* (London, Burke's Peerage, 1976).
  A Full Life by Lieutenant-General Sir Brian Horrocks (London, Collins, 1960).
  Irish Families, their Names, Arms and Origins by Edward Maclysacht (Dublin, Alan Figgis, 1978).
Papers: Dorman-Smith family; Recollections of Archbishop John Charles McQuaid.
Interviews: Mrs Mary Carney; Mr Christopher Dorman-O'Gowan; Mrs Stella Norton-Dawson; Mr Louis Smith.

Chapter 2: The Military Code

Archives: Royal Miltary Academy, Sandhurst; Royal Regiment of Fusiliers, Alnwick, Northumberland.
Interviews: Colonel Richard Trenham.

Chapter 3: A Hell of a Time

Papers: John Connell (ONT); Dorman-O'Gowan family; Basil Liddell Hart (LHC).
Archives: Royal Regiment of Fusiliers, Alnwick, Northumberland.
Interviews: Mrs Stella Norton-Dawson, Colonel Richard Trenham.

Chapter 4: Ernest Hemingway, a.d.c.

Books:
  By Ernest Hemingway:
    A Farewell To Arms (London, Jonathan Cape, 1929).
    A Moveable Feast (London, Jonathan Cape, 1964).
    By Line (London, Collins, 1968).
    Death in the Afternoon (London, Jonathan Cape, 1932).
    Green Hills of Africa (New York, Scribner's, 1935).
    The Sun Also Rises/Fiesta (New York, Scribner's, 1926).
  Being Geniuses Together by Robert McAlmon (London, Secker & Warburg, 1938).
  The Best Times by John Dos Passos (London, André Deutsch, 1968).
  Charmed Circle by James R. Mellow (Oxford, Phaidon Press, 1974).
  Ernest Hemingway: A Life Story by Carlos Baker (London, Collins, 1969).
  Ernest Hemingway, Selected Letters 1917–1961 edited by Carlos Baker (London, Granada, 1981).
  Hem and The Sun Set (particularly the interview of Donald Ogden Stewart by Donald St John) by Bertram D. Sarason (New York, NCR, 1972).
  Hemingway: A Biography by Jeffrey Meyers (Macmillan, London, 1986).
  Jurgen by James Branch Cabell (London, The Bodley Head, 1921).
  Shakespeare & Company by Sylvia Beach (London, Faber & Faber, 1960).

The Young Hemingway by Michael Reynolds (Oxford, Basil Blackwell, 1986).

Papers: Ernest Hemingway (JFK).

Achives: James Joyce Tower, Dublin; La Scala, Milan; Royal Regiment of Fusiliers, Alnwick, Northumberland.

Interviews: Mr Christopher Dorman-O'Gowan; Professor Jeffrey Meyers; Mr Robert Nicholson; Mrs Stella Norton-Dawson, Colonel Richard Trenham.

Letters: Professor Carlos Baker; Mr J. H. N. Hemingway.

Chapter 5: Leaping Ahead

Books: *The British Campaign in Ireland* by Charles Townshend (Oxford, Oxford University Press, 1975).

By Line by Ernest Hemingway (London, Collins, 1968).

Ernest Hemingway, Selected Letters 1917–1961 edited by Carlos Baker (London, Granada, 1981).

Germany Unmasked by Robert Dell (London, Martin Hopkinson, 1934).

Monty: The Making of a General by Nigel Hamilton (London, Hamish Hamilton, 1981).

Papers: John Connell (ONT); Dorman-O'Gowan family; Ernest Hemingway (JFK); General Sir Richard O'Connor and R. H. Thompson (LHC).

Archives: Defence Forces of the Republic of Ireland; Royal Military Academy, Sandhurst; Royal Regiment of Fusiliers, Alnwick, Northumberland; Staff College, Camberley.

Contemporary newspapers: *Carlow Nationalist*; *Irish Independent*; *Irish Times*.

Interviews: Mr Liam Bergin; Lieutenant-General Michael Joe Costello; General Sir John Hackett; Field Marshal Lord Harding; Lieutenant-General Sir Ian Jacob; Major-General James Lillis; Mrs Stella Norton-Dawson; Captain Mungo Park; General Sir Ouvry Roberts; Mr Louis Smith.

Letters: General Sir Philip Christison.

Chapter 6: New Food for Thought

Books: *Green Hills of Africa* by Ernest Hemingway (New York, Scribner's, 1935).

Wavell: Soldier and Scholar by John Connell (London, Collins, 1964).
Papers: John Connell (ONT); Ernest Hemingway (JFK); Basil Liddell Hart, General Sir Richard O'Connor and R. H. Thompson papers (LHC).
Archives: Royal Regiment of Fusiliers, Alnwick, Northumberland.
Interviews: Mr Correlli Barnett; Colonel Nicholas Holmes; Mrs Stella Norton-Dawson; General Sir Charles Richardson; General Sir Ouvry Roberts; Mr Louis Smith; Mr Neil Smith; Mrs Elaine Strutt.
Letters: General Sir Philip Christison; General Sir Charles Dunphie; General Sir Frank Simpson.

Chapter 7: Stepping up the Pace

Books: *Auchinleck* by John Connell (London, Cassells, 1959).
Auchinleck: The Lonely Soldier by Philip Warner (London, Buchan & Enright, 1981).
The Auk by Roger Parkinson (London, Hart Davis MacGibbon, 1977).
Mountbatten by Philip Ziegler (London, Collins, 1985).
Papers: John Connell (ONT), Basil Liddell Hart and R. H. Thompson (LHC).
Miscellaneous: *Army List*, HQ India, September 1938; *Journal of the Indian United Services Institute*, LXXI, January 1941.
Interviews: Colonel Henry Cramsie; General Sir John Hackett; Mr Michael Jackson; Lieutenant-General Sir Ian Jacob; Mrs Stella Norton-Dawson; The O'Grady; General Sir Charles Richardson; General Sir Ouvry Roberts; Mrs Elaine Strutt.

Chapter 8: Crossroads

Books: *British Intelligence in the Second World War*, vol. I, by Professor F. H. Hinsley (London, HMSO, 1979).
The Crucible of War: Western Desert 1941 by Barrie Pitt (London, Jonathan Cape, 1980).

The Desert Generals by Correlli Barnett (London, William Kimber, 1960).

Generalissimo Churchill and *Churchill and Morton* by R. W. Thompson (London, Hodder & Stoughton, 1973 and 1976).

The History of the Second World War by Captain B. H. Liddell Hart (London, Cassells, 1970).

The Official History of the Second World War, vol. 1, by Major-General I. S. O. Playfair (London, HMSO, 1954).

The Strategy of the Indirect Approach (foreword by Major-General Eric Dorman-Smith (London, Faber & Faber, 1954).

Ultra Goes to War and *The Chief* by Ronald Lewin (London, Hutchinson, 1978 and 1980).

Papers: Dorman-O'Gowan family; John Connell (ONT); Basil Liddell Hart (LHC).

Interviews: Mr Correlli Barnett; General Sir John Hackett; Field Marshal Lord Harding; Mrs Stella Norton-Dawson; Mr Barrie Pitt; General Sir Charles Richardson; Mrs Amelia Thompson.

Chapter 9: Outsider – Insider

Books: Approach To Battle by Lieutenant-General Sir Francis Tuker (London, Cassells, 1963).

Auchinleck and *Wavell* by John Connell (London, Cassells, 1959, and Collins, 1964).

British Intelligence in the Second World War, vol. II, by Professor F. H. Hinsley (London, HMSO, 1981).

The Crucible of War: Western Desert 1941 and *The Year of Alamein 1942* by Barrie Pitt (London, Jonathan Cape, 1980 and 1982).

The Desert Generals by Correlli Barnett (London, William Kimber, 1960).

The Official History of the Second World War, vol. II, by Major-General I. S. O. Playfair (London, HMSO, 1956).

The Tanks, vol. II, and *The History of the Second World War* by Captain B. H. Liddell Hart (London, Cassells, 1959 and 1970).

Papers: John Connell (ONT); Dorman-O'Gowan family; Basil Liddell Hart and R. H. Thompson (LHC).

Interviews: Mr Correlli Barnett; Field Marshal Lord Harding; General Sir John Hackett; Professor M. R. D. Foot; Mr Barrie Pitt.
Letters: Sir David Hunt.

Chapter 10: The First Battle of Alamein

Books: *Auchinleck* by John Connell (London, Cassells, 1959).
The Auk by Roger Parkinson (London, Hart Davis MacGibbon, 1977).
British Intelligence in the Second World War, vol. II by Professor F. H. Hinsley (London, HMSO, 1981).
The Crucible of War: The Year of Alamein 1942 by Barrie Pitt (London, Jonathan Cape, 1982).
The Desert Generals by Correlli Barnett (London, William Kimber, 1960).
Nine Rivers of Jordan by Denis Johnston (London, Derek Verschoyle, 1953).
The Official History of the Second World War by Major-General I. S. O. Playfair (London, HMSO, 1960).
The Rommel Papers, edited by Captain B. H. Liddell Hart (London, Collins, 1953).
Papers: Field Marshal Sir Claude Auchinleck (M); John Connell (ONT); Dorman-O'Gowan family; Denis Johnston's diary at University of Ulster at Coleraine.
Contemporary newspaper: *The Times*.
Video: Auchinleck interview (16.9.69), Manchester University.
Interviews: Mr Correlli Barnett, Professor M. R. D. Foot; Field Marshal Lord Harding; Mr Barrie Pitt; General Sir Charles Richardson.
Letters: Professor F. H. Hinsley; Sir David Hunt; General Sir Frank Simpson; Sir Edgar Williams.

Chapter 11: A Universal Blackball

Books: *Auchinleck* by John Connell (London, Cassells, 1959).
Monty: Master of the Battlefield by Nigel Hamilton (London, Hamish Hamilton, 1983).
The Montgomery Legend by R. W. Thompson (London, Hodder & Stoughton, 1967).

The *Official History of the Second World War*, vol. III, by Major-General I. S. O. Playfair (London, HMSO, 1960).

The *Alanbrooke Diaries: The Turn of the Tide* by Sir Arthur Bryant (London, Collins, 1957).

Papers: Field Marshal Lord Alanbrooke (diary and Montgomery's Situation Report, August 1942); John Connell (ONT); Dorman-Smith family; private diary of Lieutenant-General Sir Ian Jacob; Basil Liddell Hart and R. H. Thompson (LHC).

Archives: Imperial War Museum.

Contemporary newspaper: *The Times*.

Interviews: Mr Correlli Barnett; Field Marshal Lord Harding; Lieutenant-General Sir Ian Jacob; Mr Barrie Pitt; General Sir Charles Richardson.

Chapter 12: Solitary Confinement

Papers: Field Marshal Sir Claude Auchinleck (M); John Connell (ONT); Dorman-O'Gowan family; Basil Liddell Hart and R. H. Thompson (LHC).

Contemporary newspaper: *Sunday Times*.

Interviews: Sir Rex Cohen; Lady Kathleen Liddell Hart.

Chapter 13: The Mincing Machine

Books: *Anzio* by Wynford Vaughan Thomas (London, Longmans Green, 1961).

Rome 1944 by Raleigh Trevelyan (London, Secker & Warburg, 1981).

The Tanks, vol. II, by Captain B. H. Liddell Hart (London, Cassells, 1959).

Papers: John Connell (ONT); Dorman-O'Gowan family; Major-General Sir William Penney (including Colonel Careless); General Sir Sidney Kirkman and General Sir Richard O'Connor (LHC); 3rd Brigade's Anzio War Diary (PRO).

Miscellaneous: *Army List 1944*.

Archives: LHC; PRO.

Interviews: Mr Michael Elliot-Bateman; Field Marshal Lord Harding; Lieutenant-General Sir Ian Jacob; Lieutenant-General Sir Henry Leask; Mr Wynford Vaughan Thomas.

Letters: Colonel James Hackett; Sir David Hunt; General Sir Charles Loewen.

Chapter 14: Across the River . . .

Books: *Burke's Landed Gentry of Ireland* (London, Burke's Peerage, 1958).
  The History of the Second World War, vol. IV: *The Hinge of Fate*, by Winston Churchill (London, Cassells, 1951).
  The IRA by J. Bowyer Bell (Dublin, Academy Press, 1970).
  The IRA by Tim Pat Coogan (London, Pall Mall Press, 1970).
Papers: John Connell (ONT); Ernest Hemingway (JFK); Basil Liddell Hart and R. H. Thompson (LHC).
Contemporary newspapers: *Daily Express*; *Daily Mirror*; *Irish Times*; *Star* (esp. 2.7.54); *The Times*.
Interviews: Mr Noel Browne; Mr Hubert Butler; Mrs May Carney; Mr Maurice Craig; Colonel Henry Cramsie; Mr Sean Cronin; Mr Alan Figgis; Mr William Finlay SC; Captain James Kelly; Lieutenant-General Sir Ian Jacob; Mr Sean MacBride; Mrs Elizabeth Mather; Mr Gerald McCarthy; Mr Charles Murphy; Mrs Stella Norton-Dawson; Mr Ruari O'Bradaigh; Mr Ulick O'Connor; Mr Paedar O'Donnell; Lord Shawcross; Mrs Andrée Sheehy-Skeffington; Mr Daragh Smith; Mr Louis Smith; Mrs Elaine Strutt.
Letters: Mr Leslie Pine, Mr Ernest Wood SC.

Chapter 15 . . . And into the Trees

Books: *Across the River and into the Trees* by Ernest Hemingway (New York, Scribner's, 1950).
  A Moveable Feast by Ernest Hemingway (London, Jonathan Cape, 1964).
  Ernest Hemingway: A Life Story by Carlos Baker (London, Collins, 1969).
  Ernest Hemingway: Selected Letters 1917–1961 edited by Carlos Baker (London, Granada, 1981).
  Hemingway: A Biography by Jeffrey Meyers (London, Macmillan, 1986).

Papers: Field Marshal Lord Auchinleck (M); John Connell (ONT); Dorman-O'Gowan family; Ernest Hemingway (JFK); Basil Liddell Hart and R. H. Thompson (LHC).

Miscellaneous: *Journal of the Royal United Services Institute*.

Contemporary newspapers: *The Anglo-Celt*; *Daily Telegraph*; *Manchester Guardian*; *The Times*; *The Times Literary Supplement*; *Sunday Despatch*.

Interviews: Mr Correlli Barnett; Mr Hubert Butler; Mr Maurice Craig; Mr Christopher Dorman-O'Gowan; Lieutenant-Colonel John Duggan; Mr William Finlay SC; Mr M. R. D. Foot; Mr Michael Jackson; Lady Kathleen Liddell Hart; Mrs Elizabeth Mather; Professor Jeffrey Meyers; Mr Conor Cruise O'Brien; Colonel Donal O'Carroll; Mr Ulick O'Connor; Mr Tom O'Neill; Mr Barrie Pitt; Professor F. W. Ratcliffe; Mrs Ruth Connell Robertson; Mr Peter Ross; Mr Gerard Slevin; Mrs Oonagh Smith; Mr Neil Smith; Mrs Amelia Thompson.

Letters: Professor Carlos Baker; Professor F. H. Hinsley; Mrs Elise MacCormack; Mr Ernest Wood SC.

Bibliography

Auchinleck, Field Marshal Sir Claude. 'Despatches', in a supplement to the *London Gazette*, 13 February 1948

Baker, Carlos. *Ernest Hemingway, A Life Story*, London, Collins, 1969

Baker, Carlos (ed.). *Selected Letters, Ernest Hemingway*, London, Granada, 1981

Barnett, Correlli. *The Desert Generals*, London, William Kimber, 1960

Bell, J. Bowyer. *The IRA*, Dublin, Academy Press, 1970

Bryant, Sir Arthur. *The Alanbrooke Diaries: The Turn of the Tide*, London, Collins, 1957

Burgess, Anthony. *Ernest Hemingway and his World*, London, Thames & Hudson, 1978

Cabell, James Branch. *Jurgen*, London, The Bodley Head, 1921

Connell, John. *Auchinleck*, London, Cassell, 1959
   Wavell, Soldier & Scholar, London, Collins, 1964

Coogan, Tim Pat. *The IRA*, London, Pall Mall Press, 1970

Dorman-Smith, Brigadier E. E. 'Land Warfare', in *Journal of the United Service Institution of India*, vol. LXXI, January 1941

Dos Passos, John. *The Best Times*, London, André Deutsch, 1968

Guingand, Lt Gen. Sir Francis de. *Operation Victory*, London, Hodder & Stoughton, 1947
   Generals at War, London, Hodder & Stoughton, 1964

Hamilton, Nigel. *Monty – A Life of Montgomery of Alamein: I The Making of a General; II Master of the Battlefield*, London, Hamish Hamilton, 1981, 1983

Hemingway, Ernest. *A Farewell To Arms*, London, Jonathan Cape, 1929
   Death In The Afternoon, London, Jonathan Cape, 1932

Green Hills of Africa, New York, Scribner's, 1935

Men At War, Crown Publishers, 1941

Across the River and into the Trees, New York, Scribner's, 1950

A Moveable Feast, London, Jonathan Cape, 1964

By Line, London, Collins, 1968

The Sun Also Rises/Fiesta, New York, Scribner's, 1986

Hinsley, Professor F. H. *British Intelligence in the Second World War*, vols I and II, London, HMSO, 1979, 1981

Horrocks, Lt Gen. Sir Brian. *A Full Life*, London, Collins, 1960

Lewin, Ronald. *Ultra Goes to War*, London, Hutchinson, 1978

The Chief, London, Hutchinson, 1980

Liddell Hart, Captain B. H. *The Strategy of the Indirect Approach* (foreword by General Eric Dorman-Smith), London, Faber & Faber, 1954

The Tanks, London, Cassell, 1959

The History of the Second World War, London, Cassell, 1970

Liddell Hart, Captain B. H. (ed.). *The Rommel Papers*, London, Collins, 1953

McAlmon, Robert. *Being Geniuses Together*, London, Secker & Warburg, 1938

Marrinan, Patrick. *Churchill and the Irish Marshals*, Belfast, Pretani Press, 1986

Maurier, Daphne du. *The King's General*, London, Victor Gollancz, 1945; and *Not After Midnight* (particularly *A Border-line Case*), London, Victor Gollancz, 1971

Meyers, Jeffrey. *Hemingway, A Biography*, London, Macmillan, 1986

Parkinson, Roger. *The Auk*, London, Hart Davis MacGibbon, 1977

Pitt, Barrie. *The Crucible of War: I Western Desert 1941; II The Year of Alamein 1942*, London, Jonathan Cape, 1980, 1982

Playfair, Major General I. S. O. *The Official History of the Second World War*, vols I, II and III, London, HMSO, 1954, 1956, 1960

Reynolds, Michael. *The Young Hemingway*, Oxford, Blackwells, 1986

Sandilands, Brigadier H. R. *The Fifth in the Great War*, St George's Press, Dover, 1938

St George's Press. *St George's Gazette*, 1919–24, Dover, Oxford, 1920–25

Thomas, Wynford Vaughan. *Anzio*, London, Longmans, 1961

Thompson, R. V. *The Montgomery Legend*, London, Hodder & Stoughton, 1967

Generalissimo Churchill, London, Hodder & Stoughton, 1973
Churchill and Morton, London, Hodder & Stoughton, 1976
Townshend, Charles. *The British Campaign in Ireland*, Oxford, Oxford University Press, 1975
Trevelyan, Raleigh. *Rome 1944*, London, Secker & Warburg, 1981
Tuker, Lt Gen. Sir Francis. *Approach To Battle*, London, Cassell, 1963
Warner, Philip. *Auchinleck, The Lonely Soldier*, London, Buchan & Enright, 1981
Young, Desmond. *Rommel*, London, Collins, 1950

Index

Picture Acknowledgements

The photographs reproduced are from private collections with the exception of the following: *Country Life*, page 2 above. Imperial War Museum, London, pages 3 below, 6 below, 7. John F. Kennedy Library, page 4 above left and below left. Staff College, Camberley, page 5 below.